Learn Data Science from Scratch

Mastering ML and NLP with
Python in a step-by-step approach

Pratheerth Padman

www.bpbonline.com

First Edition 2024

Copyright © BPB Publications, India

ISBN: 978-93-55517-036

To View Complete
BPB Publications Catalogue
Scan the QR Code:

www.bpbonline.com

Dedicated to

Dad, **Mom**, and **Jithu** – *for being a constant source of love and support*
Keerthi – *for being my confidante, partner-in-crime, and my rock*
and
Laksh – *for being my ray of sunshine, even on the most dreary days*

About the Author

Pratheerth Padman is a data scientist who entered the field after an eclectic mix of educational and work experiences, including a stint as a production engineer in an Aluminium Extrusion Company in the Middle East. When his fascination with AI began, he dropped everything to dedicate his life to the field. He has extensive experience in creating video courses under his belt and several live training sessions as well. He also moonlights as an AI consultant and mentor, sharing his expertise with others. Pratheerth holds a Bachelor's degree in Mechatronics Engineering from India and a Master's in Engineering Management from Australia.

About the Reviewer

Supreet, an accomplished data and AI product manager, leads diverse data-driven strategies. With expertise as a Data Scientist and Strategist, she excels in crafting impactful data science use cases and spearheads the development and launch of influential data products. Apart from her strategic prowess, Supreet is a prolific writer and global speaker, sharing insights on data, AI, and product development. Acknowledged for her commitment to empowering women in technology, she serves as a Google WomenTech Makers Ambassador and holds a prominent position among the Top 25 Women in AI.

Acknowledgement

I want to express my deepest gratitude to my family and friends, whose unwavering support and encouragement have been my pillars throughout the journey of writing this book. Their belief in me was the light that guided me through the challenging process of bringing these pages to life.

I am deeply grateful to BPB Publications for their invaluable guidance and expertise in transforming my manuscript into a published reality. The journey, filled with countless revisions, was enriched by the collaborative efforts of reviewers, technical experts, and editors, each bringing a unique perspective that greatly enhanced this work.

A special acknowledgment goes to my colleagues and co-workers from my diverse professional experiences, from my time as a production engineer in the Middle East to my current role in the tech industry. The lessons learned, and the feedback received from these brilliant minds have been instrumental in shaping not only this book but also my approach to data science and AI.

Lastly, I extend my heartfelt thanks to all the readers and viewers who have shown interest in my work. Your support and enthusiasm for this book make all the effort worthwhile. Thank you for joining me on this exciting journey of discovery and learning.

Preface

Data science has revolutionized the way we understand and harness the power of information, fueling innovation and transforming industries across the globe. *Learn Data Science from Scratch* is your comprehensive guide to unlocking the potential of data.

This book provides a thorough exploration of essential data science concepts, tools, and techniques. Starting with the fundamentals of data science, you will progress through data collection, web scraping, data exploration and visualization, and data cleaning and pre-processing. You will build the required foundation in statistics and probability before diving into **Machine Learning** (**ML**) algorithms, deep learning, natural language processing, recommender systems, and data storage systems. With hands-on examples and practical advice, each chapter offers valuable insights and key takeaways, empowering you to master the art of data-driven decision-making.

Upon completing *Learn Data Science from Scratch*, you will have a deep understanding of the data science process, enabling you to apply your newfound skills to real-world projects confidently. Whether you are a beginner or an experienced professional looking to hone your abilities, this book will provide you with the required tools and knowledge. Parte superior do formulárioParte inferior do formulário

Chapter 1: Unraveling the Data Science Universe: An Introduction – Embark on your data science journey with a comprehensive introduction to the field. Explore the historical evolution, key concepts, and the significant impact of data science in shaping our world. We will discuss the roles and responsibilities of data scientists and differentiate between related fields like AI and big data.

Chapter 2: Essential Python Libraries and Tools for Data Science – Gain proficiency in Python for data science, from setting up your environment to mastering essential libraries like NumPy for numerical computing and Pandas for data manipulation. Learn to create visualizations with Matplotlib, Seaborn, and Plotly, and explore Jupyter Notebook for interactive coding.

Chapter 3: Statistics and Probability Essentials for Data Science – Build a foundational understanding of probability theory, learn about different distributions and sampling methods, and cover the principles of hypothesis testing. This chapter equips you with the statistical knowledge crucial for analyzing and interpreting data effectively.

Chapter 4: Data Mining Expedition: Web Scraping and Data Collection Techniques – Discover the art of data collection through web scraping using BeautifulSoup, understand how to harness APIs, and leverage Python libraries for efficient data gathering. The chapter also addresses ethical considerations in data collection, ensuring a responsible approach.

Chapter 5: Painting with Data: Exploration and Visualization – Uncover insights in your data through **Exploratory Data Analysis (EDA)** and descriptive statistics. Learn to use powerful visualization tools like Matplotlib, Seaborn, and Plotly to reveal patterns and trends, enhancing your data storytelling skills.

Chapter 6: Data Alchemy: Cleaning and Preprocessing Raw Data – Learn the critical steps of cleaning and preprocessing data, including handling missing values, normalizing data, and feature engineering. Understand how to tackle duplicate and inconsistent data, and the importance of encoding categorical features for analysis.

Chapter 7: Machine Learning Magic: An Introduction to Predictive Modeling – Dive into the world of **Machine Learning (ML)**, covering fundamental concepts of supervised and unsupervised learning. Understand essential algorithms, model selection, and evaluation techniques, and learn to balance overfitting and underfitting for robust models.

Chapter 8: Exploring Regression: Linear, Logistic, and Advanced Methods – Explore linear and logistic regression techniques, their assumptions, and applications. Understand how to fit, evaluate, and enhance regression models with regularization techniques and interpret their results for practical insights.

Chapter 9: Unveiling Patterns with k-Nearest Neighbors and Naïve Bayes – Get acquainted with k-Nearest Neighbors and Naïve Bayes algorithms. Learn their inner workings, applications, and fine-tune their performance with distance metrics and hyperparameters for effective classification and regression tasks.

Chapter 10: Exploring Tree-Based Models: Decision Trees to Gradient Boosting – Delve into decision trees, learn about entropy, information gain, tree pruning, and optimization. Explore ensemble methods like random forests and boosting, and understand their ability to handle complex data relationships.

Chapter 11: Support Vector Machines: Simplifying Complexity – Gain insights into **Support Vector Machines (SVMs)**, including their kernel methods for classification and regression. Learn model tuning and optimization strategies to leverage SVMs' full potential in your data science projects.

Chapter 12: Dimensionality Reduction: From PCA to Advanced Methods – Tackle the challenge of high dimensionality with techniques like **principal component analysis**

(**PCA**). Learn to visualize complex data and explore advanced methods like t-SNE and UMAP for efficient data representation.

Chapter 13: Unlocking Unsupervised Learning – Explore unsupervised learning with a focus on clustering algorithms like K-means, hierarchical clustering, and DBSCAN. Understand how to evaluate and validate clusters to derive new insights from your data.

Chapter 14: The Essence of Neural Networks and Deep Learning – Embark on a deep learning journey, understanding the basics of artificial neural networks, activation functions, and backpropagation. Dive into TensorFlow, Keras, PyTorch, CNNs, RNNs, and LSTMs, uncovering their applications and complexities.

Chapter 15: Word Play: Text Analytics and Natural Language Processing – Master text analytics and NLP techniques, including text processing, tokenization, feature extraction, sentiment analysis, text classification, topic modeling, and named entity recognition, to handle and interpret unstructured text data effectively.

Chapter 16: Crafting Recommender Systems – Develop skills to create personalized recommender systems using collaborative filtering, content-based filtering, matrix factorization, and hybrid methods. Understand these systems' principles for applications in e-commerce and entertainment.

Chapter 17: Data Storage Mastery: Databases and Efficient Data Management – Learn the fundamentals of databases, including relational and NoSQL systems, and explore SQL and Python libraries for efficient database interaction. Understand data storage formats, serialization, and the role of data warehousing and lakes in data management.

Chapter 18: Data Science in Action: A Comprehensive End-to-end Project – Apply your data science knowledge to a real-world project. Learn how to define a data science problem, collect and prepare data, select the best models, evaluate their performance, and communicate results effectively. Understand the deployment, monitoring, and maintenance of models.

Code Bundle and Coloured Images

Please follow the link to download the
Code Bundle and the *Coloured Images* of the book:

https://rebrand.ly/39fbd7

The code bundle for the book is also hosted on GitHub at
https://github.com/bpbpublications/Learn-Data-Science-from-Scratch.
In case there's an update to the code, it will be updated on the existing GitHub repository.

We have code bundles from our rich catalogue of books and videos available at **https://github.com/bpbpublications**. Check them out!

Errata

We take immense pride in our work at BPB Publications and follow best practices to ensure the accuracy of our content to provide with an indulging reading experience to our subscribers. Our readers are our mirrors, and we use their inputs to reflect and improve upon human errors, if any, that may have occurred during the publishing processes involved. To let us maintain the quality and help us reach out to any readers who might be having difficulties due to any unforeseen errors, please write to us at :

errata@bpbonline.com

Your support, suggestions and feedbacks are highly appreciated by the BPB Publications' Family.

Piracy

If you come across any illegal copies of our works in any form on the internet, we would be grateful if you would provide us with the location address or website name. Please contact us at **business@bpbonline.com** with a link to the material.

If you are interested in becoming an author

If there is a topic that you have expertise in, and you are interested in either writing or contributing to a book, please visit **www.bpbonline.com**. We have worked with thousands of developers and tech professionals, just like you, to help them share their insights with the global tech community. You can make a general application, apply for a specific hot topic that we are recruiting an author for, or submit your own idea.

Reviews

Please leave a review. Once you have read and used this book, why not leave a review on the site that you purchased it from? Potential readers can then see and use your unbiased opinion to make purchase decisions. We at BPB can understand what you think about our products, and our authors can see your feedback on their book. Thank you!

For more information about BPB, please visit **www.bpbonline.com**.

Join our book's Discord space

Join the book's Discord Workspace for Latest updates, Offers, Tech happenings around the world, New Release and Sessions with the Authors:

https://discord.bpbonline.com

Table of Contents

CHAPTER 1
Unraveling the Data Science Universe: An Introduction

Introduction

Welcome to the fascinating world of data science, where insights are extracted from the vast sea of information surrounding us. In this chapter, we will demystify data science, get a sneak peek into a day in the life of a data scientist, and delve into the data science process, familiarizing you with the key concepts and terminology you will need throughout your journey. This foundational knowledge will provide a strong platform for understanding the subsequent chapters and equip you with the essential tools to become a successful data scientist.

Structure

In this chapter, we will discuss the following topics:

- What is data science
- Data science: A fusion of fields
- History and evolution of data science as a field
- The data science process
- A day in the life of a data scientist

- How data science is shaping our world

- Differences between Artificial Intelligence, big data, and data science

Objectives

By the end of this chapter, you should have a solid understanding of the data science landscape, including its core components and processes. This foundation will serve as a springboard for diving into the more technical aspects of data science in the upcoming chapters.

What is data science

Data science is like a captivating puzzle, where different pieces from various disciplines come together to unveil hidden patterns and insights. At its core, data science is the art and science of extracting valuable information from data by employing techniques from mathematics, statistics, computer science, domain expertise, visualization and communication, and ethical considerations.

Data science: A fusion of fields

Let us expand on this phrase and explore the key components that contribute to the vibrant mosaic of data science and its interdisciplinary nature in depth:

- **Mathematics and statistics:** These pillars of data science provide the theoretical foundation and backbone for understanding patterns and relationships within data. Mathematical concepts, such as linear algebra and calculus, play a vital role in developing and optimizing algorithms, while statistical methods help quantify uncertainties, make predictions, and draw inferences from data.

- **Computer science:** In data science, computer science acts as a bridge between theory and practice. It brings mathematical and statistical concepts to life through programming, algorithms, and efficient computational methods. Additionally, computer science equips us with tools for data storage, processing, and retrieval, enabling us to deal with vast amounts of data and derive meaningful insights.

- **Domain expertise:** Like an indispensable compass, domain expertise guides data scientists in their quest to solve real-world problems. By incorporating subject matter knowledge, data scientists can ask relevant questions, identify appropriate data sources, and interpret results within the context of their specific industry or field. This allows for more impactful and targeted analyses that drive informed decision-making.

- **Visualization and communication:** A key aspect of data science is the ability to translate complex findings into digestible, compelling stories. This involves leveraging data visualization techniques to create informative and engaging graphics, and honing communication skills to effectively convey insights to diverse audiences.

- **Ethical considerations:** As data science continues to shape our world, it is crucial to recognize the ethical implications of our analyses and decisions. This interdisciplinary field must constantly balance privacy, fairness, transparency, and accountability, ensuring that data-driven insights are used responsibly and for the greater good. Take a look at the following figure:

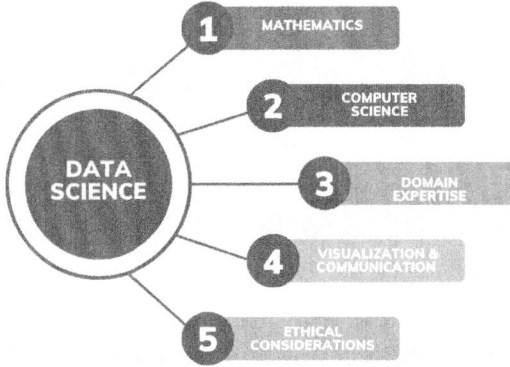

Figure 1.1: Data science: A fusion of fields

Data science is a synergistic fusion of diverse fields, each contributing its unique strengths and perspectives. This interdisciplinary character is what empowers data scientists to navigate complex problems, draw valuable insights, and make a lasting impact in today's data-driven world.

History and evolution of data science as a field

The story of data science is a fascinating one, full of exciting twists and turns that have shaped it into the dynamic field we know today. So, let us journey back in time and explore how data science has evolved over the years!

Once upon a time, in the early 20th century, statistics and probability theory were taking shape. Visionaries like *Ronald A. Fisher* and *Karl Pearson* laid the foundation for modern data analysis techniques, which would later become essential for data science.

Fast forward to the 1940s and 1950s, when the invention of computers revolutionized the world of data: pioneers like *Grace Hopper* and *Alan Turing* crafted programming languages and algorithms that would make data processing more efficient than ever before. As decades passed, databases emerged, making it easier to manage and retrieve massive amounts of data.

But the excitement did not stop there. In the 1980s and 1990s, data mining and **Machine Learning** (**ML**) burst onto the scene. Researchers like *Tom Mitchell*, *Geoffrey Hinton*, and *Yann LeCun* advanced neural networks and deep learning, unlocking new possibilities for extracting insights from data.

Things got even more interesting in the early 2000s, when the internet and digital devices caused an explosion of data, giving birth to the era of big data. Companies like Google, Facebook, and Amazon harnessed the power of big data to revolutionize their products and services, sparking a massive demand for data scientists.

By the 2010s, data science had become its own distinct field. The *Harvard Business Review* called being a data scientist the sexiest job of the 21st century in 2012! As more people pursued careers in data science, educational institutions and online platforms began offering specialized courses and degrees to meet the demand.

That brings us to today, where data science continues to evolve at breakneck speed. Cutting-edge fields like natural language processing, computer vision, and reinforcement learning are pushing the boundaries of what is possible. The future of data science is bright, with endless opportunities to make an impact across industries and worldwide.

As we embark on this thrilling adventure through the world of data science, we must appreciate the rich history that has shaped it into the vibrant and ever-changing field we know and love today.

The data science process

As we have explored the history and evolution of data science, the field has come a long way since its beginning. This rich heritage has shaped the techniques and methodologies that modern data scientists use to extract valuable insights from data. Now that we have a deeper appreciation for the journey data science has taken, let us delve into the core process that drives the work of data scientists today.

The data science process is like an exhilarating adventure, where you navigate through a series of interconnected stages, each offering its own set of challenges and rewards. This journey takes you from the initial spark of curiosity to the ultimate satisfaction of solving real-world problems using data-driven insights. Let us walk through the key steps of the data science process, exploring how they all come together to form a cohesive and structured approach:

1. **Problem definition:** Every great adventure begins with a clear purpose. In data science, this means understanding the problem you are trying to solve. You will collaborate with stakeholders to identify objectives, define goals, and translate them into actionable data-driven questions. This step lays the groundwork for the entire process and ensures that your efforts align with your organization's needs.

2. **Data collection:** With a well-defined problem, you will set out on a quest for data. This stage involves gathering relevant information from various sources, such as

databases, APIs, web scraping, or third-party providers. You must consider data quality, reliability, and representativeness, as these factors can significantly impact your analysis and subsequent insights.

3. **Data preparation:** Once you have collected the data, it is time to roll up your sleeves and dive into some data wrangling. This stage is all about cleaning, organizing, and transforming the raw data into a structured and usable format. You will address issues like missing values, inconsistencies, and outliers, ensuring that your dataset is primed for analysis.

4. **Exploratory data analysis:** With your data neatly prepped, you will be ready to embark on a journey of exploration. During **Exploratory data analysis (EDA)**, you will employ visualization techniques and summary statistics to uncover patterns, trends, and relationships within the data. This stage is essential for generating hypothesis, informing your modelling choices, and identifying potential pitfalls or areas of interest.

5. **Model development:** Now comes the moment of truth: building and training machine learning models to answer your data-driven questions. You will experiment with different algorithms, techniques, and parameter settings, iterating and refining your models to maximize their predictive power or explanatory capabilities.

6. **Model evaluation:** At this stage, you will put your models to the test, assessing their performance using appropriate metrics and validation techniques. This step is crucial for determining the reliability and robustness of your models, ensuring that they generalize well to unseen data and provide meaningful insights.

7. **Model deployment:** With a trustworthy and well-performing model at hand, it is time to bring your creation to life. You will collaborate with engineers and other team members to deploy your model into a production environment, integrating it with existing systems or building custom applications to address specific use cases.

8. **Communication and presentation:** Finally, you will weave together the story of your data science adventure, distilling complex findings into clear, compelling narratives. This stage involves crafting engaging visualizations and presenting your insights to stakeholders in an informative and actionable manner.

9. **Model maintenance and monitoring:** Just like a well-tuned car, your model requires regular maintenance to keep performing at its best. Stay ahead of the game by updating your model with fresh data and giving it a tune-up as needed. Keep a keen eye on your model's performance by tracking essential metrics and setting up alerts for any unexpected dips or hiccups. Be on the lookout for model drift, which can happen when the model's predictions start to lose accuracy due to shifts in data patterns. By being a vigilant monitor, you will be able to spot any potential issues early on and address them promptly, ensuring that your model remains a reliable tool for data-driven decision-making.

The data science process is a dynamic and iterative journey, where each stage informs and influences the others. By following this structured approach, you can tackle complex problems, uncover valuable insights, and ultimately, drive impactful change through the power of data.

A day in the life of a data scientist

Let us follow a day in the life of Mike, a data scientist working for a fast-growing healthcare start-up. Mike's days are filled with problem-solving and collaboration as he uses data to uncover insights that drive improvements in patient care and outcomes. Here is a glimpse into Mike's daily routine:

- **6:30 AM - Morning workout:** Mike starts his day with a brisk run, which helps him clear his mind and stay energized throughout the day.

- **8:00 AM - Catching up on e-mails:** After a healthy breakfast, Mike skims through his inbox, responding to any urgent messages from his team or other departments.

- **9:15 AM - Daily stand-up meeting:** Mike and his team hold a brief stand-up meeting to discuss their progress on ongoing projects, share any roadblocks they have encountered, and identify opportunities for collaboration.

- **10:00 AM - Model debugging:** Mike spends the morning investigating a performance issue with a predictive model they recently deployed. He identifies the root cause, updates the model, and documents the changes for future reference.

- **12:00 PM - Lunch and learn:** Mike attends an informal lunch and learn session led by a colleague, where he picks up new tips and techniques related to time series analysis.

- **1:00 PM - Data validation:** Mike reviews a new dataset provided by the electronic health records team, validating its accuracy and identifying any potential issues that could impact the analysis.

- **2:30 PM - Collaboration with clinical team:** Mike meets with clinicians to discuss how his team's latest model can help predict patient readmission rates. Together, they brainstorm potential improvements and identify additional data sources that could enhance the model's predictive power.

- **4:00 PM - Technical review:** Mike conducts a technical review of a junior team member's code, offering guidance on best practices and ensuring that the code is efficient, accurate, and well-documented.

- **5:30 PM - Planning an upcoming project:** Mike spends the last hour of his day planning for an upcoming project focused on optimizing patient scheduling. He outlines the project's objectives, sketches out a preliminary timeline, and identifies potential challenges.

- **6:30 PM - Evening routine:** After a fulfilling day at work, Mike heads home to unwind with a good book or practice his guitar. He knows that a healthy work-life balance is essential for maintaining his well-being and creativity.

In Mike's world, every day brings new challenges and opportunities to learn, grow, and make a real-world impact through the power of data. His experiences demonstrate that a data scientist's role goes beyond the data science process, encompassing communication, collaboration, mentorship, and continuous learning in a dynamic and multidisciplinary environment.

How data science is shaping our world

Data science has revolutionized the way we approach problem-solving, decision-making, and strategy development across a wide range of industries. By leveraging the power of data, organizations can uncover hidden patterns, make informed decisions, and drive innovation. Here are a few examples of data science applications across various industries:

- **Healthcare**
  o Predicting patient readmissions and disease outcomes
  o Identifying potential outbreaks and understanding disease spread
  o Personalizing treatment plans based on patient data
  o Optimizing hospital operations and resource allocation

- **Finance**
  o Detecting fraudulent transactions and preventing financial crimes
  o Analyzing customer data to assess credit risk and inform lending decisions
  o Developing algorithmic trading strategies for better investment returns
  o Creating personalized banking services and financial products

- **Retail and e-commerce**
  o Optimizing pricing strategies and inventory management
  o Understanding customer behavior and preferences for targeted marketing
  o Recommending products and services based on customer profiles
  o Analyzing customer feedback and reviews for insights into product improvements

- **Manufacturing**
  o Implementing predictive maintenance to reduce equipment downtime
  o Enhancing supply chain efficiency through data-driven optimization

o Identifying factors that impact product quality and production efficiency

o Forecasting demand to support better production planning

- **Energy and utilities**

    o Optimizing energy grid management and load forecasting

    o Identifying patterns in equipment performance for preventive maintenance

    o Developing more efficient energy consumption strategies for customers

    o Enhancing the integration of renewable energy sources

- **Transportation and logistics**

    o Predicting and managing traffic congestion to improve urban mobility

    o Optimizing delivery routes and schedules for efficient logistics

    o Analyzing vehicle performance data for improved maintenance and safety

    o Enhancing fleet management and resource allocation

- **Sports**

    o Analyzing player performance and injury risk for better team management

    o Developing data-driven strategies to gain a competitive edge

    o Evaluating game dynamics and tactics for improved coaching

    o Enhancing fan engagement through personalized experiences

- **Media and entertainment**

    o Analyzing user behavior to inform content creation and curation

    o Developing recommendation algorithms for personalized experiences

    o Evaluating the effectiveness of marketing campaigns and promotional strategies

    o Forecasting audience engagement and revenue generation

- **Agriculture**

    o Optimizing crop yield predictions and resource allocation

    o Analyzing soil and weather data for more efficient farming practices

    o Developing precision agriculture techniques for targeted interventions

    o Monitoring and predicting the spread of crop diseases and pests

These examples demonstrate the vast potential of data science to drive improvements and innovations across a wide range of industries. As more organizations embrace data-driven decision-making, the applications of data science will continue to grow and evolve, shaping the future of countless industries around the world.

Differences between Artificial Intelligence, big data, and data science

If you have your ear to the ground, these are terms that you must have heard for a while now. They are interconnected and are often used interchangeably, and it is easy to confuse one for the other. Before we delve into more specific, technical topics in the upcoming chapters, we will present a brief overview of the differences between these three areas.

- **Artificial Intelligence: Artificial Intelligence (AI)** is a broad field focused on developing computer systems that can perform tasks that typically require human intelligence. This includes areas such as natural language processing, computer vision, robotics, and machine learning. AI systems leverage data and algorithms to learn from experience, adapt to new inputs, and perform tasks such as image recognition, language translation, and decision-making. Data science is a subset of AI, as it relies on many AI techniques especially **Machine Learning (ML)** to analyze data and make predictions or recommendations.

- **Big data:** Big data refers to the large and complex data sets that are difficult to process and analyze using traditional data processing tools. These data sets often have high volume, velocity, and variety, requiring advanced storage, processing, and analytics solutions. Big data technologies, such as **Hadoop** and **Spark**, enable organizations to process, store, and analyze massive amounts of structured and unstructured data at scale. Data science plays a critical role in extracting value from big data by applying advanced analytics and machine learning techniques to derive insights and ensure informed decision-making.

- **Data science:** Data science is an interdisciplinary field that combines expertise in statistics, mathematics, programming, and domain knowledge to extract meaningful insights from data. It involves collecting, processing, analyzing, and interpreting complex data sets to ensure informed decision-making and develop data-driven solutions. Data scientists use various techniques, including machine learning, to create predictive models, discover patterns, and uncover hidden insights.

In summary, data science is the process of extracting insights and knowledge from data using various techniques, including machine learning. Big data refers to large and complex data sets that require advanced tools and technologies to process and analyze. AI is a broad field focused on creating computer systems that can perform tasks requiring human-like intelligence, with data science being a subset of AI. While these fields are interconnected, they each serve unique purposes and contribute to the ongoing advancement of technology and innovation.

Conclusion

In this opening chapter, we navigated the captivating world of data science, developing a clear understanding of what data science is and its interdisciplinary roots. We traced the history and evolution of the field, providing context for the development of the modern data science process. By looking at a day in the life of a data scientist, we gained insight into their daily responsibilities and challenges, while also appreciating the transformative impact data science has on our world. Furthermore, we looked at the distinctions between data science, artificial intelligence, and big data, highlighting their unique roles in shaping the future. Armed with this foundational knowledge, you are now prepared to delve deeper into the exciting universe of data science and unlock its vast potential to drive innovation and positive change.

In the next chapter, you will be introduced to all the Python libraries and tools that are essential for tackling any data science problem. You will learn how to leverage the power of **NumPy** for numerical computing, pandas for data manipulation, and visualization libraries like **Matplotlib**, **seaborn**, and **Plotly**. The chapter will also guide you to use **Jupyter Notebook**, a widely-used interactive development environment for sharing code, visualizations, and explanations.

Points to remember

- The field of data science brings together expertise from various disciplines, including statistics, programming, and domain-specific knowledge.

- The history and evolution of data science involve key milestones in statistics, computer science, data mining, machine learning, big data, and the rise of data science as a distinct discipline.

- The data science process typically includes steps such as data collection, data preprocessing, exploratory data analysis, feature engineering, model training and evaluation, and model deployment and monitoring.

- Data science is shaping our world by driving innovation and transforming industries across various sectors, from healthcare to finance and beyond.

- While data science, AI, and big data are related, they have distinct roles: data science focuses on extracting insights from data, AI involves creating algorithms that can learn from data, and big data refers to the massive amounts of data generated in the digital age.

Multiple choice questions

1. **Which of the following is not a typical step in the data science process?**

   a. Data collection

   b. Data pre-processing

   c. Model deployment

   d. Graphic design

2. **Data science is an interdisciplinary field that combines expertise from which of the following?**

   a. Chemistry, biology, and physics

   b. Music, dance, and theater

   c. Statistics, programming, and domain-specific knowledge

   d. Philosophy, history, and linguistics

3. **What is the primary goal of data science?**

   a. To create Artificial Intelligence

   b. To manage big data infrastructure

   c. To extract knowledge and insights from data

   d. To develop new programming languages

Answers

1. d

2. c

3. c

Questions

1. What are some key differences between data science, AI, and big data?

2. How has the history and evolution of data science shaped the field into what it is today?

Join our book's Discord space

Join the book's Discord Workspace for Latest updates, Offers, Tech happenings around the world, New Release and Sessions with the Authors:

https://discord.bpbonline.com

CHAPTER 2
Essential Python Libraries and Tools for Data Science

Introduction

In this chapter, we will dive into the essential Python libraries and tools that form the backbone of any data scientist's toolkit. Mastering these powerful tools will lay the foundation for your data science journey and help you become proficient in handling, analyzing, and visualizing data. We will start with the basics to help you grasp the fundamentals before moving on to more advanced techniques in the later chapters, ensuring a smooth and structured learning experience.

Structure

In this chapter, we will discuss the following topics:

- Setting up your developer environment
- Basics of NumPy
- Pandas for data manipulation
- Matplotlib, seaborn, and Plotly for data visualization
- Jupyter Notebook essentials
- Scikit-Learn: Key to streamlined Machine Learning

Objectives

By the end of this chapter, you should develop an in-depth understanding of the essential Python libraries and tools used in data science, enabling you to confidently handle, analyze, and visualize data. This foundation will prepare you for diving deeper into more advanced concepts and techniques in the upcoming chapters.

Setting up your developer environment

Before diving into data science, you must have a solid foundation, beginning with your developer environment. Installing the right tools and libraries can make all the difference in terms of productivity and ease of learning. In this section, we will guide you through setting up your developer environment using **Anaconda**, a popular and comprehensive distribution platform for Python that includes many essential packages for data science.

Anaconda simplifies the process of installing and managing packages, making it easy to get started with your data science journey. Following the steps outlined here, you can access the necessary libraries, like **NumPy**, **Pandas**, **Scikit-learn**, **Jupyter Notebook**, **Matplotlib**, **seaborn**, and **Plotly**, in no time. This will ensure you are well equipped to tackle the fascinating topics and understand the hands-on examples throughout this book.

Let us start setting up your developer environment so that you can confidently explore the world of data science and make the most of your learning experience:

1. **Download and install Anaconda:** Visit the Anaconda website (**https://www. anaconda.com/products/distribution**) and download the appropriate installer for your operating system. Follow the installation instructions to get Anaconda up and running on your computer. The following figure shows the Anaconda home page:

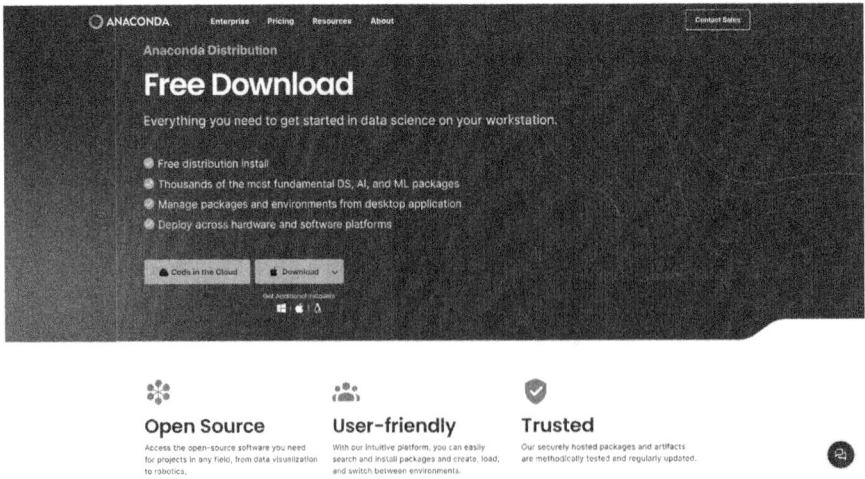

Figure 2.1: Downloading Anaconda

2. **Create a dedicated environment:** It is always a good practice to create a separate domain for each project. To do that, open the Anaconda prompt (or terminal on macOS/Linux) and run the following command, replacing **myenv** with a name of your choice. This will create a virtual environment with Python 3.11 installed. Use the following code:

```
conda create -n myenv python=3.11
```

3. **Activate your environment**: Before using your new environment, you must activate it. Run the following command, replacing **myenv** with the name you chose earlier:

```
conda activate myenv
```

4. **Install the required libraries**: Now that your environment is active, you can install the necessary libraries for this book. Run the following command in the Anaconda prompt or terminal:

```
conda install numpy pandas scikit learn jupyter matplotlib seaborn plotly
```

With your developer environment set up, you can dive into the world of data science and explore the fascinating topics covered in this book. Remember, though: this is a partial list of everything we will need for the rest of the book. We must install more packages, particularly as we go through the deep learning sections.

Basics of NumPy

Diving into the world of data science can be exciting and daunting. A secret weapon that makes working with numerical data a breeze is a library called **NumPy**, which is short for numerical Python. NumPy has been designed to help you quickly perform complex calculations and manipulate large, multi-dimensional arrays and matrices.

Imagine wielding the power of **C** and **Fortran** libraries in the familiar environment of Python. NumPy does precisely that, and as a result, it has become a tool for data scientists and researchers around the globe. Its high-performance capabilities and easy-to-use interface have made it an essential building block for many other Python libraries, such as Pandas and Scikit-learn.

In this section, we will embark on a journey to explore the fundamentals of NumPy. We will cover the creation and manipulation of arrays, learn about mathematical operations and broadcasting, and even dabble in some advanced techniques. By mastering these core concepts, you will be well on your way to becoming a data science wizard, ready to tackle complex challenges confidently and efficiently. Let us dive into the world of NumPy.

Array creation and manipulation

Arrays are the heart and soul of NumPy, and getting comfortable with creating and manipulating them is a crucial step in your data science journey. Arrays are like supercharged lists in Python; they can store large amounts of data, and NumPy allows us to perform various operations on them with lightning speed.

To create a NumPy array, we import the library and then use the **np.array()** function, passing in a list of numbers or lists for multi-dimensional arrays. For example, look at the following code:

```
import numpy as np


# Creating a 1D array
one_dim_array = np.array([1, 2, 3, 4, 5])
print(one_dim_array)  # Output: array([1, 2, 3, 4, 5])


# Creating a 2D array
two_dim_array = np.array([[1, 2], [3, 4], [5, 6]])
print(two_dim_array)  # Output: array([[1, 2], [3, 4], [5, 6]])
```

Now that we have created our arrays, let us dive into manipulating them. One common operation is accessing elements within the array. With NumPy, we can use indexing and slicing techniques similar to those with Python lists. Consider this example:

```
# Indexing
print(one_dim_array[2])  # Output: 3


# Slicing
print(one_dim_array[1:4])  # Output: array([2, 3, 4])


# Accessing elements in a 2D array
print(two_dim_array[1, 0])  # Output: 3
```

In addition to accessing individual elements, we can modify our arrays' shape and structure. Reshaping, for instance, allows us to change the dimensions of an array without altering its data. On the other hand, Transposing swaps the rows and columns of a 2D array. For example, consider the following code:

```
# Reshaping
reshaped_array = one_dim_array.reshape(5, 1)
print(reshaped_array)  # Output: array([[1], [2], [3], [4], [5]])

# Transposing
transposed_array = two_dim_array.T
print(transposed_array)  # Output: array([[1, 3, 5], [2, 4, 6]])
```

By mastering array creation and manipulation, you will unlock the true potential of NumPy and take your data analysis skills to new heights.

Mathematical operations with NumPy

As you delve deeper into data science, mathematical operations will become an indispensable part of your toolkit. NumPy shines in this area, offering various functions for performing element-wise operations, linear algebra, and statistical calculations.

Element-wise operations are performed on each element of the array independently. These operations can be as simple as addition or subtraction or more complex functions like exponentiation. NumPy makes this process incredibly efficient, allowing you to perform calculations on large arrays efficiently. Here is a quick example:

```
import numpy as np

A = np.array([1, 2, 3])
B = np.array([4, 5, 6])

# Element-wise addition
C = A + B
print(C)  # Output: array([5, 7, 9])

# Element-wise multiplication
D = A * B
print(D)  # Output: array([ 4, 10, 18])
```

Linear algebra is a branch of mathematics that deals with vector spaces and linear equations. NumPy provides a rich set of functions to handle common linear algebra tasks such as dot products, matrix multiplications, and solving systems of linear equations. Take a look at this example:

```
# Dot product
dot_product = np.dot(A, B)
print(dot_product)  # Output: 32

# Matrix multiplication
E = np.array([[1, 2], [3, 4]])
F = np.array([[5, 6], [7, 8]])
G = np.mammal(E, F)
print(G)  # Output: array([[19, 22], [43, 50]])
```

Statistical functions also play a crucial role in data analysis, allowing you to summarize and understand the properties of your data. NumPy offers statistical functions like mean, median, standard deviation, and correlation coefficients. Given an array of numbers, let us look at how to find the mean, median and standard deviation using the following code:

```
data = np.array([3, 5, 7, 9, 11])

# Mean
mean = np.mean(data)
print(mean)   # Output: 7.0

# Median
median = np.median(data)
print(median)   # Output: 7.0

# Standard deviation
std_dev = np.std(data)
print(std_dev)   # Output: 2.8284271247461903
```

Broadcasting

It is a powerful feature in NumPy that allows you to perform operations on arrays with different shapes and sizes efficiently and intuitively. It enables you to avoid explicit loops and rely on NumPy's internal optimizations for faster computations.

The term broadcasting refers to the process of automatically expanding one or more dimensions of an array so that the shapes of the arrays involved in an operation become compatible. For this to happen, NumPy follows a specific set of rules:

1. **Dimension alignment:** If the arrays have a different number of dimensions, prepend the shape of the smaller array with ones (1) until both arrays have the same number of dimensions.

2. **Shape compatibility:** Once the arrays have the same number of dimensions, check if their shapes are now compatible. Two dimensions are compatible if they are equal, or if one of them is 1. This rule means that NumPy can stretch the dimension of size 1 across the larger dimension to enable element-wise operations.

3. **Broadcasted operations:** When the shapes are deemed compatible, NumPy proceeds to perform the operation element-wise. During this operation, the smaller array is *broadcasted* over the larger array so that they behave as if they had the same shape.

Let us look at an example to understand how broadcasting works:

```
import numpy as np

A = np.array([[1, 2, 3], [4, 5, 6], [7, 8, 9]])
B = np.array([1, 0, -1])

# Broadcasting B to match the shape of A
C = A + B
print(C)
# Output:
# array([[ 2,  2,  2],
#        [ 5,  5,  5],
#        [ 8,  8,  8]])
```

In this example, array **A** has a shape of (3, 3), and array **B** has a shape of (3,). According to the broadcasting rules, **B** will be expanded along its missing dimension to match the shape of **A**, resulting in a new array with the same shape as **A**. Then, the element-wise addition will be performed.

Keep in mind that broadcasting is subject to specific rules and doesn't apply universally to all arrays with different shapes. If the arrays' shapes do not align with the broadcasting rules, NumPy will raise a **ValueError**. However, when the array shapes are compatible as per these rules, broadcasting enables efficient operations on arrays of different sizes, leading to code that is both more performant and more concise.

Advanced NumPy techniques

As you continue exploring the world of NumPy, you will encounter many advanced techniques that will empower you to manipulate and process your data more effectively. While you have already mastered the basics, this section will take you on a new journey, navigating the nuanced terrains of array reshaping, stacking and splitting. These techniques are not just about changing the structure of your data; they are about optimizing it for various analytical tasks, ensuring more efficient computations and setting the stage for more complex operations.

Array reshaping

Often, you will need to modify the shape of an array without altering its underlying data. The **reshape()** function in NumPy allows you to achieve this by specifying a new shape as a tuple of integers. Consider the following example:

```
import numpy as np
A = np.array([1, 2, 3, 4, 5, 6])
```

```
B = A.reshape((2, 3))

print(B)
# Output:
# array([[1, 2, 3],
#        [4, 5, 6]])
```

Stacking

When working with multiple arrays, you should combine them into a single array. NumPy provides the **hstack()** and **vstack()** functions for horizontal and vertical stacking, respectively. Consider the following code as an example:

```
C = np.array([1, 2, 3])
D = np.array([4, 5, 6])

# Vertical stacking
E = np.vstack((C, D))
print(E)
# Output:
# array([[1, 2, 3],
#        [4, 5, 6]])

# Horizontal stacking
F = np.hstack((C, D))
print(F)  # Output: array([1, 2, 3, 4, 5, 6])
```

Splitting

The opposite of stacking, splitting breaks an array into multiple smaller arrays along a specified axis. NumPy provides the **hsplit()** and **vsplit()** functions for horizontal and vertical splitting, respectively. For example, consider the following code:

```
G = np.array([[1, 2, 3], [4, 5, 6]])

# Vertical splitting
H, I = np.vsplit(G, 2)
print(H)  # Output: array([[1, 2, 3]])
print(I)  # Output: array([[4, 5, 6]])
# Horizontal splitting
J, K, L = np.hsplit(G, 3)
```

```
print(J)  # Output: array([[1], [4]])
print(K)  # Output: array([[2], [5]])
print(L)  # Output: array([[3], [6]])
```

Pandas for data manipulation

Pandas is a powerful, open-source Python library that has become an indispensable tool for data scientists and analysts. Designed specifically for data manipulation and analysis, Pandas provides a flexible and high-performance data structure called the **DataFrame**. With its intuitive syntax and extensive functionality, Pandas allows you to handle messy, real-world data, clean it, transform it, and extract meaningful insights.

In this section, we will explore the core features of Pandas and learn how to wield their power to manipulate, analyse, and visualize data like a pro. Get ready to dive into the world of DataFrames, slicing and dicing data and uncovering valuable patterns that will fuel your data-driven decisions.

Introducing series and DataFrame

Pandas is built upon two primary data structures: Series and DataFrames. Understanding these data structures is crucial to harnessing the full potential of Pandas for efficient data manipulation. Think of series as a single column of data, a one-dimensional array with labels; DataFrames can be visualized as a table, a collection of Series that can be of different data types. But these structures are not merely containers; they are dynamic entities equipped with a plethora of methods and attributes, designed to make data operations seamless. As we dig deeper into this section, you will come to appreciate the intricacies of these structures, understanding not just their form, but their function and significance in the broader context of data analysis.

Series

It is a one-dimensional labeled array containing any data type (integers, strings, floating point numbers, and so on). It is similar to a list in Python but with the added benefit of being indexed and labelled, making it easier to access and manipulate elements. Here is an example of how to create a series:

```
import pandas as pd


data = [1, 2, 3, 4, 5]
labels = ['a', 'b', 'c', 'd', 'e']
ser = pd.Series(data, index=labels)
```

```
print(ser)
# Output:
# a    1
# b    2
# c    3
# d    4
# e    5
# dtype: int64
```

DataFrame

It is two-dimensional and size-mutable, which means elements can be appended to or deleted from it, and it has a heterogeneous tabular data structure with labeled axes (rows and columns). It is similar to a spreadsheet or SQL table and is the most commonly used Pandas object. DataFrames can be created from various data sources, such as dictionaries, lists, and CSV files. Here is an example of creating a **DataFrame** from a dictionary:

```
data = {'Name': ['Alice', 'Bob', 'Charlie'],
        'Age': [25, 30, 35],
        'City': ['New York', 'San Francisco', 'Los Angeles']}


df = pd.DataFrame(data)


print(df)
# Output:
#       Name  Age           City
# 0    Alice   25       New York
# 1      Bob   30  San Francisco
# 2  Charlie   35    Los Angeles
```

With these two versatile data structures, you will be well equipped to tackle various data manipulation tasks. In the following sections, we will dive deeper into Pandas' rich functionality, enabling you to quickly clean, reshape, and analyze your data.

Reading and writing data from various file formats

One of the essential skills in the data science toolkit is the ability to import and export data from various file formats. As you will often find yourself working with data stored in different formats such as CSV, Excel and JSON, mastering these skills will make your life as a data scientist much easier. Pandas has covered you with its built-in functions for reading and writing data seamlessly across various formats.

Imagine receiving a CSV file containing a treasure trove of valuable data you cannot wait to analyze. With Pandas, importing this data into a DataFrame is a breeze. Let us look at how to do that using the following code:

```
import pandas as pd

csv_file = 'my_data.csv'
df = pd.read_csv(csv_file)
```

Your CSV data is now neatly organized in a DataFrame, ready for your manipulation and analysis.

Pandas is equally adept at handling data in Excel, JSON, and many more formats. For instance, to import data from an Excel file, use **read_excel**, as shown in the following code:

```
excel_file = 'my_data.xlsx'
df = pd.read_excel(excel_file)
```

And to read JSON data, you can rely on **read_json**. Execute the following code:

```
json_file = 'my_data.json'
df = pd.read_json(json_file)
```

Now, imagine you have spent hours cleaning and analyzing your data and unearthed some incredible insights. It is time to share your findings with the world. Pandas makes exporting your DataFrame to various file formats simple. To save your DataFrame as a CSV file, use the **to_csv** method and execute the following code:

```
output_csv = 'clean_data.csv'
df.to_csv(output_csv, index=False)
```

Similarly, you can export your DataFrame as an Excel file with **to_excel** or as a JSON file with **to_json**, as shown in the following code:

```
output_excel = 'clean_data.xlsx'
df.to_excel(output_excel, index=False)

output_json = 'clean_data.json'
df.to_json(output_json)
```

So, whether you are importing raw data or exporting polished insights, Pandas has your back, making it incredibly easy to work with data in diverse file formats. In the upcoming sections, we will explore more of the powerful features of Pandas.

Data cleaning and pre-processing

In the grand theater of data science, data cleaning and preprocessing play the role of unsung heroes, working diligently behind the scenes to ensure that the star performers, that is, the algorithms and models, shine brightly. Much like a sculptor who must choose and chisel a block of marble before crafting a masterpiece, a data scientist must refine and reshape raw data, stripping away its impurities and inconsistencies. While the allure of diving straight into modeling can be tempting, it is this meticulous groundwork that often dictates the quality of the final output. Pandas makes this once daunting task a structured and streamlined process. Equipped with a suite of powerful functions, Pandas ensures that your datasets, no matter how unruly, are polished and primed, ready to yield valuable insights.

Handling missing values

We have all encountered datasets with missing or incomplete data. Fortunately, Pandas makes detecting and dealing with these pesky missing values easy. The **isnull()** and **notnull()** methods help you identify missing values in your DataFrame, while the **fillna()** and **dropna()** methods allow you to fill in or remove values as needed. Let us look at how to perform these actions using the following code:

```
# Detect missing values in a DataFrame
missing_values = df.isnull()


# Fill missing values with a specified value (e.g., 0)
df_filled = df.fillna(0)


# Drop rows with missing values
df_clean = df.dropna()
```

Removing duplicates

Duplicate data can cause your analysis to go awry. Pandas has the **drop_duplicates()** method that helps you identify and remove duplicate rows in your DataFrame, keeping your data clean and unique. Here is how this is done:

```
# Remove duplicate rows from the DataFrame
df_no_duplicates = df.drop_duplicates()
```

Data type conversions

Sometimes, your data might be stored in a different format or type. Pandas provides a range of functions to convert data types, such as **astype()** and **to_numeric()**. For example, if you have a column of strings that should be integers, you can easily convert them with **astype()**. Here is an example:

```
# Convert a column from string to integer
df['column_name'] = df['column_name'].astype(int)
```

With these tools and techniques, you can transform raw, messy data into a clean, well-structured DataFrame.

Data aggregation and transformation

Data aggregation and transformation are akin to the art of sculpting your data into a masterpiece. Just as a sculptor shapes their material, Pandas allows you to mold your data into the precise form needed for meaningful analysis. Let us dive into some powerful Pandas techniques that will help you summarize and reshape your data like a pro.

Data aggregation with groupby

When you need to summarize your data by specific categories or groups, the **groupby** function is a lifesaver. It allows you to group your DataFrame by one or more columns and apply aggregate functions like **sum()**, **mean()**, or **count()** to these groups. For example, if you have a dataset of sales data and you want to calculate the total sales for each product, use the following code:

```
# Group the DataFrame by the 'product' column and calculate the total sales
total_sales = df.groupby('product')['sales'].sum()
```

Reshaping data with pivot

The **pivot** function lets you reorganize and reshape your DataFrame by creating a new table with a selected column as the index, another as columns, and a third as the data values. Suppose you have a dataset with daily sales for various products and you want to create a table where each row represents a date, each column represents a product, and the values are the sales figures. Execute the following code:

```
# Pivot the DataFrame to create a new table with dates as rows, prod-
ucts as columns, and sales as values
sales_pivot = df.pivot(index='date', columns='product', values='sales')
```

Melting data with melt

The **melt** function is the reverse of the **pivot** function. It allows you to convert a wide-format table (with multiple columns) into a long-format table (with key-value pairs). Suppose you have a table of monthly average temperatures for different cities and you want to convert it into a long format with columns for **city**, **month**, and **temperature**. Use the following code:

```
# Melt the DataFrame to create a long-format table with col-
umns for city, month, and temperature
temp_melted = df.melt(id_vars='month', var_name='city', value_name='tem-
perature')
```

With these powerful Pandas techniques in your arsenal, you will be ready to reshape and summarize your data like a skilled data artist. You will have the tools to reveal your data's hidden stories from aggregation to transformation.

Matplotlib, seaborn, and Plotly for data visualization

Three powerful Python libraries stand out in data visualization: Matplotlib, seaborn, and Plotly. They enable you to create engaging and informative plots that bring your data to life. Each library has unique strengths and capabilities, allowing you to create engaging and informative plots. While Matplotlib lays the groundwork, offering a versatile palette of plotting options, seaborn builds upon it, introducing a layer of abstraction that simplifies complex visualizations. And then there is Plotly, which elevates visualizations into interactive experiences, letting viewers dive deeper into the data. Together, these libraries form a trinity of visualization power, each complementing the other, ensuring that your data is not just seen but truly understood.

Basics of Matplotlib

Matplotlib provides the foundational tools for creating a wide array of plots and charts to reveal your data's hidden patterns and trends. Let us explore some of the basics of this versatile library as we learn to craft different plots, customize their appearance, and save our visual masterpieces for posterity.

First, you will be amazed by the variety of plots you can create with Matplotlib. From simple line and bar charts to complex scatter plots and histograms, there is a plot type for every data story you want to tell, and creating these plots is as easy as calling a few functions. Let us look at how to create a simple line plot:

```
import matplotlib.pyplot as plt

# Create a simple line plot
plt.plot(x, y)
```

Matplotlib provides an incredible array of customization options, allowing you to tweak every plot aspect from colors and markers to labels and legends. The sky is the limit when tailoring your visualizations to your unique needs and preferences. The following snippet of code lets you customize your plot with colors, markers and more:

```
# Customize the plot with colors, markers, labels, and more
plt.plot(x, y, color='red', marker='o', linestyle='--', label='My Data')
plt.legend()
```

Finally, once you have created a beautiful visualization, you will want to share it with the world (or at least save it for later). In Matplotlib, you can use the **plt.savefig** function to save your plots in various formats, as shown in the following code:

```
# Save your masterpiece as a high-quality image file
plt.savefig('my_plot.png', dpi=300)
```

Seaborn for advanced visualization

Picture this: You are ready to elevate your data visualization game and seek a powerful ally to help you achieve that goal. Enter seaborn, a Python library that specializes in statistical data visualization, and one that builds upon the solid foundation laid by Matplotlib. Seaborn simplifies the process of creating advanced visualizations, allowing you to focus on what truly matters and uncover insights from your data.

Seaborn's charm lies in its ability to generate sophisticated visualizations with minimal code, thanks to its high-level functions and built-in themes. No more fiddling with countless customization options to create a stunning plot. With seaborn, you can create a heatmap, violin plot, or swarm plot as easily as a bar chart. Here is an example:

```
import seaborn as sns

# Create an elegant heatmap with a single line of code
sns.heatmap(data)
```

The beauty of seaborn is that it does the heavy lifting for you. For instance, it automatically calculates and displays summary statistics, regression lines, and confidence intervals, allowing you to focus on interpreting the results. Execute the following code:

```
# Create a scatter plot with a regression line and confidence interval
sns.regplot(x='age', y='income', data=df)
```

And if you are feeling particularly creative, seaborn enables you to combine multiple plots into a single, cohesive visualization called a **FacetGrid**. Let us look at how to do that using the following code:

```
# Create a FacetGrid with multiple scatter plots based on adefinitel vari-
able
g = sns.FacetGrid(df, col='category')
g.map(sns.scatterplot, 'age', 'income')
```

As you can see, seaborn is a formidable partner in your data visualization journey. It empowers you to create insightful and aesthetically pleasing visualizations that reveal the hidden stories within your data. With seaborn, you can tackle even the most complex data challenges.

Interactive visualizations with Plotly

Suppose you have crafted the perfect visualization but want your audience to dive deeper and explore the data for themselves. This is where interactive visualizations come into play, and Plotly is here to make that dream a reality. Its versatile Python library allows you to create interactive, web-based plots that enable users to hover over, zoom, and select data points to uncover hidden insights.

The benefits of interactive visualizations are manifold. They empower your audience to engage with the data in a more immersive manner, fostering a deeper understanding of the underlying patterns and relationships. Moreover, interactive plots can handle large volumes of data, allowing users to focus on specific subsets without information overload.

Creating interactive visualizations with Plotly is a breeze. The library provides an extensive collection of chart types, from primary line and bar charts to more advanced plots such as contour and 3D surface plots. Here is a simple example of how to create an interactive scatter plot with Plotly:

```
import plotly.express as px


# Create an interactive scatter plot using Plotly Express
fig = px.scatter(x=df['age'], y=df['income'], hover_data=['name'])
fig.show()
```

With a few lines of code, you have created an interactive plot that allows users to hover over data points to reveal additional information, such as the individual's name in the preceding example. Plotly's functionality extends to creating dashboards, subplots, and animations, offering you a comprehensive toolkit for designing captivating and interactive data visualizations.

Choosing the right visualization

Selecting the correct visualization is essential for any data scientist, as the most compelling plot type can significantly enhance your audience's understanding of your data. When choosing a visualization, consider the following tips to ensure that your plots communicate the story behind the data effectively and engagingly:

- **Understand your data:** Familiarize yourself with the dataset, its variables, and the relationships between them. Determine whether you are working with categorical or numerical variables, and also determine the level of granularity needed to convey your message.

- **Define your goal:** Determine the critical message or insight you want to communicate with your visualization. This could showcase trends, compare values, demonstrate distribution, or reveal relationships between variables.

- **Consider your audience:** Tailor your visualization to your audience's expertise and familiarity with the subject matter. Simpler plots like bar and line charts are more accessible to a general audience, while advanced visualizations may be better suited for experts.

- **Choose the appropriate plot type:** Based on your goal, select a plot type that effectively communicates the desired message. Some standard options are listed here:

  o **Bar chart:** For comparing categorical data

  o **Line chart:** For showing trends over time

  o **Scatter plot:** For illustrating relationships between two numerical variables

  o **Histogram:** For displaying the distribution of a single numerical variable

  o **Box plot:** For comparing distributions across different categories

- **Keep it simple and clean:** Avoid clutter and unnecessary complexity in your visualizations. Stick to a minimal color palette, use clear labels, and ensure that the plot is easy to interpret.

By following these guidelines, you will be well on your way to creating impactful and engaging visualizations that effectively communicate the story behind your data. Remember that the goal of data visualization is to facilitate understanding, so always prioritize clarity and simplicity over flashy aesthetics.

Jupyter Notebook essentials

Imagine a canvas where code, visualization, and narrative merge seamlessly to paint a holistic picture of data exploration and analysis. This is the realm of Jupyter Notebooks, an indispensable tool in the toolkit of modern data scientists and analysts. Beyond just an interactive programming environment, Jupyter Notebooks serve as dynamic digital journals, capturing the entire life cycle of a data project, from the initial spark of an idea to the final insights. The beauty of these notebooks lies in their adaptability; whether you are crunching complex algorithms, penning down observations, or crafting intricate visualizations, Jupyter accommodates it all. As we delve deeper into this section, you will pick up essential skills and learn shortcuts to master Jupyter, turning it into an ally that amplifies your efficiency, fosters collaboration, and adds a touch of elegance to your data presentations.

Launching and understanding the interface

Embarking on the Jupyter journey begins with launching its intuitive interface, a gateway that melds simplicity with power. Much like the cockpit of an aircraft, the Jupyter interface might appear overwhelming at first, brimming with buttons, tabs, and panels. However, each element is meticulously designed to enhance your coding and analytical experience, ensuring smooth navigation through your data explorations. As we delve into this section, we will demystify the Jupyter dashboard, guiding you through its intricacies and revealing the logic and convenience behind each component.

You can launch Jupyter Notebook by typing **jupyter notebook** in your command prompt or terminal. This is how your terminal should look:

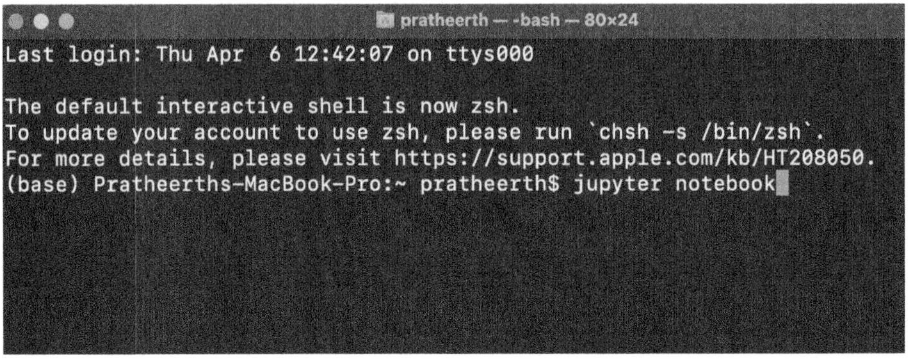

Figure 2.2: Jupyter Notebook command in terminal

This will open a new browser window with the Jupyter Notebook interface. The following figure is what you will be greeted with; it is the dashboard, where you can navigate through your files and folders, create new notebooks, or open existing ones. Take a look at the following figure:

Figure 2.3: Jupyter Notebook UI

As you explore the Jupyter Notebook interface, you will notice that it consists of cells, which are the building blocks of your notebook. Cells can contain code, Markdown text for documentation, or even raw text. Jupyter Notebook can execute code cells and display the output right below them, making it a fantastic tool for step-by-step data analysis and visualization.

Code, Markdown, and raw cells

The cells in Jupyter Notebook are the fundamental building blocks that make your notebook an all-in-one platform for coding, documentation, and output display. Notebook cells come in code, Markdown, and raw cells; let us explore each one in detail.

Code cells are where you will write and execute your Python code. You can run a code cell by pressing *Shift + Enter* or clicking the **run** button on the toolbar. The output, if any, appears right below the cell, making it easy to follow the flow of your analysis.

Markdown cells, on the other hand, allow you to write rich-text documentation to accompany your code. These cells support Markdown syntax, which means you can format text, add headings, create lists, and even include images or mathematical equations. To switch a cell to Markdown mode, select **Markdown** from the drop-down menu in the toolbar or press *Esc + M*. When ready to render your **Markdown** cell, press *Shift + Enter*.

Lastly, raw cells store text that should not be formatted or executed. This can be helpful when you want to include raw code snippets or notes that do not need to be rendered. To create a raw cell, select **Raw** from the drop-down menu in the toolbar or press *Esc + R*. With these three cell types at your disposal, Jupyter Notebook becomes a powerful and flexible tool for weaving together code, documentation, and outputs in a single, interactive document. You can easily change the type of cell using the drop-down menu, as shown in the following figure:

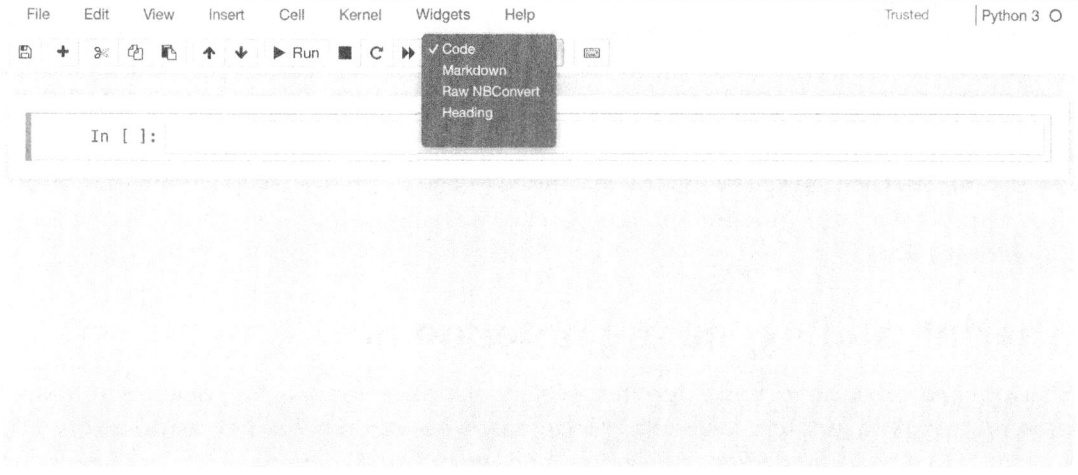

Figure 2.4: Choose from code, Markdown and Raw cells

Executing code and displaying results

Now that you know Jupyter Notebook's cell types, let us dive into executing code and displaying results. Running cells, using cell magics, and showcasing rich output are all essential to maximizing your Jupyter Notebook experience.

To execute a code cell, like we mentioned, simply press *Shift + Enter* or click the **Run** button on the toolbar. This will run the code in the cell and display the output, if any, right below it. Keep in mind that the order in which you run cells matters, as the output of one cell may depend on the code executed in the previous cells. Take a look at the following figure:

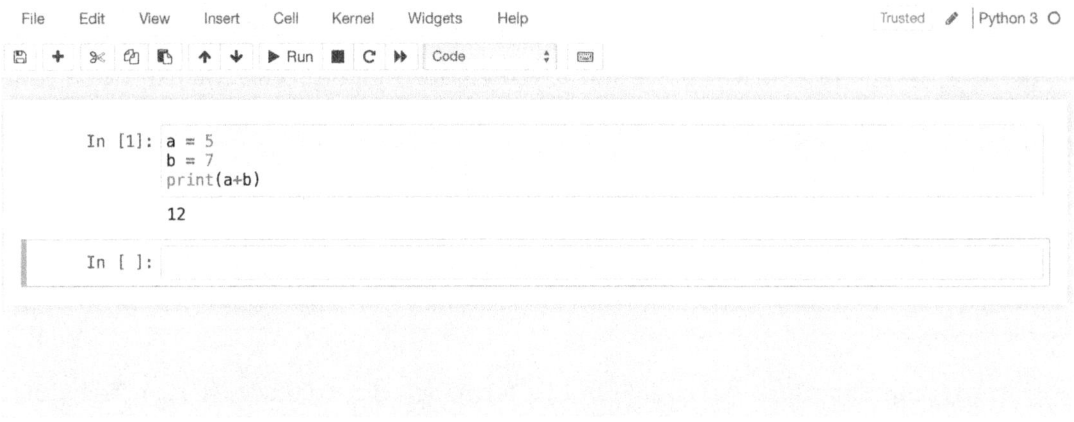

Figure 2.5: Running a code cell

Jupyter Notebook offers a powerful feature called **cell magics**, which are special commands that make your coding even more efficient. Cell magics are preceded by a percent sign (**%**) for single-line magics and a double percent sign (**%%**) for multi-line magics. For example, **%timeit** measures the execution time of a single line of code, while **%%timeit** measures the execution time of the entire cell. Many other cell magics are available, like **%run** for running external scripts or **%reset** for clearing your workspace.

Rich output is another feature of Jupyter Notebook, allowing you to display a wide variety of content types, such as images, audio, video, and interactive widgets. For instance, you can use the **IPython.display** module to embed images with the **Image()** function, audio files with the **Audio()** function, or even create interactive sliders and buttons using the **ipywidgets** library.

Sharing and exporting notebooks

Sharing and exporting your Jupyter Notebooks is essential to collaboration and presentation. With Jupyter Notebook, you can easily convert notebooks to various formats, such as HTML, PDF, and even slideshows, and work with your colleagues or share your insights with a broader audience.

To convert a notebook to a different format, you can use the **nbconvert** tool, which comes with the Jupyter installation. For instance, to convert your notebook to an HTML file, you can run the following command in your terminal or command prompt:

```
Jupyter nbconvert -to html your_notebook.ipynb
```

This will generate an HTML file that can be opened in any web browser. Similarly, you can convert your notebook to a PDF file by running Jupyter **nbconvert --to pdf your_notebook.ipynb**. Note that this may require additional dependencies, such as **LaTeX**, to be installed on your system.

Another convenient way to share your notebooks is by using Jupyter's built-in integration with various online platforms, such as **GitHub** or **Google Drive**. By pushing your notebooks to a GitHub repository, you enable others to view and interact with your work in their web browser without needing to install anything locally. Alternatively, you can upload your notebooks to Google Drive and collaborate with others in real time using Google Colaboratory.

Scikit-learn: Key to streamlined Machine Learning

The final essential tool in our data science armory is Scikit-learn.

It is a powerful and popular Python library for **Machine Learning (ML)** that offers a wide range of tools for data preprocessing, model training, and evaluation. It is designed to be easy to use, efficient, and compatible with other popular data science libraries like NumPy and Pandas. Scikit-learn provides a consistent API for various machine learning algorithms, making it easier for beginners to learn and for professionals to switch between different models.

Scikit-learn has earned its place as an indispensable tool in the data science world. It is a great library that makes machine learning approachable and efficient. Think of it as a one-stop shop for all your data pre-processing, model training, and evaluation needs, all neatly packaged in a user-friendly Python library.

What makes Scikit-learn so valuable is its seamless compatibility with other popular data science libraries like NumPy and Pandas, allowing you to integrate it into your existing data workflows effortlessly. It has a consistent API for a wide range of machine learning algorithms, so whether you are a beginner starting your data science journey or a seasoned pro, you will appreciate how easy it is to switch between models and techniques.

In a nutshell, Scikit-learn is your trusted companion on your data science adventures, offering a robust set of tools to help you uncover hidden patterns, make predictions, and ultimately, turn data into actionable insights.

Conclusion

As we wrap up this chapter, you should now have a solid understanding of essential Python libraries and tools that form the backbone of any data science project. We explored the power of NumPy and Pandas for data manipulation, Matplotlib, seaborn, and Plotly for data visualization in this chapter, and we delved into the versatile Scikit-learn library for machine learning tasks. Additionally, we introduced you to the interactive Jupyter Notebook environment for seamless code execution and documentation. With these powerful tools, you can tackle more advanced data science topics and techniques in the upcoming chapters.

In the next chapter, we will discuss the fundamental concepts of probability theory, distributions, sampling, and hypothesis testing to build a strong foundation for data analysis and decision-making.

Points to remember

- NumPy is an essential library for numerical computing, offering powerful tools for array creation, manipulation, and mathematical operations.

- Pandas provides robust data structures like Series and DataFrames, making data manipulation and cleaning a breeze.

- Matplotlib, seaborn, and Plotly are powerful visualization libraries that allow us to create static, statistical, and interactive visualizations, respectively.

- Jupyter Notebook is an interactive environment that enables seamless code execution, documentation, and sharing, making it a valuable tool for data scientists.

- Scikit-learn is a versatile library for machine learning tasks, offering built-in tools for data preprocessing, model training, and evaluation.

Multiple choice questions

1. **Which of the following Python libraries is primarily used for numerical computing?**

    a. Matplotlib

    b. NumPy

    c. Pandas

    d. Seaborn

2. **What are the two main data structures provided by Pandas for efficient data manipulation?**

   a. Arrays and tuples

   b. Lists and dictionaries

   c. Series and DataFrames

   d. Sets and queues

3. **Which library is best suited for creating interactive visualizations in Python?**

   a. Matplotlib

   b. seaborn

   c. Plotly

   d. Ggplot

4. **In Jupyter Notebook, what type of cell is primarily used for adding text, images, and formatting using Markdown?**

   a. Code cell

   b. Markdown cell

   c. Raw cell

   d. Text cell

Answers

1. b

2. c

3. c

4. b

Questions

1. What are the main advantages of using Jupyter Notebook for data science projects?

2. Explain the concept of broadcasting in NumPy and how it helps in efficient array operations.

3. Describe the differences between Matplotlib, seaborn, and Plotly in terms of their use cases and capabilities.

Join our book's Discord space

Join the book's Discord Workspace for Latest updates, Offers, Tech happenings around the world, New Release and Sessions with the Authors:

https://discord.bpbonline.com

Chapter 3
Statistics and Probability Essentials for Data Science

Introduction

Welcome to the exciting world of statistics and probability in data science! This chapter will delve into the foundational concepts that form the basis of statistical analysis and probabilistic reasoning. We will explore the principles of probability theory, understand different distributions and sampling methods, and finally, learn about hypothesis testing. These concepts will empower you to make data-driven decisions and effectively analyze and interpret data.

Structure

In this chapter, we will discuss the following topics:

- Probability theory
- Basic probability concepts
- Conditional probability and Bayes' theorem
- Discrete and continuous random variables
- Expectation, variance, and covariance of random variables
- Distributions and sampling

- Central limit theorem
- Sampling techniques
- Hypothesis testing

Objectives

By the end of this chapter, you should be well versed in essential statistical and probabilistic concepts and techniques that play an important role in data science. With this strong foundation, you will be able to understand advanced topics and apply these concepts in real-world data analysis scenarios.

Probability theory

It is the branch of mathematics that deals with the study of uncertainty, helping us make sense of random events in our lives. From figuring out the chances of getting a specific card in a deck to predicting the weather, probability is at the heart of understanding the world around us. Probability theory is the foundation for many essential concepts in data science and **Machine Learning (ML)**.

In this section, we will introduce you to the basics of probability theory, including definitions, concepts, and the different rules governing it. By the end of this topic, you should have a solid understanding of probability and its importance in the world of data science.

Basic probability concepts

Diving into probability, we will begin by exploring the core concepts of events, sample space, and probability axioms. Grasping these fundamentals will empower us to navigate probability problems and enhance our data-driven decision-making capabilities skillfully. Let us understand each one by one.

Events

Events, in probability theory, are the outcomes we are trying to predict or analyze. They represent the various possibilities that can happen in a given situation. Think about rolling a die; you might be interested in finding the likelihood of rolling a 3, or perhaps you want to know the probability of rolling an even number. In both cases, the roll of a 3 or an even number are examples of events.

There are different types of events. We have simple events, also known as elementary events, which are the most basic outcomes that cannot be broken down any further. For example, rolling a specific number on a die is a simple event. On the other hand, we have compound events, which are combinations of two or more simple events. Continuing with the die example, rolling an even number is a compound event, as it consists of rolling a 2, 4, or 6.

Then, we have **complementary events**, which are pairs of events where one event occurring means the other cannot occur, and vice versa. In other words, if one event happens, its complement will not happen. For example, when flipping a coin, the complementary events are getting a head or a tail. If you get heads, you cannot get tails in the same flip. The probability of a complementary event occurring is equal to 1 minus the probability of the original event occurring.

Finally, let us talk about the intersection and union of events. These concepts come from set theory, and they help us understand how different events can overlap or combine.

The intersection of events (denoted as $A \cap B$) refers to the situation where both events A and B occur simultaneously. In the context of probability, it represents the probability of both events happening together. For instance, if you were to draw two cards from a deck, the intersection of drawing a heart and a queen would be the probability of drawing the queen of hearts.

The union of events (denoted as $A \cup B$) signifies the scenario where either event A or event B or both occur. It represents the combined probability of A or B happening. For instance, consider drawing a single card from a deck. The union of drawing a heart or a queen includes all the hearts and all the queens. However, the queen of hearts is counted only once, although it belongs to both categories.

Sample space

When one first learns about probability, grasping the concept of sample space often proves to be a game changer. It is like a menu of all possible outcomes of an experiment, giving you the full range of what could happen.

For example, suppose you are throwing a party and want to decide a dress code. You have two options for the top (shirt or sweater) and two options for the bottom (pants or shorts). Your sample space here would be the different outfit combinations: {(shirt, pants), (shirt, shorts), (sweater, pants), (sweater, shorts)}.

Let us discuss the key aspects of sample space in more detail:

- **Listing all possibilities:** A sample space needs to cover every potential outcome, no matter how simple or complex. For instance, when flipping a coin, you have two options: heads (H) and tails (T). Likewise, when rolling a six-sided die, your sample space includes {1, 2, 3, 4, 5, 6}.

- **Discrete versus continuous:** Sample spaces can be either discrete (finite or countable) or continuous (uncountably infinite). Discrete examples include rolling dice or drawing a card from a deck, while continuous ones involve measuring temperatures or pinpointing the exact time of an event. Continuous sample spaces often need integration and probability density functions for calculations.

- **Equal chances:** Sometimes, all outcomes in the sample space have the same likelihood of happening, like rolling a fair die or flipping a fair coin. This makes probability calculations simpler, but real-life scenarios often have unequal chances, calling for more sophisticated methods.

- **Event subsets:** Events are usually part of the sample space since they represent specific outcomes we are interested in. For example, if we are looking at the chances of rolling an even number on a six-sided die, the event is the subset {2, 4, 6} within the sample space {1, 2, 3, 4, 5, 6}. By understanding the relationship between events and sample spaces, we can use set operations (intersection, union, complement) to calculate probabilities and study dependencies between events.

Conditional probability and Bayes' theorem

In the realm of probability theory, conditional probability and Bayes' theorem play a vital role in helping us assess the likelihood of an event, given new information or evidence. Conditional probability allows us to revise probabilities based on observed data, while Bayes' theorem elegantly connects prior knowledge with new observations. Together, these powerful tools enable us to refine our beliefs, make better predictions, and navigate the uncertainty inherent in the world around us.

Conditional probability

Conditional probability is an essential concept in probability theory that deals with the probability of an event occurring, given that another event has already occurred. Essentially, it enables us to adjust our understanding of the likelihood of a particular event occurring based on new evidence or information.

Let us look at a simple example to illustrate the concept of conditional probability. Suppose you have a standard deck of 52 playing cards, and you want to find the probability of drawing an ace. There are 4 aces in the deck, so the probability of drawing an ace is 4/52 or 1/13. Now, let us say you already know that the card you drew is a red card (either a heart or a diamond). Given this new information, we can recalculate the probability of drawing an ace. There are 2 red aces (ace of hearts and ace of diamonds) and 26 red cards in total, so the conditional probability of drawing an ace given that you drew a red card is 2/26 or 1/13.

Mathematically, conditional probability is expressed as $P(A \mid B)$, which reads as the probability of event A occurring, given that event B has occurred. The formula for calculating conditional probability is $P(A \mid B) = P(A \cap B) / P(B)$, where $P(A \cap B)$ represents the probability of both events A and B occurring together, and $P(B)$ is the probability of event B occurring.

Understanding conditional probability is important for making informed decisions and predictions in various fields, such as finance, medicine, and engineering. It helps us update our beliefs and expectations based on new information and contributes to the foundation of many advanced probabilistic models and techniques.

Bayes' theorem

Bayes' theorem is a powerful and widely used concept in probability theory that helps us update our beliefs and make predictions based on new evidence. Named after the *Reverend Thomas Bayes*, an 18th-century mathematician and theologian, this theorem provides a way to combine prior knowledge or beliefs with new evidence to refine our understanding of the likelihood of an event occurring. It is a fundamental tool in many fields, including finance, medicine, and even **Artificial Intelligence (AI)**.

To help you grasp Bayes' theorem, let us consider a relatable example. Suppose you have a friend named Sarah who is usually punctual. From your past experiences, you know that she is on time 90% of the time (prior probability). One day, you hear that there is heavy traffic in the city, and you know that when there is traffic, Sarah is late 75% of the time. Now, you want to calculate the probability of Sarah being late today, given the traffic situation (posterior probability). This is where Bayes' theorem comes into play.

In mathematical terms, Bayes' theorem is written as $P(A|B) = (P(B|A) * P(A)) / P(B)$. In our example, A represents the event 'Sarah is late', and B represents the event 'there is traffic'. We already know the prior probabilities $P(A) = 10\%$ (probability of Sarah being late) and $P(B|A) = 75\%$ (probability of traffic when Sarah is late). To find P(B), we can use the law of total probability: $P(B) = P(B|A) * P(A) + P(B|\neg A) * P(\neg A)$, where $\neg A$ means not A. In this case, $P(B|\neg A)$ would be the probability of traffic when Sarah is not late. Let us assume that it is 20%. So, $P(B) = (0.75 * 0.1) + (0.2 * 0.9) = 0.255$.

Now we can apply Bayes' theorem: $P(A|B) = (P(B|A) * P(A)) / P(B) = (0.75 * 0.1) / 0.255 \approx 0.294$. So, given the traffic situation, there is approximately a 29.4% chance that Sarah will be late today.

By using Bayes' theorem, we have updated our belief about Sarah's punctuality based on the new evidence (traffic). This powerful technique is applicable in numerous situations and plays an important role in decision-making, risk assessment, and even machine learning algorithms.

Discrete and continuous random variables

Building on our understanding of conditional probability and Bayes' theorem, let us now dive into the realm of discrete and continuous random variables, which will help us quantify and model the uncertainties present in various types of events and scenarios.

Discrete and continuous random variables are two key concepts in probability theory that describe different types of outcomes for experiments or events. Understanding the differences between them is essential for choosing the appropriate tools and techniques when working with data.

Before diving into that though, let us answer this question: what is a random variable?

A **random variable** is not just any variable, but rather a specific kind of variable that represents the possible outcomes of a random phenomenon or experiment. It is best understood as a rule or a mechanism that assigns numerical values to each possible outcome of a random event. For example, in a dice roll, the random variable could assign a number to each of the six possible outcomes (1 through 6).

As we know, there are two main types: discrete and continuous.

A **discrete random variable** represents a finite or countably infinite number of distinct outcomes. In other words, there is a limited set of possible values that can be enumerated. Some common examples of discrete random variables are listed here:

- The number of heads obtained when flipping a coin three times.
- The number of defective items in a production batch.
- The number of students in a classroom.

In contrast, a continuous random variable represents an uncountably infinite number of outcomes, usually corresponding to a range of values within an interval. Some common examples of continuous random variables are as follows:

- The height of a randomly chosen person.
- The exact time it takes for a chemical reaction to occur.
- The weight of a randomly picked fruit from a grocery store.

Expectation, variance, and covariance of random variables

Now that we have got a solid foundation in random variables, it is time to explore some essential concepts that will help us better understand the properties of these variables: expectation, variance, and covariance. These tools allow us to summarize and analyze the behavior of random variables, giving us insights into their central tendencies, dispersion, and the relationships between them.

Expectation

Expectation, also known as **expected value** or **mean**, is a powerful concept in probability theory that helps us understand the long-term average outcome of a random variable. Think of it as the **center of mass** of a distribution, which represents the average value we expect to see if we repeat the experiment an infinite number of times.

Let us break it down with an example. Suppose you have a fair six-sided die, and you want to find the expected value of a roll. The random variable here is the outcome of the die roll, which can take on values 1 through 6. To calculate the expected value, we need to weigh each possible outcome by its probability, which, in this case, is 1/6 for each side. So, the expected value would be as follows:

(1 * 1/6) + (2 * 1/6) + (3 * 1/6) + (4 * 1/6) + (5 * 1/6) + (6 * 1/6) = 3.5

Interestingly, the result, 3.5, is not an actual outcome on the die, but it tells us that, on average, over many die rolls, we would expect the result to be around 3.5. It is important to remember that the expected value is not a prediction of a single outcome but a measure of the central tendency of a random variable over numerous repetitions of an experiment.

Expectation also has useful properties that make it a handy tool in probability theory. For example, the expectation of a sum of random variables is equal to the sum of their expectations, and the expectation of a constant multiplied by a random variable is equal to the constant multiplied by the expectation of the random variable. These properties can simplify complex problems and make them more manageable.

Variance

Variance is another important concept in probability theory that helps us measure how much random variable deviates from its expected value, or in other words, how spread out the distribution of the variable is. A higher variance means that the values are more dispersed, while a lower variance implies that the values are clustered closer to the mean.

Let us use the same example of a fair six-sided die to illustrate variance. We already know that the expected value of a roll is 3.5. Now, we want to find out how much the outcomes vary from this average. To calculate the variance, we first find the squared difference between each possible outcome and the mean, then weigh it by its probability, and finally, sum it all up. So, the variance would be as follows:

((1-3.5)^2 * 1/6) + ((2-3.5)^2 * 1/6) + ((3-3.5)^2 * 1/6) + ((4-3.5)^2 * 1/6) + ((5-3.5)^2 * 1/6) + ((6-3.5)^2 * 1/6) ≈ 2.92

The variance we have calculated, approximately *2.92*, indicates that the die rolls are somewhat dispersed around the mean value of *3.5*. Keep in mind that variance is always non-negative, as it involves squaring the differences.

One common way to express the dispersion of a random variable more intuitively is by using the standard deviation, which is simply the square root of the variance. In our example, the standard deviation would be roughly 1.71. This value gives us a better sense of the average deviation of the die rolls from the mean since it is on the same scale as the original values.

Covariance

Covariance is a measure that tells us how two random variables change or vary together, helping us understand the relationship between them. If the covariance is positive, it means that when one variable increases, the other tends to increase as well. Conversely, if the covariance is negative, it indicates that when one variable goes up, the other tends to go down. If the covariance is close to zero, it suggests that a strong relationship does not exist between the two variables.

Let us illustrate covariance with a simple example. Suppose we have two random variables, X and Y, representing the daily temperature and ice cream sales, respectively. Intuitively, we can guess that on hotter days, ice cream sales are likely to be higher. To calculate the covariance between X and Y, we first find the expected values of both variables. Let us say the expected daily temperature (X) is 75°F, and the expected daily ice cream sales (Y) are 100 units.

Now, we want to determine how much the temperature and ice cream sales deviate from their respective means and whether they do so in the same direction. To compute the covariance, we multiply the deviations of X and Y from their means for each observation and then find the average of these products:

$Cov(X, Y) = E[(X - E[X])(Y - E[Y])]$

If the covariance value turns out to be positive, it confirms our intuition that higher temperatures coincide with increased ice cream sales. However, covariance can be difficult to interpret on its own, as it is highly dependent on the units and scales of the variables.

To overcome this limitation, we often use the correlation coefficient, which standardizes the covariance by dividing it by the product of the standard deviations of the two variables. The correlation coefficient ranges from -1 to 1, with -1 indicating a perfect negative relationship, 1 indicating a perfect positive relationship, and 0 suggesting no relationship between the variables.

Distributions and sampling

As we move further into the world of probability and statistics, it is important that we familiarize ourselves with the concepts of distributions and sampling. Distributions give us a comprehensive view of how data is spread out, helping us identify patterns and trends in the underlying population. Sampling, on the other hand, is all about selecting a representative subset of data from a larger population to make inferences and draw conclusions. Together, these two concepts form the backbone of statistical analysis. Let us see how they can improve our data-driven decision-making.

Probability distributions

In this section, we will explore some common probability distributions that frequently appear in data science and statistics. These distributions serve as convenient models for understanding the behavior and characteristics of various types of data.

Probability distributions come in two distinct types: discrete and continuous.

Discrete distributions come into play when we are working with a finite or countably infinite number of outcomes, like the number of heads in a series of coin flips or the number of visitors to a website on a given day.

Let us look at a few examples of discrete distributions:

- **Binomial distribution:** This distribution models the number of successes in a fixed number of independent Bernoulli trials with the same probability of success. It is particularly useful when looking at scenarios like the number of heads in a series of coin flips or the number of defective products in a batch.

- **Poisson distribution:** The Poisson distribution models the number of events occurring in a fixed period of time or space if these events occur independently and at a constant average rate. It is often used in situations like modeling the number of calls received at a call center or the number of emails arriving in your inbox over a certain period.

- **Geometric distribution:** This distribution describes the number of Bernoulli trials needed for the first success. It can be used to model situations like the number of attempts to pass a driving test or the number of coin flips needed to get the first head.

Continuous distributions, on the other hand, handle scenarios with an uncountably infinite number of outcomes, like the exact time someone finishes a marathon or the precise weight of a randomly chosen apple.

Just like we did with discrete distributions, let us take a quick peek at three examples of continuous distributions:

- **Uniform distribution:** The uniform distribution is the simplest continuous distribution, where all outcomes in a given interval are equally likely. It is often used to model situations where we have no reason to believe that any outcome is more likely than another, such as randomly picking a point on a line segment.

- **Normal (Gaussian) distribution:** The normal distribution, also known as the Gaussian or bell curve, is a symmetric distribution characterized by its mean and standard deviation. Many natural phenomena and measurement errors tend to follow the normal distribution, making it an essential tool in statistics and data science.

- **Exponential distribution:** The exponential distribution models the time between events in a Poisson process, where events occur continuously and independently at a constant average rate. It is useful for modeling situations like the time between customer arrival at a store or the lifespan of electronic components.

Central limit theorem

Building on our understanding of common probability distributions, the **central limit theorem (CLT)** offers significant insights into the behavior of large sample sizes, allowing us to make informed inferences about populations and simplifying our analysis by leveraging the powerful properties of the normal distribution.

The CLT is a fundamental concept in statistics with profound implications for data analysis, hypothesis testing, and confidence intervals. In essence, the theorem states that the sum or average of a large number of independent and identically distributed random variables, regardless of their underlying distribution, tends to follow a normal distribution as the sample size grows.

Let us break this down a bit further:

- **Independence:** The random variables must be independent, meaning that the outcome of one variable does not influence the outcome of another. In practice, this is often a reasonable assumption for many real-world situations.

- **Identically distributed:** The random variables must share the same probability distribution, meaning they must follow the same pattern of variation.

- **Large sample size:** The CLT holds as the sample size approaches infinity, but in practice, a sample size of 30 or more is often sufficient for the theorem to be applicable.

The implications of the CLT are far-reaching and touch many aspects of data analysis:

- **Confidence intervals:** The CLT allows us to construct confidence intervals for population parameters, such as the mean or proportion, even when the underlying population distribution is unknown.

- **Hypothesis testing:** The theorem forms the basis of many hypothesis tests, including the popular t-test and z-test, which are used to compare means or proportions between groups.

- **Simplification of analysis:** The CLT enables us to use the properties of the normal distribution to analyze data, even when the original data does not follow a normal distribution. This simplifies our analytical processes and makes it easier to draw conclusions from complex data sets.

Sampling techniques

In the context of the central limit theorem, which highlights the importance of large sample sizes, various sampling techniques become essential to ensure representative and unbiased data collection.

Sampling techniques play a significant role in gathering representative data from a larger population for statistical analysis. There are several methods to choose from, but in this section, we will focus on three popular techniques: random, stratified, and cluster sampling. Let us look at each one:

- **Random sampling:** In random sampling, each element in the population has an equal chance of being selected. This method is simple and unbiased, as it eliminates the possibility of selection bias. However, it may not always result in a sample that accurately represents the population's diverse characteristics.

- **Stratified sampling:** Stratified sampling involves dividing the population into homogeneous subgroups or strata based on specific attributes (such as age, gender, or income) and then selecting a random sample from each stratum. This technique ensures that the sample includes a proportional representation of each subgroup, leading to more accurate and reliable results.

- **Cluster sampling:** Cluster sampling entails dividing the population into clusters, typically based on geographical or organizational boundaries. Instead of sampling elements individually, entire clusters are selected at random, and all elements within those chosen clusters are included in the sample. This method is useful when dealing with large populations spread across a wide area, as it reduces the cost and effort involved in data collection.

Each of these sampling techniques has its advantages and drawbacks, and the choice of the most suitable method depends on the research objectives and the population's characteristics.

Hypothesis testing

Hypothesis testing is a significant component of statistical analysis, allowing us to make inferences and draw conclusions about population parameters based on sample data. It involves formulating a null hypothesis and an alternative hypothesis, and then using statistical methods to determine whether the observed data supports one of the hypotheses. Through hypothesis testing, we can assess the plausibility of an assumption, test the effectiveness of a treatment, or compare different groups. This process provides a rigorous, systematic way to analyze data and make informed decisions in various fields, including science, business, and social sciences.

Null and alternative hypotheses

In hypothesis testing, we begin with two competing hypotheses: the null hypothesis: let us call it **H0**; and the alternative hypothesis: let us call it **H1**.

Picture this: You are a scientist trying to determine whether a new drug is more effective than the standard treatment. You would start by assuming that there is no difference between the two treatments. This is the null hypothesis (H0): the innocent until proven guilty assumption of the statistical world. It represents the belief that there is no significant effect, relationship, or difference between the groups or variables you are studying.

Now, enter the alternative hypothesis (H1). This is the rebel idea or the one that challenges the status quo. In our example, the alternative hypothesis would propose that the new drug is indeed more effective than the standard treatment. The alternative hypothesis always directly contradicts the null hypothesis.

So, how do we decide which hypothesis to believe? Well, this is where hypothesis testing comes into the picture. We collect sample data and evaluate the evidence against the null hypothesis. If the data provides strong enough evidence against H0, we reject it in favor of H1. However, if the data does not give us a compelling reason to reject H0, we continue to accept it as the most likely explanation.

Remember, hypothesis testing does not prove either hypothesis to be absolutely true or false. Instead, it offers support for one over the other based on the available data. By understanding the logic behind hypothesis testing and the roles of null and alternative hypotheses, we can confidently draw conclusions and make data-driven decisions in various fields, from scientific research to business analytics.

Test statistics and p-values

Now that we understand the basics of null and alternative hypotheses, let us explore how we test them using test statistics and p-values. These two concepts are the most significant part of hypothesis testing, as they help us objectively evaluate the evidence and decide which hypothesis to support.

First, let us talk about test statistics. Suppose we are still examining the effectiveness of the new drug. To do this, we would collect data from two groups: one treated with the new drug and one with the standard treatment. We would then calculate a test statistic, which is a single value that summarizes the differences between the two groups. This value is calculated based on the sample data and follows a specific distribution, such as the t-distribution or the normal distribution, depending on the test being performed.

The p-value represents the probability of observing a test statistic as extreme or more extreme than the one calculated from our sample data, assuming that the null hypothesis is true. In other words, it tells us how likely it is to see the observed differences between the groups just by chance.

Let us break this down: a small p-value (usually below a predetermined threshold, like 0.05) indicates that the observed differences are unlikely to have occurred by chance alone. This means the evidence against the null hypothesis is strong, so we reject H0 and support H1. On the other hand, a large p-value suggests that the observed differences could be due to random chance, so we fail to reject H0.

In our drug effectiveness example, if we find a small p-value, we would conclude that the new drug is more effective than the standard treatment, as the difference in outcomes is unlikely to be just a coincidence.

By connecting the dots between null and alternative hypotheses, test statistics, and p-values, we can make data-driven decisions in a wide range of scenarios. Hypothesis testing is a powerful tool that enables us to navigate the world of uncertainty and draw meaningful conclusions from the data we collect.

Common hypothesis tests: Z-test, t-test, chi-square test, and ANOVA

We have just explored the basics of hypothesis testing, including null and alternative hypotheses, test statistics, and p-values. But how do we choose the right test for a specific situation? Fear not, as we will dive into some common hypothesis tests, each tailored for different data types and research questions.

The first is the z-test, a popular choice when dealing with large sample sizes and known population variances. It follows the normal distribution and is often used to compare sample means to population means or to compare the means of two independent samples. Recall the new drug example: a z-test could be employed to compare the average improvement of patients treated with the new drug to those treated with the standard one, assuming that we have a large sample and know the population variances.

Next, let us talk t-test, the z-test's close cousin. The t-test is used when the population variance is unknown, which is often the case in real-world scenarios. The t-distribution is similar to the normal distribution, but its shape depends on the sample size or degrees of freedom. There are three main types of t-tests: one-sample, independent samples (for comparing two groups), and paired samples (for comparing two related measurements).

Now, let us say we want to analyze the relationship between categorical variables like hair color and job satisfaction. We use the chi-square test, which examines the association between two categorical variables in a contingency table. It calculates the difference between the observed frequencies and the expected frequencies under the assumption of independence, allowing us to determine whether or not the variables are related.

Finally, we have **Analysis of Variance (ANOVA)**, a powerful technique for comparing the means of three or more groups. If we want to compare the effectiveness of three different drugs instead of just two, ANOVA would be our go-to method. It assesses the variability within and between groups to determine whether there is a significant difference in the means. If ANOVA detects a significant difference, we can then perform post-hoc tests to pinpoint which groups differ from each other.

We have now understood some common hypothesis tests, each with its unique strengths and applications. By understanding the differences between z-tests, t-tests, chi-square tests, and ANOVA, we can confidently choose the right test for our data and research questions, ultimately making well-informed conclusions in our data-driven world.

Type I and type II errors

We have discussed various hypothesis tests and their applications; now, it is important to be aware of the potential pitfalls we might encounter. One key aspect to consider when conducting hypothesis testing is the risk of errors. Specifically, we need to be mindful of type I and type II errors, which can have significant consequences for our conclusions. Let us dive into these errors and understand their impact on our analyses.

A type I error, also known as a **false positive**, occurs when we reject the null hypothesis when it is actually true. Imagine concluding that a new drug is more effective than the standard treatment, only to later discover that the observed difference was merely due to random chance. The probability of making a type I error is denoted by α (alpha), which is the significance level we set for our test. A common value for α is 0.05, meaning we are willing to accept a 5% chance of making a type I error.

On the other side, we have a type II error or false negative, which happens when we fail to reject the null hypothesis when it is false. Think about missing the opportunity to adopt a ground-breaking new treatment because our test did not detect a significant difference, even though one actually exists. The probability of a type II error is represented by β (beta), and the power of the test, which is the ability to detect a true effect, is given by $1 - \beta$.

Now, you might be wondering, How do we minimize both type I and type II errors? Well, it is a delicate balancing act. Reducing the risk of one error usually increases the risk of the other. Factors like sample size, effect size, and the chosen significance level (α) all play a role in determining the likelihood of these errors. A larger sample size, for example, can increase the power of the test and help detect true effects, thus reducing the chance of a type II error.

In summary, understanding type I and type II errors is essential for interpreting the results of hypothesis tests accurately. By carefully considering the potential risks and trade-offs involved, we can make more informed decisions and draw reliable conclusions from our data. Just remember, no test is perfect, and we must always weigh the consequences of these errors in the context of our specific research question.

Conclusion

As we conclude this chapter, we can reflect on the vital role that probability theory, distributions, and hypothesis testing play in data science. These concepts provide the foundation for analyzing and interpreting data, enabling us to make informed decisions and draw reliable conclusions. By understanding how to apply these principles in real-world situations, we can navigate the complexities and uncertainties inherent in our data.

Armed with this knowledge, we are better equipped to tackle the challenges that await us in the exciting world of data science.

In the next chapter, we will discuss the sources of data, explore web scraping techniques using BeautifulSoup and requests, discover useful APIs and Python libraries for data collection. We will continue to emphasize ethical considerations throughout the process, ensuring that you have the tools and ethical principles to navigate the world of data mining effectively.

Points to remember

- Probability theory is essential for understanding the likelihood of events, with concepts like sample space, events, and probability axioms forming its core.

- Distributions and sampling are crucial for analyzing data, with key ideas like the central limit theorem and various sampling techniques providing valuable insights.

- Hypothesis testing is a fundamental approach to make decisions based on data, using concepts such as null and alternative hypotheses, test statistics, and p-values.

- Various hypothesis tests, including z-test, t-test, chi-square test, and ANOVA, are designed to tackle different types of problems and data scenarios.

- Being aware of type I and type II errors helps us understand the risks and limitations of hypothesis testing, allowing us to make more informed decisions in data analysis.

Multiple choice questions

1. **Which of the following best describes a sample space?**

   a. The set of all possible outcomes for a particular event

   b. The intersection of two events

   c. The probability of an event occurring

   d. The range of values for a random variable

2. **What does the CLT state?**

   a. The sum of two normally distributed variables is always normally distributed.

   b. The distribution of sample means approaches a normal distribution as the sample size increases.

   c. The variance of a population is equal to the variance of its sample.

   d. The median of a distribution is always equal to its mode.

3. **Which of the following hypothesis tests is most appropriate for comparing the means of two independent samples?**

   a. Z-test

   b. t-test

   c. Chi-square test

   d. ANOVA

4. **When does a type I error occur?**

   a. The null hypothesis is rejected when it is actually true.

   b. The null hypothesis is not rejected when it is actually false.

   c. The alternative hypothesis is rejected when it is actually true.

   d. The alternative hypothesis is not rejected when it is actually false.

5. **In the context of hypothesis testing, what is the p-value?**

   a. The probability of the null hypothesis being true.

   b. The probability of observing the test statistic if the null hypothesis is true.

   c. The probability of the alternative hypothesis being true.

   d. The probability of observing the test statistic if the alternative hypothesis is true.

Answers

1. a

2. b

3. b

4. a

5. b

Questions

1. How do the concepts of conditional probability and Bayes' theorem help in updating our beliefs about an event based on new information?

2. Can you explain the difference between stratified sampling and cluster sampling, and when is each method preferred?

3. What is the relationship between the concepts of covariance and correlation, and how do they help in understanding the relationship between two variables?

CHAPTER 4

Data Mining Expedition: Web Scraping and Data Collection Techniques

Introduction

Embarking on a data mining expedition can be an exciting adventure in data science. In this chapter, we will delve into the practical techniques of collecting data from various sources, making sure we are well equipped for our analytical journey. From web scraping to using APIs, we will explore the tools and libraries that make data collection both efficient and fun. Along the way, we will also be mindful of the ethical considerations, ensuring that our data collection methods respect privacy and adhere to guidelines.

Structure

In this chapter, we will discuss the following topics:

- Sources of data

- Web scraping with beautiful soup and requests

- APIs and Python libraries for data collection

- Ethical considerations during data collection

Objectives

At the end of this chapter, you should be equipped with the essential skills and knowledge for effective data collection. You should be able to identify various sources of data and learn how to extract valuable information using web scraping techniques and APIs. Furthermore, you will become familiar with Python libraries that aid data collection, making the process more seamless. Lastly, we will emphasize the importance of ethical considerations, ensuring that your data collection practices remain responsible and respectful of privacy concerns.

Sources of data

Understanding where to source the data that drives our analysis is a crucial aspect of data science. In this section, we will navigate through a diverse range of data sources, including online repositories, offline databases, and real-time feeds. We will encounter structured, semi-structured, and unstructured data that can offer invaluable insights for our projects.

Publicly available datasets

One of the best starting points for any data enthusiast is publicly available datasets. These datasets are often provided by government portals and research institutions, making them accessible and free for everyone.

This source can be broadly classified into two types: government portals and research institutions.

Government portals

The government portals can be categorized into the following categories:

- **National and local government portals:** Governments worldwide, both at the national and local levels, provide vast amounts of data on diverse topics. They offer datasets related to health, education, transportation, economics, demographics, and much more. These portals can be invaluable for understanding a region's trends, challenges, and opportunities. For example, the United States has **data.gov**, which provides access to a wide range of datasets from various federal agencies. In the United Kingdom, **data.gov.uk** is the official government data portal, while in Australia, **data.gov.au** serves a similar purpose.

- **International organizations:** Agencies such as the United Nations, World Bank, and **World Health Organization** (**WHO**) often publish global datasets. This information can be vital when comparing different countries or regions, analyzing worldwide trends, or researching specific international issues. The World Bank's **World Development Indicators** (**WDI**) dataset is a comprehensive collection of global development data. Similarly, the United Nations' data portal provides access to numerous international datasets covering diverse topics such as population, health, and education.

The data from government portals is usually provided in various formats like CSV, JSON, or Excel files. Some portals even offer APIs to facilitate direct access and integration with your projects. Take a look at the following figure:

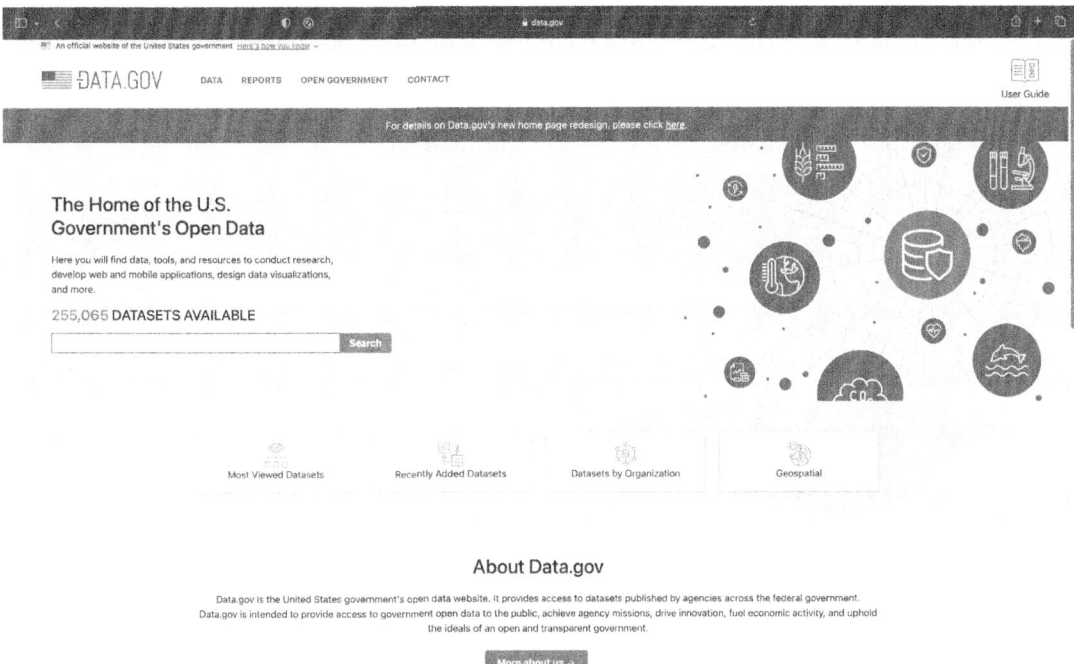

Figure 4.1: *The data.gov home page*

Research institutions

- **Universities and academic institutions:** These organizations often publish datasets related to specific fields of study or research projects. They are an excellent source of specialized data, providing insights into the latest discoveries and innovations in a wide range of disciplines. The Harvard Dataverse repository, hosted by Harvard University, is a platform for sharing and discovering research data across various disciplines. Another example is the Stanford Large Network Dataset Collection, which includes social network, web graph, and internet topology datasets, among others.

- **Industry-specific data:** Research institutions often focus on specific industries, such as agriculture, energy, or technology. These datasets can help you develop a deeper understanding of the challenges and opportunities within these sectors, informing your own research or business strategies. The **National Oceanic** and **Atmospheric Administration (NOAA)** is a research institution focused on weather, climate, and ocean data. Their **Climate Data Online (CDO)** system offers a wide range of climate and weather-related datasets.

- **Collaborative platforms:** Some research institutions have collaborative platforms that allow users to contribute, share, and access datasets. These platforms often foster a vibrant community of researchers and data enthusiasts, providing a great opportunity to learn from others and collaborate on projects. Kaggle, a platform for data science competitions and collaboration, has a rich dataset repository contributed to by users and organizations alike. Another example is the UCI Machine Learning Repository maintained by the University of California, Irvine, which is a popular resource for **Machine Learning (ML)** datasets. Take a look at the following figure:

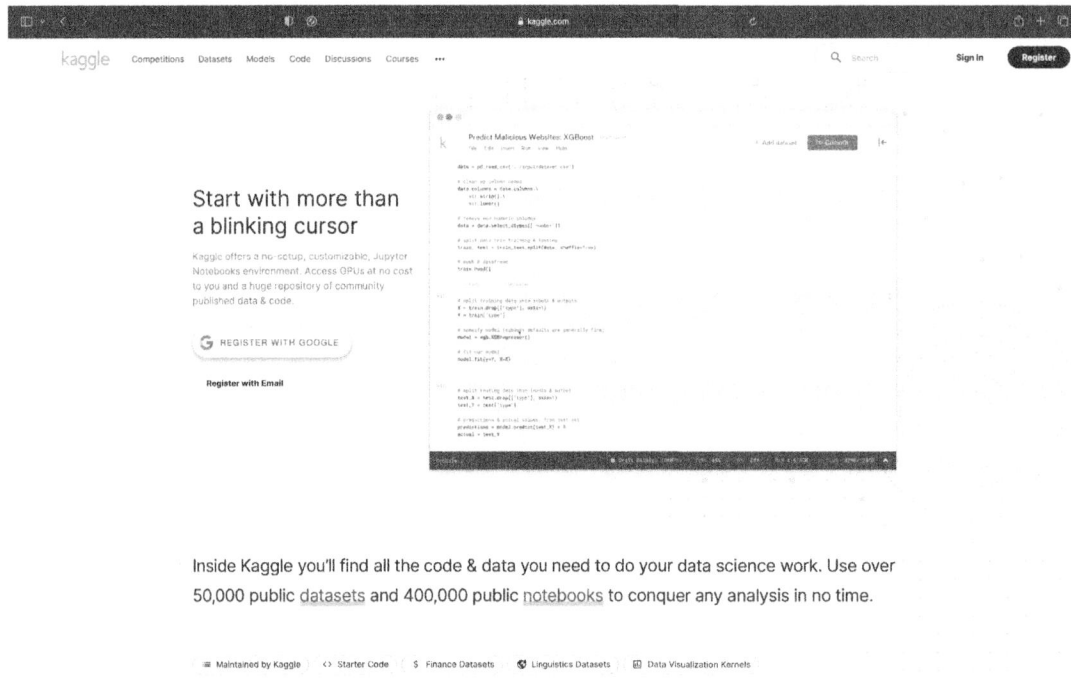

Figure 4.2: Kaggle's home page

The datasets provided by research institutions are typically well documented, with detailed information about the data collection methods, variables, and sources. This makes it easier for you to assess the quality of the data and determine its suitability for your project.

Web scraping

Unlike publicly available datasets, sometimes the data we need is not readily available in a neatly packaged dataset. In such cases, web scraping comes to the rescue, allowing us to extract valuable information from websites, blogs, and social media platforms. Web scraping is a powerful technique that involves using code to *crawl* through a web page, identify relevant content, and extract the desired information. This opens up a vast universe of data sources that can be leveraged for various data science projects.

Web scraping can be particularly useful for gathering data from dynamic websites, which may update their content frequently or have user-generated content that does not fit into a predefined structure. For instance, web scraping can help you collect news articles, forum discussions, or product reviews to analyze trends, sentiment, or user preferences. Similarly, by scraping social media platforms like X or Facebook, you can gather data on public opinion or monitor brand sentiment.

While web scraping may initially sound intimidating, numerous libraries and tools are available to simplify the process, making it more accessible to everyone. Python, a popular language for data science, offers libraries such as **BeautifulSoup** and **Requests** that make it easy to scrape and process HTML content from websites. With these libraries, you can navigate through the HTML structure of a web page, identify the elements containing the data you need, and extract the content.

As you venture into the world of web scraping, remember that different websites have varying structures and levels of complexity. Some sites require advanced techniques, such as handling JavaScript rendering or managing cookies and sessions. It is essential to be adaptable and ready to learn as you tackle the challenges of web scraping.

APIs

While web scraping offers a valuable means of extracting data from various online sources, there is another powerful technique that is often more efficient and reliable: **Application Programming Interfaces** (**APIs**). Compared to web scraping, APIs provide a more structured and convenient way to access data, typically in machine-readable formats like JSON or XML. Just like we navigated websites and extracted data through web scraping, APIs enable us to interact with online platforms and services to retrieve the information we need.

APIs are essentially a set of rules and protocols that allow different software applications to communicate with each other. Many companies and organizations offer APIs to grant developers access to their data, such as the X API for accessing tweets and user data, OpenWeatherMap API for weather data, or various financial data APIs for stock market information. This wealth of APIs can prove to be a goldmine for data scientists, as they facilitate the collection of large volumes of data in an organized and efficient manner.

To use an API, you typically need to send requests to a specific endpoint (a URL) with the required parameters, and the server responds with the requested data. Python offers several libraries, such as **Requests** and **Tweepy**, that simplify the process of making API calls and handling responses. Some APIs may require authentication, like API keys or

OAuth tokens, to verify your identity and ensure that you have the necessary permissions to access the data.

Think of an API key as a unique identifier, almost like a password, provided to developers by the API provider. This key is sent along with the request, and the server uses it to identify and verify the requester. It is a simple way to control access. However, API keys are static, meaning they do not change unless regenerated, and if they are exposed, anyone can use them to access the API.

OAuth is a more sophisticated authentication protocol. Instead of providing direct access, it allows users to grant limited access to their resources without sharing credentials, like a one-time access pass. In this process, tokens are generated. These tokens represent specific scopes and durations of access, ensuring more secure and granular control over data. Popular platforms like Google and Facebook use OAuth for third-party app integrations, ensuring that while an app may have permission to read a user's public profile, it might not have access to their private messages.

When working with APIs, it is crucial to be mindful of rate limits and usage restrictions, as many services limit the number of requests you can make within a given time frame. Moreover, always consult the API documentation to understand the available endpoints, data formats, and specific requirements. With the right tools and knowledge, APIs can be an invaluable resource for collecting diverse and up-to-date data for your data science projects.

Proprietary databases

Another option for gathering data is proprietary databases, which are typically subscription-based or organization-specific. While accessing proprietary data may come with a cost or be restricted to certain groups, proprietary databases can offer unique and high-quality information that is not readily available elsewhere.

Subscription-based databases often contain specialized datasets or information compiled by experts in various fields, providing data scientists with valuable insights. For instance, financial analysts might subscribe to **Bloomberg** or **Thomson Reuters** for extensive market data and analysis. At the same time, social scientists could turn to databases like the Pew Research Center for social and demographic data. These databases are maintained by dedicated organizations, ensuring that the data is accurate, up to date, and reliable.

Organization-specific databases, on the other hand, refer to data collected and managed internally within a company or organization. This data may include customer records, sales transactions, or even sensor data from IoT devices. Leveraging organization-specific data can be particularly advantageous, as it allows you to gain insights unique to your business, identify trends or issues, and make more informed decisions.

When working with proprietary databases, it is essential to be aware of any licensing agreements, terms of use, or data privacy concerns. Always ensure that you have the necessary permissions and adhere to any restrictions or guidelines imposed by the data provider. Additionally, companies have the option to purchase datasets from other firms like **ZoomInfo**, **Dun & Bradstreet**. By tapping into these exclusive data sources, you can enrich your data science projects with unique and valuable information that may not be accessible through other means.

Web scraping with Beautiful Soup and Requests

Web scraping often stands out as an effective method for gathering crucial information directly from websites. Beautiful Soup and Requests are popular Python libraries that simplify the web scraping process. Together, they allow you to navigate and parse HTML content, enabling you to retrieve specific data from web pages with ease. In this section, we will dive into the basics of web scraping using Beautiful Soup and Requests and explore how you can utilize their capabilities to gather essential data for your projects.

Installing and importing the Beautiful Soup and Requests libraries

Before we can start web scraping using Beautiful Soup and requests, we need to ensure that both libraries are properly installed and ready to use. To install these libraries, you can use **pip**, Python's package manager, by running the following commands in your terminal or command prompt:

```
pip install beautifulsoup4
pip install requests
```

With the libraries installed, it is time to import them into your Python script or Jupyter Notebook. To do this, simply add the following lines at the beginning of your code:

```
from bs4 import BeautifulSoup
import requests
```

Now, you have successfully installed and imported **BeautifulSoup** and requests, and you are all set to start extracting valuable information from websites using these powerful tools.

Fetching web page content using Requests

After installing and importing the Beautiful Soup and Requests libraries, we are ready to fetch web page content using the requests library. To do so, follow these steps:

1. First, pick a URL you would like to fetch content from. For demonstration purposes, let us use the Beautiful Soup documentation:

```
url = "https://beautiful-soup-4.readthedocs.io/en/latest/"
```

2. Now, use the **requests.get()** function to send a request to the URL and store the response in a variable:

```
response = requests.get(url)
```

3. You can check the status code of the response to ensure that the request was successful (status code 200 indicates success):

```
print(response.status_code)  # Should print 200 if successful
```

4. Having ascertained the success of our request, we can now extract the content of the web page. This is achieved using the **text** attribute of the response object:

```
webpage_content = response.text
```

You have successfully fetched the content of a web page using the Requests library. With the content with you, you can now move on to parsing and extracting the information you need using Beautiful Soup or other parsing tools.

Parsing HTML with Beautiful Soup and extracting data

Building upon our previous discussion, where we imported the Beautiful Soup library, let us dive into parsing the HTML with Beautiful Soup and extracting the data we need. To achieve this, follow the given steps:

1. First, let us create a **BeautifulSoup** object by passing the web page content you fetched earlier with the requests library, along with the parser you want to use (in this case, we will use the Python built-in parser **html.parser**):

```
soup = BeautifulSoup(webpage_content, 'html.parser')
```

2. With the soup object, you can now navigate and search through the HTML structure using various methods provided by BeautifulSoup. For example, you can find all the headings on the page with the **find_all()** method:

```
headings = soup.find_all('h2')
```

3. To extract the data, you can iterate through the elements returned by **find_all()** and access their attributes such as text or specific HTML attributes like **href** for links:

```
for heading in headings:
    print(heading.text)
```

Handling pagination, AJAX, and other web scraping challenges

As we discussed fetching web page content and parsing HTML with Beautiful Soup, it is important to address some common web scraping challenges, such as handling pagination, AJAX, and other issues:

- **Pagination:** Many websites display content across multiple pages to improve user experience and reduce load times. To handle pagination, you will often need to identify the URL pattern or the *next page* link and update your scraping code accordingly. For example, you can use a loop that changes the page number in the URL, or you can click the *next page* button; consider the following code:

```
for page_number in range(1, 11):  # Scraping 10 pages
    url = f"https://example.com/page/{page_number}"
    response = requests.get(url)
    soup = BeautifulSoup(response.content, 'html.parser')
    # ... Your data extraction code here ...
```

- **AJAX: Asynchronous JavaScript and XML (AJAX)** is a technique many websites use to load content dynamically without refreshing the page. When you scrape an AJAX-based site, the content you are looking for might not be available in the initial HTML source. To handle AJAX content, you can use libraries like **Selenium** or **Pyppeteer** to interact with JavaScript and load the dynamic content before parsing it with BeautifulSoup. Consider the following example:

```
from selenium import webdriver

driver = webdriver.Chrome()  # Or use Firefox, Edge, etc.
driver.get('https://example.com/ajax-page')
page_content = driver.page_source
driver.quit()

soup = BeautifulSoup(page_content, 'html.parser')
# ... Your data extraction code here ...
```

- **Rate limiting and user-agent headers:** Some websites limit the number of requests from a single IP address or require a user-agent header to allow access. To avoid getting blocked, respect the website's **robots.txt** rules, add delays between requests, and include a user-agent header in your requests. The following code demonstrates how to include a user-agent header and add a delay between requests, which are essential practices for respectful and responsible web scraping:

```
import time
```

```
headers = {'User-Agent': 'Mozilla/5.0 (Win-
dows NT 10.0; Win64; x64) AppleWebKit/537.36 (KHT-
ML, like Gecko) Chrome/58.0.3029.110 Safari/537.3'}
response = requests.get('https://example.com', headers=headers)
# ... Your data extraction code here ...
time.sleep(5)  # Wait for 5 seconds before making another request
```

- **Record fetch limits:** Another notable challenge in web scraping is the limitation some websites impose on the number of records that can be fetched. For instance, certain sites restrict data extraction to a maximum of 10,000 records per query or session. This constraint can significantly hinder the ability to gather large datasets and requires strategic planning in the scraping process to effectively collect the necessary data within these limits. Such restrictions necessitate the development of more sophisticated scraping techniques or the implementation of multiple scraping sessions to circumvent these limitations and gather comprehensive data sets.

APIs and Python libraries for data collection

Application Programming Interfaces (APIs) offer a more structured and reliable approach to data collection than web scraping. They enable developers to access a wide range of data directly from various sources, including social media platforms, weather services, and financial databases. In this section, we will explore popular APIs and Python libraries that facilitate seamless data collection for your data science projects.

RESTful APIs and their usage in data collection

RESTful APIs have become increasingly popular in recent years as they offer a more organized way to access and manage data from various sources. Compared to web scraping, RESTful APIs have quite a few perks: they are faster, more scalable, and, crucially, easier to maintain. Plus, they play nice with all sorts of programming languages, so you will have no trouble using Python to tap into their potential.

Now, you might wonder what is going on under the hood of a RESTful API. Well, they are built on the principles of **Representational State Transfer (REST)** and use resources (identified by URLs), methods like **GET** and **POST**, and standard HTTP status codes to communicate between clients and servers. And to make sure everything stays secure, you will often need an API key or token to access the data.

Python has some fantastic libraries for working with APIs, such as the requests library we used earlier for web scraping. You can easily send HTTP requests to API endpoints (URLs) and retrieve data in formats like JSON or XML. Then, you can parse that data and incorporate it into your data science projects.

But remember, with great power comes great responsibility! When using APIs, it is crucial to know the rate limits that dictate how many requests you can make within a specified time frame. Stick to the API provider's guidelines and use their resources responsibly to avoid temporary or permanent bans.

By understanding the ins and outs of RESTful APIs, you will be better equipped to harness their power and seamlessly integrate them into your data science workflows, complementing other data collection techniques like web scraping.

Authentication methods

Now that we have developed a good understanding of RESTful APIs and their role in data collection, it is time to discuss a crucial aspect that ensures the security and privacy of both users and data providers: authentication methods. As we mentioned earlier, API keys or tokens are often required to access data from an API, but why is that, and what other authentication methods are out there?

API keys are unique identifiers an API provider assigns you when you sign up for access. They allow the provider to track and monitor your usage, enforce rate limits, and ensure that only authorized users can access the API's resources. When making API requests, you usually include your API key in the header or as a query parameter.

But API keys are not the only authentication game in town. There is also OAuth, a widely used open-standard authorization protocol. OAuth allows users to grant third-party applications access to their data without sharing their credentials (like usernames and passwords). Instead, the application receives an access token representing the user's authorization, which it can use to make API requests on the user's behalf.

To use OAuth in your Python applications, you can turn to libraries like **requests-oauthlib** or **oauth2client** that handle the nitty-gritty of the OAuth flow. The process usually involves redirecting the user to the API provider's website, where they will grant your application access, and then receiving an authorization code, which you will exchange for an access token.

With a solid grasp of authentication methods like **API keys** and **OAuth**, you will be well on your way to responsibly accessing and using data from various API providers, all while keeping user credentials secure and following the API provider's guidelines.

Popular Python libraries for working with APIs

Let us now look at some popular Python libraries that can help you seamlessly interact with APIs and collect data. These libraries not only simplify API requests but also handle common tasks like data manipulation and analysis.

The requests library, which you might already be familiar with from web scraping, is a versatile tool for making HTTP requests to APIs. It allows you to easily send **GET**, **POST**,

PUT, **DELETE**, and other requests; handle responses; and parse data in various formats, like JSON or XML. This library works well with a wide range of APIs, making it an essential tool in your data collection toolkit.

If you are interested in social media data, Tweepy is a powerful Python library tailored specifically for the X API. With Tweepy, you can quickly access tweets, user profiles, timelines, and more, all while handling the nuances of the X API, such as rate limits and authentication. The library's straightforward syntax and comprehensive documentation make it accessible even to beginners.

For financial data enthusiasts, pandas-datareader is a valuable library that allows users to extract data from various sources, such as Yahoo Finance, Google Finance, and **Federal Reserve Economic Data** (**FRED**). By leveraging the power of the popular pandas library, pandas-datareader simplifies data retrieval and manipulation, returning your requested data in a convenient DataFrame format that is ready for analysis.

By exploring these popular Python libraries and others, you can efficiently tap into a wealth of data from various APIs, tailor your data collection process to specific needs, and streamline data handling and analysis in your projects.

Parsing and handling JSON, XML, and other data formats

It is time to discuss how to parse and handle the data formats that you are likely to encounter, such as JSON and XML. Since APIs often return data in these formats, so it is crucial to know how to work with them efficiently and effectively.

JSON, or JavaScript Object Notation, has become the standard data format for many APIs due to its lightweight structure and human-readable format. Python's built-in **json** library allows you to effortlessly parse JSON data into native Python data types, like dictionaries and lists. You can also convert Python objects back into JSON strings using the same library. This versatility makes handling JSON data a breeze in your Python projects.

On the other hand, **Extensible Markup Language** (**XML**), is another popular data format used by APIs, especially in older systems or specific industries. To work with XML data, you can use Python libraries like **ElementTree** or **lxml**. These libraries provide powerful parsing and data extraction capabilities, allowing you to navigate, search, and modify the XML tree structure with ease.

Sometimes, you might come across other data formats, such as CSV or plain text. For handling CSV data, the CSV library in Python's standard library is a handy tool, while pandas can be used for more complex data manipulation tasks. Plain text data can be processed using Python's built-in string methods or more advanced libraries like **re** for regular expressions.

Mastering these data formats and the tools to handle them will enable you to transform raw data into structured, usable information, setting the stage for further data processing, analysis, and visualization in your data science journey.

Ethical considerations during data collection

When discussing data collection, addressing the ethical considerations accompanying gathering and using data from various sources is of utmost importance. Being mindful of user privacy, data ownership, and the potential implications of our actions on individuals and communities is crucial. In this section, we will explore important ethical aspects to consider during data acquisition and look at some best practices for responsible data collection. By taking these factors into account, we can make more informed decisions and maintain the trust of those whose data we handle.

Respecting website terms of service and the robots.txt file

As we explore web scraping for data collection, it is important to remember that not all websites are open to being scraped. One of the first steps to ensuring responsible data collection is respecting a website's terms of service and `robots.txt` files. The terms of service often outline the acceptable use of a website's content and data, while the `robots.txt` file provides specific instructions to web crawlers about which parts of the site are off limits.

In a conversational manner, suppose you are visiting someone's home; you would not want to enter rooms you were not invited into or rummage through their belongings without permission. Similarly, when scraping a website, we need to respect the website owner's wishes and abide by any restrictions they have in place. By doing so, we can maintain a positive relationship with website owners and avoid any potential legal or ethical issues arising from unauthorized data collection.

Adhering to API rate limits and usage restrictions

When using APIs for data collection, it is essential to be mindful of rate limits and usage restrictions imposed by the service provider. Just like there are rules in place when using shared resources, APIs have guidelines to ensure fair access to data for all users. Rate limits are one way by which providers ensure that their servers are not overwhelmed by requests, which helps maintain the stability of the service for everyone.

Picture yourself at a buffet, where there is plenty of food, but it is essential to share the dishes with everyone present. In the same way, API rate limits work to prevent a single user from monopolizing the service by restricting the number of requests you can make in a given time frame. By adhering to these rate limits and other usage restrictions, we can demonstrate responsible and respectful behaviour, avoiding negative consequences such as being temporarily or permanently banned from using the API. As responsible data collectors, it is our duty to ensure that we respect these guidelines and use the data provided ethically and responsibly.

User privacy and data anonymization

While collecting data, especially from public platforms, it is crucial to be mindful of user privacy and consider data anonymization. Suppose you are walking through a park and overhear a conversation that interests you. Even though the conversation is public, you would not share the details with everyone you know. Similarly, when collecting data, it is essential to treat people's personal information respectfully and consider the potential consequences of sharing or using it.

Data anonymization involves removing or altering any **personally identifiable information (PII)** in a dataset, making it impossible to trace the data back to specific individuals. This process is vital because, as data collectors and analysts, we need to strike a balance between extracting valuable insights and respecting the privacy of the individuals whose data we are working with. By anonymizing the data, we protect users' privacy and prevent potential misuse of their information. It is not just about following legal requirements but also about upholding ethical principles and ensuring that our data collection practices promote trust and transparency.

Ethics and law in data management

When handling data storage and sharing, it is crucial to comply with legal and ethical standards. Just as you would take care of a borrowed book and return it in the same condition, you should treat data responsibly and securely, abiding by relevant laws and ethical guidelines.

Legal standards, such as data protection laws (like the GDPR in the European Union), dictate how data should be collected, stored, and shared. These laws protect individual privacy and ensure that organizations handle data responsibly. It is essential to be aware of the laws that apply to your specific region or the regions where your data subjects reside and to follow them meticulously.

Beyond legal compliance, ethical standards should also be considered. This involves obtaining user consent, if required, and ensuring that data is used only for the intended purposes. Maintaining transparency with data subjects and implementing proper security measures to protect data from unauthorized access or breaches is crucial. By adhering to legal and ethical standards, you create a trustworthy environment for data collection, storage, and sharing, enabling the extraction of valuable insights without compromising the rights and privacy of those whose data is being handled.

Conclusion

In this chapter, we delved into the exciting world of web scraping and data collection techniques, covering various methods to gather valuable insights from various sources. We explored publicly available datasets, web scraping with Beautiful Soup and requests, APIs, and proprietary databases, all while keeping ethical considerations at the forefront. By understanding the importance of adhering to website terms of service and API restrictions and prioritizing user privacy, we can ensure that our data collection practices are legally and ethically sound. With the knowledge gained from this chapter, you can embark on your data mining expedition, responsibly collecting and utilizing data to drive your projects and analyses forward.

Now, as we transition into the next chapter, we will harness the data collected in innovative ways, exploring exploratory data analysis, descriptive statistics, and mastering data visualization with Matplotlib, seaborn, and Plotly to identify patterns and trends that will further enhance your data-driven insights.

Points to remember

- Web scraping and APIs are powerful tools for data collection, but it is crucial to respect website terms of service, `robots.txt` files, and API rate limits.

- Beautiful Soup and requests are popular Python libraries for web scraping, while libraries like Tweepy and pandas-datareader can help with APIs.

- Always prioritize user privacy and data anonymization when handling sensitive information or personal data.

- Ensure that your data storage and sharing practices comply with legal and ethical standards to maintain trust and avoid potential issues.

Multiple choice questions

1. **Which Python library is commonly used for web scraping?**

    a. Tweepy

    b. pandas-datareader

    c. BeautifulSoup

    d. NumPy

2. **What should you check before web scraping to ensure that you are respecting a website's rules?**

    a. `sitemap.xml`

    b. `robots.txt`

    c. `index.html`

    d. `README.md`

3. **Which of the following is an example of a popular Python library used for working with X's API?**

    a. Tweepy

    b. Beautiful Soup

    c. Requests

    d. Pandas

4. **Which of the following is an essential ethical consideration when collecting and handling data?**

    a. Ignoring API rate limits

    b. Bypassing website terms of service

    c. Ensuring user privacy and data anonymization

    d. Scraping without checking `robots.txt`

Answers

1. c

2. b

3. a

4. c

Questions

1. What are some of the challenges you might encounter when web scraping, and how can you handle them?

2. How do RESTful APIs facilitate data collection, and what are some common authentication methods used with APIs?

3. What are the key ethical considerations to keep in mind when collecting, storing, and sharing data obtained through web scraping and APIs?

CHAPTER 5

Painting with Data: Exploration and Visualization

Introduction

This chapter will delve into the fascinating world of data exploration and visualization to unlock the hidden stories within your datasets. Starting with exploratory data analysis, we will preprocess and familiarize ourselves with the data we are working with. We will then use descriptive statistics to summarize our findings and highlight key insights effectively.

As we progress, we will explore various data visualization techniques using Python libraries such as Matplotlib, seaborn, and Plotly. We aim to identify patterns and trends that will enable us to transform raw data into valuable, actionable knowledge.

Structure

In this chapter, we will discuss the following topics:

- Exploratory data analysis
- Descriptive statistics
- Data visualization with Matplotlib, seaborn, and Plotly
- Discovering trends and relationships

Objectives

This chapter aims to equip you with the skills and knowledge required to effectively explore, analyze, and visualize data using various Python tools and techniques. You will learn how to perform exploratory data analysis, apply descriptive statistics, and create impactful visualizations that reveal patterns and trends. By the end of this chapter, you will be well prepared to extract valuable insights from datasets and communicate your findings to others clearly and compellingly.

Exploratory data analysis

Exploratory data analysis (EDA) is the crucial first step in the data analysis process. It is all about understanding your data by summarizing, visualizing, and examining its main characteristics. This stage helps you identify potential trends, patterns, and anomalies while also revealing any data quality issues that need to be addressed. With a solid grasp of EDA, you will be better equipped to make informed decisions, develop hypotheses, and ultimately, build effective models to solve real-world problems.

Why do we need exploratory data analysis

So, why is EDA significant in the data analysis process? Well, let us consider EDA as the detective work of data science. It entails a thorough examination of the data, posing pertinent questions and delving into undiscovered aspects. The primary purpose of EDA is to help you build a solid foundation for subsequent data analysis and modeling.

By diving into EDA, you will identify trends, patterns, and potential outliers that might otherwise go unnoticed. This can be extremely helpful when formulating hypotheses and understanding the relationships between variables. Moreover, EDA helps you detect data quality issues, such as missing values, duplicates, or inconsistencies, allowing you to address them before they impact your analysis.

One thing to keep in mind is that EDA is an iterative process. As you explore and uncover new insights, you will likely generate more questions and ideas for further investigation. This continuous back and forth between exploration and hypothesis refinement ultimately leads to a deeper understanding of the data and more robust analytical models.

In short, EDA is an essential step in the data analysis process because it helps you make sense of your data, uncover hidden patterns, and set the stage for more advanced analytical techniques. So, grab your magnifying glass and let us start uncovering the secrets hidden within your data!

Cleaning and preprocessing data for exploratory data analysis

Now that we have discussed the importance of EDA, let us talk about a crucial step before diving into any analysis: cleaning and preprocessing the data. Data is often messy and full of imperfections, so getting it into shape is an essential part of the process.

First things first, let us look at handling missing values. Missing data can be a real headache, leading to biased or incorrect conclusions. To tackle this issue, you can either impute the missing values using a suitable method (such as mean, median, or mode imputation) or simply remove the instances with missing data. The choice depends on the nature of the data and the percentage of missing values.

Next up, we have duplicates. Duplicates can occur for various reasons, and they can distort your analysis if not dealt with properly. So, always check for duplicates and decide whether to keep, remove, or merge them based on the context and the data quality.

Another aspect of data preprocessing is dealing with inconsistent or incorrect data. This might include things like different units of measurement, varying date formats, or even typos. Identifying and correcting these inconsistencies is crucial to ensure the accuracy of your analysis.

Finally, let us talk about feature engineering. Sometimes, the variables in your dataset are not directly suitable for analysis or modeling. In such cases, you may need to create new variables or transform existing ones to represent the underlying relationships in the data better. This could involve, for example, creating dummy variables for categorical data or normalizing continuous variables.

Univariate and multivariate analysis techniques

Univariate and multivariate analysis techniques are essential tools in the EDA process, as they help us explore the data and understand its underlying patterns, trends, and relationships. Let us dive into these techniques and learn how they can be used in our data exploration journey.

Univariate analysis focuses on a single variable, exploring its distribution, central tendency, and dispersion. Common techniques include creating histograms, box plots, or calculating summary statistics like mean, median, and standard deviation. For example, if we have a dataset of people's ages, a histogram can help us visualize the age distribution, while summary statistics can tell us about the average age and the spread of **ages** in the dataset.

Here is a simple example using Python and pandas:

```python
import pandas as pd

data = {'ages': [25, 30, 35, 40, 45, 50, 55, 60]}
df = pd.DataFrame(data)


print(df['ages'].describe())
```

The output of this piece of code will be as shown in the following figure:

```
count      8.000000
mean      42.500000
std       12.247449
min       25.000000
25%       33.750000
50%       42.500000
75%       51.250000
max       60.000000
Name: ages, dtype: float64
```

Figure 5.1: Summary statistics

Multivariate analysis, on the other hand, examines the relationships between two or more variables. Scatter plots, correlation matrices, and pair plots are common techniques for visualizing and analyzing multivariate relationships. For instance, if we have a dataset of people's ages and their incomes, a scatter plot can reveal any patterns or trends between these two variables, such as a positive correlation between age and income.

Here is an example using Python and seaborn:

```python
import pandas as pd
import seaborn as sns
import matplotlib.pyplot as plt

data = {'ages': [25, 30, 35, 40, 45, 50, 55, 60],
        'incomes': [30000, 35000, 40000, 45000, 50000, 55000, 60000, 65000]}
df = pd.DataFrame(data)

sns.scatterplot(x='ages', y='incomes', data=df)
plt.show()
```

The following figure shows the plot you get once you run the code:

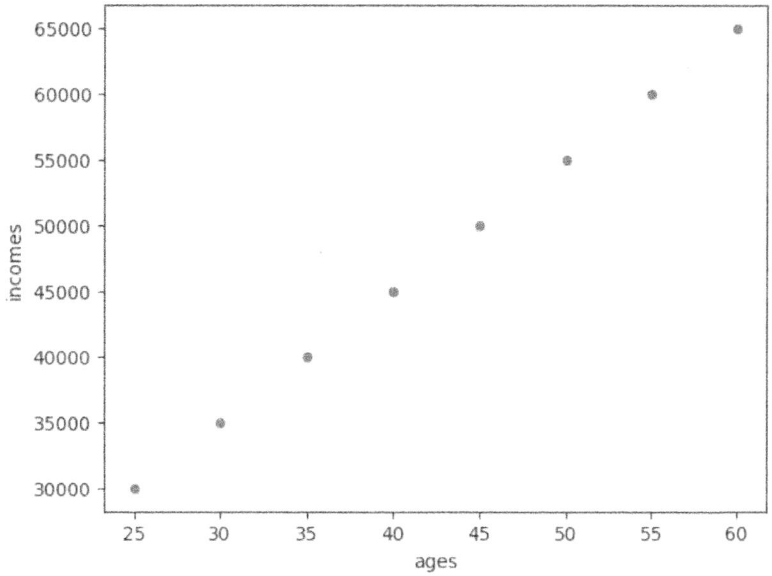

Figure 5.2: Scatter plot showing incomes versus ages

As you can see, univariate and multivariate analysis techniques allow us to explore our data from different perspectives, ultimately providing a more comprehensive understanding of the dataset. Using these techniques, along with appropriate visualizations, can lead to exciting discoveries and insights that might otherwise remain hidden.

Descriptive statistics

In the context of data exploration, descriptive statistics play a vital role in helping us gain a deeper understanding of the dataset at hand. These summary measures provide quick insights into the central tendency, dispersion, and shape of a dataset's distribution. As we dive into this subtopic, we will explore how descriptive statistics can be effectively used in exploratory data analysis. Furthermore, we will discuss how Python libraries like **pandas** and **NumPy** can be leveraged to compute these statistics, enabling us to analyze and interpret our data more efficiently.

Measures of central tendency: mean, mode and median

Measures of central tendency, such as the mean, mode, and median, are essential tools in our data exploration toolkit. They help us pinpoint the middle ground or central value of a dataset, providing a quick summary of its overall nature.

Take the **mean**, for example. It is calculated by adding all the data points in a dataset and dividing the sum by the total number of points. In Python, we can effortlessly compute the mean using the **numpy** library; consider the following code:

```
import numpy as np

data = [10, 15, 20, 25, 30, 35, 40]
mean = np.mean(data)
print("Mean:", mean)
```

On the other hand, the **median** represents the middle value in a dataset when the data points are sorted in ascending order. For an even number of data points, the median is the average of the two middle values. Computing the **median** with Python is a breeze using the **numpy** library:

```
median = np.median(data)
print("Median:", median)
```

Lastly, the **mode** is the most frequently occurring value in a dataset. It is particularly useful for understanding the most common patterns in categorical or discrete data. The **scipy** library provides a convenient method for finding the **mode**; consider the following code:

```
from scipy import stats

data = [1, 2, 2, 3, 4, 4, 4, 5, 6, 7]
mode = stats.mode(data)
print("Mode:", mode.mode[0])
```

In summary, mean, mode, and median are powerful measures of central tendency that help us grasp the essence of our data, guiding us in our exploratory data analysis journey.

Exploring data spread: Range, variance, and standard deviation

While central tendency measures give us a glimpse into the average of a dataset, it is crucial to consider how the data points are dispersed or spread out. To achieve this, we use measures of dispersion such as range, variance, and standard deviation.

The **range** is the simplest measure of dispersion. It is the difference between the maximum and minimum values in a dataset. Calculating the range in Python is quite easy; use the following code:

```
import numpy as np
```

```
data = [10, 15, 20, 25, 30, 35, 40]
range_data = np.max(data) - np.min(data)
print("Range:", range_data)
```

Variance, on the other hand, quantifies the average squared deviation of the data points from the mean. It tells us how spread out the data points are in the dataset. To calculate **variance** using Python and the **numpy** library, we use the following code:

```
variance = np.var(data)
print("Variance:", variance)
```

Standard deviation, which is the square root of the variance, is another essential measure of dispersion. It is expressed in the same units as the data, making it easier to interpret. A higher standard deviation indicates greater variability in the data. Computing the **Standard deviation** in Python is fairly simple using the **numpy** library; use the following code:

```
std_dev = np.std(data)
print("Standard Deviation:", std_dev)
```

By understanding measures of dispersion like range, variance, and standard deviation, we can gain deeper insights into our data, such as how consistent or spread out the values are. These measures help us make more informed decisions in our data exploration and visualization process.

Skewness and kurtosis

To develop a deeper understanding of our data, it is essential to explore the shape of its distribution. Skewness and kurtosis are two key aspects that can reveal important information about the data. Skewness gives us an idea of the asymmetry in the distribution. In other words, it tells us how much the data is leaning to one side. If the distribution is symmetric, the skewness will be 0, whereas a positive skewness indicates a longer tail on the right side and a negative skewness indicates a longer tail on the left side.

Kurtosis, on the other hand, provides insights into the **tailedness** or **peakedness** of the distribution. A high kurtosis value indicates a distribution with more extreme values, leading to heavier tails and a sharper peak compared to a normal distribution. Conversely, a low kurtosis value means the distribution has fewer extreme values, resulting in lighter tails and a flatter peak.

By examining skewness and kurtosis, we can identify unique features and relationships within the data, guiding our choice of appropriate statistical methods for further analysis. Remember that skewness and kurtosis are just two ways to understand your data's distribution better, allowing you to make more informed decisions during your data analysis journey.

Understanding descriptive statistics in data analysis

Descriptive statistics provide a quick and insightful dataset summary, helping us understand its structure and characteristics. But how do we interpret these statistics and gauge their relevance to our data?

Consider a dataset of movie ratings on a scale of 1 to 10. The mean, median, and mode reveal the central tendency of the ratings, which helps us understand the overall sentiment of the viewers. If the mean and median are close, it indicates that the data is likely symmetric. At the same time, a significant difference between them could suggest the presence of outliers or a skewed distribution.

Measures of dispersion, such as range, variance, and standard deviation, give us an idea of how spread out the ratings are. A small standard deviation implies that the ratings are clustered closely around the mean, while a larger standard deviation indicates more variation among the scores. This information can be valuable in understanding user preferences and tailoring content to specific audience segments.

Finally, skewness and kurtosis shed light on the shape of the distribution. If the skewness is close to 0, it indicates a symmetric distribution, while positive or negative values suggest a skewed distribution. High kurtosis implies a sharper peak and heavier tails, whereas low kurtosis indicates a flatter peak and lighter tails. These characteristics can help us identify patterns and trends in the data that could inform our decisions and strategies.

Interpreting descriptive statistics is crucial for drawing meaningful insights and understanding the relevance of these measures to our dataset. By considering central tendency, dispersion, and distribution shape, we can effectively analyze and make informed decisions based on our data.

Data visualization with Matplotlib, seaborn, and Plotly

Data visualization plays a pivotal role in conveying complex information in an easily digestible format, enabling us to identify patterns, trends, and relationships within our data. Matplotlib, seaborn, and Plotly are the three powerful Python libraries that help us create visually appealing and informative graphs and charts. By harnessing the capabilities of these libraries, we can transform raw data into visually engaging stories that drive insights and decision-making. In this section, we will explore the diverse range of visualization options these libraries offer and demonstrate how to communicate the insights hidden within our data effectively.

Getting acquainted with Matplotlib, seaborn, and Plotly

Matplotlib, seaborn, and Plotly are widely used Python libraries that cater to different visualization needs and preferences. Matplotlib, the foundation of many other visualization libraries, offers a versatile and customizable approach to plotting various types of graphs, making it a go-to option for many data scientists. It is particularly handy when you need control over the appearance of your visualizations.

Seaborn, built on top of Matplotlib, brings a more modern and aesthetically pleasing touch to the visualizations. It simplifies the creation of complex plots and offers numerous built-in themes and color palettes, making it a popular choice for creating visually appealing and informative graphics with less effort.

Plotly, on the other hand, is a library that excels in creating interactive and web-based visualizations. Its ability to generate responsive and dynamic charts enables users to explore the data more thoroughly, providing a deeper understanding. Plotly's appeal lies in its capacity to create engaging visualizations that cater to diverse audiences and facilitate more interactive data exploration experiences.

A guide to visualizing data with common chart types

Diving into the world of data visualization, there is an array of plot types at our disposal, each serving a unique purpose in showcasing various aspects of our dataset. Let us explore some common chart types with examples to help you bring your data to life.

Bar plots are an excellent choice when comparing discrete categories or displaying counts. For instance, imagine visualizing the number of items sold across different product categories in a store. You can use a bar plot with product categories on the x-axis and the number of items sold on the y-axis. Matplotlib makes it easy to create a simple bar plot. Use the following code:

```
import matplotlib.pyplot as plt


categories = ['Electronics', 'Clothing', 'Toys']
items_sold = [120, 200, 150]

plt.bar(categories, items_sold)
plt.xlabel('Categories')
plt.ylabel('Items Sold')
plt.show()
```

The bar plot looks like the following figure:

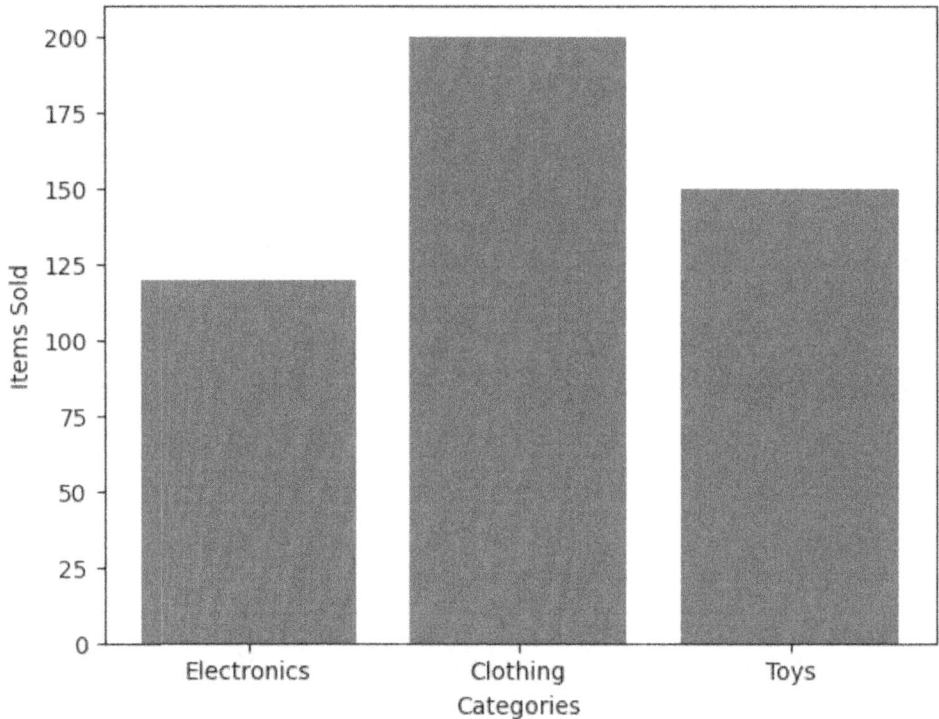

Figure 5.3: *An example of a bar plot*

Line plots, on the other hand, excel at displaying trends over time or continuous data. For example, you could create a line plot to track the daily temperature over a month. Use the following code:

```
import seaborn as sns
import matplotlib.pyplot as plt

days = list(range(1, 31))
temperatures = [23, 24, 26, 24, 22, 20, 25, 23, 24, 26, 28, 27, 24, 22, 23,
25, 27, 26, 24, 23, 25, 26, 27, 29, 28, 26, 25, 24, 26, 27]

sns.lineplot(x=days, y=temperatures)
plt.xlabel('Days')
plt.ylabel('Temperature')
plt.show()
```

The line plot is shown in the following figure:

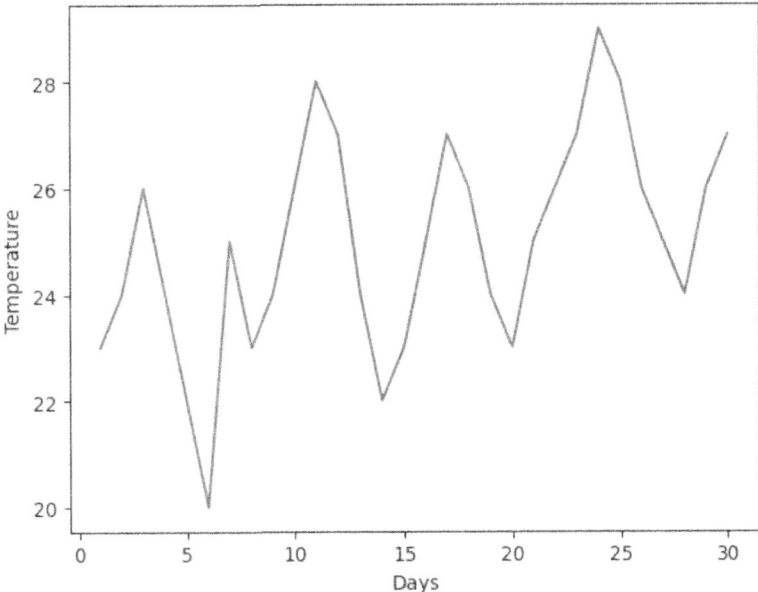

Figure 5.4: *An example of a line plot*

Scatter plots are great for visualizing relationships between two continuous variables. Suppose you want to examine the relationship between the size of a house and its price. Use the following code:

```
import matplotlib.pyplot as plt

house_sizes = [1000, 1500, 1200, 1800, 2300, 1900, 1700, 2100, 1300, 1600]
house_prices = [100000, 200000, 150000, 250000, 320000, 230000, 210000, 280000, 140000, 190000]

plt.scatter(house_sizes, house_prices)
plt.xlabel('House Size (sq ft)')
plt.ylabel('House Price ($)')
plt.title('House Size vs. Price')
plt.show()
```

The scatter plot looks like the following figure:

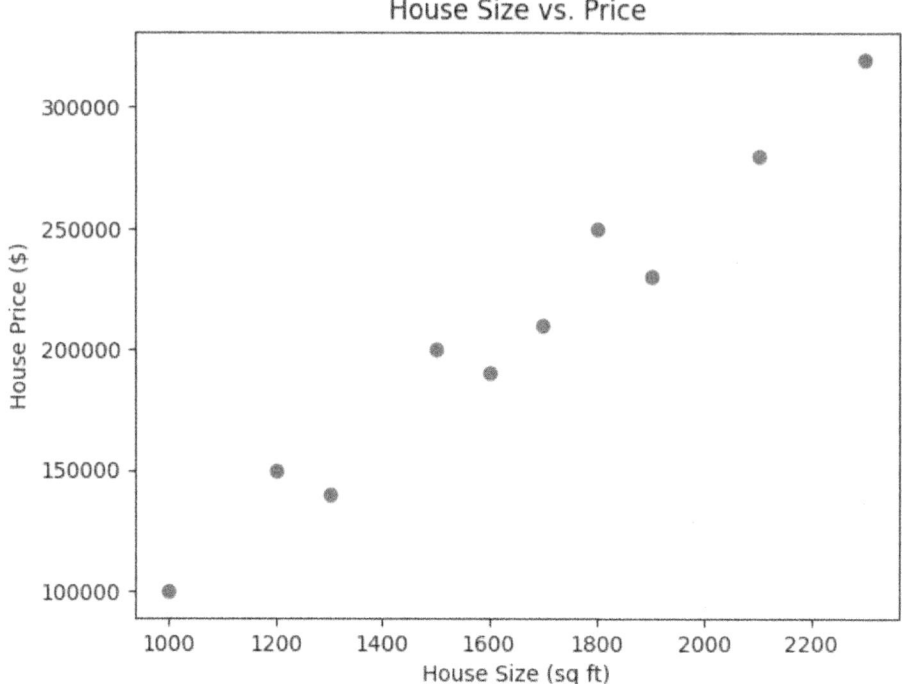

Figure 5.5: An example of a scatter plot

Histograms help visualize the distribution of a continuous variable by dividing the data into bins and displaying the count of observations within each bin. For instance, if you want to examine the distribution of **ages** in a group of people, you could use a histogram. Use the following code:

```
import matplotlib.pyplot as plt

ages = [20, 25, 30, 29, 35, 40, 45, 50, 55, 60, 65, 70, 75, 80, 85, 90]

plt.hist(ages, bins=10)
plt.xlabel('Age')
plt.ylabel('Count')
plt.title('Age Distribution')
plt.show()
```

The histogram looks like the following figure:

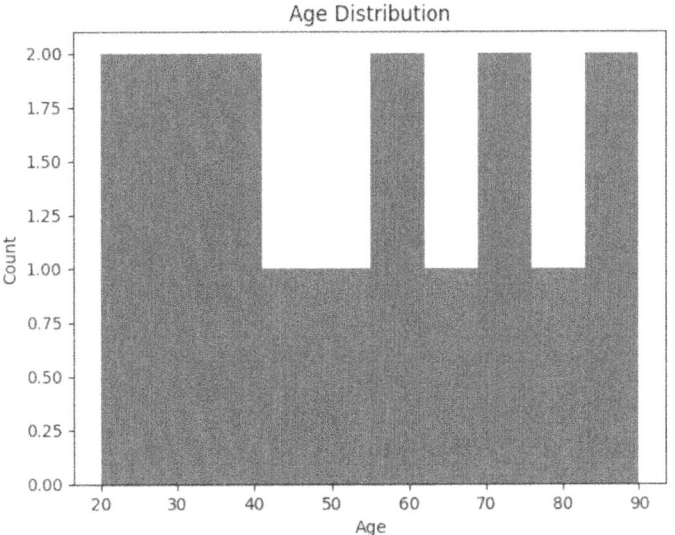

Figure 5.6: *An example of a histogram*

With these versatile chart types in your arsenal, you will be well equipped to tackle various data visualization tasks.

Customization techniques for engaging visualizations

When it comes to data visualization, customization is key to making your plots not only informative but also visually appealing. Let us delve into various customization options, such as colors, labels, and legends, that can elevate your plots to the next level using a simple dataset. Use the following code to plot your graph:

```
import matplotlib.pyplot as plt
import seaborn as sns


x = [1, 2, 3, 4, 5]
y1 = [2, 4, 6, 8, 10]
y2 = [1, 3, 5, 7, 9]
```

Colors play a significant role in making your plots more engaging and easier to interpret. You can customize colors in Matplotlib using the **color** parameter shown in the following code:

```
plt.plot(x, y1, color='magenta', label="Dataset 1")
plt.plot(x, y2, color='cyan', label="Dataset 2")
```

Seaborn's built-in color palettes can also be used for a more sophisticated look, as shown in the following code:

```
sns.set_palette("husl")
sns.scatterplot(x=x, y=y1, label="Dataset 1")
sns.scatterplot(x=x, y=y2, label="Dataset 2")
```

Labels and legends help provide context to your visualizations. In Matplotlib, you can add axis labels using **xlabel** and **ylabel**, and a title with **title** using the following code:

```
plt.xlabel("X-axis Label")
plt.ylabel("Y-axis Label")
plt.title("Customized Plot")
```

Legends are particularly useful when displaying multiple datasets in a single plot. You can add a legend in Matplotlib by calling **legend()**:

```
plt.legend()
```

Customizing other aspects of your plots, like markers and line styles, is also easy with Matplotlib and seaborn:

```
plt.plot(x, y1, color='magenta', linestyle='dashed', marker='o',
label="Dataset 1")
plt.plot(x, y2, color='cyan', linestyle='dotted', marker='s',
label="Dataset 2")
```

Finally, you can display your customized plot using the following code:

```
plt.show()
```

And this will be the final plot:

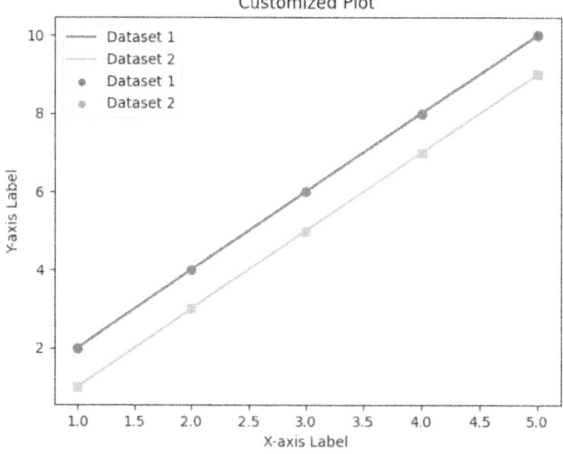

Figure 5.7: A customized plot

By mastering these customization techniques, you will be able to create visualizations that are both informative and visually captivating, ensuring that your audience remains engaged with your data story.

Creating interactive visualizations with Plotly

Interactive and dynamic visualizations are a game changer when it comes to data storytelling, as they allow your audience to engage more deeply with the data. Plotly is a powerful library that lets you create interactive plots with ease. Let us explore how to use Plotly to create an interactive scatter plot.

First, let us import the library and create some sample data using the following code:

```
import plotly.express as px
```

```
x = [1, 2, 3, 4, 5]
y1 = [2, 4, 6, 8, 10]
y2 = [1, 3, 5, 7, 9]
```

Instead of importing Plotly, we are importing **Plotly Express**. Why?

Plotly Express is a high-level wrapper around the base Plotly library, which aims to make it simpler and more efficient to create common types of plots. It provides a concise syntax for creating visualizations with a single line of code in many cases, making it more convenient for data exploration and quick visualization tasks.

While the base Plotly library offers more fine-grained control over the plot's appearance and customization, it requires more code and a deeper understanding of the library's structure. Plotly Express, on the other hand, is designed for ease of use and rapid development. It is particularly well suited for situations wherein you need to create visualizations quickly or for users who are new to Plotly. Execute the following code:

```
fig = px.scatter(x=x, y=y1, labels={"x": "X-axis Label", "y": "Y-axis La-
bel"}, title="Interactive Scatter Plot")
```

To make the plot even more informative, you can add a hover feature, which displays additional information when you hover over data points:

```
fig.update_traces(hovertemplate="X: %{x}<br>Y: %{y}")
```

You can also customize the appearance of the plot by updating its layout, marker style, and text properties using the following code:

```
fig.update_layout(
    font_family="Arial",
    font_size=14,
```

```
        title_font=dict(size=24, color='blue'),
        plot_bgcolor='rgba(230, 230, 230, 0.8)',
        xaxis_title="X-axis Label",
        yaxis_title="Y-axis Label"
)

fig.update_traces(
        marker=dict(size=12, color='red', symbol='star'),
        selector=dict(mode='markers')
)
```

To display the interactive plot, simply call the **show** method; execute the following code:

```
fig.show()
```

Let us look at the output of the preceding code:

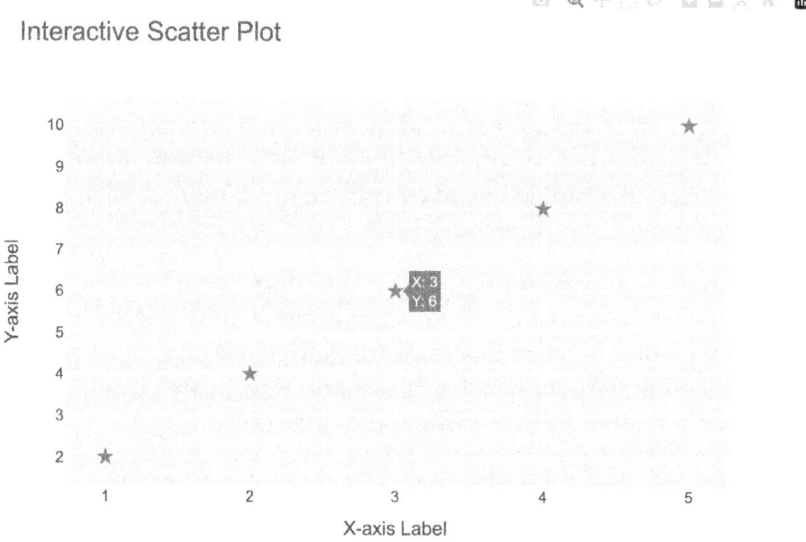

Figure 5.8: An example of an interactive plot

We can now explore the data by hovering over the points, zooming in and out, and panning across the plot. With Plotly's interactive and dynamic visualizations, you can engage your audience and provide them with in-depth understanding of your data.

Discovering trends and relationships

Identifying patterns and trends in our data is a vital aspect of extracting valuable insights. In this section, we will delve into techniques for discovering meaningful relationships, trends, and anomalies in our datasets. By recognizing these patterns, we can better understand the underlying structure of the data and make informed decisions based on our findings. So, let us explore various approaches to uncover the hidden gems within our data and bring them to light, ultimately empowering us to make well-informed decisions.

Unraveling linear and non-linear relationships

Understanding the relationships between variables is a fundamental aspect of data analysis, as it helps identify trends and make informed decisions. Let us dive deeper into linear and non-linear relationships and see how they manifest in real-world situations.

In a linear relationship, the change in one variable is directly proportional to the change in another. For example, suppose you are investigating the relationship between the number of hours spent studying and test scores. You might notice that for every additional hour of study, there is a consistent increase in test scores. In this case, the relationship can be represented by a straight line in a scatterplot, which indicates a linear relationship. Analyzing linear relationships can provide valuable insights into the predictability of outcomes based on changes in input variables.

On the other hand, non-linear relationships are more complex, as the change in one variable is not directly proportional to the change in another. Let us consider the example of an advertising campaign. Initially, you might observe that increasing ad spending leads to a significant rise in sales. However, after a certain point, the sales growth starts to level off, despite further increases in ad spending. This could be represented by a curve in a scatterplot, indicating a non-linear relationship. Non-linear relationships can be more challenging to analyze but understanding them can unveil essential patterns and help optimize resource allocation.

Recognizing and interpreting linear and non-linear relationships between variables in your data can uncover valuable insights, allowing you to make informed decisions and optimize your strategy. By utilizing visualization tools and statistical methods, you can better understand these relationships and ensure a comprehensive understanding of the data at hand.

Unraveling time series data: Trends and seasonality

Time series data is a type of data collected at regular intervals over time, which makes it particularly useful for understanding patterns, trends, and seasonality. When working with time series data, it is crucial to analyze how the data changes over time to spot any underlying patterns that could inform your decision-making process.

For example, let us consider a company that wants to forecast its sales for the upcoming year. By examining the historical sales data, we might find that sales have been consistently growing each year, indicating an overall upward trend. We might also notice a recurring pattern of higher sales during specific months or seasons, such as the holiday season, which suggests seasonality in the data.

To analyze time series data effectively, you can use various visualization techniques like line charts or bar charts, which help display the data over time and make it easier to spot trends and seasonal patterns. Additionally, there are specialized techniques and models, such as moving averages or exponential smoothing, that can help smooth out the noise in the data and reveal underlying trends more clearly. By understanding the patterns and trends in time series data, you will be better equipped to make informed predictions and strategic decisions for your organization.

Outliers: Uncovering their impact on data analysis

Outliers are data points that deviate significantly from the overall pattern or trend observed in the dataset. While they may appear to be a mere anomaly, it is essential to understand their impact on the analysis as they can sometimes carry crucial insights or indicate potential issues with the data collection process.

Let us say you are analyzing the average temperature in a city over the past 100 years. You notice that most of the data points are clustered around a particular range, but there is one temperature value that is extremely high, way above the others. This point is an outlier, and it may be worth investigating further. It could be the result of a data entry error, a rare heatwave, or even an indication of an emerging trend due to climate change.

Detecting outliers can be accomplished through various methods, including visual inspection of plots like scatterplots or boxplots, and statistical techniques like the **IQR rule** or **Z-scores**. Once you have identified outliers, it is essential to assess their impact on the overall analysis. In some cases, removing outliers might improve the accuracy of your models or give you a clearer picture of the general trend. In other cases, keeping the outliers and understanding their underlying causes can lead to valuable insights that would have otherwise gone unnoticed.

When dealing with outliers, remember to exercise caution and consider the context of your analysis. Taking the time to understand their impact can help you make better-informed decisions and enhance your overall data analysis process.

Revealing hidden patterns through visualization techniques

Visualization techniques can be powerful tools for uncovering hidden patterns within complex datasets. They allow us to transform raw data into visual representations that make it easier to identify trends, relationships, and anomalies that might be difficult to spot using raw numbers alone.

For instance, let us say you are working with a dataset containing information about the sales of a retail store. Using a heatmap, you can visualize the sales data across different product categories and time periods. This could reveal patterns such as higher sales of winter clothing during colder months or a sudden spike in the sales of a specific product after a promotional campaign.

Another example could be analyzing social network data to understand relationships and interactions among users. By creating a network graph, you can visually represent connections between users, helping you identify influential individuals, tightly knit communities, or even potential bottlenecks in the flow of information.

Choropleth maps are another powerful visualization technique that can reveal geographic patterns. By mapping data onto a geographic area and using color to represent the value of a variable, you can quickly identify regions with high or low values, revealing trends and relationships that might not be apparent from a simple table of numbers.

Remember, the key to uncovering hidden patterns through visualization is to choose the appropriate technique for your dataset and the questions you are trying to answer. Experimenting with different visualizations and adjusting their parameters can often reveal insights that would have remained buried in the data, ultimately leading to better-informed decisions and more effective data-driven strategies.

Conclusion

As we wrap up this chapter on data exploration and visualization, it is important to remember the value these techniques bring to the data analysis process. By conducting exploratory data analysis, using descriptive statistics, and creating meaningful visualizations, you can discover patterns, trends, and relationships within your dataset. These insights can help drive better decision-making, inform strategy, and contribute to a more thorough understanding of the data at hand. Keep experimenting with various techniques and tools to uncover the hidden gems in your data, and never underestimate the power of a well-crafted visualization in telling a compelling data-driven story.

In the next chapter, we will explore these techniques in greater detail, along with other strategies and tools for cleaning and preprocessing data.

Points to remember

- Exploratory data analysis is a crucial step in the data analysis process to clean, preprocess, and understand the dataset.

- Descriptive statistics, including measures of central tendency, dispersion, skewness, and kurtosis, provide valuable insights into a dataset's characteristics.

- Data visualization tools like Matplotlib, seaborn, and Plotly enable the creation of informative and engaging plots that reveal patterns, trends, and relationships in the data.

- Identifying linear and non-linear relationships, analyzing time series data, detecting outliers, and using visualization techniques are essential for uncovering hidden patterns and enhancing data analysis.

Multiple choice questions

1. **Which of the following libraries is not commonly used for data visualization in Python?**

   a. Matplotlib

   b. Seaborn

   c. Plotly

   d. NumPy

2. **What is the measure of central tendency that represents the most frequently occurring value in a dataset?**

   a. Mean

   b. Median

   c. Mode

   d. Range

3. **Which term describes the measure of how much data values deviate from the mean in a dataset?**

   a. Variance

   b. Skewness

   c. Kurtosis

   d. Range

4. **In the context of data analysis, what is the primary purpose of exploratory data analysis?**

   a. To build predictive models

   b. To create visually appealing graphs

   c. To understand the structure and characteristics of the dataset

   d. To test hypotheses

Answers

1. d

2. c

3. a

4. c

Questions

1. What are the key differences between Matplotlib, seaborn, and Plotly when it comes to data visualization in Python, and when might you choose one library over another?

2. How can you detect and handle outliers in a dataset during the data exploration phase, and why is it important to consider their impact on your analysis?

3. How can exploratory data analysis and descriptive statistics be used together to better understand the structure of and the relationships within a dataset before proceeding with more advanced analysis or modeling?

Join our book's Discord space

Join the book's Discord Workspace for Latest updates, Offers, Tech happenings around the world, New Release and Sessions with the Authors:

https://discord.bpbonline.com

CHAPTER 6
Data Alchemy: Cleaning and Preprocessing Raw Data

Introduction

Data is the driving force behind every analysis, model, and visualization that we create. However, raw data is often messy, inconsistent, or even missing crucial pieces of information. In this chapter, we will explore the art of Data Alchemy, where we clean and preprocess raw data to transform it into a valuable resource for our projects. We will delve into techniques for handling missing data, transforming and normalizing variables, de-duplicating records, and more. By the end of this chapter, you should have the tools and knowledge to turn even the most chaotic dataset into meaningful insights.

Structure

In this chapter, we will discuss the following topics:

- Handling missing data

- Data transformation and normalization

- Addressing duplication and data inconsistencies

- Feature engineering and selection

- Encoding categorical features

Objectives

The objective of this chapter is to equip readers with the essential skills to clean and preprocess raw data effectively, enabling them to transform it into a format suitable for in-depth analysis, modeling, and visualization. Through this process, readers will learn to identify and address common data issues, such as missing values, inconsistencies, and duplicates, while also gaining an understanding of data transformation, normalization, feature engineering, and encoding categorical variables.

Handling missing data

Missing data is a common and significant obstacle in data processing. It refers to values that should logically exist but are absent from the data for several reasons. How we handle these missing values can greatly influence the results of our data analysis and model outcomes. In this section, we will explore different strategies to deal with missing data, look at their implications, and learn how to choose the best method based on the context of the problem at hand.

Detecting missing data

Missing data can be a bit of a paradox: it is a piece of information that is not there but tells a story all the same. As we just mentioned, missing data can show up in many forms. An empty cell is the most straightforward, but sometimes placeholders are used: perhaps a *-1* where it is impossible to have a negative, a *9999* that is outside the feasible range, or simply a *?* that is literally a question mark where the answer should be. Recognizing these disguised forms of missing data can make or break your data analysis pipeline.

Now, how do we go about identifying this missing data in Python, particularly when we are working with Pandas DataFrames?

Let us start simple. Say we have a DataFrame *df*. We can use the **isnull()** function in Pandas, which returns another DataFrame, but this one is full of Boolean values: *True* if the original cell was missing data, *False* if it was not. Here is how you can do it; consider the following code:

```
missing_data = df.isnull()
print(missing_data)
```

Executing the preceding lines of code will give you a snapshot of where exactly your missing values are in the DataFrame. But what if your DataFrame is a gigantic one with thousands of rows and columns? The output from the **isnull()** function could be overwhelming and not particularly helpful in that case. We need something more concise. That is where the combination of **isnull()** and **sum()** functions comes to our rescue. By chaining the **sum()** function, we get a count of how many missing values there are in each column. Execute the following code:

```
missing_count = df.isnull().sum()
print(missing_count)
```

This way, you get a column-wise sum of missing values, giving you a clear picture of how scattered or concentrated your missing data is. It is like having a bird's-eye view of the battlefield before you plunge into the nitty-gritty of handling the missing data.

Consider calculating the percentage of missing data in each column, especially when working with large datasets. This can provide you with a relative measure and can be easily done by modifying the previous code as follows:

```
missing_percent = df.isnull().sum() * 100 / len(df)
print(missing_percent)
```

This exploration of missing data is like detective work: you pick up clues, and each clue provides insight into the next step of your data cleaning process. Therefore, be patient, be thorough, and let the story of your data unfold.

Strategies for tackling missing data

In an ideal scenario, every dataset would be pristine, comprehensive, and primed for analysis. However, this is not always the case. In the real world, we encounter missing data more often than we would like. However, we are not defenseless. We have a range of strategies at our disposal to tackle missing data, and in this section, we will discuss them in detail.

The simplest approach is to ignore the missing data. However, this should be reserved only for situations where the missing data is negligible and does not impact the overall analysis. In practice, such situations are quite rare.

Another strategy is to remove observations or variables that contain missing data. Known as **listwise deletion**, this approach can be followed using the **dropna()** method in pandas. However, be careful with this approach as it could potentially result in you losing a lot of information. Here is how you can do it:

```
df_clean = df.dropna()
```

The mentioned line of code will remove all rows where at least one column has missing data. If you want to remove only those rows where all columns have missing data, you can do so by specifying **how** parameter as **all**. Execute the following code in this case:

```
df_clean = df.dropna(how='all')
```

Imputation is a more sophisticated way of handling missing data, where we fill in missing values with some statistical measure like mean, median, or mode. Imputation maintains the size of the data, which can be especially helpful if you are dealing with a small dataset and do not want to lose precious data points. It is like a guessing game, but with the help of statistics; your guesses can be pretty informed. Here is an example of **mean** imputation:

```
df_filled = df.fillna(df.mean())
```

However, it is important to note that while imputation can be highly beneficial, it also has its associated challenges. Imputing with mean, median, or mode can potentially reduce the variance of your data and lead to incorrect estimates of standard errors. So, we need to do it carefully.

Another strategy to handle missing data, especially non-random, is to use predictive models. Methods like regression, **K-Nearest Neighbors** (**KNN**), or even **Machine Learning** (**ML**) models like random forests can be used to predict and fill in the missing values. This strategy, although more complex, can provide a more accurate result.

Finally, a more nuanced approach is to treat missing data as just another category, especially when dealing with categorical variables. Here, the missing data is not filled with any imputed or predicted value but is recognized and marked missing. This strategy might be useful when the fact that the data is missing carries some meaningful information in itself.

All these strategies come with their own sets of advantages and challenges. As a data scientist, it is essential to understand the nature of your data, the reason for the data being missing, and the potential implications of each strategy before choosing the one that fits your specific scenario. It is a bit like a strategic game: know your players, understand the rules and make your move.

Pandas and NumPy for missing data handling

With a basic understanding of identifying missing data, we will now approach the heart of our operation: managing missing data using Python's in-house toolkits, that is, Pandas and NumPy. These libraries have a collection of powerful tools tailored to make the handling of missing data easier.

So, we have already seen how Pandas can flag missing values with **isnull()** and how we can tally these missing values with **isnull().sum()**. It also offers a useful tool to fill these missing values: the **fillna()** function. This function allows us to replace all missing values with a specific value, such as *backfill* or *ffill*, or even along an axis. Execute the following code:

```
df_filled = df.fillna(0)  # Replace all missing values with 0

df_filled_previous = df.fillna(method='ffill')  # Forward fill to replace miss-
ing values with the previous value

df_filled_next = df.fillna(method='bfill')  # Backward fill to replace miss-
ing values with the next value
```

And then there is NumPy, the bedrock of scientific computing in Python. Though we mainly use NumPy for lower-level operations, it has its method to deal with missing data. In NumPy, missing data is typically represented as **np.nan**. We can use this to replace missing or empty values in our data. Use the following code:

```
df_nan = df.replace(" ", np.nan)  # Replace all empty strings with np.nan
```

While NumPy and Pandas both offer missing data handling capabilities, their utility is often best realized when they are used in tandem. With these tools, we can handle the twists and turns that missing data often present. Always remember: the data cleaning journey may be challenging, but with Python's Pandas and NumPy, we are never ill prepared.

Data transformation and normalization

Navigating the realm of data analysis often means dealing with data in all shapes and forms. Data transformation and normalization are like the backstage crew of a grand theater performance: you might not see them, but they play a vital role in making the show successful. They help reshape and rescale our data, ensuring that it can be analyzed effectively and accurately. By the end of this section, you should understand why these techniques are essential, when to apply them, and how they can improve the quality of your analysis and predictive modeling.

Importance of data transformation and normalization

Working with raw data can feel like choreographing a dance where everyone is moving to a different rhythm. It is chaotic and confusing and makes it nearly impossible to identify any meaningful patterns or relationships. Data transformation and normalization are equivalent to setting a common tempo so that all the data points move in harmony, allowing you to discern structure and draw valuable insights.

The importance of these techniques arises from the various hurdles that raw data often presents. For instance, your dataset might consist of variables with drastically different scales. Imagine trying to directly compare the age of a house (measured in years) to its price (measured in thousands or millions). The disparity in these scales can heavily skew the results of your analysis or the performance of your machine learning model.

Moreover, many statistical and machine learning models make assumptions about your data. They might expect your data to follow a normal distribution or have linear relationships between variables. However, raw data rarely fits these assumptions perfectly. This is where data transformation steps in: by applying mathematical functions to your data (like log, square root, or reciprocal), you can mold your data to meet these assumptions more closely.

Normalization, on the other hand, helps to level the playing field. It adjusts your data such that different variables have a common scale without distorting the differences in the range of values or losing information. This is particularly useful when you are working with machine learning algorithms that use a distance-based metric to make predictions, such as KNN or **Support Vector Machines (SVM)**.

By the end of it, data transformation and normalization make your data dance beautifully to the same beat, making your job as a data analyst or data scientist much easier and more effective. They ensure that your models are not just fitting to the data but also to the inherent structure and patterns within the data.

Overview of data transformation techniques

In our quest to make our data more amenable to analysis and modeling, various data transformation techniques come into play. Just like a potter molds clay into various forms to serve different purposes, we can apply various mathematical functions to our data to meet the requirements of specific analysis or machine learning models.

One such transformation is the logarithmic transformation, fondly known as the **log transform**. The log transform is a powerful tool for dealing with situations where your data is highly skewed or when it spans several orders of magnitude. By compressing the high values and stretching out the low values, the log transform can help stabilize variance and make patterns more visible.

Consider this scenario: you are studying income distribution in a city. You are likely to find that the majority of people earn around a certain amount, but a few earn significantly more. A histogram of the raw data might show a peak with a long tail toward the higher end, which is not very useful for visual analysis or modeling. By applying a log transform, you bring that long tail back in line with the rest of the data, making your histogram look more like the familiar bell curve.

The square root and cube root transformations work similarly. They are less dramatic than the log transform and are best suited for moderately skewed data.

The reciprocal transformation (or taking the inverse of each data point) is another method. This transformation results in a significant change in the distribution shape and is more likely to be used when your data shows a hyperbolic pattern.

It is important to remember that there is no one-size-fits-all transformation; the choice of technique will always depend on the characteristics of your specific dataset and the requirements of your analysis or model. After applying a transformation, it is crucial to revisit your data with visualizations and statistical tests to ensure that the transformation has made your data more analysis friendly.

Scaling techniques in data normalization

In our ongoing journey through the realms of data, we sometimes encounter a situation where the range of values in our dataset is so vast that it dwarfs the nuances we are interested in. For example, suppose you are building a machine learning model to predict house prices using the size of the house and the number of rooms as input variables. The size of the house might range from a few hundred to a few thousand square feet, while the number of rooms will typically be between 1 and 10. The huge discrepancy in these scales could mean that the size variable ends up dominating the number of rooms in your model, which is not what we want. This is where scaling techniques come to the rescue, putting our giants and dwarfs on an equal footing.

One such technique is **min-max Scaling,** also known as **normalization**. In this process, we rescale our values so that they fall within a specified range, typically 0 to 1. The transformation is simple: for each value, subtract the minimum value of the feature and then divide the answer by the range of the feature. The result is that your maximum value becomes 1, your minimum value 0, and everything else a decimal somewhere in between.

A second technique is **Z-score standardization**, or simply standard scaling. Instead of squishing the values between 0 and 1, standard scaling transforms the values such that the mean of the feature becomes 0 and the standard deviation becomes 1. This does not bind values to a specific range like min-max scaling does, but it does handle outliers better, which can be a major advantage.

Both these techniques can be easily implemented in Python using the `sklearn.preprocessing` module, which contains the `MinMaxScaler` and `StandardScaler` classes.

Always remember, the choice of scaling technique depends on your specific situation: what kind of data you have, what you know about its distribution, and which algorithm you intend to use afterward. Like much of data science, it is as much an art as a science.

Mastering data alchemy with Python libraries

Data transformation and normalization can sound complex, but the beauty of Python is that it comes with powerful libraries that make these processes straightforward. Let us start this adventure by scaling the giants and dwarfs of our data with scikit-learn and Pandas.

Scikit-learn is an amazing machine learning library with built-in classes for both Min-Max scaling and standard scaling. Let us assume we have a feature in our dataset with values ranging from 20 to 200. Using `MinMaxScaler`, we can normalize this data to be within the range of 0 to 1. Execute the following code:

```
from sklearn.preprocessing import MinMaxScaler
```

```
# Initialize the Scaler
scaler = MinMaxScaler()

# Fit and transform the data
data_normalized = scaler.fit_transform(data)
```

The preceding code creates a **MinMaxScaler** object, fits it to the data, and then transforms the data. The result is a new array where all the values lie between 0 and 1.

Similarly, we can apply Z-score standardization to our data using the **StandardScaler** class. Execute the following code:

```
from sklearn.preprocessing import StandardScaler

# Initialize the Scaler
scaler = StandardScaler()

# Fit and transform the data
data_standardized = scaler.fit_transform(data)
```

Pandas, another great library, also allows us to perform data transformation. For instance, we can easily perform a logarithmic transformation on our dataset. Use the following code:

```
import pandas as pd

# Apply log transformation
data_log_transformed = pd.DataFrame(data).apply(np.log)
```

In the preceding example, the **apply** function is used to apply the **np.log** function to every element of the DataFrame.

These examples just scratch the surface of what you can do with scikit-learn and Pandas. As you venture deeper into data transformation and normalization, always consider the nature of your data and the requirements of the analysis or model you are building. The right tools are in your hands, and it is up to you to wield them effectively.

Addressing duplication and data inconsistencies

Data cleaning does not end at handling missing data or normalization; another major part of the cleaning process is de-duplication and addressing inconsistent or incorrect data. Duplicate data entries can mislead our analysis or training models, while inconsistencies or incorrect values can often stem from human error or system glitches. Furthermore, the way we deal with such issues can largely depend on the nature of the inconsistency or the duplicate data itself. This section will walk you through the common causes of these problems and some effective strategies to rectify them, arming you with the skills to maintain the integrity of your data.

Spotting and eliminating duplicate entries

Duplicates in your dataset can be more than a minor nuisance; they can lead to skewed results and flawed interpretations. Python, armed with Pandas, provides powerful methods to spot and remove such duplications effectively.

Consider a hypothetical dataset that contains information about employees in a company and create it using the following code:

```
import pandas as pd

data = {
    'Name': ['John', 'Anna', 'Peter', 'John', 'Anna'],
    'Age': [28, 25, 32, 28, 25],
    'Department': ['Sales', 'Marketing', 'HR', 'Sales', 'Marketing']
}

df = pd.DataFrame(data)
print(df)
```

The output is as shown in the following figure:

	Name	Age	Department
0	John	28	Sales
1	Anna	25	Marketing
2	Peter	32	HR
3	John	28	Sales
4	Anna	25	Marketing

Figure 6.1: DataFrame before de-duplication

When you print the DataFrame, you will notice that **John** and **Anna** have duplicate entries. To identify these duplicates, we can use the **duplicated()** function in pandas. This function returns a Boolean series, where True indicates a row is a duplicate of an earlier row. Let us execute the following code to see which rows in our DataFrame are duplicates:

```
print(df.duplicated())
```

The output will indicate true for the duplicate entries. In this case, the fourth and fifth entries are duplicates of the first and second entries, respectively.

To remove these duplicates, we use the **drop_duplicates()** function, as follows:

```
df = df.drop_duplicates()
print(df)
```

The output is shown in the following figure:

	Name	Age	Department
0	John	28	Sales
1	Anna	25	Marketing
2	Peter	32	HR

Figure 6.2: DataFrame after de-duplication

This will yield a cleaned DataFrame where the duplicates have been removed. You will notice that **John** and **Anna** now appear only once in the dataset. It is important to note that by default, **drop_duplicates()** considers all columns. If you want to specify certain columns for duplicate checking, you can pass those column names in the parentheses.

In the real world, your data can be much more complex and larger, but these fundamental concepts will hold as you scale up your data cleaning efforts. Always remember, maintaining the integrity of your data is paramount in data analysis.

Handling inconsistent and incorrect data

Dealing with inconsistent or incorrect data is like untangling a knot. It is tricky, sometimes frustrating, but ultimately a necessary step to maintain data integrity. Here are a few strategies to untwist the tangles in your data.

First, we can have inconsistent data types for the same attribute. For example, in a column intended for dates, you might find some entries in the *DD-MM-YYYY* format and others in the *YYYY-MM-DD* format. In this case, we use the **to_datetime()** function in pandas to unify the date format. Execute the following code:

```
df['Date'] = pd.to_datetime(df['Date'], errors='coerce')
```

The **errors=coerce** argument forces any values that cannot be converted into dates into Python's **NaT**, or **Not a Time**, which is like a null value for dates. This makes it easy to identify and handle them later.

Second, you may encounter inconsistent case usage, especially in text data. For example, *New York, new york,* and *NEW YORK* should ideally be treated the same. To make them consistent, you can convert all text to lower case using the following code:

```
df['City'] = df['City'].str.lower()
```

Third, dealing with incorrect data is more complex because it requires a certain degree of domain knowledge and often, manual inspection. For instance, if you are working with a dataset about humans and see an age value of 150, that is likely incorrect. Depending on the extent of these errors and the nature of your analysis, you may decide to remove these entries, correct them if you have enough information, or even leave them as they are but treat them as outliers in your analysis.

Lastly, it is important to validate the data against a known standard or rule. For example, a **ZIP** code column in a US dataset should not contain any non-numeric or null values. We can set conditions to flag or filter out such incorrect entries. Execute the following code:

```
df = df[df['ZIP'].apply(lambda x: str(x).isdigit())]
```

Handling inconsistent or incorrect data is like polishing a rough gem; with some effort and patience, you can uncover the true value beneath. Remember, the cleaner and more consistent the data, the more reliable your analysis will be.

Feature engineering and selection

Feature engineering and selection are like the secret ingredients of a winning data analysis recipe. They allow us to take raw data and transform it into a format that is more conducive to the particular algorithms we are planning to use. With feature engineering, we can create new variables that can improve the performance of our models. In contrast, feature selection helps us to avoid the curse of dimensionality by reducing the number of input variables. In this section, we will delve into the art and science of crafting and choosing the right features to make our models shine.

Role of feature engineering and selection

Feature engineering and selection are the twin engines propelling the data analysis process forward. They are the invisible threads that weave together raw data and predictive models, determining the overall quality and accuracy of our analysis. Think of feature engineering as a form of translation: it converts raw data, which is often noisy and unstructured, into a language that our models can understand and learn from.

Feature engineering is about capturing domain knowledge and using it to create variables that make the data more representative and meaningful. For instance, if you are working with a dataset about houses and have the width and length of the house, you could engineer a new feature that represents the total area. This new feature could turn out to be a stronger predictor of the house price than either the length or the width alone, thereby improving your model's performance.

On the other hand, feature selection is all about simplicity and focus. It helps us to gradually decrease the feature set to the bare essentials, the significant variables. This is especially important when dealing with high-dimensional datasets, where the sheer number of features can lead to overfitting and degrade the performance of our model. Feature selection techniques, such as **Recursive Feature Elimination (RFE)** or using feature importance from tree-based models, can help identify and retain the most important features, ensuring that our models are both effective and efficient.

In a nutshell, feature engineering and selection are crucial for the data analysis process, acting as a bridge between raw data and effective models. They are the tools we use to shape, refine, and optimize our data, ensuring that it is in the best possible form to feed into our models. And when done right, they can significantly improve the performance of our data analysis and predictive modeling.

The art of crafting features

Creating new features from existing variables is a significant part of feature engineering, akin to an artist crafting a masterpiece from raw materials. Suppose you are working on a dataset that is all about houses. You have variables such as the length and width of the house. Alone, these variables provide some insights, but when multiplied together to create a new feature, that is, the house area, they become much more informative. This house area is a feature that is engineered from existing variables, and it is likely to be a more potent predictor of something like house price than either the length or the width alone.

This approach of creating interaction features can be extended to several situations. For instance, in a dataset about cars, we might have engine size and fuel efficiency as separate features. By creating an interaction term, we can examine the relationship between engine size and fuel efficiency; perhaps larger engines tend to be less fuel-efficient.

Polynomial features are another powerful tool in our feature engineering toolbox. These are features that raise an existing variable to a power. For instance, if we have a variable x, we could create the features x^2, x^3, and so on. Polynomial features can be helpful when the relationship between the feature and the target variable is non-linear.

Creating new features from existing variables blends creativity and domain knowledge. As you work with your dataset, you will understand which interactions or polynomial features might be informative. Python's scikit-learn library has convenient functions to help you generate these features automatically, making it easier for you to experiment and find the best set of features for your model. Ultimately, this process is all about enhancing the *signal* in your data—making the meaningful patterns more pronounced and accessible for your models to learn.

Picking the A-team: Methods for effective feature selection

Think of feature selection as forming an elite team, where each member (or feature) brings unique skills and insights to the table to solve a complex problem (or model a tricky dataset). Not all features are created equal; some may bring crucial insights, while others may simply add noise. We employ various strategies for selecting the best subset of features for our models.

Let us dive into these strategies, categorized broadly into filter methods, wrapper methods, and embedded methods.

Filter methods

Filter methods involve evaluating the relevance of each feature independently of any machine learning algorithm. These methods assess the statistical properties of the data, such as correlation or mutual information, to gauge the relationship between each feature and the target variable. Features with a stronger relationship are given priority.

Wrapper methods

Unlike filter methods, wrapper methods evaluate subsets of features within the context of a specific machine-learning model. Essentially, we are wrapping the feature selection process around a particular model. These methods often use a search strategy (like backward elimination, forward selection, or recursive feature elimination) to identify the best subset of features that optimizes the model's performance.

Embedded methods

Embedded methods integrate the feature selection process within the model training process. This means that the model itself determines which features are important during the learning phase. Techniques like LASSO and decision trees fall into this category. For instance, LASSO performs regularization, which can lead to some feature coefficients becoming zero, effectively selecting out those features.

Each method has its strengths and weaknesses, and the choice often depends on the specifics of your dataset and the problem at hand. While filter methods can be fast and not prone to overfitting, they may miss out on important interactions between features. On the other hand, wrapper methods may provide the best performance, but they can be computationally intensive and overfit the data if not carefully controlled. Embedded methods offer a good compromise, balancing performance and computational efficiency.

Feature selection is a crucial step that helps in reducing dimensionality, improving model performance, and enhancing interpretability. It is an art and science requiring a mixture of statistical knowledge, machine learning expertise, and a dose of intuition.

Feature engineering with Pandas and Scikit-Learn

We have talked about the theories and strategies behind feature engineering and selection. Now it is time to bring them to life using the power of Python. Pandas and scikit-learn are two of the most widely used libraries for data manipulation and machine learning.

Pandas is like a Swiss Army Knife for data manipulation. It offers numerous functionalities to create new features out of existing ones. Remember how we spoke about creating polynomial features or interactions? Well, with Pandas, it just needs a few lines of code. For instance, if you have two columns, height and weight, and you would like to create a new feature representing the **body mass index** (**BMI**), the following code can be used:

```
import pandas as pd


# Assuming df is your DataFrame and it has columns 'height' and 'weight'
df['BMI'] = df['weight'] / df['height'] ** 2
```

Using the preceding code, you created a new feature using Pandas. This was a simple example, but you can imagine how you could create more complex features or interactions.

Scikit-learn, on the other hand, comes into play for feature selection. The library provides several classes for implementing filter, wrapper, and embedded methods. For example, if you want to use a filter method based on chi-square statistics for a classification problem, you can use the **SelectKBest** class along with the **chi2** function, as follows:

```
from sklearn.feature_selection import SelectKBest, chi2


# Assuming X is your feature matrix and y is the target vector
selector = SelectKBest(chi2, k=5) # Select top 5 features
X_new = selector.fit_transform(X, y)
```

Similarly, if you prefer an embedded method like LASSO for feature selection, it is pretty straightforward too. Execute the following code:

```
from sklearn.linear_model import LassoCV


lasso = LassoCV().fit(X, y)
importance = np.abs(lasso.coef_)
print(importance)
```

In the preceding example, the absolute values of the LASSO coefficients represent the importance of each feature. Features with zero coefficients can be considered for removal as they do not contribute to the model.

Using these libraries, we can create new features and select the most relevant ones easily and efficiently. This enables us to focus on understanding the data and improving the model rather than being bogged down by technicalities.

Encoding categorical features

This is our last stop in this journey of data cleaning and preprocessing. Handling categorical variables is a vital step to preparing your data, especially when dealing with machine learning models. As most algorithms work with numerical inputs, we need an effective way to convert categorical data into a format our models can understand. This is where encoding comes into play, serving as a translator between the language of categories and numbers, helping us extract valuable insights from our data.

Rationale for encoding categorical features

Categorical variables carry a great deal of information. In the field of data science, they often serve as descriptive agents, adding a layer of qualitative insights to the quantitative facts. This makes them an integral part of our data. However, despite their immense value, categorical variables pose a unique challenge in data analysis. This challenge lies in their innate character; they are not inherently numerical.

The foundation of data analysis and machine learning rests on mathematical and statistical operations, which, to be executed, necessitate numeric data. Imagine trying to feed the text red, green, and blue into a model and expecting the model to perform mathematical operations on it. It would simply be impossible. The model is equipped to deal with numbers, not words. This is where encoding comes into play.

Encoding is a method that transforms categorical variables into a numerical format that our models can understand. Simply put, it is like having a translator who can convert the language of categories into the language of numbers. Let us consider an example. Suppose we have a clothing store dataset where the sizes of items are denoted as S, M, and L. Our machine learning model would not understand what S, M, or L means. However, if we encode S as 1, M as 2, and L as 3, our model can process these values, maintaining the essence of their categorical distinctions.

It is important to note that encoding should be done thoughtfully, as the type of encoding used can influence the performance of the model. The relationship between the categories should be considered before choosing an encoding technique.

Encoding is not just a technical necessity; it is an instrumental step in maintaining the integrity of the data while making it compatible with the requirements of our analysis tools. It allows us to tap into the depth of insights that categorical variables hold and harness their full analytical potential.

Diverse pathways of encoding: One-hot and ordinal techniques unveiled

Handling categorical data is an art that data scientists need to master. There are numerous strategies to approach this task, each serving a unique purpose and providing its own set of advantages. Today, we will take a closer look at two common techniques: one-hot encoding and ordinal encoding.

Let us start with one-hot encoding, a widely used method for handling nominal categorical variables, that is, categories that lack any inherent order. Suppose you have a dataset that has the color of cars with three categories: red, blue, and green. A simple way to encode this information is to assign each color a unique number. But what if our model misconstrues these numbers as having an order or weight? That is where one-hot encoding comes to the rescue.

In one-hot encoding, each category is represented as a binary vector. Each element of this vector corresponds to a category and is set to 1 if the category is present and 0 if it is not. For our car color example, we would end up with three new features: `is_red`, `is_blue`, and `is_green`. If a car is red, it is represented as [1, 0, 0]; if it is blue, as [0, 1, 0]; and if it is green, as [0, 0, 1]. Thus, one-hot encoding successfully transforms our categorical data without imposing any artificial order.

On the other hand, we have ordinal encoding, designed specifically for ordinal categorical variables, that is, categories that have clear and meaningful order. Let us take the example of t-shirt sizes: small, medium, and large. Unlike car colors, these categories have an inherent order: small is less than medium, which is less than large.

In ordinal encoding, we assign each category a unique number, similar to label encoding. However, the crucial difference lies in the fact that we assign these numbers in a way that respects the order of the categories. In our t-shirt size example, we might encode small as 1, medium as 2, and large as 3. The model can then understand and use this order in its learning process.

Choosing the right encoding technique is crucial as it directly affects the quality of our data analysis and the performance of our models. Therefore, understanding the nature of your categorical data and the implications of each encoding technique is a fundamental step in the data preprocessing journey.

Conjuring the magic of encoding: A pythonic approach

Encoding categorical variables is not just about understanding the theoretical framework behind different techniques; it is also about executing them proficiently with the right tools. Python, with its robust libraries like Pandas and scikit-learn, offers excellent functionalities for implementing these encoding techniques.

Let us start by revisiting the concept of one-hot encoding, which is ideal for handling nominal variables. We will employ the pandas library's **get_dummies** function, which automates the process of one-hot encoding, using the following code:

```
import pandas as pd

df = pd.DataFrame({
    'color': ['blue', 'green', 'red', 'blue', 'red']
})

df_encoded = pd.get_dummies(df, columns=['color'])

print(df_encoded)
```

In this simple snippet, we first import pandas and define a DataFrame representing a nominal variable color. By invoking the **get_dummies** function on the DataFrame, we get a one-hot encoded representation of our color variable. Each color now has its own column, and the presence of a color in a row is denoted by a 1 in the corresponding column.

On the other hand, for ordinal variables, scikit-learn offers the **OrdinalEncoder**. Let us see how we can use it; consider the following code:

```
from sklearn.preprocessing import OrdinalEncoder

df = pd.DataFrame({
    'education': ['high_school', 'undergraduate', 'postgraduate', 'high_
school', 'undergraduate']
})

encoder = OrdinalEncoder(categories=[['high_
school', 'undergraduate', 'postgraduate']])
df['education_encoded'] = encoder.fit_transform(df[['education']])

print(df)
```

In the preceding example, we created an **OrdinalEncoder** object and specified the order of the categories. We then called **fit_transform** on the education column to create a new column with the encoded values.

Note that the order you give in the **OrdinalEncoder** initializer corresponds to the order of the categories. Here, **high_school** is encoded as 0, undergraduate as 1, and postgraduate as 2.

Both Pandas and scikit-learn offer versatile and efficient ways to encode categorical variables. With a clear understanding of your categorical variables and the right Python tools, you can transform your data into a format ready for high-performing machine learning models.

Conclusion

Wrapping up our journey into Data Alchemy, we have discovered the criticality of transforming raw data into a gold mine of insights. From dealing with missing data to transforming and normalizing variables, removing duplicates, engineering features, and encoding categorical variables, every step brings us closer to creating a refined, ready-to-use dataset. The art and science of cleaning and preprocessing data are indispensable skills in any data professional's toolkit. Python, with its powerful libraries, makes these tasks more manageable, helping us unveil the true value of our data. Remember, the quality of your data analysis and predictions is directly proportional to the quality of your preprocessing efforts, making this an essential part of any data-related endeavor.

In the next chapter, we will apply these meticulously prepared datasets to explore supervised and unsupervised learning, essential algorithms and model selection, the intricacies of training, testing, and evaluation, all while understanding the pitfalls of overfitting and underfitting, guiding you into the captivating world of predictive modeling.

Points to remember

- Identifying and properly handling missing data is crucial, and strategies can include removal or various imputation methods. Python's pandas and NumPy libraries can assist with these tasks.

- Data may require transformation (like log and square root transformations) to meet the assumptions of certain statistical analyses or machine learning algorithms. Normalization techniques like Min-Max scaling and Z-score standardization ensure that variables are on the same scale.

- Removing duplicates and dealing with inconsistent or incorrect data is vital for maintaining data integrity and accuracy. This could involve correcting errors, removing inaccuracies, or addressing formatting inconsistencies.

- Creating new features from existing ones and selecting the most relevant features can enhance the performance of data models. Techniques to do this include interaction features, polynomial features, and filter, wrapper, or embedded methods for selection.

- Categorical variables need to be encoded in numerical form for most algorithms. This could involve one-hot encoding for nominal or ordinal encoding for ordinal variables. Python's pandas and scikit-learn libraries offer functions to implement these encoding techniques easily.

Multiple choice questions

1. **Which of the following is not a common strategy for handling missing data?**

   a. Deletion

   b. Mean imputation

   c. One-hot encoding

   d. Regression imputation

2. **Which technique would be best suited for scaling data to a fixed range between 0 and1?**

   a. Z-score standardization

   b. Min-Max scaling

   c. Square root transformation

   d. Log transformation

3. **Which of the following techniques is not related to feature engineering and selection?**

   a. Creating interaction features

   b. Polynomial feature creation

   c. One-hot encoding

   d. Filter methods

4. **What does one-hot encoding do for nominal categorical variables?**

   a. It transforms the categories into numerical order

   b. It assigns each category a unique numerical ID

   c. It creates new binary features for each category

   d. It calculates the mean value for each category

Answers

1. c

2. b

3. c

4. c

Questions

1. Discuss the potential consequences of ignoring missing data in a dataset and how you can address these issues.

2. Explain the differences between the three common scaling techniques for data normalization: Min-Max scaling, Z-score standardization, and log transformation.

3. How do filter, wrapper, and embedded methods differ in terms of feature selection? Discuss each method's pros and cons.

Join our book's Discord space

Join the book's Discord Workspace for Latest updates, Offers, Tech happenings around the world, New Release and Sessions with the Authors:

https://discord.bpbonline.com

CHAPTER 7
Machine Learning Magic: An Introduction to Predictive Modeling

Introduction

Embarking on the journey of predictive modeling feels like unlocking a magical toolbox filled with algorithms, methods, and strategies to transform raw data into insightful predictions. This chapter will demystify this realm by diving into supervised and unsupervised learning, the two pillars of the **Machine Learning (ML)** universe. We will also guide you through the intricate maze of algorithms, model selection, training, testing, and evaluation. Plus, we will delve into understanding and mitigating the common challenges of overfitting and underfitting. As we uncover these essential elements, you will have the knowledge to turn numbers into narratives and predictions into actionable insights.

Structure

In this chapter, we will discuss the following topics:

- Supervised and unsupervised learning
- Essential algorithms and model selection
- Training, testing, and evaluation
- Overfitting and underfitting

Objectives

By the end of this chapter, readers should gain a solid understanding of the fundamental concepts of machine learning. They will explore the differences between supervised and unsupervised learning, discover essential machine learning algorithms, and learn the process of training, testing, and evaluating models. Additionally, they will develop an understanding of common challenges in machine learning, such as overfitting and underfitting, and learn techniques to address these issues. The ultimate objective is to equip readers with the knowledge to select appropriate machine learning algorithms and effectively apply them to solve real-world problems.

Supervised and unsupervised learning

Machine learning can be thought of as a powerful wizard that uses algorithms to make sense of data, making predictions and finding patterns along the way. The two most common types of machine learning wizards that you will encounter in this magical realm are supervised and unsupervised learning. Supervised learning learns from labeled data, predicting outcomes based on what it has seen before. Unsupervised learning, on the other hand, explores unlabeled data, discovering hidden structures and interesting patterns. These two paradigms form the bedrock of machine learning, and understanding their workings is crucial for any data science endeavor.

Supervised versus unsupervised learning

Machine learning can be compared to an eager apprentice who learns by observing and doing. Suppose our eager apprentice has a master who clearly labels everything, demonstrating what is good and bad, guiding the apprentice step by step. This is what supervised learning is. In this approach, the algorithm learns from a labeled dataset: think of this as a textbook where all the problems have known answers. The algorithm uses this information to predict the same kind of labels when it encounters new, similar problems. This makes supervised learning great for classification and regression tasks such as spam detection (whether or not email is spam) or house price prediction (predicting house price based on size and location).

But what happens when our apprentice does not have a guiding master or a textbook with the answers? What if they only have a heap of tools and materials but no clue what they should make? This is where unsupervised learning comes into play. In unsupervised learning, the algorithm is not given labels or right answers. Instead, it is left to find interesting structures and patterns in the data on its own. This type of learning is suited for clustering and association tasks like customer segmentation (grouping similar customers) or association rule mining in market basket analysis (finding associations between products in transaction data).

The key difference between the two lies in the data they learn from. Supervised learning requires labeled data learning the relationship between the features (inputs) and the target (output). Unsupervised learning does not have a target output. It looks at the features and tries to find patterns or structures within them. In terms of application, this makes supervised learning a tool for predictive modeling, while unsupervised learning shines in exploratory data analysis.

Impact of supervised and unsupervised learning

It is one thing to understand the technical differences between supervised and unsupervised learning, but what brings these concepts to life are their applications in our day-to-day world. Let us dive deeper into a few real-life examples.

We will start with supervised learning, which excels in predictive modeling. Think about your email inbox, which is a mix of personal emails, work-related communication, promotional emails, and unwanted spam. Spam detection is a classic example of a supervised learning application. Using a dataset of emails labeled as spam or not spam, a machine learning algorithm can be trained to recognize characteristics of spam emails and filter them out from your inbox.

Another important application is in healthcare, where supervised learning algorithms can predict disease progression. For instance, algorithms can be trained on a dataset of patient records with labels indicating the presence or progression of a disease, enabling them to predict disease outcomes in new patients based on their records.

Unsupervised learning, on the other hand, excels in unearthing hidden structures and revealing insights from unlabeled data. For example, suppose a large supermarket wants to understand shopping behavior to optimize store layout. They could use unsupervised learning techniques like clustering to group customers based on their buying habits, revealing patterns such as customers who buy diapers often buy baby food too.

Similarly, in the world of social media, unsupervised learning algorithms help power recommendation systems. By analyzing user behavior patterns, these systems can identify similar users and recommend content based on the preferences of those similar users, all without the need for explicit labels.

In essence, while supervised learning has a guiding hand directing its path, unsupervised learning ventures into the unknown, making discoveries that can often lead to profound insights. Both have their unique applications and, when used appropriately, can create quite an impact.

Essential algorithms and model selection

We will now venture into essential algorithms and the art of model selection. In the grand theater of predictive modeling, algorithms are the actors, each with a unique role. However, not all algorithms are suited for every role, just as not all actors can portray every character. Understanding the essential algorithms and how to select the right one for your unique dataset is like casting the perfect actor for a role, setting the stage for a blockbuster performance in predictive modeling.

Understanding the role of algorithms in machine learning

As our journey into machine learning continues, we will now encounter the mystics that weave the magic of predictive modeling: the algorithms. Remember our discussion on supervised and unsupervised learning? Well, each of those learning paradigms has specific algorithms that work best. Let us look at some of these prominent algorithms.

Starting with supervised learning, equipped with labeled data, we have **linear regression**, an old faithful in machine learning. As its name suggests, linear regression models the relationship between two variables by fitting a linear equation to observed data.

Logistic regression, another commonly used supervised learning algorithm, is a go-to option when dealing with binary classification problems. Despite its name suggesting regression, it is used for classification.

Decision trees, with their simple yet powerful structure of nodes, branches, and leaves, are easy to understand and visually interpret. They can handle both numerical and categorical data, making them a versatile choice for many problems.

Then we have **random forests**, which are groups of decision trees working together. They are an ensemble learning method that operates by constructing multiple decision trees at training time and outputting the class that is the mode of the classes for classification or by mean prediction of the individual trees for regression.

Support Vector Machines (**SVMs**) are also part of the supervised learning family. They excel at binary classification tasks and can work well in higher dimensional spaces or when the number of dimensions exceeds the number of samples.

Shifting our focus to unsupervised learning, where we deal with unlabeled data, we can see clustering algorithms. These algorithms aim to group sets of objects in a way that objects in the same group (called a **cluster**) are more similar to each other than to those in other groups.

Among the clustering algorithms, **K-means** is the most popular. It partitions the data into K non-overlapping clusters based on their distances from the K centroids.

Hierarchical clustering is another interesting unsupervised learning algorithm that creates a tree of clusters. Unlike K-means, it does not require us to prespecify the number of clusters, which can be a big plus.

These algorithms, like diverse tools in a toolbox, each have their strengths, their preferred tasks, and their nuances. Understanding their roles and knowing when to use each one is a crucial skill in machine learning. Stay tuned as look at how to select the best algorithm for a given task.

Finding the right model for your data

Just like choosing a champion in a game, selecting the right machine learning model is an art that involves considering various factors. Let us look at some of these considerations.

First, it is essential to understand the problem at hand thoroughly. Are we predicting a continuous outcome, classifying objects into distinct categories, or finding hidden patterns in our data? Each problem type will lean toward different algorithms. For instance, if we are predicting house prices, a regression model like linear regression would be suitable, while if we are trying to categorize emails as spam or not spam, a classification model like logistic regression or a support vector machine would be more apt.

Next, we must assess the nature of our data. Is it linear or nonlinear? Do we have a few strong features or a multitude of weak ones? Are there any outliers? Are our variables categorical or continuous? The answers to these questions influence our model choice. For instance, linear regression assumes a linear relationship between the features and the target variable. At the same time, decision trees and random forests are more versatile and can handle both categorical and continuous data, as well as nonlinear relationships.

The complexity of the model is another critical factor to consider. A more complex model might give us a better fit with our training data but risks overfitting, where the model performs well on the training data but poorly on new, unseen data. Simpler models may not fit the training data that well, but they often have better generalizability, meaning they perform better on new data.

The interpretability of the model can also be a key deciding factor. In many industries, it is not enough to have a model that makes accurate predictions; it is also crucial to understand why it is making those predictions. For example, decision trees and linear/logistic regression models offer good interpretability as you can see how the model makes decisions or predictions.

Finally, practical considerations like computational resources, time constraints, and the availability of pretrained models may also play a role in model selection. Some models may be computationally expensive or time-consuming to train, especially on large datasets.

Choosing the right model is a blend of art and science, requiring a mix of technical knowledge, practical experience, and a dash of intuition. Remember, there is often no single correct model for a given problem. Rather, it is about finding the model that best meets your specific needs and constraints. Next, we will explore how we train these models and evaluate their performance.

Balancing bias, variance, and accuracy in model selection

Assume that you are a tightrope walker, high above the ground, balancing with a long pole in your hands. On one end of the pole, you have bias and accuracy, and on the other, you have variance and complexity. The key to staying on the rope is maintaining the perfect balance.

Choosing a machine learning model is a similar act of balance, as it involves making critical trade-offs between various aspects. Two of the most important trade-offs are the bias-variance trade-off and the accuracy-complexity trade-off.

Bias and variance are two fundamental sources of error in our models. High bias means our model is oversimplified, not considering all the available information, and therefore, missing critical relationships in the data, leading to underfitting. High variance, on the other hand, indicates that our model is overcomplicated and fits our training data too closely, even capturing its noise, leading to overfitting.

The challenge lies in striking a balance to minimize both bias and variance. Overemphasis on either aspect can compromise the model's effectiveness on new, previously unseen data. Many machine learning algorithms come with hyperparameters that let us tune this balance. For example, in a decision tree, the tree depth is a hyperparameter that we can adjust. A shallow tree might have high bias and low variance, while a deep tree could exhibit low bias but high variance.

Similarly, there is a delicate balance between model accuracy and complexity. A complex model might offer high accuracy on the training data but could be difficult to interpret, slow to run, and prone to overfitting. On the other hand, a simple model might be quicker to run and easier to understand but might not capture all the nuances in the data, leading to lower accuracy.

This accuracy-complexity trade-off becomes especially crucial in real-world scenarios. For instance, in industries where model interpretability is key, a simpler, slightly less accurate model might be preferred over a more complex, slightly more accurate one.

Thus, the art of model selection is about walking this tightrope, finding a model that offers a just-right balance of bias and variance, accuracy, and complexity. And as with any balancing act, it requires practice, precision, and patience. Now, let us move on and explore how we bring our chosen model to life through training and testing.

Training, testing, and evaluation'

Now that we have chosen our machine learning model, it is time to put it through its paces. This is where training, testing, and evaluation come into play. Picture this process as a triathlon, where our model must swim, bike, and run to the finish line. At each stage, we challenge the model, push its limits, and evaluate its performance. By the end, we will know how well our model can handle unseen data and whether it is ready for deployment.

Learning the ropes of the training process

If you think about it, the machine learning model is like an athlete preparing for the big race. Training is where the model hits the gym, so to speak. It sweats it out with the data, lifting and lowering weights to strengthen its predictive muscles. It learns from the examples in the training data, adjusting its parameters to minimize errors and maximize accuracy.

This process is like a coach guiding an athlete. The coach presents different scenarios or exercises (the training data), and the athlete (our model) learns how to respond effectively. The end goal? It is to enable the athlete to face new scenarios in the future with confidence and accuracy.

Let us wade a little deeper into this analogy. We have our athlete (the model) and our coach (the algorithm), but what does the training look like? In machine learning, training is not about physical exertion but iterative refinement.

First off, our model is initiated with a set of random parameters (weights and biases). Consider it to be an athlete that never played the sport before. It is enthusiastic but lacks knowledge and experience.

The coach (the algorithm) comes with a strategy (objective function) and a playbook (training data). The coach starts by showing the athlete a few plays from the book, and the athlete tries to predict the outcomes. In the early stages, the predictions can be wildly off. This is where the magic happens. The coach does not scold the athlete but gently corrects them, adjusting the parameters slightly to reduce the error.

This process of making a prediction, comparing it with the actual result, and making corrections based on the error is repeated over and over, with each repetition being known as an epoch in machine learning lingo. With every epoch, the model becomes a bit more tuned to the data, slowly but steadily improving its performance.

The beauty of this process is that it is all driven by mathematics. The algorithm leverages calculus (specifically, a method called **gradient descent**) to find the direction in which the model's parameters should be adjusted to minimize the error. It is like a compass guiding the athlete to improve performance.

But remember, training is not a sprint; it is a marathon. It is a delicate balance of learning enough to make accurate predictions but not so much that the model becomes over-specialized to the training data. This concept, known as **overfitting**, is something we will delve into later.

In summary, the training process is a fascinating dance between the model and the data, orchestrated by the algorithm. It is where raw data transforms into valuable insights, enabling machines to learn from past examples and make accurate predictions in the future. Understanding this process is crucial to mastering the art and science of machine learning.

Understanding training, testing, and holdout sets

Do you recall the age-old strategy of divide and conquer? This principle applies just as aptly in machine learning. We divide our dataset into two primary subsets – training set and testing set – to conquer the challenge of building robust, reliable predictive models.

Consider our machine learning model to be a student prepping for a big exam. The training data is akin to all the material the student studies and learns from. This is the major chunk of data that the model uses to learn patterns and nuances, or in other words, train.

Now, how do we know if our student – the model – is truly ready for the final test – predicting unseen data? This is where the testing set enters the scene, playing the role of a surprise quiz. It is a smaller, separate portion of data that the model has never seen during training.

We use the testing set to evaluate how well our model generalizes its learning to unseen data. It is like a reality check, helping us determine whether our model is truly learning patterns or merely memorizing the training data.

The train-test split is a critical step in machine learning. It safeguards us from a common pitfall known as overfitting, where the model becomes a crammer rather than a learner. It might ace the training data but fails miserably when presented with new, unseen data.

It is important to remember, though, that there is no fixed rule for the split ratio between training and testing sets. A commonly used one is 80:20, but it can vary based on the specificities of the dataset and the problem at hand.

While we have discussed dividing our dataset into training and testing sets, there is another critical component in the machine learning process that you should know about: the **holdout set**. Think of the holdout set as an additional layer of validation, a final exam after our model has passed its surprise quiz (the testing set).

After training on the training set and being evaluated on the testing set, the model is exposed to the holdout set. This is yet another subset of the data that the model has not encountered before. The key purpose of the holdout set is to provide a final, unbiased evaluation of the model's performance.

The holdout set is particularly important in scenarios where model tuning is an iterative process. As we tweak and refine our model – perhaps adjusting parameters or introducing new features – there is a risk of inadvertently tuning the model to perform too well on the testing set, a phenomenon known as test set overfitting. The holdout set helps mitigate this risk by objectively assessing the model's true predictive power on entirely unseen data.

In practice, the dataset might be split into a 70:20:10 ratio, where 70% is used for training, 20% for testing, and the remaining 10% for the holdout set. However, similar to the train-test split, these proportions can vary based on the dataset's size and the specific requirements of the project.

By dividing our data into training, testing and holdout sets, we ensure that our model learns well and tests well. This step gives us confidence that our model is ready to face the real world and make reliable predictions.

Grading the machine: Understanding model evaluation metrics

Suppose you are participating in a cooking competition. You have done the work, selecting the perfect ingredients, following the recipe meticulously, and presenting your dish with flair. But how do you know if you have truly nailed it? The answer lies in the feedback from the judges, who score your dish based on criteria such as taste, presentation, and originality.

Much like this scenario, after training our machine learning model (preparing the dish) and making predictions on the test data (presenting the dish), we need a way to measure how well our model has performed. These measures, or metrics, are equivalents of our cooking competition judges.

In the world of machine learning, these judges are many and varied. The choice of metric depends on the type of problem you are solving. Let us focus on two main types: classification tasks and regression tasks.

For **classification tasks**, where we predict discrete categories, we have metrics like the confusion matrix, accuracy, precision, recall, and the F1 score. These metrics are like our taste judges: each measures a unique aspect of the model's performance.

On the flip side, we have **regression tasks**, where we predict continuous values. Here, our metrics are **mean absolute error (MAE)**, **mean squared error (MSE)**, and R-squared. These are like our presentation judges, evaluating how close our predictions are to the actual values.

In the end, like in the cooking competition, no single judge or metric can tell the whole story. Combining these evaluation metrics gives us a comprehensive picture of our model's performance, helping us identify areas of strength and opportunities for improvement. Remember, the right choice of metrics leads to better models and, ultimately, more effective solutions to our problems.

Evaluating classification models

Let us understand the nitty-gritty of some of the most widely used evaluation metrics for classification models:

- **Accuracy:** Suppose you have built a model to predict whether or not a given email is spam. Accuracy is simply the proportion of predictions your model gets right. So, if your model correctly identified 90 out of 100 emails, its accuracy would be 90%. It is like the report card of your model: a single figure that gives you a general idea of how well your model did. However, it can be misleading when classes are imbalanced. Let us say only 10 out of 100 emails are spam, and your model simply predicts everything to be non-spam. It would still have an accuracy of 90% even though it did not identify any spam emails correctly!

- **Precision and recall:** These are like two best friends who always go together, especially when dealing with imbalanced datasets. Precision measures the proportion of positive identifications that were actually correct. So, if your model flagged 50 emails as spam, and only 40 of them truly were spam, the precision would be 80%. On the other hand, recall measures the proportion of actual positives that were identified correctly. So, if there were 60 actual spam emails and the model correctly identified 40, the recall would be 66.67%. One tells you how precise your model is, while the other tells you its completeness or recall capability.

- **F1 score:** Meet the harmonic mean of precision and recall: the F1 score. It is a single metric combining precision and recall, giving them equal weightage. If you are finding it hard to strike a balance between precision and recall, look no further than the F1 score. A higher F1 score means your model has a good balance of precision and recall.

- **Confusion matrix:** The confusion matrix, an essential tool in machine learning, gives us a more detailed view of our model's performance, beyond just accuracy. This table has four components: **True Positives (TP)**, **False Positives (FP)**, **True Negatives (TN)**, and **False Negatives (FN)**. These terms represent correct and incorrect predictions of our model for both positive and negative classes. By understanding these, we can compute other important metrics like precision, recall, and F1-score, which provide a more nuanced view of our model's performance.

- **ROC-AUC: Receiver Operating Characteristic (ROC)** is a probability curve, and **Area Under the Curve (AUC)** represents the degree or measure of separability. It tells how much the model is capable of distinguishing between classes. The higher the AUC, the better the model distinguishes between spam and non-spam emails.

Evaluating regression models

Now that we have gained some insights into classification metrics, we will shift gears and delve into the world of regression. Whether you are predicting house prices, forecasting sales, or estimating life expectancies, regression metrics are the tools you will need to evaluate your model's performance. Let us look at the most common ones closely:

- **MAE:** Let us say you have built a model to predict the prices of used cars. The MAE gives you the average magnitude of errors your model makes, regardless of the direction of the mistakes. It is as if the model says, "On average, I will be off by about $x". It is a metric that is easy to understand, but it does not indicate how grave an error can be. For example, an MAE of $200 might be acceptable for predicting house prices but not so much for predicting the cost of books.

- **MSE:** This is a little tougher on your model because it squares the errors before averaging them. This means larger errors are penalized more than smaller ones, giving you a more nuanced picture of your model's performance. It is a bit like a strict teacher who is not content with an average performance and is keen on catching those glaring mistakes.

- **R-squared:** This is the coefficient of determination or R-squared. This metric tells you the proportion of the variance in the dependent variable that can be predicted using the independent variable(s). In other words, it shows how well your model fits the data. An R-squared of 1 indicates a perfect fit (which can be a warning sign of overfitting), while an R-squared closer to 0 means your model is struggling.

- **Root mean squared error (RMSE):** The RMSE is like the hyped-up version of MSE. We arrive at the RMSE by taking the square root of the MSE. This metric is useful because it allows us to interpret the error in the same units as the target variable. For instance, if our target variable is in dollars, our MSE would be in squared dollars, while the RMSE would be in dollars, making it more intuitive.

Overfitting and underfitting

Picture a seesaw on a playground, striving to maintain perfect balance. On one end of this seesaw is underfitting, a simplistic model that just cannot quite grasp the complexity of our data. On the opposite end, we have overfitting, a model so entangled in the details that it loses sight of the big picture. Our journey in this section is to find that sweet spot in the middle, where the model is just right: complex enough to capture relevant patterns yet simple enough to generalize well to new data. This equilibrium is a crucial aspect of building effective machine learning models, and understanding the concepts of overfitting and underfitting is key to achieving it.

Striking the right balance: Overfitting and underfitting explained

In machine learning, the performance of a model is deeply influenced by its complexity. A model can err in two primary ways: by being overly simplistic or exceedingly intricate.

When a model is underfitting, it is too basic. Such a model does not capture the underlying patterns in the data. Imagine fitting a straight line to a dataset that exhibits a curved trend. No matter how you adjust this line, it would not accurately represent the data's inherent curve.

Conversely, an overfitting model is exceedingly detailed. It not only captures the primary patterns but also the noise, outliers, and minor fluctuations in the training data. Visualize a model trying to pass through every data point on a scatter plot. While it might excel in the training data, its performance on new, unseen data would likely be subpar due to its excessive specificity.

The essence of machine learning is to find a model that sits between these two extremes. It should capture the essential patterns without getting bogged down by every minor detail. Achieving this balance while navigating the pitfalls of overfitting and underfitting is crucial for model efficacy.

Techniques to tackle overfitting and underfitting

Navigating the world of machine learning can sometimes feel like performing a high-wire act. Our journey involves a constant battle against the dual perils of underfitting and overfitting. However, we are not without tools and strategies to maintain the balance and ensure good performance of our models.

Our first ally in this battle is **cross-validation**. Consider the act of rehearsing for a major performance. We would not merely rehearse the whole act once; instead, we would break it down into sections, fine-tuning each part before bringing it all together. Cross-validation works similarly. Instead of solely training our model on the training set, we segregate the set into several partitions, or folds. We successively train the model on most folds (the training part) and evaluate it on the remaining one (the validation part). This process repeats until each fold has had a turn at validation. This way, we obtain a more holistic assessment of our model's performance and its ability to generalize to unseen data, without touching our actual test set.

Our second tool to combat overfitting is regularization. It is like using a balance pole in our high-wire act. Regularization methods, such as **Ridge** and **Lasso**, help us by introducing a penalty for excessive complexity in our models. By penalizing models with many parameters or overly large coefficients, regularization helps us keep our balance on the high wire, preventing our models from becoming overly complex and reducing the likelihood of overfitting.

Finally, we have direct control over the complexity of our models. If we are tilting toward underfitting, we can increase the complexity of our model by adding more features, creating polynomial features, or choosing a more intricate model type. Conversely, if our model sways towards overfitting, we can simplify our model by using fewer features, removing polynomial features, or opting for a less complex model.

Applying these techniques requires an in-depth understanding of our data and a keen sense of our model's performance. But by employing cross-validation, regularization, and complexity control, we can walk the high wire of machine learning with skill, ensuring that our models perform admirably on both our training and unseen data. And that is how we make the magic of machine learning come alive!

Conclusion

This chapter took us on a thrilling journey into the heart of predictive modeling, starting with a grounding understanding of supervised and unsupervised learning and then exploring essential machine learning algorithms. We delved into the intricacies of model selection and learned how to navigate the trade-offs inherent in choosing the right model for our data. Furthermore, we dug deep into the critical process of training, testing, and evaluating our models, understanding the importance of different metrics to gauge their performance accurately. Finally, we grappled with the twin challenges of overfitting and underfitting, developing a better understanding of these phenomena and how to mitigate them, thereby ensuring that our models are capable and reliable predictors.

As we step into the next chapter, we will focus on regression techniques, including linear and logistic regression, and explore the world of regularization techniques that enhance the robustness of our models and their applicability to real-world scenarios.

Points to remember

- Understanding the difference between supervised and unsupervised learning is important. While supervised learning uses labeled data to make predictions, unsupervised learning uncovers hidden structures in unlabeled data.

- The choice of which machine learning algorithm to use depends on various factors, including the nature of your data and the problem you are trying to solve. It is essential to consider the trade-offs between bias and variance, complexity, and interpretability.

- Training, testing, and evaluating your model are crucial steps in the machine learning pipeline. Splitting your data into training and testing sets and choosing the right evaluation metric ensures that your model is robust and can generalize well to unseen data.

- Overfitting and underfitting are two common pitfalls in machine learning. By leveraging techniques like cross-validation, regularization, and controlling model complexity, you can improve the balance and performance of your model.

Multiple choice questions

1. **Which of the following is a supervised learning algorithm?**

    a. Linear regression

    b. K-means clustering

    c. Hierarchical clustering

    d. None of the above

2. **When selecting a model for a machine learning problem, which of these is not typically a consideration?**

    a. The nature of the data

    b. The problem you are trying to solve

    c. The brand of the computer you are using

    d. The complexity of the model

3. **Why do we split our data into training and testing sets in machine learning?**

    a. To ensure that our model can generalize well to unseen data

    b. To avoid using all our data

    c. Because it is mandatory in all machine learning projects

    d. None of the above

4. **Overfitting in a machine learning model signifies which of the following?**

    a. The model performs poorly on both the training and testing sets.

    b. The model performs well on the training set but poorly on the testing set.

    c. The model performs poorly on the training set but well on the testing set.

    d. The model performs well on both the training and testing sets.

Answers

1. a

2. c

3. a

4. b

Questions

1. What are the key differences between supervised and unsupervised learning?

2. What are some of the factors to consider when selecting a machine learning algorithm for your problem?

3. How can we address the issue of overfitting in a machine learning model?

## CHAPTER 8

Exploring Regression: Linear, Logistic, and Advanced Methods

Introduction

Welcome to our journey through the intriguing realm of regression. In this chapter, we will explore some of the most fundamental and widely used algorithms in **Machine Learning** (**ML**): linear and logistic regression. We will delve into the core concepts, the assumptions, and the mathematics underlying these algorithms, allowing us to understand their workings and application better. We will then confront a common issue in machine learning, which is overfitting, and we will introduce powerful tools called **regularization techniques** to combat it. By the end of this chapter, you should have a solid foundation in regression techniques, equipping you to build effective predictive models.

Structure

In this chapter, we will discuss the following topics:

- Linear regression
- Logistic regression
- Regularization techniques

Objectives

The aim of the chapter is to help you develop a comprehensive understanding of key regression techniques. We aim to dissect the theories behind linear and logistic regression, explore their assumptions, and demonstrate their practical applications. We will also discuss the concept of overfitting and introduce regularization as a solution to manage this challenge. We aim to equip readers with the knowledge to correctly choose, implement, and evaluate these regression methods in various real-world predictive modeling scenarios.

Linear regression

Linear regression, an essential tool in the machine learning toolkit, is where we begin our journey into the world of regression. This powerful statistical technique allows us to understand the relationship between a dependent variable and one or more independent variables. It serves as a simple yet effective model for predicting a quantitative response. In this section, we will unlock the mystery behind this crucial algorithm, explore its assumptions, and learn about its applications in predictive modeling.

What is linear regression

At first glance, the term 'linear regression' might seem daunting with its mathematical undertones. Consider it a fun puzzle where you are trying to draw the best straight line through a scatterplot of data points. This line is our mathematical model: a way to predict y based on x. Let us break it down with a real-world scenario.

Suppose you are a real estate agent trying to predict the selling price of a house. You have a rich dataset of past sales, with each record containing details of the house's age, the number of bedrooms, and the sale price. In this scenario, the house's price is the dependent variable we are trying to predict, and the other attributes (like age and bedrooms) are the independent variables that we expect to influence the price.

With linear regression, we will build a model that best captures the relationship between these variables. The model will establish a formula, allowing us to plug in the independent variables (age and number of bedrooms) and get an estimate of the dependent variable (the price).

It is like a recipe where you control the ingredients (independent variables), and the cake (dependent variable) comes out differently depending on what and how much you put in. The beauty of this model lies in its simplicity and interpretability: you can directly see how changes in your independent variables could potentially affect your dependent variable.

But it is not all smooth sailing. Several assumptions underpin a valid linear regression model, which we will get into in the next section. Plus, it is crucial to remember that while the model can help us predict, it does not always imply causation.

Despite its potential complexities, linear regression remains a staple in the statistical toolset. From economics to ecology, it is a fundamental technique with wide-reaching applications. As we move further in this chapter, we will uncover more about this versatile, practical approach to prediction. So, let us dive right in!

Understanding linear regression: Four fundamental assumptions'

Linear regression is a powerful statistical tool, but it is crucial to understand that it comes with a set of assumptions that should ideally be met to work most effectively. It is like inviting someone to a party: You want to make sure you have all the right conditions in place for your guests to shine.

The assumption of **linearity** states that there is a linear relationship between the independent and dependent variables. Think of it like a straight road, where knowing how far you have traveled directly tells you how far you have moved from the starting point.

Next comes the assumption of **independence**, which asserts that the observations are independent of each other. It is like a roll of the dice: what you roll now does not depend on what you rolled earlier.

The third assumption is called **homoscedasticity**. In simpler terms, it means that the spread of the errors remains consistent regardless of the value of the independent variables. Consider a scatter plot of residuals (errors); these should appear as a band with a consistent width from one end to the other.

The final assumption is that of **normality**, which assumes that the errors of the model are normally distributed. Consider a bell curve here: this shape is the classic symbol of a normal distribution.

Building a linear regression model: An overview

When building a linear regression model, we try to find the best-fitting line through our data points. In the case of simple linear regression (one predictor), this is easy to visualize: Imagine a scatterplot of data points and that you are trying to draw a straight line that best represents the general trend.

The best-fitting line is defined as the line that minimizes the sum of the squared residuals, where a residual is the difference between the observed and predicted values. This method is called the method of least squares.

In the simple linear regression model, our formula is straightforward: $y = \beta 0 + \beta 1 x + \varepsilon$. Here, y is the dependent variable we want to predict, x is our independent variable or predictor, $\beta 0$ is the y-intercept (the value of y when x = 0), $\beta 1$ is the slope of the line (the change in y for a one-unit change in x), and ε is the error term.

But when we move to multiple linear regression, things get a bit more complex. We are no longer dealing with a straight line but with a multidimensional hyperplane. Our formula expands to accommodate multiple predictors: $y = \beta0 + \beta1x1 + \beta2x2 + ... + \beta nxn + \varepsilon$. Now, each xi represents a different predictor, and each corresponding βi represents the change in y for a one unit change in xi while keeping all other predictors constant.

Selecting the right predictors requires careful statistical analysis, domain knowledge, and an understanding of the problem at hand. There are techniques like forward selection, backward elimination, and stepwise regression that can help in this process.

Coefficients, predictions, and model evaluation

Delving into the heart of a linear regression model requires us to understand the regression coefficients and how they influence the predictions our model makes. The coefficients in our linear equation, which are the beta values, signify the change in our response variable for each one unit change in a predictor, assuming all other predictors stay the same.

Consider an example where we are predicting house prices using the size of the house and the number of rooms as predictors. If the coefficient for size is 3000, it means for each additional square foot of space, we predict the house price to increase by $3000, given that the number of rooms stays the same. Similarly, if the coefficient for the number of rooms is 10000, we predict a house price increase of $10000 for each additional room, assuming that the house's size remains constant. It is a bit like saying, *If I increase the size of my house by one square foot, leaving the number of rooms the same, I would expect my house value to go up by $3000.*

But merely fitting the model is not enough. We need to know how well our model is performing. For that, we look at evaluation metrics like the R-squared value, also known as the **coefficient of determination**. This metric tells us the proportion of variance in our dependent variable that's predictable from our independent variables. So, if we get an R-squared value of 0.85, our model explains 85% of the variability in house prices using the size and number of rooms.

However, we should not rely solely on R-squared because it tends to increase as we add more predictors, even if they do not contribute much to the model's predictive ability. That is why we also consider adjusted R-squared, which adjusts the statistic based on the number of predictors in the model. It is like the responsible older sibling to R-squared, keeping things in check and preventing us from getting carried away with adding too many predictors.

Alongside this, we should check the p-values of our predictors to ensure that they are statistically significant and contribute to our model.

A step-by-step guide to linear regression with Python's scikit-learn

Let us dive in and build our first linear regression model using the scikit-learn library in Python. Before we start, make sure you have the necessary tools installed: Python, scikit-learn, and Pandas.

For this guide, we will use the Boston housing dataset, a classic dataset in the scikit-learn datasets module. The goal is to predict the median value of owner-occupied homes (in $1000s) in Boston based on 13 features (inputs), such as crime rate and average number of rooms per dwelling.

First things first, let us load the dataset using the following code:

```
from sklearn.datasets import fetch_california_housing
housing = fetch_california_housing()
```

Now, let us create a **DataFrame** to make it easier to visualize; consider the following code:

```
import pandas as pd
california_df = pd.DataFrame(housing.data, columns=housing.feature_names)
california_df['MEDV'] = housing.target
```

At this stage, it is always good to explore the data, perhaps use **california_df.head()** to see the first few rows or **california_df.info()** to get a summary.

The **head()** function will give you the following output:

	MedInc	HouseAge	AveRooms	AveBedrms	Population	AveOccup	Latitude	Longitude	MEDV
0	8.3252	41.0	6.984127	1.023810	322.0	2.555556	37.88	-122.23	4.526
1	8.3014	21.0	6.238137	0.971880	2401.0	2.109842	37.86	-122.22	3.585
2	7.2574	52.0	8.288136	1.073446	496.0	2.802260	37.85	-122.24	3.521
3	5.6431	52.0	5.817352	1.073059	558.0	2.547945	37.85	-122.25	3.413
4	3.8462	52.0	6.281853	1.081081	565.0	2.181467	37.85	-122.25	3.422

Figure 8.1: First five rows of the California housing dataset

We will first split our data into the predictors (X) and the target variable (y); consider the following code:

```
X = california_df.drop('MEDV', axis=1)
y = california_df['MEDV']
```

Now, we will split our data into training and testing sets, and we will be using the **train_test_split** function in **sklearn** to do so; consider the following code:

```
from sklearn.model_selection import train_test_split
```

```
X_train, X_test, y_train, y_test = train_test_split(X, y, test_
size=0.2, random_state=42)
```

By giving **test_size** as 0.2, we want to use 80% of the dataset for training and 20% for testing. You can also see something called **random_state**; it is a parameter that is often used in machine learning models and functions that involve randomness.

In the case of **train_test_split**, which we used to divide our data into a training set and a testing set, the **random_state** parameter controls how the data is split. If you consider shuffling a deck of cards before dealing them, **random_state** is like a seed for the random number generator that decides how to shuffle the deck.

By setting **random_state** to a fixed number (like 42 in our example), we ensure that we get the exact same shuffle every time we run the code. This is useful in cases where we want our results to be reproducible, especially when troubleshooting or comparing models. Without a fixed **random_state**, every run could generate different results due to the different splits in the data, even if all other parameters remained the same.

X_train, **X_test**, **y_train**, and **y_test** are the four variables to which the output from **train_test_split** will be assigned. **X_train** and **X_test** are the features for the training and testing sets, respectively. **y_train** and **y_test** are the corresponding labels or targets.

Finally, it is time to train our model now. We will import the **LinearRegression** class from **sklearn**, create its instance, and then **fit** it on our training data using the following code:

```
from sklearn.linear_model import LinearRegression
lm = LinearRegression()
lm.fit(X_train, y_train)
```

You have just built your linear regression model. The **fit** method calculates the best-fit line for the provided data. It determines the coefficients (parameters) for the linear regression equation that will best predict the target variable (**y_train**) based on the features (**X_train**).

And now, we will use this model to predict the outcomes of the test data:

```
y_pred = lm.predict(X_test)
```

But it does not stop here. We need to evaluate the model using our test data. To do that, you could calculate the **mean squared error** (**MSE**) or R-squared:

```
from sklearn.metrics import mean_squared_error
mse = mean_squared_error(y_test, y_pred)
print('Mean Squared Error:', mse)
```

In this case, the mean squared error comes up to 0.555. Would that be considered good or bad? It strictly depends on the context:

- **Scale of the data:** If your target values range between 0 and 1, then an MSE of 0.555 might be considered high. However, if your target values range in the hundreds or thousands, an MSE of 0.555 might be considered quite good. Given the scale and context of the California housing dataset, an MSE of 0.555 is relatively high since the target variable is scaled between 0.14999 to 5.00001.

- **Baseline models:** It is useful for comparing the MSE of your model to that of a simple baseline model (like predicting the mean of the target variable for all observations). If your model's MSE is significantly lower than the baseline's, it suggests that your model is capturing some patterns in the data.

- **Domain specifics:** In some domains, a small error can be very costly, while in others, it is negligible.

You have successfully built and evaluated a linear regression model using scikit-learn!

Logistic regression

There is another player in the regression league, that is, logistic regression. Now, why a different form of regression? Not all problems we encounter are suited for linear regression, particularly when our target variable is categorical. As we dive into logistic regression, we will explore how it handles situations in which we need to make binary predictions, like diagnosing a disease (yes or no), predicting customer churn (will churn or would not), or classifying emails (spam or not spam).

Logistic regression: Deciphering binary decisions

If we take a step back and look at the world around us, we will realize that so many of our daily decisions are binary. Will it rain today? Will this customer make a purchase? Will the stock prices go up or down? All these questions require yes or no answers. In the machine learning world, this is where logistic regression comes into play.

While its name includes the term regression, logistic regression is not just another player in the regression team. It is actually a statistical method for predicting binary outcomes. So, rather than predicting continuous values, logistic regression helps us estimate the probability of an instance belonging to a particular class. If the estimated probability is greater than 50%, then the model predicts that the instance belongs to that class, or else it predicts that it does not.

An everyday application of logistic regression can be seen in the medical field. For instance, hospitals might use logistic regression to predict whether a patient will have a heart attack within a certain period based on features like age, sex, body mass index, results of various blood tests, and the like.

In the corporate world, logistic regression is widely used in predictive analytics. Companies may use it to predict whether a customer will buy a product, subscribe to a service, or churn.

In essence, whenever we are faced with a *this or that* situation, logistic regression is our go-to tool. It is a powerful algorithm that helps in classifying, or predicting, the odds of a binary outcome. With the fundamentals in place, we will now explore how to build a logistic regression model in the upcoming sections.

The sigmoid function: An essential cog in logistic regression

Now that we have a fair understanding of what logistic regression is and where it can be used, let us dive a bit deeper and see what really powers this machine learning algorithm. At the heart of logistic regression is the **sigmoid function**, also known as the **logistic function**. This function acts as a magical transformational gate that helps us morph our data into the format we need.

Think of the sigmoid function as a very skilled artist who takes in raw, unstructured clay and meticulously shapes it into a beautiful, symmetrical pot. In our case, the *raw, unstructured clay* is the input data, and the *beautiful, symmetrical pot* is the output in the form of probabilities ranging between 0 and 1. This artist of ours follows a specific blueprint: the sigmoid function.

So, what does this sigmoid function look like? Well, if we were to plot it, it would take the shape of an S curve. Why this specific shape, you might wonder? The beauty of this S shape is that it can take any real-valued number and transform it into a value between 0 and 1. If we were to put this in mathematical terms, the sigmoid function looks like this:

sigmoid(x) = 1 / (1 + e-x)

Take a look at the following figure:

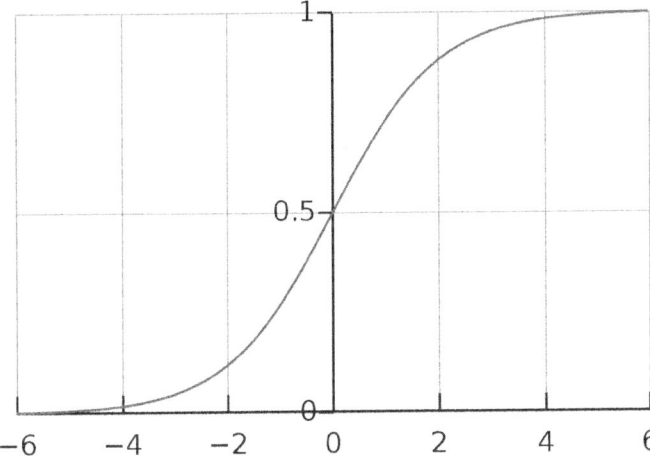

Figure 8.2: *The sigmoid function*

In this equation, e is the base of the natural logarithm (approximately 2.718), and x is the input to the function. This function ensures that even if x is very large, the output will be constrained within the range of 0 to 1, creating an S-shaped curve.

Having this S-shaped toolkit in our arsenal is what allows logistic regression to make those critical binary predictions. The linchpin holds the logistic regression model together, letting us classify our data into two distinct groups. As we delve further into logistic regression, we will see how this logistic function plays a key role in building our predictive model.

Building a logistic regression model: An overview

When we think about logistic regression, we primarily think about binary classification problems, which are situations wherein we have exactly two outcomes. For instance, predicting whether a student will pass or fail, whether or not an email is spam, whether a tumor is malignant or benign; you get the idea. These are your classic binary logistic regression problems.

Picture this: We are standing at a soccer match, and we have to predict the outcome. In a classic match, there are only two teams, so that is a binary outcome: either team A wins or team B wins. But what happens if it is a tournament and there are multiple teams involved? Suddenly, we are not just dealing with many outcomes. This is where multiclass classification comes into play.

Let us build on our soccer analogy. In a tournament, let us say we have team A, team B, team C, and team D. Now, we have to predict which team will win the tournament. This is not a binary problem anymore, as there are more than two possible outcomes. The way logistic regression handles this is using a strategy called *one-vs-all* or *one-vs-rest*. It breaks the problem down into multiple binary classification problems.

This is how it works: First, it takes one class and puts it against all other classes. Using our example, first, we would compare team A (one class) with teams B, C, and D (all other classes). Then, we would move on to comparing team B with teams A, C, D, and so on. This results in n binary logistic regression models, where n is the number of classes. Finally, when we need to make a prediction, all n models predict the probabilities of their respective classes. The class with the highest probability is considered the final prediction.

Whether you are dealing with binary or multiclass classification, the principles remain the same. It is all about taking your data, using logistic regression to draw the best decision boundary you can, and then classifying new data based on where it falls in relation to that boundary. Now that we have built our logistic regression models, in the upcoming sections, we will see how we can further refine them for better performance.

Deciphering coefficients and model evaluation in logistic regression

Diving headfirst into logistic regression, we encounter two things that often seem cryptic: the coefficients and model evaluation metrics.

Interpreting coefficients in logistic regression is slightly trickier than in linear regression. In linear regression, the coefficients directly represent the change in the dependent variable for each unit change in the predictor. But with logistic regression, due to the logistic function (remember our S-curve?), we are not dealing with a straight line anymore. Instead, we are predicting the logit of the outcome variable, which is the log of the odds.

This makes the interpretation of coefficients in logistic regression quite different. A positive coefficient indicates that as the value of the predictor variable increases, the event defined as *1* in the outcome variable is more likely, whereas a negative coefficient indicates the opposite. But remember, the magnitude of change is not constant across the range of the predictor variable, courtesy of our S-shaped logistic function. Thus, the impact of changing the predictor variable is not as straightforward to summarize as it is in linear regression. It is all about odds and probability in the logistic world!

Let us switch gears and talk about model evaluation. In classification problems, accuracy is not always the best metric, especially when dealing with imbalanced classes. For instance, if 95% of emails are not spam, even a naive model that predicts *not spam* for all emails will have a 95% accuracy, but it is useless for identifying spam emails.

This is where metrics like precision (the accuracy of positive predictions), recall (the ratio of correctly predicted positive observations to all observations in actual class), the F1 score (the weighted average of precision and recall), and the ROC-AUC curve (which tells us how much the model is capable of distinguishing between classes) come into play. Each of these metrics provides a different perspective on what is going on with your model, and choosing the right one depends on what is most important for your specific problem.

So, while coefficients help you understand your model's behavior, the evaluation metrics assist you in assessing its performance. Understanding both these aspects of logistic regression will equip you with a sharper toolset to build and evaluate effective models!

Logistic regression analysis: A study of the Titanic dataset

We will use the popular **Titanic dataset** for our logistic regression example. The Titanic dataset is well known in the data science community, as it provides information about passengers onboard the ill-fated Titanic, including whether or not they survived.

In the infamous Titanic shipwreck, numerous factors such as age, gender, and class, played a role in determining the survival of a passenger. Our goal is to build a model that uses these factors to predict whether or not a passenger would survive. This binary classification problem serves as a practical introduction to logistic regression.

We will start by loading the necessary libraries and dataset. The Titanic dataset can be directly fetched from seaborn datasets using the following code:

```
import seaborn as sns
from sklearn.model_selection import train_test_split
from sklearn.linear_model import LogisticRegression
from sklearn.metrics import confusion_matrix, classification_report

# Load the titanic dataset
titanic = sns.load_dataset('titanic')

# Display the first few rows of the dataset
print(titanic.head())
```

Output

The output is shown in the following figure:

	survived	pclass	sex	age	sibsp	parch	fare	embarked	class	who	adult_male	deck	embark_town	alive	alone
0	0	3	male	22.0	1	0	7.2500	S	Third	man	True	NaN	Southampton	no	False
1	1	1	female	38.0	1	0	71.2833	C	First	woman	False	C	Cherbourg	yes	False
2	1	3	female	26.0	0	0	7.9250	S	Third	woman	False	NaN	Southampton	yes	True
3	1	1	female	35.0	1	0	53.1000	S	First	woman	False	C	Southampton	yes	False
4	0	3	male	35.0	0	0	8.0500	S	Third	man	True	NaN	Southampton	no	True

Figure 8.3: The Titanic dataset

The **survived** column in the dataset is our target variable. Other columns like **pclass**, **sex**, **age**, and so on are the features that we will use to predict survival.

But before moving forward, we need to preprocess the data. The **sex** column is categorical, so we will transform it into numeric values. We will also handle the missing values in **age** by filling them with the **median** age using the following code:

```
# Preprocess the data
titanic['sex'] = titanic['sex'].map({'male': 0, 'female': 1})
titanic['age'].fillna(titanic['age'].median(), inplace=True)

# Define the features and the target
X = titanic[['pclass', 'sex', 'age']]
y = titanic['survived']

# Split the data into train and test sets
X_train,  X_test,  y_train,  y_test  =  train_test_split(X,  y,  test_
size=0.2, random_state=42)
```

Now, let us implement our logistic regression model; consider the following code:

```
# Create an instance of LogisticRegression
log_reg = LogisticRegression()

# Fit the model to the training data
log_reg.fit(X_train, y_train)

# Predict the labels of the test set
y_pred = log_reg.predict(X_test)
```

We have built our model, and it is time to evaluate its performance. We will use the confusion matrix and the classification report provided by scikit-learn:

```
# Print the confusion matrix
print(confusion_matrix(y_test, y_pred))

# Print the classification report
print(classification_report(y_test, y_pred))
```

Output

The output is shown in the following figure:

	precision	recall	f1-score	support
0	0.82	0.87	0.84	105
1	0.79	0.73	0.76	74
accuracy			0.81	179
macro avg	0.81	0.80	0.80	179
weighted avg	0.81	0.81	0.81	179

Figure 8.4: Classification report

The classification report provides a comprehensive overview of our model's performance. It includes **precision** (the proportion of positive identifications that were actually correct), **recall** (the proportion of actual positives that were identified correctly), and **F1 score** (a balanced blend of precision and recall) for each class.

This has been a complete run-through of building a logistic regression model in Python. You can tweak this basic pipeline by adding more features, tweaking the logistic regression parameters, or even using different preprocessing steps. It is all part of the fun of exploring machine learning!

Harnessing regularization: Techniques to rein in your model

Regularization is a term that echoes through the hallowed halls of machine learning. It is the solution to a problem that has tormented data scientists for ages. Think of regularization as a tool to name your model, to prevent it from getting too engrossed in the training data and losing sight of its goal, which is to perform well on unseen data. With regularization, we will learn how to infuse just the right amount of bias into our model, helping it generalize better.

Balancing variance, bias, and overfitting

Remember how, in the previous chapter, we briefly touched upon the concepts of bias and variance? We had likened them to two ends of a seesaw and understood that trying to strike a balance is a tricky task.

Variance, to remind you, refers to how much the predictions of our model would change if we used a different training dataset. If a model has high variance, it implies that it is extremely sensitive to the exact data it is trained on. Picture an overeager artist who tries to capture every minute detail in a landscape, including the insignificant ones. This is what a high variance model does: it tries to fit every data point, including the noise and outliers. While this model might do well on the training data (because it has learned all the details by heart), it might fail terribly when it comes to new data because the noise and outliers are different. This is what is called overfitting.

Bias, on the other hand, is how far off our predictions are from reality due to flawed assumptions in our algorithm. When we have high bias, our model is too simplistic; it does not pay enough attention to the data, misses out on important patterns, and ends up underperforming. It is like a painter who only uses broad strokes and fails to capture the fine details of the landscape. This type of model oversimplifies the reality and underfits the data.

The challenge here is that there is a trade-off between bias and variance. If you try to reduce variance (and prevent overfitting), you will have to simplify your model, which increases bias (and the risk of underfitting). Similarly, if you try to reduce bias (and prevent underfitting), you will have to make your model more complex, but this increases variance (and the risk of overfitting). This dilemma is often referred to as the Bias-Variance trade-off. In the following sections, we will explore regularization, a technique that allows us to navigate this tricky trade-off more effectively.

Navigating the complexity maze: Unravelling regularization

Let us picture machine learning as a challenging trek. You have a backpack filled with data, and your goal is to reach the peak of predictive performance. As we have seen earlier, this journey is filled with potential pitfalls of overfitting and underfitting.

Regularization is the art of balancing. It is a technique used to prevent our model from learning the noise in the data, which results in overfitting. Remember, an overfit model is like that overeager artist we discussed, capturing every minute detail, even the insignificant ones. While this model might excel in the training data, it stumbles when introduced to new data because the noise is different. Regularization helps prevent this by adding a penalty to the loss function, forcing the model to be simpler and thus, reducing the risk of overfitting.

But here is the intriguing part: By simplifying the model, are we not risking underfitting? Well, yes. That is why regularization is a balancing act. We need to find the right amount of simplicity. Too much, and we will miss out on important patterns (underfitting). Too little, and we will learn too much noise (overfitting). But when we get it just right, we will have a model that generalizes well to new data, which is our ultimate goal.

So, how exactly does regularization impose this penalty, and how can we control it? That is what we will explore in the next section as we delve into the most popular regularization techniques: Ridge, Lasso, and Elastic Net. We will also look at how we can implement these techniques in Python. So, strap in, because our trek through the machine learning landscape is about to get even more exciting!

Regularization rumble: Lasso, Ridge, And Elastic Net

Let us think of regularization as a superhero team assembled to combat the villain of overfitting. The team has three members: Lasso, Ridge, and Elastic Net. Each of these superheroes, or techniques, has their special powers that they bring to the table.

Lasso, also known as **L1 regularization**, is the first member of our team. Its special power is feature selection. When we apply Lasso regularization, it can reduce some feature coefficients to zero. This means that it completely removes those features from the model, effectively performing feature selection. This can be especially helpful when dealing with a large dataset with many features and we suspect that only a subset of them are actually useful.

Next up, we have Ridge, or **L2 regularization**. Ridge does not have the feature selection ability of Lasso. Instead, it is more of a team player, distributing the weight evenly across all features. This can help reduce the impact of any one feature dominating the model, making Ridge especially useful when we believe that all our features contribute to the output, but we are worried about overfitting.

Finally, there is Elastic Net, which combines the powers of both Lasso and Ridge. Elastic Net uses a mix of L1 and L2 regularization, giving us the best of both worlds. It can perform feature selection like Lasso and distribute weights evenly like Ridge. Elastic Net is great when we have many features and are unsure of whether or not all of them are useful.

Choosing between these techniques depends on our specific situation: our data, our problem, and our goals. But no matter which technique we choose, we will need to decide how much regularization to apply. Too much, and our model might be too simple and underfit the data. Too little, and we might not combat overfitting effectively. Selecting the right level of regularization usually involves a bit of trial and error, and techniques like cross-validation can be very helpful in this process.

So, there you have it, our superhero team ready to combat overfitting. In the next section, we will take a look at how we can call upon these superheroes using Python.

Implementing regularization techniques in Python with Scikit-Learn

Now that we have met our superheroes, let us figure out how to summon them using Python. Armed with the scikit-learn library, we can get these regularization techniques in action to save our machine learning models from overfitting.

The Lasso, Ridge, and Elastic Net regularization techniques can be called upon in Python using scikit-learn's `linear_model` module. Let us start by including Lasso. After importing `linear_model`, we can create a `Lasso` object and specify the strength of the regularization using the alpha parameter. Once our **Lasso** object is ready, we can train it on our data using the **fit** method. Execute the following code:

```
from sklearn.linear_model import Lasso
lasso = Lasso(alpha=0.1)
lasso.fit(X_train, y_train)
```

Ridge can be summoned in a similar way, using the following code:

```
from sklearn.linear_model import Ridge
ridge = Ridge(alpha=0.1)
ridge.fit(X_train, y_train)
```

For Elastic Net, we need to specify an additional parameter: **l1_ratio**. This parameter controls the mix of L1 and L2 regularization. If **l1_ratio = 1**, we get L1 regularization, and if **l1_ratio = 0**, we get L2 regularization. For anything in between, we get a mix of both. Execute the following code:

```
from sklearn.linear_model import ElasticNet
elasticnet = ElasticNet(alpha=0.1, l1_ratio=0.5)
elasticnet.fit(X_train, y_train)
```

One important thing to remember when using regularization is to ensure that the features are on the same scale. Regularization is sensitive to the scale of features, so it is generally a good practice to normalize or standardize your data before applying these techniques.

So now, you know how to summon the regularization superheroes and prevent overfitting in your models. But remember, with great power comes great responsibility. Use these techniques judiciously, and always validate your model's performance on a test or validation set.

Conclusion

In this chapter, we took a significant stride in our exploration of machine learning, specifically in the land of regression techniques. We began our journey with linear regression, understanding its core concepts, assumptions, and applications. We then looked at logistic regression, learning how it helps in scenarios where we need to predict categorical outcomes. Regularization techniques entered the spotlight next, helping us deal with overfitting and model complexity. In each section, we were keen to put theory into practice, using Python and scikit-learn to implement these models. As we close this chapter, remember that the concepts we have grasped form the foundation for many advanced machine learning models.

In the next chapter, we will learn about **k-Nearest Neighbors** (**KNN**) and Naïve Bayes.

Points to remember

- Linear regression is used for predicting continuous outcomes, while logistic regression is used for predicting categorical outcomes with their unique assumptions and applications.

- Regularization techniques like Ridge (L2), Lasso (L1), and Elastic Net prevent overfitting by adding a penalty term to the loss function, controlling model complexity.

- Always be aware of the Bias-Variance trade-off. We need to strike a balance between a model that is too simple (high bias) and one that is too complex (high variance).

Multiple choice questions

1. **Which of the following is not an assumption of linear regression?**

    a. Independence of errors

    b. Homoscedasticity

    c. Multicollinearity

    d. All variables must be categorical

2. **Which regularization technique should you choose if you believe many features are irrelevant?**

    a. Ridge (L2)

    b. Lasso (L1)

    c. Elastic Net

    d. All of the above

3. **In the context of logistic regression, what is the sigmoid function used for?**

    a. Transforming any value into a value between 0 and 1

    b. Calculating the error term

    c. Determining the best-fit line

    d. None of the above

4. **Which of the following evaluation metrics is typically used for a regression task?**

    a. Accuracy

    b. Precision

    c. Recall

    d. Mean squared error

Answers

1. d

2. b

3. a

4. d

Questions

1. What is the key difference between linear regression and logistic regression, and where are they typically used?

2. Explain what is meant by the Bias-Variance trade-off and why it is important in machine learning.

3. Describe how you would implement a Lasso (L1) regularization in a linear regression model using scikit-learn in Python.

Join our book's Discord space

Join the book's Discord Workspace for Latest updates, Offers, Tech happenings around the world, New Release and Sessions with the Authors:

https://discord.bpbonline.com

## CHAPTER 9

Unveiling Patterns with k-Nearest Neighbors and Naïve Bayes

Introduction

Welcome to the fascinating world of **k-Nearest Neighbors** (**KNN**) and Naïve Bayes, two exceptionally versatile and intuitive algorithms in **Machine Learning** (**ML**). This chapter dives deep into the realm of these algorithms, unveiling the patterns and wisdom they use to classify data with astounding precision. As we navigate through the KNN algorithm, we will delve into the importance of distance metrics and how they govern neighborhood rules. Shifting our focus to Naïve Bayes, we will explore the world of conditional probability and how simple assumptions can lead to powerful predictions. Finally, we will master the art of hyperparameter tuning, a crucial step to creating optimal models that can outperform the rest.

Structure

In this chapter, we will discuss the following topics:

- k-Nearest Neighbors
- Naïve Bayes classifier
- Hyperparameter tuning

Objectives

By the time you turn the last page of this chapter, we aim to equip you with a firm understanding of the KNN algorithm, including its inner workings and the essential role distance metrics play in determining its function. But we would not stop there. We will also dive deep into the Naïve Bayes classifier, demystifying its foundational assumptions and illustrating how it leverages the power of conditional probability to accomplish classification tasks. One of the key objectives of this chapter is to introduce you to the art and science of model evaluation, particularly for the KNN and Naïve Bayes models. This will empower you to critically assess the performance of your models and refine them for better results. Lastly, we will delve into the exciting world of hyperparameter tuning, which is a critical step in improving model performance, and you will learn how to fine-tune the parameters of both KNN and Naïve Bayes classifiers. And, of course, all of this theoretical knowledge will be complemented with practical Python-based examples to provide a comprehensive, end-to-end understanding of these algorithms.

Understanding the k-Nearest Neighbors algorithm

As we navigate the complex world of machine learning, we often encounter problems that ask us to classify a new data point based on its proximity to known data points. This is where the KNN algorithm comes to the rescue, acting as a beacon in the vast sea of data. This intuitive, easy-to-understand algorithm has an essential role in both classification and regression tasks, relying on a principle as old as time: like attracts like. As we take a step-by-step journey through this topic, we will uncover the unique traits of KNN that make it such a powerful tool for solving machine learning problems.

Unraveling the threads of k-Nearest Neighbors

In machine learning, you will come across numerous algorithms, each with its unique way of learning from data. The KNN is one such simple yet powerful algorithm that is based on the concept of proximity or closeness.

Think of KNN as the machine learning equivalent of the old saying 'birds of a feather flock together'. It operates on the idea that similar data points will likely have the same class labels or output values. So, when a new, unknown data point enters the scene, KNN takes a look at its neighbors: the points that are closest to it based on a certain distance metric (more on this later). It then decides on the label of this new point based on the labels of its neighbors.

Let us say we have a two-dimensional scatter plot of height and weight, with each data point representing an individual, and each individual is classified as either a child or an adult. Now, if we have a new individual (that is, a new data point) whose classification is unknown, the KNN algorithm looks at the k individuals closest to our new individual. If most of these k individuals are adults, then the new individual is classified as an adult, and vice versa.

An intriguing aspect of KNN is that it is an instance-based learning algorithm. While many machine learning algorithms like linear regression and logistic regression require a model to be trained, KNN makes predictions by referring directly to the training dataset, thus earning the title of a lazy learner.

The KNN algorithm can be used for both classification (when the output variable is a category) and regression (when the output variable is a real value), making it a versatile tool to have in your machine learning toolbox.

There you have it, an overview of the KNN algorithm, a method grounded in the simple notion of *similarity*. But this is just the tip of the iceberg; as we dive deeper, we will uncover more details and complexities.

Exploring distance metrics: Euclidean to Hamming

Following the introduction to the KNN algorithm, a pertinent question arises: How does the algorithm determine the proximity of data points to a new point? This is determined by what is termed as distance metrics. As the name suggests, these metrics are rules or formulas used to calculate the distance or similarity between data points. The choice of distance metric plays a pivotal role in the KNN algorithm, affecting the definition of *nearest*. Now, let us understand some common distance metrics:

- **Euclidean distance:** This is arguably the most familiar distance metric for most. It is the straight-line distance we usually think of when we hear distance. Suppose you are in a flat park, and you want to get to a point directly visible to you; you would likely take a straight-line path; that is Euclidean distance. Mathematically, it is calculated as the square root of the sum of the squared differences between the corresponding values of two points.

- **Manhattan distance:** Suppose you are in a city with a grid-like street structure (like Manhattan in New York City). Now, if you want to get from one intersection to another, you cannot simply cut through the buildings in a straight line (like we did in the park). You have to move along the grid, right? That is the concept of the Manhattan distance. It is computed as the sum of the absolute differences between the corresponding values of two points.

- **Minkowski distance:** This is the most generalized form of distance metric. You can think of it as a parent to both the Euclidean and Manhattan distances. It has a parameter p that can be adjusted to give different distance metrics. When p=2, Minkowski distance is the same as Euclidean distance, and when p=1, it turns into Manhattan distance.

- **Cosine distance:** This distance metric is frequently used in high-dimensional spaces, such as text data, where the data is represented as word frequencies. It measures the cosine of the angle between two vectors, capturing their directional relationship rather than the absolute distance. This is particularly useful when the magnitude of the vectors is less relevant than their orientation.

- **Hamming distance:** This is a popular choice when dealing with categorical data. It calculates the number of positions at which the corresponding values are different. For example, for two binary strings, 1101 and 1001, the Hamming distance would be 1 since they differ at one position.

The choice of distance metric largely depends on the nature of your data and what you are trying to achieve with your model.

How do distance metrics affect the performance of KNN

The relationship between distance metrics and the performance of the KNN algorithm is a critical one, not too different from how an engine's performance is influenced by the quality of fuel it uses.

You see, KNN works by identifying the k instances in your training set that are closest to a given test instance and then assigns a label based on the majority class among these neighbors. The concept of closeness here is quantified by distance metrics. This is why the choice of distance metric can significantly influence the output of your KNN model.

If you use Euclidean distance metric, your KNN model operates like a person walking in a park who defines nearness as the straight-line or bird's flight distance to other people. However, suppose you decide to use Manhattan distance. In that case, your model acts more like a taxi driver in New York, defining nearness as the sum of horizontal and vertical distances since it cannot fly over buildings.

These differences in perception of nearness can lead to different sets of k nearest neighbors for the same test instance and, thus, potentially different classification outcomes. This implies that no single metric is universally the best. Depending on the nature of your data and the specific problem context, different distance metrics may lead to better model performance.

For instance, if your features represent dimensions like height and weight, using Euclidean distance might make sense since it effectively captures the concept of physical distance in a 3D space. On the other hand, if your data is binary or categorical, Hamming distance might be a better choice.

In essence, the choice of distance metric in KNN is like choosing the right fuel for an engine. The right choice can lead to efficient and accurate predictions, while a poor choice might lead to performance issues or misclassifications. Hence, understanding and choosing the right distance metric is essential for harnessing the full power of the KNN algorithm.

Constructing the KNN model: A step-by-step approach with Python

Building a k-Nearest Neighbors model is not a difficult task, especially if you have got Python and scikit-learn in your toolkit. Let us plunge into the details and explore how to build a KNN model from scratch.

Before we delve into constructing our k-Nearest Neighbours model, let us take a step back and introduce our dataset. For this exercise, we will create a synthetic dataset using Python's Numpy and Pandas libraries. This synthetic dataset will simulate a real-world scenario in an educational context. Let us call this dataset **student_scores**.

Here is how we will structure it:

- **hours_studied:** This feature, a float value, represents the number of hours a student has spent studying. As you might guess, we expect it to have a positive correlation with the test score.

- **hours_slept:** This is another float value feature that represents the number of hours a student sleeps per day. Adequate sleep is crucial for cognitive functioning and overall productivity, so we also expect a positive correlation with the test score.

- **test_score:** This is our target variable, which is also a float value. It indicates the score a student achieved on a test, measured as a percentage.

Here is the code to generate this dataset:

```python
import numpy as np
import pandas as pd

np.random.seed(0)
n = 100
hours_studied = np.random.normal(30.0, 10.0, n)
hours_slept = np.random.normal(8.0, 3.0, n)

# We make the test score a func-
tion of study hours and sleep, plus some noise
test_score = hours_studied + hours_slept + np.random.normal(0, 10.0, n)

student_scores_df = pd.DataFrame({'hours_studied': hours_studied, 'hours_
slept': hours_slept, 'test_score': test_score})

# Let's print the first few rows of the dataframe
print(student_scores_df.head())
```

Output

The output is shown in the following figure:

	hours_studied	hours_slept	test_score
0	47.640523	13.649452	57.598157
1	34.001572	3.956723	35.564503
2	39.787380	4.188545	54.972521
3	52.408932	10.908190	69.869759
4	48.675580	4.480630	59.557525

Figure 9.1: Student scores dataset

The preceding code creates a dataframe of 100 students' study hours, sleep hours, and their corresponding test scores. The test scores are generated as a function of study hours and sleep hours, plus some random noise to simulate real-world unpredictability.

With our dataset now in place, let us create a KNN model.

Our aim will be to predict the test score of a student, given the number of hours they studied and slept.

Since we already have the dataset with us, here are the next steps we will follow:

1. **Split the dataset into a training set and a testing set:** We will use 80% of the data for training and set aside 20% for testing our model. Execute the following code:

```
from sklearn.model_selection import train_test_split

X = student_scores_df[['hours_studied', 'hours_slept']]

y = student_scores_df['test_score']

X_train, X_test, y_train, y_test = train_test_split(X, y, test_size=0.2, random_state=42)
```

Here, **X** and **y** are the features and target variable. The **train_test_split()** function splits **X** and **y** into training (**X_train, y_train**) and testing (**X_test, y_test**) sets.

2. **Create and train the KNN model:** We will use scikit-learn's **KNeighborsClassifier** for this. Here, **k** refers to the number of neighbors the classifier will consider when it predicts the class of a given point. We will start by setting **k=3**. Now, execute the following code:

```
from sklearn.neighbors import KNeighborsRegressor

knn = KNeighborsRegressor(n_neighbors=3)

knn.fit(X_train, y_train)
```

In the first line, we create an instance of **KNeighborsRegressor** with **k=3**. In the second line, we train this model on our training data using the **.fit()** method.

Here, we have not explicitly specified a distance metric, so the algorithm used the default one, which is the Euclidean distance. This is typically a good starting point as it is simple and intuitive.

3. **Test the model:** Once the model is trained, we will use it to predict test scores for our test data and assess the accuracy of these predictions. Execute the following code:

```
y_pred = knn.predict(X_test)
print("Test set predictions:\n", y_pred)
```

4. **Evaluate the model:** Finally, we will evaluate our model by calculating the mean squared error of our predictions. Use the following code:

```
from sklearn.metrics import mean_squared_error
mse = mean_squared_error(y_test, y_pred)
print('Mean Squared Error:', mse)
```

When you run the preceding code, you will have a not-so-great score. Feel free to play around with the distance metric and the number of neighbors and see what you get.

You have successfully built your first KNN model in Python. We took a simple dataset, built a model, and assessed its accuracy.

Now that we have taken a comprehensive look at the k-Nearest Neighbors algorithm, let us focus on another fundamental algorithm in machine learning: the Naïve Bayes classifier.

Naïve Bayes classifier

Next up in our data science exploration is the world of Naïve Bayes, a powerful yet simple technique in machine learning. Named after *Thomas Bayes*, who provided an equation to calculate a posterior probability, Naïve Bayes classifiers are a collection of probabilistic algorithms that utilize this principle. A striking feature of these classifiers is their *naïve* assumption of feature independence, meaning they consider all the features contributing to the outcome as independent of each other. This assumption, despite seeming overly simplistic, works surprisingly well for many real-world scenarios, making Naïve Bayes a popular choice in text mining, spam filtering, and sentiment analysis.

Unraveling the simplicity and power of Naïve Bayes

Naïve Bayes classifiers offer a remarkably straightforward and effective approach to classification problems. They are called **Naïve** because they operate under the assumption that all the features in a dataset are independent of each other. This implies that the presence or absence of a particular feature does not influence the presence or absence of any other feature. For instance, if we want to classify a fruit as an apple or a banana based on its color, shape, and size, a Naïve Bayes classifier assumes that these characteristics do not depend on each other.

Now, while this assumption of independence seems rather naive, hence the name, it is this simplicity that often makes these classifiers highly efficient and particularly suitable for large datasets. Despite the apparent oversimplification, Naïve Bayes classifiers often outperform more complex models, particularly in tasks like text classification, spam filtering, sentiment analysis, and disease prediction.

In Naïve Bayes classifiers, we use Bayes' Theorem to compute the probabilities. Bayes' Theorem provides a way to calculate the probability of a data point belonging to a particular class, given our prior knowledge. It is expressed mathematically as follows:

$P(A \mid B) = [P(B \mid A) * P(A)] / P(B)$

Where,

$P(A \mid B)$ is the posterior probability of class (A) given predictor (B).

$P(A)$ is the prior probability of class.

$P(B \mid A)$ is the likelihood, which is the probability of the predictor given class.

$P(B)$ is the prior probability of the predictor.

While the theory and the formula might appear complicated at first, their application in Python is rather simple, thanks to the scikit-learn library, which has ready-to-use Naïve Bayes classifier implementations that we will dive into in the section titled *Crafting a Naïve Bayes classifier from scratch with Python*. But before that, we need to understand different types of Naïve Bayes classifiers, that is, Gaussian, Multinomial, and Bernoulli, each of which is best suited for different kinds of data distribution.

In the following sections, we will explore how to create Naïve Bayes models, interpret their outputs, and evaluate their performance.

Crafting a Naïve Bayes Bayes classifier from scratch with Python

After understanding the foundations of Naïve Bayes, it is time to put the theory into practice. We will step into the shoes of a data scientist and construct our very own Naïve Bayes classifier using Python. This exercise will give you a first-hand experience of the process and, of course, the thrill of seeing a model you built make predictions.

To do this, we will be using The Breast Cancer Wisconsin dataset. This dataset is a classification dataset that includes the measurements from the digitized images of breast mass cell nuclei. It is used to build models to predict whether a tumor is malignant or benign. It is included in scikit-learn's datasets module and is often used as a beginner-friendly dataset that provides a slightly more complex challenge than the Iris dataset.

For this task, we will employ the Gaussian Naïve Bayes classifier as it assumes that features follow a normal distribution, which is often the case in many real-world scenarios. Python's scikit-learn library has a simple and intuitive implementation of this classifier. Let us dive right in and execute the following code:

```python
from sklearn.datasets import load_breast_cancer
from sklearn.model_selection import train_test_split
from sklearn.naive_bayes import GaussianNB
from sklearn.metrics import accuracy_score


# Load the breast cancer dataset
data = load_breast_cancer()


# Split the data into input features (X) and target variable (y)
X, y = data.data, data.target


# Split the data into training set and test set
X_train, X_test, y_train, y_test = train_test_split(X, y, test_size=0.2, random_state=42)


# Create a Gaussian Naive Bayes object
gnb = GaussianNB()


# Train the model using the training sets
gnb.fit(X_train, y_train)


# Predict the response for the test dataset
y_pred = gnb.predict(X_test)


# Print the accuracy score of the model
print("Accuracy: ", accuracy_score(y_test, y_pred))
```

In the preceding code snippet, we first import the necessary libraries and split our dataset into a training set and a test set. We then create a Gaussian Naïve Bayes object and train the model using our training data. After our model is trained, we use it to make predictions on our test data and evaluate the model's accuracy.

Building and employing a Naïve Bayes classifier is as straightforward as this. However, understanding its output and properly evaluating its performance may require a bit more nuance, which is explained in the next section.

Deciphering Naïve Bayes: Understanding outputs and performance evaluation

Having constructed the initial Naïve Bayes classifier, it is imperative to analyze the model's output further and evaluate its performance.

When we use a Naïve Bayes classifier, it provides us with the probabilities of each class for a given instance. For example, with our breast cancer dataset, the model will provide probabilities indicating whether the tumor is malignant or benign. These probabilities represent the model's confidence in assigning each class to the instance.

If you remember, after training the model, we used it to make predictions on the test set. This is how we can get these probabilities, using the following code:

```
# predict probabilities
probabilities = gnb.predict_proba(X_test)
print(probabilities)
```

In the output, each row corresponds to a single observation from the test set, and the columns represent the classes. The value in each cell is the probability that the observation belongs to the respective class.

While these probabilities can be insightful, what we are often interested in is how well our model is performing. This is where performance evaluation comes into the picture. The most straightforward metric we can use is accuracy, which we have already seen. However, when dealing with imbalanced classes, precision, recall, and the F1 score might be more suitable metrics. We can get all of these in the classification report using the following code:

```
from sklearn.metrics import classification_report

# get the classification report
report = classification_report(y_test, y_pred)
print(report)
```

By understanding model outputs and performance evaluation metrics, we equip ourselves with the essential skills to build effective and reliable Naïve Bayes models. Now, with these skills in your data science toolkit, you are ready to tackle more complex data challenges.

Hyperparameter tuning

While building machine learning models, we often encounter parameters we do not learn from the training data. Instead, these are knobs that we adjust to optimize model performance. Welcome to the fascinating world of hyperparameter tuning, where we explore these control settings, fine-tune them, and unlock our models' potential to predict better and accurately.

What are hyperparameters

Suppose you are driving a manual transmission car. You can adjust the speed by changing the gear according to your needs. Here, the gears act like the hyperparameters of your car, which you need to tune for a smooth and efficient ride. Similarly, in the realm of machine learning, we have model parameters that are learned during training, and then we have hyperparameters that we, the drivers, need to set before training.

In the simplest terms, hyperparameters are external configurations to your model that cannot be estimated from the data itself. They need to be predefined by the practitioner, who might choose to follow best practices, intuition, or optimization procedures to set them. For instance, in a k-Nearest Neighbors algorithm, the number of neighbors (k) is a hyperparameter. You must decide the best k before you start training your model.

While parameters and hyperparameters may sound similar, they play entirely different roles. Model parameters are internal to your model, and they are the part that learns from your data. They adjust themselves as the model gets trained. For instance, in a linear regression model, the coefficients are model parameters.

Hyperparameters and parameters together govern the learning process of your model, but in different ways. Hyperparameters set the conditions for the learning process, while parameters evolve and adapt through the learning process itself. It is a dynamic duo that makes our machine learning models powerful and flexible.

Getting the hyperparameters right is crucial as they directly influence how well a model can learn from the data. Hence, they can significantly impact the performance of your model. So, let us dive deeper into hyperparameter tuning, an exciting, although sometimes challenging, part of building successful machine learning models.

Why does hyperparameter tuning matter

Like a tightrope walker making minute adjustments to maintain balance, the art of hyperparameter tuning refers to fine-tuning your machine learning model for optimal performance. Let us understand why it matters.

At its core, the importance of hyperparameter tuning can be summed up in one word: performance. The right choice of hyperparameters can make the difference between a mediocre model and a great one. While a model's parameters learn from the data during training, the hyperparameters are like the guiding stars, setting the conditions for the learning process.

But it is not just about accuracy. Hyperparameter tuning can also influence your model's complexity, speed of training, and resource consumption. For instance, increasing the depth of a decision tree or the number of hidden layers in a neural network (both hyperparameters) will undoubtedly make your model learn better from the data. However, it might also increase the computational requirements, risk overfitting, and slow down the training process. Thus, there is always a trade-off, and striking the right balance is where the skill of tuning comes in.

Furthermore, each dataset and problem is unique. The **one-size-fits-all** approach does not work in the machine learning domain. The best set of hyperparameters for one problem might not work as well for another, even with similar datasets. Hence, it is important to experiment and tune the hyperparameters specific to your task.

Finally, hyperparameters are like the knobs and dials of your machine learning model. They allow you to control the learning process, customize your model, and enhance its performance. As a data scientist or machine learning practitioner, mastering the art of hyperparameter tuning is a critical skill that can set you apart. It is a journey of exploration and continuous learning, where you learn to harness the true potential of your models. And there is nothing quite like seeing your model's performance boost after a successful tuning session.

Hyperparameter tuning: Grid and random search methods

With numerous combinations to explore, how do we find that perfect setting for our model? That is where methods like grid search and random search come to our rescue.

Imagine having to cook a new dish but being unsure about the proportions of spices to use. You could start by trying every possible combination of spices in a systematic way: this is what we call **grid search** in the realm of hyperparameters. Grid search is a systematic way of combing through a grid of hyperparameters to find the optimal values. For every possible combination of hyperparameters in a predefined grid, we train our model, evaluate its performance, and keep track of the results. The set of hyperparameters that deliver the best performance is our winning combination.

Grid search can be computationally expensive, particularly if we have many hyperparameters to tune. It is like tasting every dish in a huge buffet: it is thorough but can be overwhelming.

Now, let us understand random search in detail. It is like tossing a dart on the hyperparameter board and seeing where it lands. Instead of systematically traversing the entire grid, random search randomly selects combinations of hyperparameters for model training and evaluation. It might sound chaotic, but it is surprisingly effective and efficient. The beauty of random search is that it can explore the hyperparameter space more diversely, and it often takes less time to find a good, if not the best, set of hyperparameters.

Remember, both grid search and random search have their strengths and weaknesses, and the choice between them depends on your specific scenario. Sometimes, combining both methods can lead to efficient and effective hyperparameter tuning. So, think of these methods as tools in your tuning toolkit, ready to be used per the task at hand.

Fine-tuning the k-Nearest Neighbors model

Returning to the world of k-Nearest Neighbors, let us see how hyperparameter tuning can significantly boost our model's performance. Remember, our chief hyperparameter in KNN is the number of neighbors k. The selection of k can drastically impact the results of our model. A smaller value of k might make our model sensitive to noise, while a larger k might make it too generalized. So, finding the right k is like hitting the bull's eye in the dartboard of model performance.

To navigate the hyperparameter space, we will use the **GridSearchCV** function from the scikit-learn library. Let us go back to our wine dataset and see this in action using the following code:

```
from sklearn.model_selection import GridSearchCV
from sklearn.neighbors import KNeighborsClassifier

# Define the parameter values that should be searched
k_range = list(range(1, 31))

# Create a parameter grid: map the parameter names to the values that should be searched
param_grid = dict(n_neighbors=k_range)

# instantiate the grid
knn = KNeighborsClassifier()
grid = GridSearchCV(knn, param_grid, cv=10, scoring='accuracy')

# fit the grid with data
grid.fit(X_train, y_train)

# view the complete results
```

```
grid.cv_results_
```

```
# examine the best model
print("Best Score: ", grid.best_score_)
print("Best Parameters: ", grid.best_params_)
print("Best Estimator: ", grid.best_estimator_)
```

Here, we have used a range of 1 to 30 for k, and **GridSearchCV** runs the KNN algorithm for each of these k values. We have set the scoring parameter as accuracy to maximize accuracy.

The output will give us the best score obtained and the k value that led to this score. We could then use this k value to train our model. Remember that the best hyperparameters can change based on the dataset, so it is good practice to always check for the optimal hyperparameters when working on a new problem.

Fine-tuning the Naïve Bayes model

Now that we have fine-tuned the k-Nearest Neighbours algorithm, let us switch gears and navigate the hyperparameters of the Naïve Bayes algorithm. The Naïve Bayes algorithm, especially the Gaussian Naïve Bayes version, does not have many hyperparameters to tune. However, one common parameter that can be tuned in some variants of Naïve Bayes, like multinomial and complement Naïve Bayes, is the smoothing parameter alpha.

This parameter helps handle cases when our test data has a category that was not observed in the training data. A higher value of alpha will mean that we are assigning a higher probability to the unseen categories, which can influence the overall predictions. Thus, tuning alpha can be quite crucial.

Let us take an example where we are using the multinomial Naïve Bayes algorithm. We will use the **GridSearchCV** method, just like we did with the KNN algorithm. Use the following code:

```
from sklearn.model_selection import GridSearchCV
from sklearn.naive_bayes import MultinomialNB


# Define the parameter values that should be searched
alpha_range = list(range(1, 11))


# Create a parameter grid: map the parameter names to the val-
ues that should be searched
param_grid = dict(alpha=alpha_range)
```

```
# instantiate the grid
nb = MultinomialNB()
grid = GridSearchCV(nb, param_grid, cv=10, scoring='accuracy')

# fit the grid with data
grid.fit(X_train, y_train)

# view the complete results
grid.cv_results_

# examine the best model
print("Best Score: ", grid.best_score_)
print("Best Parameters: ", grid.best_params_)
print("Best Estimator: ", grid.best_estimator_)
```

Here, the **GridSearchCV** method will iterate over the alpha values from 1 to 10 and find the value that gives us the highest accuracy. The optimal alpha value can then be used for our final model.

Even though Naïve Bayes seems quite simple, adjusting its hyperparameters can significantly affect your model's performance.

Conclusion

In this chapter, we embarked on a thrilling journey, exploring the world of the k-Nearest Neighbours and Naïve Bayes classifiers, two remarkably simple yet powerful machine learning algorithms. We saw how distance metrics and choice of k value can significantly influence our k-Nearest Neighbours model's performance. We then delved into the Naïve Bayes classifier, understanding its underlying principles of conditional probability and independence. We also discussed its variants and saw how to build and evaluate a Naïve Bayes model.

In the latter part of the chapter, we introduced you to the critical concept of hyperparameters, helping you learn to distinguish them from model parameters. Understanding the significance of tuning these hyperparameters, we used grid search and random search to find the optimal values, boosting our models' performance. Finally, we applied our newfound knowledge of hyperparameter tuning on both the k-Nearest Neighbours and Naïve Bayes models.

Now, as we transition into the next chapter, we will discuss decision trees, entropy and information gain, tree pruning, optimization techniques, and the power of ensemble methods, building on the foundations of predictive modeling to enhance our understanding and capabilities in machine learning.

Points to remember

- The k-Nearest Neighbors algorithm is a type of instance-based learning that classifies new instances based on their distance to existing instances. The choice of distance metric (for example, Euclidean and Manhattan) and the value of k can greatly influence model performance.

- The Naïve Bayes classifier is a probabilistic classifier that leverages Bayes' theorem and assumes independence among features. Despite its simplicity and the naive assumption, it can be highly effective, particularly in text classification problems.

- Hyperparameters are model settings that we need to decide before training, unlike parameters, which the model learns during training. Tuning hyperparameters, such as through methods like grid search and random search, is essential for optimizing model performance.

Multiple choice questions

1. **Which of the following is not a common distance metric in the k-Nearest Neighbors algorithm?**

    a. Euclidean

    b. Manhattan

    c. Minkowski

    d. Hyperbolic

2. **In the Naïve Bayes classifier, the Naïve term refers to which of the following?**

    a. The simplicity of the algorithm

    b. The assumption of independence among features

    c. The fact that it is based on Bayes' theorem

    d. The assumption that the prior probabilities are equal for all classes

3. **Which method can we use for hyperparameter tuning?**

    a. Grid search

    b. Random search

    c. Hill climbing

    d. Both a) and b)

Answers

1. d

2. b

3. d

Questions

1. How does the choice of distance metric affect the performance of a k-Nearest Neighbors model?

2. Can you explain how hyperparameter tuning using grid search works and why it might be useful in improving your model performance?

Join our book's Discord space

Join the book's Discord Workspace for Latest updates, Offers, Tech happenings around the world, New Release and Sessions with the Authors:

https://discord.bpbonline.com

## CHAPTER 10

Exploring Tree-Based Models: Decision Trees to Gradient Boosting

Introduction

Welcome to the fascinating world of decision trees and their ensemble counterparts. In this chapter, we will dive deep into the workings of these powerful algorithms and explore how they make predictions. Decision trees, in their simplicity, offer intuitive decision-making models, which we can then improve with ensemble methods like random forests and boosting techniques. The enigmatic concept of entropy and information gain, which drives decision tree splitting, will be unfolded. Lastly, to ensure that our trees are optimally structured, we will delve into tree pruning and optimization, thereby maintaining a balance between model complexity and predictive power.

Structure

In this chapter, we will discuss the following topics:

- Decision trees
- Entropy and information gain
- Tree pruning and optimization
- Ensemble methods

Objectives

The objective of this chapter is to provide a solid understanding of decision trees, including the concepts of entropy and information gain, and methods for tree pruning and optimization. We aim to introduce you to and delve into the specifics of ensemble methods, specifically, random forests, bagging, boosting, and gradient boosted trees. Through detailed explanations, engaging discussions, practical examples, and Python code snippets, we aim to ensure that by the end of this chapter, you will be confident in your ability to understand, implement, and optimize these algorithms in a data science context.

Decision trees

Decision trees are tree-like models of decisions. A decision tree uses a tree structure to represent several possible decision paths and an outcome for each path. It is one of the most straightforward and widely used algorithms because it is easy to understand, does not require any scaling, and can handle both numerical and categorical data. Strap in as we journey deep into decision trees!

Getting acquainted with decision trees

Have you ever played the game 20 questions? If you did, you already have an intuitive understanding of how decision trees work. This machine learning algorithm operates under a concept that is simple yet extraordinarily powerful. Let us explore this intriguing concept together.

Picture this: We start at the top with the entire set of data, just as we would start the game 20 questions, knowing that our object could be, well, anything. As we move down the tree, each node in the tree represents a question or decision, effectively splitting the data into subsets that resemble each other most closely.

As we answer questions and make decisions, we filter down through the branches of the tree until we get to a leaf node—an endpoint of the tree, where we make a final prediction based on our input.

One of the unique strengths of decision trees is their transparency. We can easily visualize the tree and its decision-making process, making it a great choice when interpretability is crucial. Unlike some other **Machine Learning (ML)** models, which might seem like impenetrable black boxes, decision trees offer a comprehensible way to understand the mechanics behind predictions.

In the world of machine learning, decision trees are versatile all-rounders. They handle both regression and classification tasks, dealing with both numerical and categorical data.

However, they can sometimes create overly complex structures that could be more generalized to new data, a problem we call overfitting. To mitigate this issue, we use tree pruning and ensemble methods, which we will dive into later in this chapter.

Let us dig deeper into their roots and learn about entropy and information gain, two key concepts that drive the decision-making process in this impressive algorithm.

Constructing a decision tree

The process of building a decision tree involves various steps, and just like constructing a building, each step is crucial for a sturdy outcome.

We start the process at the tree's root with the entire dataset. Here, we ask a question that splits the data into two subsets. But what question should we ask? This is where concepts like entropy and information gain come into play. These allow us to quantify the best possible question, or split, that leads to the most informative branching of the data. Essentially, they help us make the most of each question we ask.

Once we have asked our question and divided the data, we move to the resulting subsets and repeat the process, asking another question to split each subset further. This process continues recursively until we reach a condition that tells us to stop, such as when no further information can be gained or when we reach a preset limit to the tree's depth.

Each time we make a split, we create a decision node, and when we cannot split the data any further, we have a leaf node. The leaf nodes represent the final predictions, the categories in a classification task, or the numerical values in a regression task.

As we construct our decision tree, we may experience some bumps along the road. A common challenge is overfitting, where the tree becomes too complex and starts to model the noise in the data rather than the underlying pattern. It is like a building that has become so complicated it is no longer functional. To deal with this, we can prune the tree, simplifying it to improve its predictive power.

The beauty of decision trees lies in their simplicity. They break down a complex decision-making process into a series of simple questions, each leading us closer to the answer. And the best part? Once the tree is built, making a prediction is as easy as following a path from the root to a leaf.

So, that is the blueprint for constructing a decision tree. We will understand the math behind these concepts later in the chapter. Let us continue our journey by exploring the concepts of entropy and information gain further.

The twin branches: Classification and regression trees

How about we get acquainted with the two main types of decision trees that rule the landscape of decision tree models? We are talking about classification trees and regression trees. These siblings, while sharing the same roots, serve distinct purposes.

Let us understand both the concepts briefly:

- **Classification trees:** Classification trees are used when the outcome or the target variable is categorical or discrete in nature. In other words, when we want to classify our data into specific categories, we use classification trees. For example, if we want to predict whether an email is spam or whether a loan applicant will default, we would use a classification tree. Each leaf of the classification tree represents a category, and the branches represent combinations of feature values that lead to those categories.

- **Regression trees:** On the other hand, when our target variable is continuous or numerical, we use regression trees. These are used for prediction tasks where the output is a real number, like predicting the price of a house or the height of a person. Instead of categories, each leaf in a regression tree represents a numerical value.

So, a major distinction between the two trees is the target variable type they deal with. They both follow the same construction process and use the same decision-making mechanism. The only difference lies in how they reach the final output at the leaf nodes.

For classification trees, the most commonly occurring class of the observations within that node becomes the predicted class. Regression trees, however, predict the average value of the observations within the node.

Remember, whether you are using classification trees or regression trees, the principle remains the same. You are still asking simple questions to divide your data, slowly but surely getting closer to your final prediction. Keep this duality in mind as we explore the forest of decision tree models. Next, we will delve into some of the fundamental mathematical concepts used in building these trees: entropy and information gain.

Entropy and information gain

Entropy and information gain are two essential mechanics that guide the growth of a decision tree. You can think of entropy as a measure of disorder or uncertainty in the data. Information gain is just the opposite, quantifying how much we reduce this uncertainty by splitting the data a certain way. Together, these concepts help us make the crucial decisions on splitting the data at each node. By the end of this section, you will have a solid grasp of these concepts and their significant role in creating efficient and effective decision trees.

Diving into entropy: Unraveling chaos in decision trees

You have probably come across the term entropy in a physics class, signifying chaos or randomness. It turns out this term is borrowed by the world of decision trees in machine learning, but with a slight twist. In our case, entropy is a measure of impurity, disorder, or uncertainty. Specifically, it quantifies the impurity of an input set.

In the case of decision trees, think of entropy as a measure of randomness in the information being processed. We use it to decide which feature to split on at each step in the tree. The goal of the tree is to reduce the entropy, that is, reduce the randomness, making the information as specific as possible.

Consider a binary classification problem where our classes are positives (+) and negatives (-). The entropy of the entire dataset would be at its maximum if half of our instances are positive and the other half negative (meaning our dataset is very chaotic and random). If, however, all instances are positive or all are negative, then entropy would be zero, indicating no chaos or randomness (a very orderly dataset).

Here is the mathematical formula for entropy for a binary classification problem:

$E(S) = - p+ * log2(p+) - p- * log2(p-)$

Here,

- $E(S)$ is the entropy of set S.

- $p+$ is the proportion of positive instances in the dataset.

- $p-$ is the proportion of negative instances in the dataset.

As you can see, the entropy function only considers the proportions of instances in each class. Therefore, it is mainly concerned with how mixed the classes are.

In the next section, we will discuss how we use this measure of chaos to create an effective decision tree.

Demystifying information gain

Now that we have seen entropy, a measure of chaos or randomness in a set of data, how do we make sense of it and use it to make decisions? This is where the concept of **information gain (IG)** comes into play.

Information gain in decision trees is a statistical property that measures how well a given attribute separates the training examples according to their target classification. This separation is crucial as it impacts the efficiency and accuracy of our decision tree.

The information gain of a feature is defined as the decrease in entropy after the dataset is split on that feature. A feature with a high information gain means that by using that feature for splitting, we reduce the randomness and bring order into our dataset, achieving a more significant separation of our classes.

Mathematically, the IG can be defined as the entropy of the dataset before the split *(T)* minus the weighted entropy $H(T, F)$ after the split of the dataset T over feature F. This is as follows:

IG(T, F) = H(T) - H(T, F)

From this, it is clear that a feature with maximum information gain is chosen as the splitting attribute. The same process recursively continues on the sub-datasets until one of the stopping criteria is met, leading to a complete decision tree.

Therefore, understanding and calculating information gain is crucial in the decision-making process of a decision tree model. It helps us decide which features are most significant and which ones can be ignored, allowing us to construct efficient and effective decision trees.

In the next sections, we will further discuss how we can enhance the effectiveness of decision trees. We will also delve into more complexities like tree pruning and optimization. So, stick around and keep exploring.

Role of entropy and information gain in constructing a decision tree

Let us go ahead and delve deeper into how these two concepts govern the process of decision tree formation.

Remember that a decision tree splits its nodes such that the outcomes are as homogeneous as possible. It is like organizing a messy room where you want to put similar things together to bring about a sense of order. But how does the decision tree know where to start or which feature to use for splitting the data? This is where entropy and information gain take the stage as the main conductors.

Entropy measures the impurity or disorder in the data, providing an indication of how mixed the classes in our dataset are. In the context of decision trees, a node with entropy of 0 is pure, meaning that it contains instances from a single class only. High entropy, on the other hand, suggests a more mixed set of instances. The aim is to build a tree that reduces the entropy with each split.

So, how do we decide where to split? This is where information gain steps in. We calculate the information gain for each feature, which tells us how much additional information we would obtain or how much entropy we would reduce by splitting on this feature. The feature with the highest information gain gets selected for the split. Essentially, the decision tree algorithm is on a quest to reduce entropy and maximize information gain.

The journey from root to leaf nodes in a decision tree is essentially an entropy-minimizing and information gain-maximizing process. By iteratively using entropy and information gain, the decision tree sorts the data into increasingly pure subsets, leading to efficient and effective decisions.

Understanding the roles of entropy and information gain in decision trees not only helps you comprehend how decision trees make decisions but also empowers you to optimize them for your specific needs. Next, we will look at how we can further fine-tune our decision trees through tree pruning and optimization.

Tree pruning and optimization

With our understanding of decision trees and their underlying concepts, such as entropy and information gain, we have now arrived at an important phase in the life of a decision tree: pruning and optimization. While decision trees can be quite effective, they can also become overly complex, leading to overfitting. To combat this, we can introduce the concept of tree pruning, a process of trimming down a tree to reduce its complexity and improve its predictive power. In this section, we will explore how tree pruning works, why it is important, and how we can optimize our decision trees for better performance.

Pruning a decision tree

Tree pruning is an essential technique in decision tree modeling and for good reasons. If you think of a decision tree as a literal tree, pruning is like trimming off some branches to help the tree grow healthier.

Let us delve into this a bit more. As we have seen, decision trees, if left unchecked, can grow very complex branches that perfectly fit the training data but perform poorly with new data, and that is exactly what we want to avoid. Tree pruning helps by simplifying the tree structure. This reduces the model's complexity, making it more generalizable to unseen data, thus improving its performance.

There are several techniques for pruning a tree, each with its advantages and potential drawbacks. The most common ones are pre-pruning (or early stopping) and post-pruning (also known as cost complexity pruning).

Pre-pruning involves setting constraints on the tree before it is fully developed. For example, limiting the maximum depth of the tree, setting a minimum number of samples required to split an internal node or a minimum number of samples required to be at a leaf node.

Post-pruning, on the other hand, allows the tree to grow to its full extent, and then the unnecessary or overfitted nodes are pruned. A complexity parameter is used to define a metric, where the sum of error and the complexity of the tree are minimized.

The choice of pruning method often depends on the specific task at hand and the nature of the data. But regardless of the method used, tree pruning is all about striking the right balance between model accuracy and complexity. So, the next time you are building a decision tree model, remember to prune that tree, and watch it flourish.

Hyperparameters in decision trees

Decision trees, like other machine learning models, come with a host of hyperparameters that we can tune to try and achieve better performance. So, let us dig into some of the most crucial hyperparameters in decision trees and learn how we can play around with them using Python.

The most important hyperparameter regarding decision trees is the tree depth, controlled by the `max_depth` parameter in scikit-learn's `DecisionTreeClassifier`. This parameter decides how deep our tree can grow and, thus, how complex our model can get. A shallow tree might only capture some of the intricacies of the data, leading to underfitting. On the other hand, a tree that is too deep could overfit the training data, leading to poor generalization of unseen data.

Here is an example of how you can set the `max_depth` parameter when creating a decision tree:

```
# Create a DecisionTreeClassifier with max_depth of 5
tree = DecisionTreeClassifier(max_depth=5, random_state=42)
```

Another critical hyperparameter is `min_samples_split`, which defines the minimum number of samples required to split an internal node. If this number is too high, it could prevent the tree from splitting enough times to capture the data's complexity, leading to underfitting. Conversely, if it is too low, the tree could make splits that are too specific to the training data, leading to overfitting.

Here is how to set the `min_samples_split` parameter:

```
# Create a DecisionTreeClassifier with min_samples_split of 10
tree = DecisionTreeClassifier(min_samples_split=10, random_state=42)
```

Bear in mind that these hyperparameters are not independent of each other, and changing one could affect how the others behave. It is all about finding the right balance, which brings us to hyperparameter tuning, a topic that is an adventure in itself. But for now, we will stop here, leaving you armed with a good starting point for exploring decision tree hyperparameters in your projects.

Crafting and refining a decision tree

We have been deep in the theoretical forest, dissecting the many aspects of decision trees. Now, we will venture into the practical woods, putting theory into action to create and refine our decision tree. For this exercise, we will use the famous Titanic Dataset, which we can download from **Kaggle** using this link: **https://www.kaggle.com/c/titanic.**

The Titanic Dataset is one of the most iconic datasets in the world of data science. Originating from the tragic sinking of the RMS Titanic in 1912, this dataset encapsulates the information of passengers aboard. Features such as class, age, gender, fare, and others serve as predictors for the ultimate outcome: did the passenger survive or not?

Using this dataset, our aim is two-fold:

- Build a baseline model with a decision tree classifier to predict survival.

- Attempt to improve our model's accuracy using hyperparameter tuning with grid search.

Let us first build our baseline model using the following code:

```
# Importing essential libraries
import pandas as pd
from sklearn.model_selection import train_test_split
from sklearn.tree import DecisionTreeClassifier
from sklearn.metrics import accuracy_score


# Loading the dataset (assuming you've downloaded it from Kag-
gle and it's in the same directory)
titanic_data = pd.read_csv("titanic.csv")


# Some preprocessing might be needed, like handling missing values and con-
verting categorical features.
# Here's a simplified version:
titanic_data.dropna(inplace=True)
titanic_data.drop(["Name", "Ticket", "Cabin"], axis=1, inplace=True)
titanic_data = pd.get_dummies(titanic_data, columns=["Sex", "Em-
barked"], drop_first=True)


# Splitting the dataset into features and target
X = titanic_data.drop("Survived", axis=1)
y = titanic_data["Survived"]


# Splitting data into training and test sets
X_train, X_test, y_train, y_test = train_test_split(X, y, test_
size=0.2, random_state=42)


# Training our baseline decision tree classifier
clf_baseline = DecisionTreeClassifier(random_state=42)
clf_baseline.fit(X_train, y_train)
```

```
# Making predictions
y_pred_baseline = clf_baseline.predict(X_test)
```

```
# Measuring accuracy
print("Baseline Model Accuracy:", accuracy_score(y_test, y_pred_baseline))
```

The accuracy in this case is 72.97%.

Now, let us attempt to tune our tree. As you have seen, trees have various parameters, like how deep they should grow or how many samples they should split at each node. By tuning these parameters, we might improve our prediction. Take a look at the following code:

```
# Setting the parameters for hyperparameter tuning
from sklearn.model_selection import GridSearchCV
parameters = {'max_depth':range(2,15), 'min_samples_
split':range(2,10), 'min_samples_leaf':range(1,10)}
```

```
# Using Grid Search for hyperparameter tuning
clf = GridSearchCV(DecisionTreeClassifier(random_state=42), parameters, n_
jobs=4)
clf.fit(X=X_train, y=y_train)
best_tree = clf.best_estimator_
print('Hyperparameters of the best model:', clf.best_params_)
```

```
# Predicting using the best model
y_pred_tuned = best_tree.predict(X_test)
```

```
# Measuring accuracy of the tuned model
print("Tuned Model Accuracy:", accuracy_score(y_test, y_pred_tuned))
```

The accuracy has now jumped up to 81.08%.

It is amazing how our accuracy improved with a bit of fine-tuning. With the right parameters, our tree is now a more discerning evaluator of wine, much like a seasoned sommelier. This example demonstrates how pruning and tuning can enhance the performance of decision trees and prevent overfitting.

The power of ensemble methods in machine learning

In our journey to understand machine learning algorithms, we come upon a powerful category of techniques known as **ensemble methods**. Ensemble methods are meta-algorithms that combine several machine learning models to create more powerful and robust models. In this section, we will delve into the concept of bagging, explore the fascinating forest of random forests, get boosted with boosting, and finally, venture into the territory of gradient-boosted trees. These are all distinctive yet interrelated methodologies, each with its unique strength in dealing with different types of data and problems, contributing to the versatility of machine learning.

Embarking on the ensemble journey

Ensemble methods, at their core, are all about bringing together a collection of individual models to improve overall prediction accuracy. Rather than relying on a single model's output, ensemble methods create multiple models and combine their predictions. This strategy often results in a model that is more robust and accurate than any of its individual components.

The beauty of ensemble methods is that they help us address the limitations of individual models. Imagine trying to complete a complex puzzle. You might make some progress on your own, but things will likely move faster if you get help from your friends, each working on a different part of the puzzle. That is precisely how ensemble methods operate. They pool together the abilities of various models, thereby enhancing overall performance.

Now, the ensemble approach is more than just a one-size-fits-all solution. There are several ensemble methods, each with its strengths and suitability for different scenarios. We will explore the popular ones in this chapter, namely, bagging, random forests, boosting, and gradient boosted trees.

Understanding the bagging method

Let us kick off our journey into the world of ensemble methods by exploring bagging. For bootstrap aggregating, bagging is an ensemble method designed to improve the stability and accuracy of machine learning algorithms. It is like a team-building exercise for models, bringing together a group of slightly different models to tackle a problem.

Now, let us see how bagging works. It starts by creating multiple subsets of the original data, each of the same size as the original. This is done through bootstrapping, a resampling method that allows a few instances to appear multiple times in a subset while leaving out others. Each of these subsets is then used to train a separate model. The final prediction is made by aggregating the individual predictions of all models. For regression problems, we often use the mean or median of the predictions, while for classification, we use a majority vote.

So, what is the beauty of bagging? It reduces overfitting. By creating a bunch of models, each with a different subset of the data, we are likely to get models with slightly different perspectives of the problem. This diversity reduces the chances of overfitting the training data, making our final model more robust.

But just like most things, bagging could be better. The method tends to be computationally intensive because of the number of models it needs to train. Plus, if the models are too similar (think high bias), bagging may not provide substantial benefits. And if your data has a little noise, simpler methods may suffice.

Despite these limitations, bagging is a powerful strategy to have in your machine-learning toolkit, particularly for models that have high variance.

Unearthing the forest within data

Once we have grasped the concept of bagging, stepping into the forest, that is, the random forest, feels almost like a natural progression. The random forest algorithm extends the bagging technique, specifically tailored for decision trees. Like bagging, random forests train numerous decision trees on bootstrapped subsets of the data, but it also introduces an extra sprinkle of randomness. When determining the best split at each node, only a random subset of features is considered. This extra randomness, while seemingly insignificant, actually plays a key role in decreasing the correlation between the trees, thereby adding to the diversity of the models within the ensemble. The result? A generally superior prediction performance. But let us not rush ahead. Let us stroll through the details of random forests, understanding their unique strengths and acknowledging their limitations.

A random forest, much like its name suggests, creates a forest of decision trees. Here is the twist: it is not just any forest but a randomly created one. The method starts by building a multitude of decision trees, each trained on a different bootstrap sample of the data. But there is another level of randomness: when splitting nodes, a random forest considers only a subset of the features chosen at random. This way, it creates a broad spectrum of trees, each with its unique perspective of the data.

Once the forest is ready, making a prediction involves getting each tree to make its prediction and then combining them. In the case of regression, we take the average, while for classification, we go with the majority vote.

But what makes random forests so appealing? They significantly reduce the overfitting problem plaguing individual decision trees. They also handle many features quite well, and they do not require feature scaling. Furthermore, random forests can provide insights into feature importance, making them not only predictive but also descriptive tools.

Training a large number of deep trees can be computationally expensive and slow. Also, random forest models are quite complex and can be difficult to interpret as compared to individual decision trees.

Having learned about the principles and pros and cons of random forests, let us take a quick peek at deploying a **RandomForestClassifier** model. Use the following code:

```
from sklearn.ensemble import RandomForestClassifier

# Define the model with 100 trees
model_rf = RandomForestClassifier(n_estimators=100, random_state=42)
```

In essence, with these lines of code, you are setting up a random forest classifier made up of **100** decision trees. When you train this model on data, each of the **100** trees will learn from a slightly different set of data. When making predictions, the model will aggregate the predictions of all **100** trees to give a final answer.

Boosting power: The strengths and shortcomings of boosting

Instead of treating each model equally, boosting learns from the mistakes of its predecessors to improve the prediction.

Starting with a weak learner (a model slightly better than random guessing), boosting adds new models that attempt to correct the errors made by the existing ensemble. Each subsequent model is influenced more by the data points that were previously predicted incorrectly, thereby focusing its attention on the hard-to-learn examples. This sequential learning from errors is the core principle of boosting.

In the next section, we will dig deeper into a particularly popular boosting flavor, known as **gradient boosting,** to enhance our understanding of how these powerful ensemble techniques can be leveraged.

Boosting with a twist: Introducing gradient boosting

Gradient boosting is a powerful machine learning algorithm that falls under the umbrella of ensemble learning methods. It is an iterative strategy combining weak learners to create a strong learner. In essence, gradient boosting fine-tunes the predictions by continually reducing the residuals of the previous models, hence boosting the overall performance. This is done by building new models that predict the errors or residuals of the prior model and then adding these new predictions to the final prediction.

The *gradient* in gradient boosting comes from the fact that the algorithm uses gradient descent to minimize errors. Just like a hiker descending a mountain by following the path of the steepest descent, gradient boosting identifies the direction the model should take to minimize errors.

While traditional boosting methods might employ a predefined loss function, gradient boosting is more flexible. It can optimize any differentiable loss function, making it a more generalized approach.

The strength of gradient boosting comes from its ability to learn complex, non-linear relationships and its adaptability in handling various data types, whether numerical, categorical, or a mixture of both. It is a top performer in many machine learning competitions and is widely used in the industry for predictive tasks.

However, as powerful as gradient boosting is, it has weaknesses. It can be computationally intensive, and due to its sequential nature, it can be difficult to parallelize, making it slower than some other algorithms. It also has several hyperparameters that require tuning, which can be a complex task, especially for beginners.

Now that we have a theoretical understanding of gradient-boosted trees, let us move to the practical side. Let us use Python's popular scikit-learn library, which offers an easy-to-use interface for working with gradient-boosted trees. We will stick with our wine quality dataset to maintain continuity.

Before we move on to the code, you need to know about a key ingredient in every algorithm based on gradient descent: learning rate. As far as gradient-boosted trees are concerned, this hyperparameter determines how much each tree contributes to the final prediction. A lower learning rate means each tree has a smaller influence, which can make the model more resistant to overfitting but requires more trees (and thus more time) to train. Conversely, a larger learning rate means each tree has a larger influence, potentially allowing the model to learn faster and making it more susceptible to overfitting.

We initialize a gradient boosted regressor model using the following code:

```
from sklearn.ensemble import GradientBoostingRegressor
# Initialize Gradient Boosting Regressor
gbr = GradientBoostingRegressor(n_estimators=100, learning_rate=0.1, max_
depth=3, random_state=42)
```

In this code, we are initializing a **GradientBoostingRegressor** from sklearn's ensemble module. We set the number of boosting stages (**n_estimators**) to **100**, the learning rate (**learning_rate**) to **0.1**, and the maximum depth of the decision tree estimators (**max_depth**) to **3**. These hyperparameters were chosen arbitrarily for this demonstration, but in practice, you would likely want to tune them for your specific problem and dataset.

The power of gradient boosting trees – as you would know by now – lies in their ability to combine weak learners to create a model that can make accurate predictions. As with all models, hyperparameter tuning is critical in the model's ability to generalize well to unseen data.

Picking the right ensemble method

Ensemble methods are robust machine learning techniques that combine multiple models to deliver more reliable and accurate predictions. But when faced with a myriad of options such as bagging, random forests, boosting, and gradient-boosted trees, how do you decide which one to use? This decision mainly depends on the problem at hand, the dataset, and the specific characteristics of each method.

Bagging involves creating multiple subsets of the original dataset (with replacement), training a model on each, and then averaging the prediction results. It is particularly useful for reducing the variance of models that tend to overfit, like decision trees. This technique works well with a large enough dataset and computational power, as it does not require tuning. However, the models can be complex and time-consuming to train.

Random forests are a good default choice for many applications due to their simplicity, robustness, and often excellent performance. However, they may need help with very high-dimensional data or sparse data.

Boosting models, especially gradient boosting, are widely used due to their high performance on various problems. However, they can be more sensitive to the choice of hyperparameters and take longer to train.

In a nutshell, if you are dealing with a complex problem where accuracy is the priority, boosting methods, especially gradient boosted trees, might be the best choice. But if you are working with a large, noisy dataset and are more concerned about overfitting, bagging or random forests could be the way to go. Remember, no one size fits all in machine learning; the best method is often found through experimentation and validation.

Conclusion

As we wrap up this chapter on decision trees and ensemble methods, let us take a moment to appreciate the journey we have been on. We began by diving into decision trees, understanding their structure, the role of entropy, and the concept of information gain. We got our hands dirty by building and optimizing decision trees with Python, making strategic decisions to avoid overfitting.

We then branched off into the fascinating world of ensemble methods, understanding how bagging, random forests, and boosting work. We further enhanced our understanding by exploring gradient-boosted trees, looking into their strengths and limitations. To make things practical, we coded these algorithms in Python, demonstrating their efficacy on real-world datasets.

In the end, we also learned that there is no one-size-fits-all solution in machine learning. The choice of algorithm depends greatly on the problem at hand, the nature of the data, and the computational resources available. The journey of a machine learning practitioner is one of continuous learning, exploration, and constant fine-tuning.

In the next chapter, we will explore the fascinating world of **Support Vector Machines (SVMs)**, understanding their power and versatility, the role of kernel methods, and how to harness SVMs for classification and regression tasks, further expanding our toolkit for tackling complex real-world problems.

Points to remember

- Decision trees are intuitive, versatile, and easy-to-interpret machine learning models that can handle both categorical and numerical data.

- Entropy and information gain are fundamental concepts in building decision trees; they help determine the best splits by measuring the impurity of the nodes and the information provided by each attribute.

- Tree pruning and hyperparameter tuning are critical techniques to prevent overfitting in decision trees and improve model performance.

- Ensemble methods like bagging (random forests) and boosting (gradient boosted trees) can substantially improve prediction accuracy by combining multiple weak learners to form a strong learner. They are particularly effective for reducing variance (bagging) and bias (boosting).

- The choice of a machine learning model (including decision trees or ensemble methods) should depend on the specific characteristics of the problem and the dataset. Understanding the strengths and limitations of each method is crucial to making the right choice.

Multiple choice questions

1. **Which of the following is true about decision trees?**

   a. Decision trees cannot handle categorical data.

   b. Overfitting is not a problem with decision trees.

   c. Tree pruning is used to prevent overfitting in decision trees.

   d. Decision trees cannot be used for regression problems.

2. **What is the role of entropy in decision trees?**

   a. Determines the split at each node in the tree

   b. Measures the impurity of a node

   c. Measures the overall performance of the tree

   d. Determines the depth of the tree

3. **What is the principle idea behind ensemble methods like random forests and gradient boosting?**

   a. To use a single complex model for prediction

   b. To combine the predictions of several weak models to form a strong model

   c. To increase the bias in the models

   d. None of the above

4. **In the context of decision tree building, what is Information Gain?**

   a. It measures the difference in entropy before and after the split.

   b. It indicates the amount of information a feature provides about the target.

   c. It calculates the total amount of information in the dataset.

   d. Both A and B

Answers

1. c

2. b

3. b

4. d

Questions

1. How does tree pruning help in optimizing a decision tree?

2. Discuss the benefits and limitations of random forests and gradient boosted trees.

3. How can hyperparameter tuning improve the performance of a decision tree model?

Join our book's Discord space

Join the book's Discord Workspace for Latest updates, Offers, Tech happenings around the world, New Release and Sessions with the Authors:

https://discord.bpbonline.com

CHAPTER 11

Support Vector Machines: Simplifying Complexity

Introduction

In this chapter, we will unveil the power of **support vector machines (SVM)**, a versatile and powerful **Machine Learning (ML)** model adept at dealing with intricate patterns and complex decision boundaries. Coupled with kernel methods, SVM provides us with a robust toolset to tackle non-linear problems that other algorithms might struggle with. Within these pages, we will explore the mathematical principles that guide SVMs and use them for both classification and regression tasks. By exploring the art of model tuning and optimization, we will ensure that our SVM models are tuned for optimal performance, balanced to avoid overfitting and underfitting.

Structure

In this chapter, we will discuss the following topics:

- Introduction to support vector machines
- Understanding kernel methods
- SVM for classification and regression
- Real-world SVM: From processing to evaluation
- Balancing the bias: Variance trade off in SVM

Objectives

Our aim with this chapter is to develop a comprehensive understanding of SVM and kernel methods. We will learn the key concepts behind these techniques, discover how to apply them for classification and regression tasks, and explore ways to tune and optimize our models. By the end of the chapter, we should feel confident in creating, implementing, and fine-tuning SVM models to solve various complex, real-world data problems.

Introduction to support vector machines

In this first section, we are going to acquaint ourselves with a machine learning powerhouse: SVM. SVM is an algorithm that excels in both classification and regression tasks, carving out decision boundaries that separate data with an impressive level of precision. Born out of statistical learning theory and the work of *Vapnik* and *Chervonenkis*, SVMs are particularly noted for their ability to handle high-dimensional data and complex patterns. As we unpack the mechanics of SVMs, you will see why they are often a go-to tool in a data scientists' arsenal when it comes to both linear and non-linear machine learning problems.

Mastering the mechanics of support vector machines

To truly understand SVM, let us imagine we are throwing a party, and we need to separate our two groups of guests: cat lovers and dog lovers. Now, we could simply draw a line between these two groups, right? But wait, there are so many possible lines we could draw. So, how do we choose the best one?

That is exactly the principle behind SVM; it searches for the optimal boundary line (or hyperplane, in higher dimensions) that maximizes the margin between two classes. This optimal line is the one that has the largest distance to the nearest data point of any class, creating a street or margin between classes. The wider this street, the better our SVM model can generalize to unseen data.

Now, the support vectors in SVM are essentially the coordinates of individual data points that lay on the edge of the street, and these are what support or define the hyperplane. These points are the critical elements of our data set. The positioning of the rest of our data can be changed without impacting the hyperplane, as long as these support vectors remain in place.

In the case where our cat and dog lovers cannot be separated by a straight line, SVM uses a trick called the **kernel trick**. This essentially transforms our party space such that our groups become separable. Imagine adding a third dimension, like a love for fish dimension, where we can lift all our cat lovers up into this new dimensional space. Suddenly, we can separate our two groups with a plane.

And that is the beauty of SVMs; they are capable of creating complex boundaries, thanks to these kernels, making them incredibly flexible and powerful for various machine learning tasks.

Uniqueness of SVM in the machine learning ensemble

Alright, now let us picture ourselves at a global machine learning conference. Here, every algorithm is a participant with unique abilities, showcasing their prowess to solve problems. While each algorithm has its specialty, our special guest, SVM, has a distinctive charm. Let us explore why.

The essence of SVMs lies in their principle of maximizing the margin. Think of it as a safety buffer. Most classification algorithms would be satisfied with any decision boundary that correctly separates the classes, but not SVM. It demands the widest possible street between classes. This ensures a robust classification, even if new data points sneak in close to the decision boundary.

Moreover, SVMs have the extraordinary capability of morphing the problem space with kernel tricks. Suppose you are an artist trying to paint a clear sky, but there are birds and planes flying around, making it difficult to depict the vastness. Now, imagine that you could momentarily elevate yourself above the atmosphere, where only space exists, allowing you to paint that clear sky easily. Afterward, you return to the ground, with a perfect painting. That elevation and perspective change is similar to what SVMs do with data. They transform complex, inseparable data to a higher dimension where separation becomes easier. Only few other algorithms have such in-built transformation abilities.

Finally, SVMs are versatile. They can perform linear classification, nonlinear classification, and even regression. They do not shy away from multi-dimensional or multi-class problems either. Moreover, SVMs are deterministic, meaning given the same data, they will always produce the same model. This makes them reliable and reproducible, a significant advantage in many applications.

Overall, SVMs are like a multi-tool in our machine learning toolbox, equipped with a distinctive set of abilities that make them stand out. They are unique, reliable, and remarkably flexible, capable of performing a wide array of machine learning tasks.

Numerical craft behind support vector machines

When you walk into the mathematical art gallery of SVM, there is a beautiful piece of craftsmanship that stands out; it is called the **large margin classification**.

The central tenet of SVM is not just to separate the data points of different classes but to do so in a way that ensures the maximum possible distance (or margin) between them.

Mathematically, this is achieved by solving an optimization problem: *Minimize* $||w||$ (the norm of the weight vector) subject to $y(i)(w^T x(i) + b) \geq 1$ for all *i*, where w is the weight vector, *x(i)* represents the feature vectors, *y(i)* are the class labels, and b is the bias term. The function we are trying to minimize effectively controls the width of the margin, while the constraint ensures that all instances are off the street and on the right side.

Now, we have data that is not as friendly and refuses to be cleanly separated. This is where soft margin classification comes into the picture. It allows SVM to flex its muscles and handle such cases by allowing some instances to end up on the street, even on the wrong side. This is managed by introducing slack variables, $\xi(i)$, for each instance. The optimization problem then balances between making the street as wide as possible and limiting the margin violations.

Finally, there is a touch of magic: the kernel trick. This lets SVM deal with nonlinear datasets by moving them into a higher-dimensional space where they can be separated linearly. Kernels, like the **radial basis function** (**RBF**), transform the feature space without having to compute the coordinates of the data in that high-dimensional space. It is like bending the rules of the universe to make it work for you.

In the grand scheme, the numerical artistry of SVM combines optimization, linear algebra, and even a bit of quantum leaping (thanks to kernels) to classify data points.

The art of drawing lines: Hyperplanes and support vectors

Hyperplanes are our superheroes in the high-dimensional world of SVM. In a two-dimensional world, a hyperplane is just a line, and in a three-dimensional world, it is a flat plane. But when we have data with more than three features, things get a bit tricky. Here, the hyperplane can be thought of as a multi-dimensional extension of a flat plane, slicing through the feature space to separate data of different classes.

Now, picture a knife slicing through a loaf of bread. The knife is our hyperplane, and the biggest slices of bread that touch the knife on either side are our support vectors. These support vectors are data points that are closest to the hyperplane and essentially support the creation and positioning of the hyperplane. They are the critical elements of our dataset that directly influence how the decision boundary is formed. If the support vectors were to change, the position of the hyperplane would change too.

Something is fascinating about the location of these support vectors. They are always on the edge of the margin or the wrong side of the margin in the case of soft margin classification. They are like the rebels of our dataset, those boundary pushers that keep the SVM in check.

Understanding hyperplanes and support vectors is like learning to see the world in 4D or more; it challenges our imagination, but once we grasp it, we gain a powerful tool for separating our data, no matter how many dimensions it lives in. Armed with this knowledge, we are ready to delve even deeper into the caverns of support vector machines in the next section.

Understanding kernel methods

In the realm of support vector machines, we have been walking through the high-dimensional landscapes with the help of hyperplanes. But what happens when the data is not easily separable by a simple line or a flat plane? That is where our trusty companion, kernel methods, comes into play. So, put on your explorer's hat and brace yourself as we delve into the fascinating world of kernel methods, a sophisticated approach that allows us to explore and conquer even the most intricate data structures.

The power of kernel functions

Kernel functions are like secret weapons we can use to solve complex problems in our data science adventures. Picture them as special transformational maps, guiding us from a low-dimensional world where our data seems entangled and impossible to separate into a higher-dimensional space where the same data points magically appear separate and structured.

Suppose we have a map of an intricate maze drawn on a piece of paper. To the naked eye, it seems impossible to navigate through. But what if we could add another dimension to this map? Suddenly, the walls of the maze lift off the page, creating tunnels and bridges, and the path through becomes clear.

These mathematical marvels take our input data and transform them, adding more dimensions and revealing hidden structures. They allow us to handle nonlinear relationships without actually increasing the computational complexity of our models. It is like getting a superpower to see structures and relationships we could not see before in our data. The kernel trick, as it is commonly called, offers us the ability to run computations in higher-dimensional space without paying the computational price.

This technique is used not only in SVMs but also in various other machine learning algorithms where we need to deal with complex, nonlinear data structures. As we will see in this section, understanding and effectively utilizing kernel functions will give us a substantial edge in crafting powerful, insightful models.

Data transformation with kernel methods

Kernel methods have an uncanny ability to illuminate our path through the winding complexities of our data. They are like our private set of night-vision goggles, showing us the structures and patterns hiding beneath the surface. But how exactly does this process of data transformation with kernel methods work?

The first step in the kernel method is to select the right kernel function. We have a few different types: linear, polynomial, radial basis functions and sigmoid are among the most popular. But remember, picking the right kernel is like choosing the right tool for the job. We have to consider the nature and complexity of our data, the computational resources available, and the specific problem we are trying to solve.

Once we have chosen our kernel, we apply it to our data, transforming it into a higher-dimensional space. It is like taking a flat, 2D map and turning it into a 3D model. This new space, created by the kernel method, allows us to see and manipulate our data in ways we could not before. Intricate patterns become clear, and classes that seemed hopelessly entwined are now cleanly separated.

For instance, let us say we are trying to classify a dataset that looks like a circular target, with one class in the middle and the other forming a ring around it. In the original 2D space, these two classes are inseparable with a straight line. However, by applying a radial basis function kernel, we can transform this data into 3D space where the classes become separable by a plane.

They allow us to work in this higher-dimensional space without actually having to calculate the coordinates of the data in that space.

In the end, the power of kernel methods is not just about transforming data. It is about revealing the potential of our models to understand and learn from this data in new ways. As we continue our journey, we will see how these methods underpin the strength and versatility of SVMs.

Kernel functions: Linear, polynomial, and radial basis

In our exploration of kernel methods, we are going to encounter various tools. Just like a master chef has an array of utensils and ingredients at their disposal, we have a selection of kernel functions to help us create the perfect recipe for our data. Let us dive into this delectable smorgasbord and understand the characteristics and uses of linear, polynomial, and RBF kernels:

- **Linear kernel:** The linear kernel, as the name suggests, is a straightforward function that allows us to capture linear relationships in the data. It is like our reliable, everyday chef's knife: it might not be the fanciest tool in the drawer, but it is versatile, efficient, and the right choice for many tasks. With a linear kernel, we are mapping our data directly into a higher-dimensional space without any additional transformation, making it an ideal choice when dealing with linearly separable data or high-dimensional datasets.

- **Polynomial kernel:** The polynomial kernel, like the whisk in our kitchen metaphor, is all about mixing things up. It helps us capture not only the linear relationships but also the interactions between our features. This is achieved by mapping our data into a higher-dimensional space where the degree of the polynomial determines the complexity of the relationships we can capture. A higher degree allows us to model more intricate relationships. Just like over-whisking can make our mixture too stiff or cause it to separate, overcomplicating our model can lead to overfitting.

- **RBF kernel:** This is the food processor of our kitchen. The RBF kernel is a powerful tool capable of mapping our data into an infinite-dimensional space. It is especially handy when dealing with non-linear, complex data because it can carve out radial boundaries around our data points. The RBF kernel is like our go-to gadget when the data gets tough and linear or polynomial transformations just would not cut it.

Choosing the right kernel for your SVM

Choosing the right kernel function is an art form in itself, and it heavily depends on the data at hand and the problem we are trying to solve. But with a little practice and a good understanding of each kernel's strengths and weaknesses, we will be able to select the best kernel for our task, creating an SVM model that is not only robust but also performs brilliantly.

Let us dive into some hands-on strategies to pick out the star kernel for your dataset:

- **Experimenting with different kernels:** One straightforward approach is to try various kernels and observe their performance. Common kernels include linear, polynomial, RBF, and sigmoid. Each has its characteristics and suits different types of data. For example, the RBF kernel is often a good starting point due to its flexibility, while the linear kernel may suffice for linearly separable data.

- **Grid search for hyperparameter tuning:** Employing grid search is an effective way to find the best combination of kernel and its parameters (like C, gamma, and degree). Grid search systematically works through multiple combinations of parameter values and cross-validates as it goes to determine which combination yields the best model performance.

- **Ensemble methods with different kernels:** Sometimes, a single kernel may not be sufficient to capture the complexities of the data. Using ensemble methods, such as bagging or boosting, with different kernels can combine their strengths. This approach involves training multiple SVMs, each with a different kernel, and then aggregating their predictions. This method can potentially lead to more robust and accurate models.

Incorporating these techniques into your SVM workflow can significantly enhance your model's accuracy and generalizability. It is important to remember that there is no one-size-fits-all kernel; the choice largely depends on the nature of the data and the specific problem at hand. As such, thorough experimentation and validation are key to identifying the most suitable kernel function for your SVM model.

SVM for classification and regression roles

SVM excels in classifying your data, but it is equally adept at predicting numerical outcomes. Just as an accomplished actor can take on various roles, SVM gracefully takes on the roles of both a classifier and a regressor, delivering standout performances each time. In this section, we will explore how SVM employs its unique techniques to perform these two distinct tasks. Let us first see how it steps into the shoes of a classifier.

SVM in binary and multiclass scenarios

Suppose you have a data set and need to classify it. If it is a binary problem, SVM can probably handle it with ease. It excels at sorting data into two distinct groups. But what if we have more than two categories? Can SVM still come to our rescue? Of course, it can. SVM does not shy away from multiclass problems. It embraces the complexity with various strategies, such as one-vs-one and one-vs-all, to keep the classes in check. Let us dive deeper and see how SVM manages this juggling act between binary and multiclass classification.

In binary classification, SVMs construct a hyperplane in multidimensional space to separate different classes. The data points from each class closest to the constructed hyperplane are known as **support vectors**. The hyperplane is positioned to have the maximum possible distance, or margin, from these support vectors, hence creating the largest gap between classes. This is what makes SVM an excellent choice for binary classification tasks; its fundamental design is to create the optimal boundary that best separates the classes.

But things get a little trickier when we deal with multiclass classification. Here, we have more than two categories to predict. SVMs, in their original form, are not designed to handle multiclass problems directly. But that does not mean they are out of the race. On the contrary, they have evolved to conquer this challenge in two main ways: one-vs-one and one-vs-all strategies.

The one-vs-one strategy involves training a separate SVM for each pair of classes. For a problem with N classes, this results in $N(N-1)/2$ classifiers. Each classifier is then used to vote on the class, and the class with the most votes is the predicted class. Although this approach can be computationally expensive, it is quite effective as each classifier only needs to be trained on the part of the data set involving the pair of classes it is responsible for.

The one-vs-all strategy, on the other hand, involves training one SVM per class, with the samples of that class as positive instances and all other samples as negatives. This results in N classifiers for N classes. For an unseen sample, each of the N classifiers determines if this particular sample falls into the class they represent. The classifier that predicts with the highest confidence score is considered the predicted class.

Both strategies have their merits, and the choice between one-vs-one and one-vs-all often depends on the specifics of the problem at hand. But one thing is clear: whether it is a binary or multiclass problem, SVMs have the versatility and strength to deliver reliable results.

SVM in the world of regression

SVM's powers extend beyond the realm of classification and into the world of regression. This technique, known as **Support Vector Regression (SVR)**, applies the same principles used in SVM to solve regression problems. In a nutshell, it fits a hyperplane that deviates from the actual output by a value no greater than a specified tolerance ε, while trying to maximize the margin.

Let us unravel this a bit. In classification tasks, we aim to create a boundary that separates different classes while maintaining the largest margin. On the other hand, in SVR, our goal is not to separate classes but to predict continuous values. So, we create a sort of boundary of a fixed width ε around the regression line (or hyperplane in higher dimensions) and try to make sure all our data points fall within this boundary. Those do not are considered as violations, similar to the concept of support vectors in classification.

The ε-insensitive loss function used in SVR means that errors within the specified boundary are ignored. This technique makes SVR robust to outliers. The epsilon parameter can be tuned to achieve the desired balance between margin size and the tolerance of violations.

The other fascinating aspect of SVR is that it, too, employs the kernel trick to solve nonlinear regression problems. By mapping input features to a higher-dimensional space, SVR enables the construction of nonlinear regression surfaces.

So, whether it is classification or regression, linear or nonlinear problems, SVMs have you covered. They truly break boundaries and prove to be versatile and powerful tools in the world of machine learning.

Real-world SVM: From preprocessing to evaluation

We have learned the principles of SVM and looked at the math under the hood; now, let us see how it performs in the wild. In this section, we will walk through the steps of applying SVM to both a classification and a regression problem.

Let us begin with classification. Suppose we are working with the popular Iris dataset, aiming to classify different species of Iris flowers based on their petal and sepal lengths and widths.

Execute the following code:

```
# Importing necessary libraries
from sklearn import datasets
from sklearn.model_selection import train_test_split
from sklearn.preprocessing import StandardScaler
from sklearn import svm
from sklearn.metrics import accuracy_score, confusion_matrix

# Load the iris dataset
iris = datasets.load_iris()
X = iris.data
y = iris.target

# Split the dataset into a training set and a test set
X_train, X_test, y_train, y_test = train_test_split(X, y, test_
size=0.3, random_state=42)

# Standardize the features
scaler = StandardScaler()
X_train_std = scaler.fit_transform(X_train)
X_test_std = scaler.transform(X_test)

# Create a SVM classifier using the radial basis function (RBF) kernel
clf = svm.SVC(kernel='rbf', random_state=42)

# Train the classifier
clf.fit(X_train_std, y_train)

# Make predictions
y_pred = clf.predict(X_test_std)

# Evaluate the model
print('Accuracy:', accuracy_score(y_test, y_pred))
print('Confusion Matrix:\n', confusion_matrix(y_test, y_pred))
```

This will give you the accuracy of the classification and a confusion matrix that shows the number of correct and incorrect predictions classified by the actual class.

You might be wondering why we are standardizing the features here. Standardization, as you know, is a common requirement for many machine learning algorithms, including SVMs.

In the case of SVMs, they try to fit the widest possible street between the classes in the feature space, also known as the maximization of the margin. This means that SVMs are sensitive to the scales of the features. If one feature has a range of values that is vastly larger than another feature, the larger feature would dominate when calculating the distance between the data points. This could potentially lead to sub-optimal solutions where the SVM does not perform as well as it could.

By standardizing the features, we are making sure that all features contribute equally to the distance calculation, preventing any one feature from dominating simply because of its scale. This results in a model that can make better predictions.

It is important to fit the **StandardScaler** on the training data only, then standardize both training and test sets using this scaler. This ensures that the same transformation is applied to both the training and test sets, preserving the distribution of the data.

It is worth mentioning that in certain cases, you might not want to standardize your data. For instance, if your features represent counts or proportions and you know that they follow a specific distribution, then standardization might not be the best preprocessing step. However, in many common situations, standardization is a safe and useful preprocessing step to perform.

Next, let us see how SVM can be used for regression problems. This time, we will be predicting the median value of owner-occupied homes in Boston using the Boston housing dataset. Use the following code:

```
# Importing necessary libraries
from sklearn import datasets
from sklearn.model_selection import train_test_split
from sklearn.preprocessing import StandardScaler
from sklearn import svm
from sklearn.metrics import mean_squared_error

# Load the California housing dataset
california = datasets.fetch_california_housing()
X = california.data
y = california.target
```

```
# Split the dataset into a training set and a test set
X_train,  X_test,  y_train,  y_test  =  train_test_split(X,  y,  test_
size=0.3, random_state=42)

# Standardize the features
scaler = StandardScaler()
X_train_std = scaler.fit_transform(X_train)
X_test_std = scaler.transform(X_test)

# Create a SVM regressor
regr = svm.SVR(kernel='linear')

# Train the regressor
regr.fit(X_train_std, y_train)

# Make predictions
y_pred = regr.predict(X_test_std)

# Evaluate the model
print('Mean Squared Error:', mean_squared_error(y_test, y_pred))
```

The output here will be the **mean squared error** (**MSE**), which tells you how close your predictions are to the actual values in the test set. The lower the MSE, the better your model.

We have used SVM to solve both a classification and a regression problem from end-to-end, from data preprocessing to model evaluation.

Handling imbalanced data in support vector machines

Now, let us explore a common challenge in machine learning: dealing with imbalanced data. Imbalanced data refers to a situation where the classes in the target variable are not represented equally. For instance, in a binary classification problem, you might have 90% of samples belonging to Class A and just 10% belonging to Class B. This could pose a problem as our SVM might be biased toward the majority class and might fail to predict the minority class accurately.

SVMs have built-in capabilities to manage this issue. They utilize a parameter known as C, which regulates the penalty of misclassifications in the optimization function that SVMs aim to minimize. By adjusting this C parameter, we can control the balance between having a wide street and limiting the margin violations (instances that end up in the middle of the street or on the wrong side).

However, sometimes adjusting the C parameter is not enough. Another common technique to deal with imbalanced data is to use a different weight for different classes. In the case of SVM, you can assign a larger penalty to misclassifications of the minority class. This can be done by setting the **class_weight** parameter to balanced when defining your SVM in scikit-learn, which automatically adjusts weights inversely proportional to class frequencies.

Let us see how this can be done in Python:

```python
from sklearn import svm

# Assign class_weight='balanced' to handle imbalanced classes
clf = svm.SVC(kernel='linear', class_weight='balanced')

# Fit the model on your training data
clf.fit(X_train_std, y_train)

# Make predictions on your test data
y_pred = clf.predict(X_test_std)
```

Remember, though, that addressing imbalanced data is not a one-size-fits-all kind of deal. The techniques to handle it will vary depending on the context, the dataset, and the specific problem at hand. The best approach is usually to try several methods and see which one works best for your particular situation.

With that, you have got a new tool in your SVM toolbox: the ability to handle imbalanced data and make your SVM model even more effective.

Perfecting your support vector machines

In this crucial phase, we take our SVM model from good to great. If you have wondered how to fine-tune your model to squeeze out the best performance, this is the section for you. We will be delving into the depths of the key SVM parameters, exploring strategies to combat overfitting and underfitting, and learning how to evaluate our model's performance with the appropriate metrics.

Impact of the C parameter and kernel coefficients on your SVM model

Let us put on our data scientist hats and think about tuning parameters for a moment. Specifically, we will examine two essential elements in our SVM toolbox: the C parameter and kernel coefficients. You can think of the C parameter as a kind of strictness enforcer: the higher the C value, the less tolerance the model has for misclassification. On the other hand, lower C values allow for more misclassification but aim for a more general decision boundary.

Now, on to the kernel coefficients, also known as **gamma**, in the context of the radial basis function kernel. Gamma dictates how far the influence of a single training example reaches. If it has a low value, each example's range is broad, and the decision boundary ends up smoother. In contrast, a high gamma means that each example has a close reach, creating a more complex, wavy boundary, potentially overfitting the data.

Are you curious about how these parameters affect your model in practice? Here is an example:

```
from sklearn import svm, datasets
from sklearn.model_selection import GridSearchCV

# Load iris dataset as an example
iris = datasets.load_iris()
parameters = {'kernel':('linear', 'rbf'), 'C':[1, 10]}

svc = svm.SVC()

clf = GridSearchCV(svc, parameters)

clf.fit(iris.data, iris.target)

# Let's print the best parameters found by GridSearchCV
print("Best parameters found: ", clf.best_params_)
```

In this code, we are setting up a parameter grid with two possible kernels (*linear* and *rbf*) and two different values for the C parameter (1 and 10). The **GridSearchCV** function then tests all the combinations of parameters for us, and in the end, we print the best parameters found for our SVM model.

Remember, the best parameters will always be dependent on your specific dataset and the problem you are trying to solve. Therefore, tuning is an art and requires some experimentation.

Balancing the bias-variance trade-off in SVM

When working with SVM, overfitting and underfitting are two key challenges that must be managed.

Both situations are, of course, undesirable, and their presence can often be inferred from the model's performance on training and validation datasets. If the model performs exceptionally well on the training data but poorly on the validation data, it is likely overfitting. If it performs poorly on both, it is likely underfitting.

There are several strategies to prevent these issues in SVM:

- **Regularization:** The C parameter in SVM is a regularization parameter. It controls the trade-off between achieving a low error on the training data and minimizing the complexity of the model. A high C will classify as many samples correctly as possible (leading to potential overfitting), while a low C will create a wider margin, even if that means misclassifying more points (which could lead to underfitting). Therefore, tuning the C parameter is crucial.

- **Kernel choice and parameters:** The choice of the kernel and its parameters can greatly influence overfitting. Using more complex kernels (like RBF or polynomial kernels) increases the risk of overfitting, particularly if the data does not require such complexity. Therefore, starting with a simpler kernel like the linear one, then experimenting with more complex ones, and tuning the kernel parameters can help prevent overfitting.

- **Cross-validation:** K-fold cross-validation helps prevent overfitting by splitting the training data into K folds and then training the model K times, each time using a different fold as a validation set and the remaining data as the training set. The average error across all K trials is computed to give an overall error metric for the model.

Remember, the key is to find a balance. You want a model that is just right, capturing the underlying patterns in your data without being overly complex or too simplistic.

Conclusion

We have journeyed through the landscape of support vector machines and kernel methods, witnessing the power these algorithms hold for both classification and regression tasks. We have explored the theory behind these techniques, delved into the mechanics of kernels, and discovered how to optimize our models for maximum performance. Most importantly, we have learned that a solid grasp of the underlying principles of these methods equips us with the tools needed to select the right parameters and avoid common pitfalls such as overfitting. By understanding and implementing these lessons, you are now well-positioned to harness the capabilities of SVMs in your data science projects, whether you are predicting house prices or classifying text documents.

In the next chapter, we will tackle the challenge of high dimensionality in data, exploring techniques like **principal component analysis (PCA)**, visualization of high-dimensional data, and advanced methods such as t-SNE and UMAP, which will empower you to handle complex datasets and extract meaningful insights efficiently.

Points to remember

- Support vector machines are powerful supervised learning methods used for classification and regression. They work on the principle of maximizing the margin between the closest samples of different classes, termed as support vectors.

- Kernel methods are a cornerstone of SVM, allowing us to handle non-linearly separable data by mapping it to a higher-dimensional space. Different kernel functions can be used depending on the structure of the data, including linear, polynomial, and radial basis function.

- Careful tuning of the SVM parameters, such as the C regularization parameter and the choice of kernel, is critical to avoid overfitting or underfitting and achieve optimal model performance.

- Dealing with imbalanced data and using techniques like cross-validation for model evaluation are key steps to creating robust and reliable SVM models.

Multiple choice questions

1. **Which of the following is not a type of kernel used in SVM?**

    a. Linear

    b. Polynomial

    c. RBF

    d. Logarithmic

2. **How does SVM handle non-linearly separable data?**

    a. By mapping it to a lower-dimensional space

    b. By mapping it to a higher-dimensional space

    c. By adding more support vectors

    d. By reducing the regularization parameter

3. **What is the role of the regularization parameter C in SVM?**

    a. It determines the complexity of the kernel function.

    b. It determines the margin width between classes.

    c. It determines the learning rate of the model.

    d. It determines the number of support vectors.

Answers

1. d

2. b

3. b

Questions

1. What are support vectors in SVM, and why are they important?

2. Explain the concept of kernel trick in SVM and how it helps in dealing with non-linear data.

3. What steps can be taken to prevent overfitting in SVM?

Join our book's Discord space

Join the book's Discord Workspace for Latest updates, Offers, Tech happenings around the world, New Release and Sessions with the Authors:

https://discord.bpbonline.com

## CHAPTER 12

Dimensionality Reduction: From PCA to Advanced Methods

Introduction

In data analysis, we frequently encounter datasets with a multitude of features. While these features may carry valuable information, their sheer number can lead to challenges that obstruct efficient data analysis and **Machine Learning (ML)**: a phenomenon known as the curse of dimensionality. This chapter will guide you through the labyrinth of high-dimensional data, focusing primarily on a widely used technique called **principal component analysis (PCA)**, which simplifies data without substantial loss of information. We will also introduce you to dimension reduction methods like **t-Distributed Stochastic Neighbor Embedding (t-SNE)** and **Uniform Manifold Approximation and Projection (UMAP)**, allowing you to compare their utility and pick the best fit for your specific use case.

Structure

In this chapter, we will discuss the following topics:

- Understanding the problem of high dimensionality
- Principal component analysis
- Visualizing high-dimensional data
- Exploring beyond PCA: t-SNE and UMAP

Objectives

By the end of this chapter, you should have a clear understanding of the problems associated with high-dimensional data and how dimensionality reduction techniques, especially PCA, can help mitigate these issues. You will also learn how to implement PCA, visualize high-dimensional data, and develop a basic understanding of other dimension reduction techniques like t-SNE and UMAP. This knowledge will equip you to handle complex, high-dimensional datasets more effectively in future data science endeavors.

Understanding the problem of high dimensionality

High-dimensional datasets, those with many features, might at first seem like a data scientist's dream, promising a wealth of information. However, they can quickly turn into a nightmare due to an issue known as the curse of dimensionality. This curse manifests in various ways, including increased computational complexity, overfitting, and reduced model performance. In this section, we will examine these challenges more closely, exploring why high dimensionality poses a problem and how it can affect our ability to carry out successful data analysis and modeling.

The curse of dimensionality

High dimensionality, at its core, refers to datasets with a large number of features or variables. While this may seem like a rich source of information for analysis, it can easily become a complex challenge, an effect known as the curse of dimensionality. This curse can transform what was initially an expedition into a treasure trove of data into a complex puzzle loaded with numerous obstacles and pitfalls.

One might ask, what makes high-dimensional data so challenging? Well, when we have many dimensions, our data points tend to spread out and become sparse. This dispersion can turn our data into a vast, empty space with observations thinly scattered about, making it difficult for algorithms to discern meaningful patterns or structures.

Additionally, as the number of features grows, so does the computational demand. This increase can significantly slow down the training process of our machine learning models. But it is not just about speed; the demand on computational resources can limit the complexity of the models we can use and the size of the datasets we can handle, restricting our exploration of the data.

Here is another pitfall on our trek: overfitting. With an abundance of features, our models might lean on irrelevant ones, crafting a complex narrative that fits the training data perfectly but fails to generalize to unseen data. This overcomplexity is like taking unnecessary detours on our hike, exhausting our resources without getting us closer to our destination.

Last but not least, high-dimensional data can also make our journey confusing. With a handful of features, it is easy to understand and visualize the relationships in our data. But when the dimensionality shoots up, mapping out these relationships becomes a formidable task.

While high-dimensionality presents some formidable hurdles, it also opens up a fascinating avenue of exploration. In the upcoming sections, we will uncover techniques to manage this high-dimensional complexity, including our main guide for this chapter: Principal component analysis. With the right tools, we can navigate the high-dimension maze and unearth valuable insights hidden in the data.

High-dimensionality at play: Encounters in the real world

Let us now walk into real-life scenarios where we encounter high-dimensional data, making this concept more tangible. This high-dimensional data encounter is ubiquitous, often unnoticed in our day-to-day interactions with technology.

Our first stop is a field that is seeing explosive growth: genomics. Genomics is the study of an organism's entire set of DNA, including all of its genes. Genomic datasets are intrinsically high-dimensional, with each gene representing a different dimension. In human genomes, we are talking about 20,000+ genes. Researchers use this high-dimensional data to identify genes responsible for diseases, a challenging but rewarding endeavor.

Next, we turn to text analysis. When dealing with a corpus of text, common practices like a bag of words or **Term Frequency-Inverse Document Frequency (TF IDF)** represent each unique word as a separate dimension. If you have ever dealt with textual data, you know that the number of unique words can skyrocket quickly, creating a high-dimensional data problem.

Stepping into the field of image recognition, we encounter another high-dimensional titan. Each pixel in an image is treated as a separate feature or dimension. Consider a modest-sized color image of 100x100 pixels. That is already 30,000 dimensions: 100 height pixels x 100 width pixels x 3 color channels (red, green, blue). And usually, the images we deal with are much larger than this.

Last but not least, customer behavior data also tends to be high-dimensional. Think about an e-commerce platform that collects data on customer demographics, browsing behavior, past purchases, and more. Each type of information represents a separate dimension. With the richness of data available, the feature space can easily extend into the hundreds, if not thousands.

High dimensionality is truly all around us, tucked into the corners of various fields. Recognizing it is the first step to managing it effectively and making the most of the valuable insights it can offer. So, armed with a deeper understanding of what high dimensionality looks like in practice, we can now move forward to explore how we can unravel this complexity with tools like PCA.

Tackling high-dimensional data

When faced with the challenges of high-dimensional data, we have several effective strategies to help us grapple with this complexity, each with its own trade-offs and best use cases.

The first strategy is **feature selection**, which involves identifying and using only the most important features for our model. This method can be highly effective, but it also requires a solid understanding of the dataset and the problem domain.

The second strategy, **feature extraction**, is where we create new, fewer features from combinations of the original ones. PCA, which we will delve into later in this chapter, is a classic example of feature extraction.

Data sampling is another strategy. We can take a representative sample of our data rather than using the entire dataset. This can simplify the computations and improve model performance, but there is also a risk of losing important information.

Dimension reduction techniques, which we will explore extensively in this chapter, can be another powerful way to handle high-dimensional data. These techniques can help us to compress the data, reducing the number of dimensions while retaining the most critical information.

Lastly, we have regularization methods that add constraints to the learning algorithms. This helps to manage high-dimensional data by discouraging complex models that are likely to overfit. These methods, such as **Lasso** and **Ridge regression**, add a penalty term to the loss function that increases as the complexity of the model increases.

These strategies, used alone or in combination, can help to demystify high-dimensional data and bring it within the reach of our analytical methods. As we move on to discussing specific techniques like PCA, keep in mind that these are all part of a broader toolkit for managing the curse of dimensionality.

Principal component analysis

PCA is a technique known for its versatility and simplicity. PCA is a statistical procedure that orthogonally transforms the original n coordinates of a data set into a new set of n coordinates known as **principal components**. This makes PCA a valuable tool when we are faced with data of high dimensionality. Over the next few sections, we will dissect the mathematical foundation of PCA, its applications, and how we can harness it to uncover the hidden structures within our data.

Decoding principal component analysis

At its core, PCA is a technique that simplifies the complexity of high-dimensional datasets while retaining their critical structure. Imagine having a vast dataset with hundreds, maybe thousands of variables. Analyzing and visualizing such a dataset can be a real challenge, not to mention the computation resources it demands. That is where PCA comes in.

It is like packing for a trip. You have a ton of clothes you would like to bring along, but your suitcase can only hold a few. PCA is the method used to decide which clothes are the most important to pack. Similarly, in data terms, PCA identifies the most significant directions in your data or the principal components where the variation in the data is the greatest.

But how does it do that? PCA performs a coordinate transformation, turning the original data dimensions into a set of linearly uncorrelated variables known as principal components. The first principal component accounts for the most variance, the second principal component (orthogonal to the first) accounts for the second most, and so on. By doing so, PCA allows you to focus on a few components instead of an entire high-dimensional dataset.

In a nutshell, PCA is like a data reduction superstar, allowing us to simplify complex high-dimensional data into a lower-dimensional form, making it easier to analyze, visualize, and model. It does this while still retaining as much of the essential information as possible.

Understanding PCA: The role of eigenvalues and eigenvectors

Let us dive a little deeper into the world of PCA and understand how it works its magic to reduce dimensionality. It is a thrilling journey that starts with our old friends from linear algebra: eigenvalues and eigenvectors.

Firstly, it is essential to consider the roles of eigenvalues and eigenvectors in this context. When PCA gets hold of your data, it calculates the covariance matrix of your dataset. Think of the covariance matrix as a way of understanding how different variables in your data relate to one another.

Once we have the covariance matrix, we can calculate the eigenvalues and eigenvectors. Eigenvalues tell us about the length or magnitude of the eigenvectors. Larger eigenvalues correspond to larger amounts of variation within the data along that eigenvector. Meanwhile, the eigenvectors represent directions in your data. They are unit vectors (having length 1) and are orthogonal (or perpendicular) to each other in the feature space.

The eigenvectors corresponding to the largest eigenvalues (the principal components) are the ones where the data varies the most. By selecting these eigenvectors, we can effectively reduce the dimensionality of our data.

Here is an analogy. Suppose you are an artist, and you have just finished a sculpture. You can look at it from several different angles, but only a few of those views capture the essence of your work. In the same way, PCA finds the essential views or directions (principal components) of your data, helping to reduce its dimensionality.

That is how PCA reduces dimensionality, all the way from eigenvalues to eigenvectors. It is like PCA paints a simpler picture of your data, capturing its essence without all the extra dimensions.

PCA in action: A step-by-step guide

Now that we have explored the foundations of PCA, it is time to see it in action. Here is a step-by-step guide to implementing PCA using Python and the sklearn library:

1. **Import the necessary libraries**

   Python's sklearn provides a straightforward PCA implementation, but we will also need NumPy for some numerical operations and matplotlib for visualizations. Use the following code:

   ```
   import numpy as np

   from sklearn.decomposition import PCA

   import matplotlib.pyplot as plt

   from sklearn.preprocessing import StandardScaler

   from sklearn.datasets import load_iris
   ```

2. **Prepare the data**

   For demonstrating PCA, let us go ahead with the Iris dataset. The data should be standardized such that each feature has a mean of 0 and a standard deviation of 1. Use the following code:

   ```
   # Loading the Iris dataset

   data = load_iris()

   X = data.data

   y = data.target

   labels = data.target_names


   # Standardizing the dataset

   scaler = StandardScaler()

   X_std = scaler.fit_transform(X)
   ```

3. **Perform PCA**

   We will initialize a PCA object and fit it to our standardized data. For this example, let us extract two principal components. Use the following code:

```
# Applying PCA and reducing to 2 components
pca = PCA(n_components=2)
principalComponents = pca.fit_transform(X_std)
```

4. **Analyze the results**

   The output **principalComponents** now holds the values for two principal components. You can explore these values, plot them, or use them in further analysis. Use the following code:

```
# Plotting the 2D data
plt.figure(figsize =(8, 6))

# Using different markers for different classes in the Iris dataset
markers = ['^', 's', 'o']
labels = ['Setosa', 'Versicolour', 'Virginica']

# Loop over the classes
for i, marker in zip(range(len(labels)), markers):
    plt.scatter(principalComponents[y == i, 0],
                principalComponents[y == i, 1],
                marker=marker,
                label=labels[i])

plt.xlabel('First Principal Component')
plt.ylabel('Second Principal Component')
plt.legend(loc="best")
plt.title("PCA of Iris Dataset")
plt.show()
```

The output is shown in the following figure:

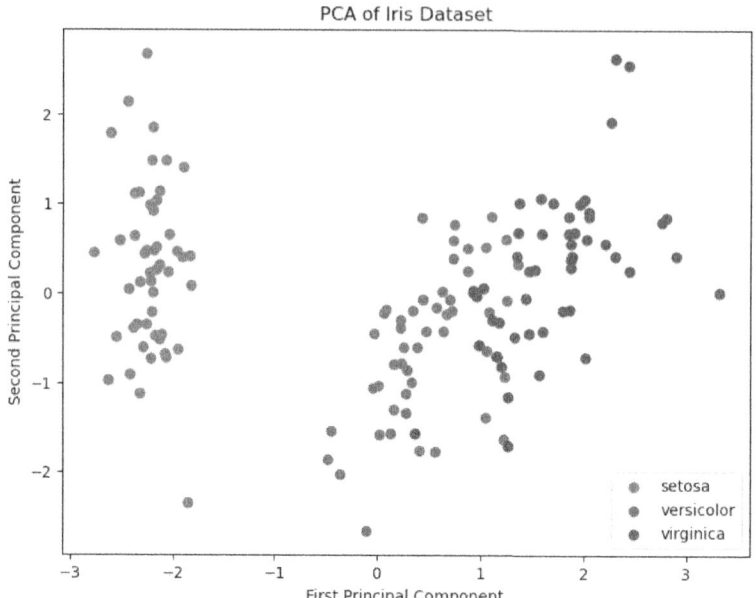

Figure 12.1: Visualization of PCA

5. **Evaluate the PCA**

A useful method to evaluate the PCA is to examine the explained variance ratio, which shows the amount of variance explained by each of the selected components. Use the following code:

```
print(pca.explained_variance_ratio_)
```

In this case, two values are given as output: **0.72962445** and **0.22850762**

That is a quick run-through of how you implement PCA in Python using sklearn. With this in your toolkit, you are ready to tackle the beast of high dimensionality.

Tuning into the right number of dimensions in PCA

Picking the right number of components in PCA is like tuning a radio to get the clearest signal. Too few, and you might miss out on important information; too many, and you might just be adding noise. So, how do we find that? Let us look at some handy methods:

- **The elbow method:** Suppose you are plotting the explained variance against the number of components: it is a bit like looking at a mountain slope. As you add more components, the amount of variance explained by the model increases. But after a certain point, this increase becomes marginal, and that is where you find your elbow, the point where adding more components does not give you a greater return on investment. It is a visual and intuitive method to pinpoint the right number of components. You will find more details about this method in *Chapter 13, Cluster Conquerors: Unsupervised Learning Adventures.*

- **Cumulative explained variance:** This method involves choosing the smallest number of components that still capture a good portion of the variance in your data. Set a threshold – say, 95% – and then select the minimum number of components needed to explain that percentage of the variance. It is like packing the most essential items until your suitcase is 95% full, ensuring that you have what you need but not burdening yourself with excess weight.

Both these methods have their charm. The elbow method gives you a visual and intuitive understanding, while the cumulative variance method is more systematic and quantitative. The key is to align your choice with your specific data and the goals of your analysis. It is a crucial step to ensure that your PCA model is both efficient and effective, providing clarity without sacrificing crucial insights.

Visualizing high-dimensional data

As we work our way through high-dimensional data, we often encounter the challenge of visualizing this information effectively. While we, as humans, are bound by three-dimensional understanding, our data is not. In this section, we will explore how we can visualize our high-dimensional data. This process not only provides us with insightful graphics but also helps us understand the underlying structure of our data and make better-informed decisions.

High dimensional data: Visualization techniques and challenges

Visualizing high-dimensional data is like being a cosmic explorer trying to make sense of a vast universe teeming with dimensions that go beyond the normal perception of space. This task is crucial as it not only provides insightful snapshots of our data galaxy but also helps identify patterns, trends, and anomalies that could get lost in the high-dimensional space.

However, it is not without its own unique set of challenges. High-dimensional data inherently defies our three-dimensional intuition, leading to issues in comprehending relationships, spotting clusters, and interpreting outliers. On top of this, real-world data often contains noise, missing values, and irrelevant dimensions, which further complicate the visualization process. Despite these challenges, visualization remains a powerful tool, serving as a bridge between high-dimensional data complexity and human cognitive capabilities.

Now, coming to the techniques, scatter plots are like the workhorse of high-dimensional data visualization, allowing us to perceive patterns in two or three dimensions. While they are straightforward, scatter plots become limited in effectively representing data as the number of dimensions increases beyond three. This limitation arises because scatter plots can only display data in two or three dimensions at a time, making it challenging to visualize and interpret relationships in datasets with more complex, multidimensional structures. This is where parallel coordinates come to the rescue. Think of them as multi-dimensional scatter plots that let you view all dimensions at once. Each axis represents a dimension, and data points are lines crossing these axes. This way, it helps to track individual data points across multiple dimensions.

Real-world high-dimensional data visualization

When we talk about high-dimensional data visualization, it is not about abstract mathematical concepts; it is about making real-world data accessible, understandable, and actionable. Let us consider some examples.

Suppose we are working with a health dataset, with hundreds of variables including patients' age, weight, blood pressure, and cholesterol levels. Visualizing this data in its original form would be impossible. But with PCA, we can reduce these hundreds of variables down to just a few principal components that capture the most important information. By plotting these components, we might be able to spot clusters that correspond to different health conditions.

Or consider a marketing dataset with information about customers' demographics, buying habits, browsing behaviour, and more. Again, trying to visualize this data in its raw form would be like trying to look at every star in the universe at once. But with PCA and other visualization techniques, we can highlight the features that matter most, perhaps identifying segments of customers with similar behaviors or spotting trends that could inform future marketing campaigns.

In these examples and many others, high-dimensional data visualization is not just a theoretical exercise but a practical tool that can lead to valuable insights. Remember, our aim here is not to see all dimensions at once but to understand the key patterns and relationships within our data.

Exploring beyond PCA: t-SNE and UMAP

While PCA is a powerful and commonly used technique for dimension reduction, it is far from the only tool in the box. The field of dimensionality reduction is rich and varied, with many techniques designed to address different challenges and use cases. In this section, we will introduce two additional methods that have gained popularity in recent years: t-SNE and UMAP. Each of these techniques has its unique strengths and considerations, offering new ways to simplify and explore high-dimensional data.

t-SNE unveiled: Functionality and use cases

Have you ever come across a situation where PCA just does not quite cut it for your visualization needs? If so, you might want to consider t-SNE. As a technique, t-SNE is particularly good at maintaining local relationships within your data, which makes it an excellent choice when you are dealing with complex or convoluted clusters.

Now, let us uncover how t-SNE actually works. In layman's terms, it calculates the similarity between points in a high-dimensional space and then maps these similarities to a lower-dimensional space, say 2D or 3D, for easy visualization. The t in t-SNE stands for t-distribution, which is used as the basis for creating this similarity-based map.

One key characteristic of t-SNE is that it tends to create well-separated clusters of points, which makes it highly valuable when working with data where distinct groups are present. On the other hand, you need to be aware that t-SNE might not always perfectly maintain the global structure of the data. It is a tool with a specific set of strengths and one that requires a considered and thoughtful approach to its use. But used well, t-SNE can be an extraordinary addition to your dimensionality reduction toolbox.

Unfolding the UMAP technique: Operation and best use scenarios

In our journey through the landscape of dimensionality reduction, we have now arrived at UMAP. UMAP is one of the newer kids on the block but has quickly garnered attention for its balance between speed and performance. But let us cut the jargon and understand what this technique does and when it is best used.

UMAP is a nonlinear dimensionality reduction technique similar to t-SNE but with some key differences. The underlying mathematics of UMAP are quite advanced, involving the concept of a manifold from topology, a branch of mathematics. To simplify it, UMAP, like t-SNE, also aims to preserve the local and global structure of the data when reducing dimensions. However, UMAP achieves this in a slightly different way, with the goal of creating a uniform representation of the data across different scales.

In practice, UMAP has a reputation for being faster than t-SNE, especially on larger datasets, and it also tends to preserve more of the global data structure. This makes it an excellent tool for tasks where understanding the overall relationships between clusters is important.

Like all techniques, UMAP is not a one-size-fits-all solution. It is essential to understand your data and your specific needs when choosing a dimensionality reduction technique. But in the right situations, UMAP can truly shine, providing valuable insights and helping uncover the underlying structure of complex, high-dimensional data.

PCA, t-SNE, and UMAP: A comparative analysis

As we have journeyed through the various dimension reduction techniques, you may have asked yourself, 'When should I use PCA, t-SNE, or UMAP?' Well, it is time we explore their unique strengths and limitations and see how they compare.

PCA, our oldest friend, is a linear method that works great when the data exhibits linear correlations and patterns. It is speedy, deterministic and preserves the global structure of the data, meaning it gives us a broad view of how data points relate to each other. However, its linearity can be a limitation when dealing with complex, non-linear data structures where the real story is not just a straight line.

t-SNE, which is a non-linear technique, excels at maintaining the local structure of data, meaning it keeps data points close together in the high-dimensional space and close together in the low-dimensional representation. This makes it fantastic for creating intuitive and interpretable visualizations. On the flip side, t-SNE is computationally intensive, particularly on large datasets, and it does not preserve the global structure of the data as well as PCA or UMAP. Moreover, it can provide different results with different runs due to its stochastic nature.

UMAP technique is a balance between PCA and t-SNE; it is nonlinear like t-SNE, so it is good at handling complex data structures, but it also preserves more of the global structure, similar to PCA. UMAP is also generally faster than t-SNE, making it a good choice for larger datasets. But remember, it is still relatively new and might not be as universally supported or understood as PCA.

In conclusion, the choice between PCA, t-SNE, and UMAP will depend on the nature of your data and what you want to achieve. If you need to maintain the broad structure of the data, PCA might be your best bet. If you are looking for more detailed, local structure and do not mind the computational intensity, t-SNE could be the way to go. And if you are after a balance between local and global structure, especially for large datasets, UMAP could be your star player.

Let us use the Iris dataset for a comparative visual analysis.

We will use scikit-learn for PCA and t-SNE, and **umap-learn** for UMAP. You can install u-map learn by running the following command in your Jupyter notebook:

```
!pip install umap-learn
```

Or you can run the following command in your terminal:

```
pip install umap-learn
```

Now, execute the following code:

```
# Re-importing the necessary libraries and re-loading the dataset since the
previous execution did not succeed.
```

```python
from sklearn.decomposition import PCA
from sklearn.manifold import TSNE
from sklearn.datasets import load_iris
import matplotlib.pyplot as plt
import umap

# Load Iris dataset again
iris = load_iris()
X = iris.data
y = iris.target

# PCA
pca = PCA(n_components=2)
X_pca = pca.fit_transform(X)

# t-SNE
tsne = TSNE(n_components=2, random_state=42)   # Set a random_state for
reproducibility
X_tsne = tsne.fit_transform(X)

# umap
reducer = umap.UMAP()
X_umap = reducer.fit_transform(X)

# Visualization
fig, axs = plt.subplots(1, 3, figsize=(20, 5))  # Adjust for 2 subplots

# Define markers and loop over each class for PCA plot
markers = ['o', 's', 'x'] # circle, square, diamond
for i, marker in zip(range(3), markers):
    axs[0].scatter(X_pca[y == i, 0], X_pca[y == i, 1], marker=marker)
axs[0].set_title('PCA')

# Repeat for t-SNE plot
for i, marker in zip(range(3), markers):
    axs[1].scatter(X_tsne[y == i, 0], X_tsne[y == i, 1], marker=marker)
axs[1].set_title('t-SNE')
```

```
# Repeat for UMAP
for i, marker in zip(range(3), markers):
    axs[2].scatter(X_umap[y == i, 0], X_umap[y == i, 1], marker=marker)
axs[2].set_title('UMAP')

# Save the figure
image_path = "iris_dimensionality_reduction_shapes.png"
plt.savefig(image_path)
plt.show()
```

The output is shown in the following figure:

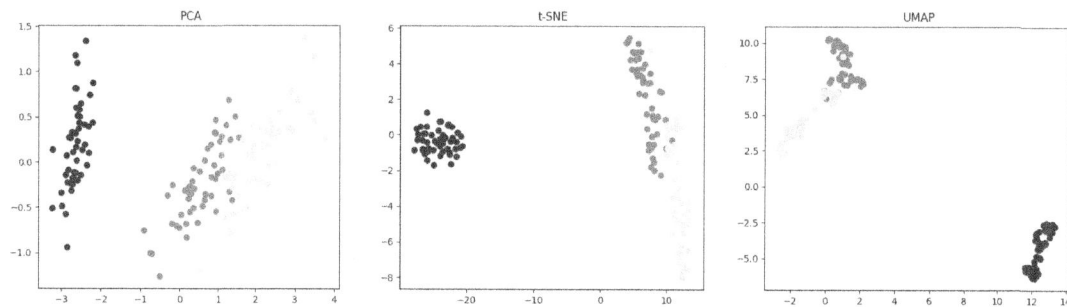

Figure 12.2: Visualization for PCA, t-SNE and UMAP

Conclusion

We have reached the end of our journey through the multidimensional maze. It has been a challenging hike, ascending through high-dimensional data and finding ways to navigate it all. By understanding and applying techniques like PCA, t-SNE, and UMAP, we have taken a significant step in making high-dimensional data more manageable and less daunting. These powerful tools allow us to simplify complex data while preserving crucial information, providing invaluable insights into our data's structure and relationships.

In the next chapter, we will learn more about text analytics and natural language processing.

Points to remember

- High-dimensional data, despite its challenges, is abundant in real-world scenarios. It is essential to understand the curse of dimensionality and its impact on our models.

- PCA is a powerful tool for reducing dimensionality and simplifying data without losing critical information. It transforms the original features into a set of linearly uncorrelated new principal components.

- Data visualization techniques, including PCA, are essential in understanding our data's underlying structure. Visualizing high-dimensional data can unveil patterns and relationships that might not be apparent in the raw data.

- Other dimension reduction techniques, like t-SNE and UMAP, have unique advantages and applications. They can sometimes provide better results than PCA, especially when dealing with complex, non-linear data.

Multiple choice questions

1. **What is the curse of dimensionality in the context of machine learning?**

    a. The phenomenon where machine learning models perform better with more features.

    b. The phenomenon where the volume of the feature space increases so fast that the available data becomes sparse.

    c. The phenomenon where adding more dimensions improves the visualization of the data.

    d. The phenomenon where reducing the dimensions of the data improves the performance of the model.

2. **Which of the following best describes PCA?**

    a. PCA is a data visualization technique for high-dimensional data.

    b. PCA is a clustering algorithm used in unsupervised learning.

    c. PCA is a dimension reduction technique that transforms the original variables into a new set of variables, which are linear combinations of the original variables.

    d. PCA is a type of neural network used for regression tasks.

3. **Which of the following is not a technique for dimension reduction?**

    a. principal component analysis

    b. t-SNE

    c. UMAP

    d. **Long Short-Term Memory (LSTM)**

4. **When might you prefer using t-SNE or UMAP over PCA for dimensionality reduction?**

   a. When the data is perfectly linear.

   b. When there is a lot of noise in the data.

   c. When the data contains non-linear relationships.

   d. When you have a small dataset.

Answers

1. b

2. c

3. d

4. c

Questions

1. Can you explain why high-dimensional data might pose a problem in machine learning?

2. How does PCA reduce the dimensionality of a dataset?

3. In what kind of scenarios would you prefer to use t-SNE or UMAP over PCA for dimensionality reduction?

Join our book's Discord space

Join the book's Discord Workspace for Latest updates, Offers, Tech happenings around the world, New Release and Sessions with the Authors:

https://discord.bpbonline.com

CHAPTER 13
Unlocking Unsupervised Learning

Introduction

Welcome to the fascinating world of unsupervised learning, where we venture to find hidden structures within the data, unsupervised and unguided. Clustering is one of the most widely used techniques in this domain, which helps group similar data points together. In this chapter, we will delve into some of the most popular clustering algorithms, such as K-means, hierarchical clustering, and DBSCAN. We will explore each technique in depth, understand its unique characteristics, limitations, and learn to evaluate and validate the resulting clusters.

Structure

In this chapter, we will discuss the following topics:

- K-means clustering
- Hierarchical clustering
- DBSCAN and other density-based methods
- Cluster evaluation and validation

Objectives

By the end of this chapter, you should have a comprehensive understanding of key clustering algorithms used in unsupervised learning. This includes K-means, hierarchical, and density-based clustering methods, each with their unique characteristics, strengths, and limitations. You will be proficient in choosing appropriate parameters for each algorithm, managing their constraints and understanding their applicability. Moreover, you will appreciate the importance of cluster validation and be familiarized to a range of internal and external validation indices. Furthermore, you will have the skills to apply these clustering methods to real-world datasets in Python and, more importantly, interpret the results to derive meaningful insights.

K-means clustering

As we embark on our journey into the world of unsupervised learning, let us start with one of the most popular and accessible clustering methods: K-means clustering. This algorithm is widely used due to its simplicity and efficiency in handling large datasets. At its core, K-means seeks to partition a dataset into distinct clusters where each data point belongs to the cluster with the nearest mean value. As we delve into the intricacies of K-means, we will uncover how it forms these clusters, its strengths and limitations, and its applications in real-world scenarios.

Exploring K-means: From principles to practice

This unsupervised learning method is about partitioning data into distinct groups or clusters. The K in K-means signifies the number of these clusters that you, as a data scientist, choose to create. But how does it determine what goes where? That is where the means part of the name comes in. It hints at the fact that this algorithm uses the mean value of the cluster's points to determine the cluster's center, the so-called centroid.

Let us get a closer look at its step-by-step process:

1. **Initialization:** Firstly, we choose the number of clusters, K. The algorithm then randomly picks K data points from the dataset. These are the initial centroids.

2. **Assignment:** Each data point in the dataset is assigned to the nearest centroid. This nearness is typically determined by calculating the Euclidean distance, though other distance metrics can also be used.

3. **Centroid update:** The centroids are recalculated by taking the mean of all data points in the cluster. Hence, each centroid moves according to its cluster members.

4. **Iteration:** Steps 2 and 3 are repeated until the centroids no longer change significantly or a certain number of iterations have been reached.

This simple and elegant process is widely applicable and extremely powerful, helping us make sense of the most sprawling and complex datasets. It is a true gem in the realm of unsupervised learning.

The enigma of optimal K

Selecting the number of clusters, k, in K-means is one of the trickiest parts. How many clusters?

K-means is like the **Goldilocks problem**. You do not want too many clusters; that is overkill. But too few, and you are oversimplifying your data. You want the number of clusters to be just right.

The most common method for this challenge is the elbow method. It involves running the K-means algorithm multiple times over a loop with an increasing number of cluster choices and then plotting a clustering score as a function of the number of clusters. The score could be **Within the Cluster Sum of Squares (WCSS)**, which we try to minimize. The point where the rate of decrease sharply shifts (the elbow of the plot) can be a good indication of the optimal number of clusters.

Another method is the silhouette method, which measures how similar a point is to its own cluster (cohesion) compared to other clusters (separation). The silhouette score ranges from 1 (a poor clustering) to +1 (a very dense clustering), with 0 denoting the situation where clusters overlap. There are some points to note, though; while a higher silhouette score is generally better, it does not favor clustering of a higher number.

Remember, these methods are more like guiding principles rather than hard-and-fast rules. They provide a good start but do not always lead to the best number of clusters. Sometimes, domain knowledge, the purpose of the analysis, or other factors can also influence the selection of the number of clusters.

So, while there is no foolproof method for choosing k, understanding your data, combined with these heuristic methods, can guide you toward a sensible choice. Remember, clustering is as much an art as it is a science.

Bringing K-means to life: A real-world clustering journey

Let us understand K-means clustering with a hands-on example. We will use the scikit-learn library, and we will use the Iris dataset, which comprises four measurements (sepal length, sepal width, petal length, and petal width) from three types of Iris flowers: a dataset you must be familiar with by now.

Let us start our journey by importing the necessary libraries and loading the dataset using the following code:

```python
from sklearn.cluster import KMeans
from sklearn.datasets import load_iris
import matplotlib.pyplot as plt

iris = load_iris()
X = iris.data
```

Now, let us find an optimal number of clusters using the **Elbow method**. Use the following code:

```python
wcss = []
for i in range(1, 11):
    kmeans = KMeans(n_clusters=i, init='k-means++', max_iter=300, n_init=10, random_state=0)
    kmeans.fit(X)
    wcss.append(kmeans.inertia_)

plt.plot(range(1, 11), wcss)
plt.title('The Elbow Method')
plt.xlabel('Number of clusters')
plt.ylabel('WCSS')
plt.show()
```

The output is shown in the following figure:

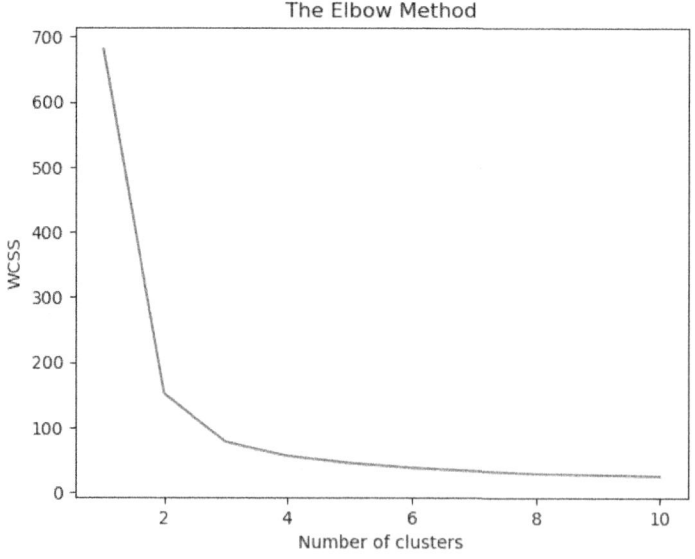

Figure 13.1: Elbow method on the Iris dataset

You will notice that the optimal number of clusters is at the elbow point in the plot, which, as you can see in *Figure 13.1*, is 3 in this dataset.

Now, armed with the optimal k, we are ready to perform the actual K-means clustering. Execute the following code:

```
kmeans = KMeans(n_clusters=3, init='k-means++', max_iter=300, n_init=10,
random_state=0)
pred_y = kmeans.fit_predict(X)
```

Let us visualize the clusters along with their centroids using the following code:

```
plt.scatter(X[pred_y == 0, 0], X[pred_y == 0, 1], s=100, marker='^', label
='Cluster 1')
plt.scatter(X[pred_y == 1, 0], X[pred_y == 1, 1], s=100, marker='s', label
='Cluster 2')
plt.scatter(X[pred_y == 2, 0], X[pred_y == 2, 1], s=100, marker='o', label
='Cluster 3')
plt.scatter(kmeans.cluster_centers_[:, 0], kmeans.cluster_centers_[:, 1],
s=300, marker='*', c='yellow', label = 'Centroids')
plt.title('Clusters of Iris')
plt.legend()
plt.show()
```

The output is shown in the following figure:

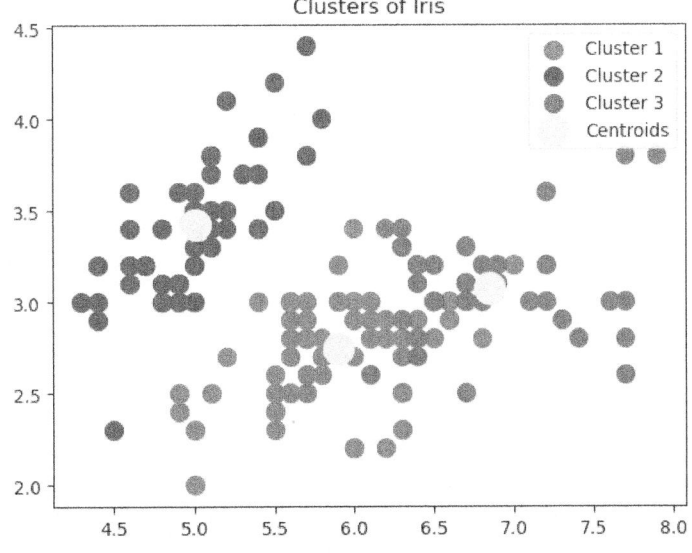

Figure 13.2: Iris dataset clusters

You have just experienced the journey of K-means clustering in action. Note how the clusters are formed and how each centroid, marked in yellow, signifies the heart of each cluster. Now, you are ready to conquer clustering with K-means in your **Machine Learning (ML)** quests.

Hierarchical clustering

Let us shift our gears and dive into the world of hierarchical clustering, a different yet powerful clustering technique. Unlike K-means, which partitions the data into separate clusters, hierarchical clustering creates a tree-like model of data, visualized as a dendrogram. This approach allows us to not only witness the clusters but also understand the hierarchy and relationships between them. Whether we are dealing with gene-level data or social network analysis, hierarchical clustering helps us paint a vivid picture of the complex relationships that exist within our data.

Intricacies of hierarchical clustering

Hierarchical clustering is a compelling method in unsupervised learning that gives us a comprehensive view of our data. Unlike the flat clustering methods like K-means, which partition the data into distinct clusters in one step, hierarchical clustering allows us to infer the data's structure over multiple levels of granularity. This added dimension of depth makes it an invaluable tool in our data scientist's toolkit.

Hierarchical clustering works on two essential principles: agglomerative, which is a bottom-up approach, and divisive, which is a top-down approach. They each provide different views of the data and its inherent structures.

Let us start with the agglomerative approach: it considers each data point as an individual cluster at the outset. It then sequentially links these singleton clusters into larger clusters based on the similarity between data points. The process continues iteratively, creating a multi-tier hierarchy until all points are merged into a single cluster at the top of the hierarchy. One common strategy for measuring this similarity is the average linkage method, which considers the average distances between all pairs of observations in the two clusters.

On the flip side, the divisive method starts with a single cluster that encompasses all data points. It then splits the cluster into smaller ones, moving down the hierarchy until each data point forms an individual cluster. The choice of how to split a cluster is generally based on minimizing a given objective function.

An important aspect of hierarchical clustering is the dendrogram, a tree-like diagram that records the sequences of merges or splits. This visualization tool not only shows the final clusters but also beautifully portrays their hierarchical relationships.

However, hierarchical clustering is not without its challenges. One key issue is that once a merge or split is done, it can never be undone. This greedy localization can lead to sub-optimal results. Also, the algorithm can be computationally intensive for large datasets, which can be a limiting factor.

The choice between the agglomerative and divisive strategies, and indeed whether to use hierarchical clustering at all, will depend largely on the nature of the data and the specific objectives of the analysis. However, when the conditions are right, hierarchical clustering can provide insights that might be difficult to achieve with other methods.

Hierarchical clustering: Exploring linkage criteria

When we talk about hierarchical clustering, a critical concept that comes into play is the linkage criterion. The linkage criterion determines how the distance between clusters is measured, which, in turn, influences the shape of the clusters and the hierarchical structure of the dendrogram. There are several different linkage criteria, each with its own strengths and considerations. Let us delve into four common ones: single, complete, average, and ward's method:

- **Single linkage:** Also known as the nearest point algorithm, single linkage measures the shortest distance between clusters, that is, the distance between the closest pair of data points or where one point is from each cluster. Single linkage can result in clusters that are long and loose, extending toward other clusters.

- **Complete linkage:** Also known as the farthest point algorithm, complete linkage takes the opposite approach to single linkage. It measures the longest distance between clusters, that is, the distance between the farthest pair of data points, or again, where one point is from each cluster. This method results in more compact clusters, but they may not always be spherical.

- **Average linkage:** This method takes a balanced approach, calculating the average of the distances between all pairs of data points in two clusters. By taking into account all these distances, average linkage tends to create clusters that are reasonably compact and well separated.

- **Ward's method:** This method is slightly different. Instead of focusing on distances between individual data points, it looks at the total variance within clusters. At each step, it merges the clusters that will result in the smallest increase in total within-cluster variance. This method often produces compact, spherical clusters.

Choosing the appropriate linkage method depends heavily on the dataset and the specific requirements of your task. It is often a good idea to try different methods and evaluate their results.

Understanding DBSCAN: A comprehensive guide

Dendrograms are a crucial part of hierarchical clustering, offering a visual representation of the clustering process that can provide valuable insights into the structure of your data. But to fully leverage their power, you need to know how to read and interpret them. So, let us demystify dendrograms.

At its most basic, a dendrogram is a tree-like diagram where each leaf represents a data point, and the branches represent the linkages between them based on their similarity. The root of the tree represents the final single cluster that includes all data points. Here is how to decipher it:

- **Branch lengths:** The lengths of the branches in a dendrogram represent the distance (or dissimilarity) between clusters or data points. Longer branches mean greater dissimilarity.

- **Linkage point:** When two branches merge, they form a new branch. The height of this new branch (that is, the point where the link occurs) corresponds to the distance between the two clusters at the time of merging. A higher linkage point indicates that the clusters are quite different, while a lower linkage point suggests the clusters are very similar.

- **Clusters:** Cutting the dendrogram at a specific height gives us our clusters. All the branches (and the leaves connected to them) below the cut become separate clusters.

When it comes to interpretation, dendrograms can help you identify the number of clusters in your data by observing where large jumps in the merging distances occur; these jumps often suggest a natural cluster structure. They also show how well separated your clusters are. They can reveal hierarchical relationships within the data, such as whether one cluster can be seen as a super-cluster of several smaller clusters.

In essence, dendrograms are a powerful tool for understanding your data, guiding the clustering process, and communicating your results. As with all visualizations, though, it is important to approach them with a critical eye and consider the context and the specifics of your analysis.

Navigating the dendrogram: Hierarchical clustering in action

When dealing with hierarchical clustering, theory only gets us so far; seeing it in action is where the real learning happens. Let us explore a practical example that illustrates how hierarchical clustering works, again, using the iris dataset:

```
# Import necessary libraries
from sklearn.datasets import load_iris
from sklearn.preprocessing import StandardScaler
from scipy.cluster.hierarchy import dendrogram, linkage
from matplotlib import pyplot as plt

# Load the iris dataset
iris = load_iris()
X = iris.data

# Standardize the features for better results
scaler = StandardScaler()
X_scaled = scaler.fit_transform(X)

# Perform hierarchical clustering
linked = linkage(X_scaled, 'ward')

# Plot the dendrogram
plt.figure(figsize=(10, 7))
dendrogram(linked,
           orientation='top',
           distance_sort='descending',
           show_leaf_counts=True)
plt.show()
```

The output is shown in the following figure:

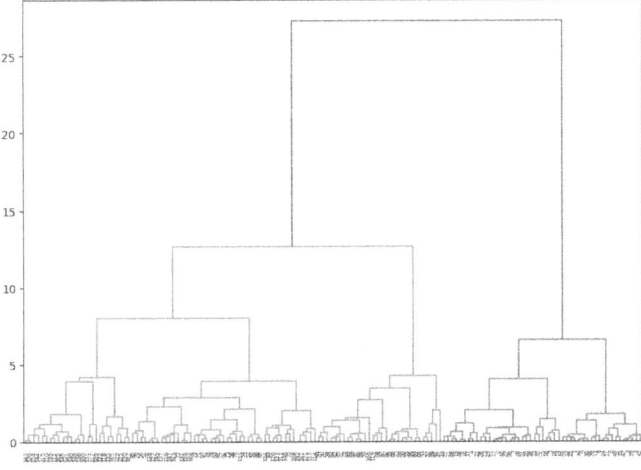

Figure 13.3: Hierarchical clustering

Let us break down what this particular dendrogram (refer to *Figure 13.3*) reveals:

- **Cluster separation**: The dendrogram displays how the clustering algorithm progressively merges data points into clusters. Here, we see three distinct vertical lines above the rest, suggesting that there are three primary clusters within the data. Given our knowledge of the Iris dataset, it is reasonable to deduce that these three clusters may correspond to the three species of Iris flowers.

- **Height of merges:** The vertical lines represent the hierarchical merging of clusters. Their height indicates the distance or dissimilarity at which clusters were merged. A taller line suggests that the clusters merged at that point had a greater dissimilarity. In this dendrogram, the tallest vertical line (in blue) separates one large cluster from two closer clusters (in orange and green).

- **Determining the number of clusters:** An elbow, or a significant jump in the height of the vertical lines, can help determine the number of clusters. If we were to draw a horizontal line (known as a **cut-off threshold**) just below the height of the tallest line, we would cut across three vertical lines, reinforcing the idea of three clusters.

- **Leaf counts:** Each leaf at the bottom represents an individual sample from the dataset. Leaves that are grouped together at the lower part of the dendrogram are more similar to each other. The numbers at the bottom indicate the number of samples in each final cluster when the dendrogram is cut at a certain threshold.

By examining this dendrogram, one can conclude that the Iris dataset has one species that is distinctly different from the other two (indicated by the blue line), and the other two species are more similar to each other but still distinct (as indicated by the orange and green lines). This aligns with the scientific understanding that Iris setosa is generally more distinct from Iris versicolor and Iris virginica, which are more similar to each other but can still be separated based on specific features.

DBSCAN and other density-based methods

In the vast landscape of clustering techniques, density-based methods stand out for their unique approach. One of the most renowned members of this family is DBSCAN, which is an acronym for density-based spatial clustering of applications with noise. Unlike K-means or hierarchical clustering, DBSCAN does not require us to specify the number of clusters upfront and is particularly adept at identifying noise and discovering clusters of any shape. As we delve into this section, we will unmask the mechanics of DBSCAN, explore other density-based clustering methods, and see how they tackle real-world problems.

DBSCAN clustering: Unveiling its unique approach

In the ocean of clustering algorithms, DBSCAN stands apart with its distinctive methodology. While other techniques, such as K-means or hierarchical clustering, focus on distance or linkage, DBSCAN defines clusters based on dense regions of data points, thereby bringing a fresh perspective to unsupervised learning.

When you consider K-means or hierarchical clustering, you will notice they rely heavily on centroid distances or tree structures, often requiring us to specify the number of clusters in advance. However, DBSCAN operates on a different premise. It identifies clusters as high-density regions separated by areas of low density, freeing us from determining the number of clusters beforehand.

But how does DBSCAN achieve this? The secret lies in its concept of core points, border points, and noise.

DBSCAN is guided by two main parameters: **epsilon (eps)** and **minimum points (MinPts)**. Here, epsilon marks the maximum radius of the neighborhood around a data point, and MinPts is the minimum number of data points needed in a neighborhood to define a cluster. Now, if a point has at least MinPts within its epsilon neighborhood, we have a core point, the backbone of any cluster.

Border points are the next piece of our clustering puzzle. While these points are part of a cluster, they do not meet the criteria to be core points. Although they are within an epsilon distance of a core point, they themselves do not have the MinPts within their epsilon neighborhood.

Lastly, we encounter noise or outlier points, which are not part of any cluster. These are the lone wolves, distant from both core and border points, as they neither fall within the epsilon radius of a core point nor satisfy the MinPts requirement.

The beauty of DBSCAN is that it takes a simple approach to form clusters. It first pinpoints all core points and assigns distinct clusters to each. Then, it brings in the border points, assigning each to the cluster of its nearest core point. Noise points, on the other hand, are left unassigned, often representing outliers in our data.

By offering a unique take on cluster formation, DBSCAN brings added depth to our understanding of unsupervised learning. The interplay of core points, border points, and noise not only distinguishes DBSCAN from its peers but also makes it an appealing choice for many real-world applications.

Tuning DBSCAN

DBSCAN is a powerful clustering algorithm that automatically determines the number of clusters based on the data. However, its performance is heavily dependent on its two main parameters: eps and MinPts. Selecting the appropriate values for these parameters is vital for the algorithm to work effectively, and in this section, we will delve into how you can tune these parameters for optimal results.

The eps parameter is the maximum distance allowed between two samples for them to be considered in the same neighborhood. If we choose a very small value for eps, most of the data will not be clustered at all (it will be labeled as noise). On the other hand, a very large value might result in all data points belonging to the same cluster. An optimal eps can be determined based on the knowledge of the data and by using techniques like k-distance graph, where the average distances to the k nearest neighbors are plotted for each point in ascending order. A significant bend in the graph (also known as an **elbow**) can indicate a good eps value.

The MinPts parameter defines the minimum number of samples needed in a neighborhood for a data point to qualify as a core point. Its selection largely depends on the density of the dataset. Generally, a larger dataset would require a larger MinPts value. A low MinPts means that noise points that are close to a cluster will be included in the cluster, making the clusters fuzzy. A high value means that only areas of high density are considered as clusters. As a rule of thumb, a minimum MinPts can be derived from the number of dimensions D in the data set, as $MinPts \geq D + 1$.

In conclusion, tuning DBSCAN involves striking a balance between sensitivity to cluster size (through eps) and robustness to noise (through MinPts). It is a matter of understanding your data and using a bit of trial and error.

Putting DBSCAN into action

Let us use the evergreen Iris dataset again to demonstrate **DBSCAN** in the real world using the following code:

```
from sklearn.cluster import DBSCAN
from sklearn import datasets

# Load Iris data
iris = datasets.load_iris()
X = iris.data

# Apply DBSCAN
DBSCAN = DBSCAN(eps=0.5, min_samples=5)
clusters = DBSCAN.fit_predict(X)

print("DBSCAN cluster labels: ", clusters)
```

In this example, we used an **epsilon (eps)** of **0.5** and a minimum number of samples (**min_samples**) of **5**, which are fairly common initial values for these parameters. However, remember that these values might need to be adjusted depending on the specificities of different datasets.

This example should give you a feel for how DBSCAN can be applied in practice. Feel free to experiment with different datasets and parameters to understand how DBSCAN performs under various circumstances.

Cluster evaluation and validation

Talking about clustering algorithms and applying them in practice can be quite an adventure. But how do we know we have done a good job? The importance of cluster evaluation and validation cannot be overstated in unsupervised learning. This section unfolds the mystery behind evaluating the quality of the clusters formed, helping you understand how well your model has performed and whether the clusters make sense.

Importance of cluster validation

As we journey further into unsupervised learning, we come across a fundamental question: Why do we need to validate clusters? To put it simply, cluster validation helps us gauge the reliability and quality of our formed clusters.

Clustering is an exploratory technique that aims to discover hidden structures or groupings in data. However, without a validation step, we risk forming clusters that might not have any real meaning, significance, or usefulness. This is especially important because, unlike supervised learning, we do not have a ground truth or target variable to check our results against.

Furthermore, different clustering algorithms or even different parameters in the same algorithm can lead to different clustering outcomes. Cluster validation helps us compare these different outcomes and select the one that best suits our data and purpose.

Another essential aspect is the impact of the dimensionality of the data. High-dimensional data can often lead to spurious clusters that exist just because of the high dimensionality and not because there is any meaningful grouping in the data. Cluster validation techniques can help detect such scenarios.

Validating our clusters ensures that we are not just seeing patterns due to randomness or chance. Instead, we are capturing the underlying and often hidden structures in the data that can provide meaningful insights, maximizing the value of our unsupervised learning efforts.

Cluster validation with internal indices

Cluster validation measures, also known as **validation indices**, come in two types: internal and external. As we proceed, let us focus on internal validation indices, which evaluate the goodness of a clustering structure without reference to external information.

Our first stop is the silhouette score. Think of the silhouette score as a way of measuring how well each instance lies within its cluster. It gives a score of between -1 and 1, where a higher value indicates that the instance is well matched to its own cluster and poorly matched to its neighboring clusters. If most instances have a high score, then the clustering configuration is appropriate.

Next, let us consider the **Dunn index**. Here is an analogy to understand it better: If the silhouette score is a measure of a student's fit in their group, the Dunn index would be the ratio of the size of the smallest group to the distance between groups. A higher Dunn index is desirable as it signifies denser, well-separated clusters.

While the silhouette score and Dunn index are the more common ones, there are numerous other internal validation indices, like the **Davies-Bouldin index** or the **Calinski-Harabasz index**. Each of these indices has its own strengths and weaknesses, and the choice often depends on the data and the specific requirements of the task at hand.

Cluster validation with external indices

Just as we embraced the internal validation indices, let us now turn our attention to their counterparts: the external validation indices. Unlike internal indices, these scores require knowledge of the ground truth labels. They assess how the clusters discovered by our algorithms match the actual groups in the data.

One classic example of an external validation index is the Rand index, named after its creator, *William Rand*. This index assesses the similarity between two sets of data clusters. It does so by examining all pairs of samples, and counts how many are assigned to the same or to different clusters in both the predicted and actual clustering results. The Rand index provides a score ranging from 0 to 1, with 1 indicating a perfect match between the two sets of clusters.

The Jaccard coefficient, on the other hand, is a measure of the overlap between two sets. In the context of clustering, it gauges the similarity between the predicted clusters and the actual classes by taking the intersection (the common members) of the two sets divided by their union (all members). Just like the Rand index, a higher Jaccard coefficient is a sign of better clustering.

While these two indices are widely used, there are also others, like the **Fowlkes-Mallows index** or the **Adjusted Rand index**, each offering a different perspective on the quality of the clustering. Remember, though, that these indices are not a one-size-fits-all solution. They serve as a guide and should be used with your knowledge of the data and the problem at hand. After all, machine learning is not just about algorithms and data; it is about understanding and intuition too.

Ensuring robust clusters with stability-based validation

When measuring the quality of clustering algorithms, stability-based validation methods have their unique place. Stability, in the context of clustering, refers to the algorithm's ability to produce similar results when applied multiple times on slightly perturbed versions of the same dataset.

Here is how it works. We create multiple subsets of the data by resampling and then run our clustering algorithm on each subset. If our clusters are stable, we should be getting similar clustering results across these subsets.

One key aspect to keep an eye on is the stability measure. This can be anything from simple similarity metrics such as Jaccard index to more sophisticated measures such as variation of information or normalized mutual information. The idea is the same: If the clustering results from different subsets are similar, the stability measure will be high, indicating a stable and reliable clustering.

But wait, there is a catch. This method assumes that our data contains genuine clusters. If this is not the case, we might achieve high stability for the wrong number of clusters. This is where domain knowledge comes into play, guiding us in our quest to uncover the underlying structure of the data.

In conclusion, stability-based validation methods are an essential part of our clustering toolbox, complementing other internal and external validation indices. They not only give us a measure of quality but also a sense of reliability, helping us build robust and trustworthy machine learning models.

Demonstrating cluster evaluation and validation

As we discussed, an integral part of any machine learning workflow, including clustering, is assessing the performance of your model. But it can be a bit abstract to think about silhouette scores or Rand indexes without seeing them in action. Let us take a look at how to apply these validation methods in practice using Python's popular scikit-learn library.

Suppose we have performed K-means clustering on our dataset and want to evaluate the quality of our clusters. For simplicity, let us say we have a 2D array X representing our data and a list of labels representing the cluster assignments of each data point.

To compute the silhouette score, we can use the **silhouette_score** function; consider the following code:

```
from sklearn.metrics import import silhouette_score

# Assuming labels are the predicted cluster labels from our KMeans model
sil_score = silhouette_score(X, labels)
print(f'Silhouette Score: {sil_score}')
```

The silhouette score ranges from -1 to +1, with higher values indicating that samples are well matched to their own clusters and poorly matched to neighboring clusters.

If we have the true labels of our data points (which is often not the case in unsupervised learning, but just for the sake of an example), we can also compute the Rand index or Jaccard coefficient. Use the following code:

```
from sklearn.metrics import jaccard_score

# Assuming true_labels are the true labels
jac_score = jaccard_score(true_labels, labels, average='micro')
print(f'Jaccard Coefficient: {jac_score}')
```

The Jaccard coefficient, or Jaccard similarity index, measures the similarity between the true labels and the predicted labels. A score of 1.0 indicates a perfect match.

It is also important to note that validation measures should not be used in isolation. Instead, they should be part of a more comprehensive evaluation strategy, considering the problem context, the data properties, and other practical considerations. And remember, a model is only as good as its ability to perform on unseen data.

Conclusion

In this journey through the landscapes of unsupervised learning, we navigated the terrain of different clustering techniques. We discussed K-means, hierarchical clustering, and DBSCAN, highlighting the unique strengths and applications. But we did not stop at merely learning these techniques; we also emphasized the importance of evaluation and validation, illuminating different ways to assess cluster quality and the reliability of our models. As we continue our exploration of the vast machine learning realm, let us carry forward the core principles of these unsupervised learning techniques, applying them when we encounter similar scenarios in our data science adventures.

In the next chapter, we will learn about the recommender system.

Points to remember

- Clustering is an unsupervised learning technique used to categorize data points into groups or clusters, where points in the same cluster are more similar to each other than to points in other clusters.

- K-means clustering is based on the principle of minimizing the within-cluster sum of squares. It is simple and efficient but requires the number of clusters to be specified upfront and may be sensitive to initialization and outliers.

- Hierarchical clustering builds a tree-like model of clusters, which can be visualized with a dendrogram, enabling an intuitive understanding of the cluster relationships. It can produce clusters of various sizes and shapes, but it can be more computationally intensive than K-means.

- Density-based clustering methods, such as DBSCAN, create clusters based on areas of high density separated by low density areas. They can find arbitrary-shaped clusters and handle noise, but choosing the appropriate parameters can be challenging.

- Evaluating and validating clusters is crucial in clustering analysis. Internal validation indices, such as the silhouette score, measure the compactness and separation of the clusters, while external validation indices, such as the Rand index or Jaccard coefficient, compare the clustering result with known ground truth. Stability-based validation methods aim to measure the consistency of clustering results under perturbations of the data.

Multiple choice questions

1. **Which of the following best describes the K-means clustering algorithm?**

    a. It groups data points based on a pre-determined number of clusters.

    b. It organizes data into a tree-like structure.

    c. It clusters data based on areas of high density separated by areas of low density.

    d. It groups data points based on the label of the data.

2. **In the context of DBSCAN clustering, what are core points, border points, and noise?**

    a. Core points are in high-density regions, border points are on the edges of these regions, and noise are outliers.

    b. Core points are outliers, border points are in high-density regions, and noise are in low-density regions.

    c. Core points are on the edges of high-density regions, border points are in the middle of these regions, and noise are in low-density regions.

    d. Core points, border points, and noise all refer to the same type of data points in a cluster.

3. **Which of the following methods would you use to determine the optimal number of clusters in K-means clustering?**

    a. Jaccard coefficient

    b. Rand index

    c. Silhouette score

    d. Dunn index

4. **What is a dendrogram in the context of hierarchical clustering?**

    a. A chart showing the optimal number of clusters.

    b. A tree-like diagram illustrating the arrangement of the clusters.

      c. A graph displaying the density of the clusters.

      d. A plot showing the locations of the cluster centers.

Answers

    1. a

    2. a

    3. c

    4. b

Questions

    1. What are some advantages and disadvantages of K-means clustering as compared to hierarchical clustering?

    2. What is the difference between internal and external validation indices when evaluating the quality of clusters?

    3. How does DBSCAN clustering handle noise in the dataset, and how does this compare to the handling of noise in K-means and hierarchical clustering?

Join our book's Discord space

Join the book's Discord Workspace for Latest updates, Offers, Tech happenings around the world, New Release and Sessions with the Authors:

https://discord.bpbonline.com

## CHAPTER 14

The Essence of Neural Networks and Deep Learning

Introduction

Deep learning, a subset of **Machine Learning (ML)**, is akin to a magic wand that has transformed countless fields, including image recognition, **Natural Language Processing (NLP)** and even healthcare. At the heart of deep learning are neural networks, which are inspired by the human brain's neural architecture. In this chapter, we will start by understanding what deep learning is all about and how it differs from its counterpart, shallow learning. We will then introduce you to the spellbooks of deep learning wizards, TensorFlow, Keras, and PyTorch, which are among the most powerful libraries for building neural networks. We will further dive into the depths of **artificial neural networks (ANNs)**, **convolutional neural networks (CNNs)**, and **recurrent neural networks (RNNs)**, including the mighty **long short-term memory networks (LSTMs)**. Along the way, we will cover activation functions, backpropagation, and various neural network architectures.

Structure

In this chapter, we will discuss the following topics:

- Deep learning: Beyond conventional machine learning
- Deep learning as artificial intelligence's game changer
- Data and processing power

- Introduction to deep learning libraries

- The intricate web of artificial neural networks

- Importance of data and feature engineering in deep learning

- Feature crafting versus self-learning

- Overfitting: A deep learning perspective

- Convolutional neural networks

- Recurrent neural networks

- Long short-term memory networks

Objectives

By the end of this chapter, you should have gained a strong foundation in deep learning and neural networks. You should be proficient in differentiating between shallow learning and deep learning. Also, you should understand the key role that neural networks play in deep learning. We will also empower you with the knowledge and practice of TensorFlow, Keras, and PyTorch, which are essential tools in any deep learning magician's arsenal. You should understand the fundamental concepts and architectures of ANNs, CNNs, and RNNs and how they can be trained and optimized once you have completed the chapter. Through hands-on exercises and practical examples, you will learn how to wield these tools and techniques to conjure powerful deep learning models capable of solving complex real-world problems. Prepare to become a deep learning conjurer, adept at crafting intelligent systems to learn from and make predictions or decisions based on data.

Deep learning: Beyond conventional machine learning

Let us play a game of imagination: Suppose you have found a magical book in your attic. It is old and dusty, but as you open it, you realize that it contains spells to create enchanted forests, conjure dragons, and pretty much create a world akin to the mystical realms you have read about in fiction. Well, folks, deep learning is like that book for the realms of **Artificial Intelligence (AI)**. It allows computers to create worlds far beyond what traditional machine learning can muster.

Traditional machine learning is like planting a sapling, tending to it, and watching it grow into a tree. It is simple, it is neat, and it does the job. Deep learning is more like planting a seed that sprouts into a dense forest with layers of interconnected trees and wildlife. You see, deep learning is a subset of machine learning that deals with algorithms inspired by the structure and function of the human brain, called artificial neural networks.

Deep learning takes these neural networks to the next level. It lets them tackle complex problems, like recognizing objects in images, understanding natural language, and even mastering games like chess and Go, stuff that traditional machine learning can only dream about.

Sure, traditional machine learning has its perks. It is less computationally intensive, sometimes easier to understand, and often requires less data. Deep learning is reserved for more challenging tasks that require significant computational power. It is not merely an extension of machine learning but an advancement that enables a higher level of data interpretation and problem-solving.

Deep learning as artificial intelligence's game changer

Deep learning helps computers to mimic the human brain's ability to learn from experience. This is why it is a core component of AI. It allows machines to recognize patterns and make decisions like humans. It is like giving the machine a brain, albeit one that runs on electricity.

Deep learning algorithms are the backbone of the AI renaissance. They are why Siri can understand your requests, why self-driving cars are becoming a reality, and how Facebook can automatically tag your friends in photos. This technology is not just for Silicon Valley elites; it is everywhere, from healthcare institutions diagnosing diseases to financial institutions detecting fraud.

As computing power increases and datasets become even more massive, deep learning will take us to new horizons. We are discussing AI companions, automated cities, and solving humanity's biggest mysteries. Deep learning is not just a tool, and it is an adventure, an ongoing quest that might as well define our future.

Data and processing power

Think of deep learning models as insatiable creatures with a bottomless appetite for data. The more they consume, the smarter they become. They seem never to get enough, always yearning for more and more data. Like gourmet chefs trying to perfect a recipe, they need an array of ingredients to make sure everything is just right.

They need more than just heaps of data. They require a high-performance kitchen to process all the ingredients. This is where computational power enters the picture. Deep learning involves layers upon layers of calculations; this is no job for your everyday calculator.

Now, let us talk about GPUs, the lightning-fast processors that are indispensable in deep learning. Consider a processor that is built for speed and can handle multiple tasks simultaneously. That is what a GPU is in comparison to a regular CPU. They are like the top-of-the-line kitchen gadgets that chefs dream of, able to slice and dice through calculations at astonishing speeds.

Combining an endless stream of data with the blistering pace of GPU processing, deep learning models can construct incredibly sophisticated representations and predictions. They are like master artisans, sculpting and refining their creations until they are nothing short of masterpieces.

In a nutshell, deep learning needs two key ingredients for success: a treasure trove of data to learn from and the computational might to process it all. It is this dynamic duo that makes waves in the AI world, transforming industries from healthcare to automotive. Whether it is recognizing images, understanding speech, or predicting trends, deep learning is at the forefront, and it is hungry for data and speed.

Transformative applications of deep learning in the modern world

Deep learning is like a swiss army knife in the world of AI: versatile, powerful, and indispensable. From sifting through medical data to help diagnose diseases to mastering video games, deep learning is the superstar everyone wants on their team. Let us embark on an exploration of the incredible ways in which this technology is reshaping industries and lives:

- **Healthcare: A healer in disguise**

  In the medical field, deep learning is like a highly skilled diagnostician. With the ability to sift through medical images, deep learning models can identify patterns and anomalies that might be missed by the human eye. Whether it is detecting tumors in X-rays or monitoring the vital signs of patients in ICUs, deep learning is revolutionizing healthcare by providing early diagnosis and personalized treatment plans.

- **Autonomous vehicles: Taking the wheel**

  Imagine sitting back and relaxing while your car drives you to your destination. Autonomous vehicles are no longer a sci-fi dream. Deep learning is in the driver's seat, navigating through traffic, obeying traffic signals, and making real-time decisions. These vehicles learn to understand and interpret the world around them through an array of sensors and cameras.

- **Natural language processing: Conversing with machines**

  From chatbots to virtual assistants, deep learning is making machines more conversational. **NLP** is a subfield of AI, which is empowered by deep learning to analyze and generate human language. Next time you ask your smartphone for the weather or chat with customer support online, know that you are interacting with a deep learning model.

- **Personalized recommendations: Tailored with care**

  Remember when you last binged a TV series or shopped online? There is a high probability that deep learning played a matchmaker. Recommendation engines use deep learning to analyze your preferences and behavior. Like a personal concierge, they curate content and products tailored to your tastes.

- **Facial recognition: Identifying in the crowd**

  Deep learning models can scan through a sea of faces and pinpoint individuals with astonishing accuracy. From unlocking your smartphone to enhancing security systems, facial recognition is deeply woven into our daily lives.

- **Creative AI: The artistic touch**

  Deep learning is not all about numbers and analysis; it has a creative side, too. It is learning to paint, compose music, and even write stories. Through techniques like neural style transfer, AI can recreate images in the style of iconic artists.

In conclusion, deep learning is like a tide, steadily advancing and reshaping the landscape of countless industries. Its ability to learn from data and adapt makes it an invaluable tool in the technological toolkit. As deep learning continues to evolve, who knows what astonishing applications we will witness in the years to come.

Introduction to deep learning libraries

Embarking on a deep learning journey without the right tools is like setting sail without a compass. That is where deep learning libraries come to the rescue. TensorFlow, Keras, and PyTorch are the juggernauts of the deep learning world that arm you with tools, functions, and resources. These libraries, each with its own strengths and unique characteristics, streamline the process of building, training, and deploying deep learning models. So, let us grab our gear and delve into what each of these power-packed libraries brings to the table.

Navigating TensorFlow, Keras, and PyTorch

Suppose there are three master chefs in the kitchen of deep learning, each having unique skills and flavors. TensorFlow, Keras, and PyTorch are these master chefs, working tirelessly to serve up delectable deep learning dishes.

Let us begin with TensorFlow, which was crafted by the ingenious minds at Google. TensorFlow is akin to the multi-talented chef who can whip up a range of dishes, from the simplest to the most intricate. Its ability to create complex neural networks and deploy models across various platforms, including mobile and embedded systems, is awe-inspiring. The vibrant community and well-structured documentation act as secret recipes available to anyone who ventures into the TensorFlow kitchen.

Now, let us discuss Keras, the swift and efficient maestro. Keras is all about making things uncomplicated and efficient. Think of it as the chef always ready to quickly prepare tasty snacks for unexpected guests. Its user-friendly nature makes it perfect for fast prototyping and playing around with ideas. The simple structure and intuitive APIs are a hit among those who want to focus on the bigger picture rather than the underlying mechanics.

Lastly, we have PyTorch, the alchemist of deep learning, brought to you by the artisans at Facebook's AI research lab. PyTorch is ideal for those who wish to delve into the art and science of deep learning, experimenting, and innovating. Picture a meticulous chef who carefully selects ingredients, adjusts temperatures, and garnishes the dish to perfection. Its dynamic computational graph and efficient memory usage offer a real-time coding experience that is loved by researchers and academics.

These libraries have risen to prominence for good reasons: their sheer power, flexibility, and the robust communities rallying behind them. TensorFlow, with its versatility; Keras, with its simplicity; and PyTorch, with its dynamism are invaluable assets for anyone eager to tackle deep learning. From developing autonomous systems to advancing healthcare, these libraries are your faithful companions on the path to innovation and discovery.

The seamless integration of Keras and TensorFlow

Suppose you are assembling the ultimate band where each member's distinct rhythm and style blend into a harmonious melody. In our deep learning band, Keras is like the talented lead singer, while TensorFlow is the incredible band backing it up. The integration of Keras with TensorFlow is like creating chart-topping hits with everyone dancing to their tunes.

Keras, with its simplicity, was always the go-to for both beginners and seasoned professionals. But it needed a powerful band – or, in technical terms, a backend engine – to run on. Initially, Keras was compatible with several engines, including **Theano** and **CNTK**. However, TensorFlow, with its versatility, caught Keras' eye.

The big moment arrived when TensorFlow 2.0 was launched. Keras officially tied the knot with TensorFlow and became its default high-level API. This integration is akin to a lead singer committing to one incredibly dynamic band.

So, how does this power duo work together? Keras provides an easier and more intuitive set of tools to design and build neural networks, whereas TensorFlow handles the heavy lifting in the background. Think of Keras as the conductor guiding an orchestra (TensorFlow) to produce an amazing symphony (the neural network).

Using Keras within TensorFlow has made life a lot easier. You just need to import TensorFlow and access Keras directly from it. It is as simple as using *import tensorflow as tf* and then defining your models with **tf.keras**. There is no need for a separate Keras installation. Plus, Keras can now harness all of TensorFlow's powerful features, like eager execution and TensorFlow datasets.

This partnership also means that you can create Keras models and then tinker with the TensorFlow core, giving you much more flexibility.

With Keras and TensorFlow combined, the sky is the limit! Whether you are just getting started in deep learning or looking to build something with world-changing potential, this dynamic duo ensures that you have all the tools you need to make it happen.

Installing TensorFlow and PyTorch

Alright, let us set up our deep learning toolbox. Setting up TensorFlow and PyTorch is like stocking up your workshop with all the tools you will need for some fantastic DIY projects. Think of it as being the handyman or handywoman of deep learning.

We will begin with TensorFlow. Installing TensorFlow is a breeze. There is a high probability that you only need one command to do it. If you are using Python, just open your terminal or command prompt and type in the following command:

```
pip install tensorflow
```

Now, let us talk about PyTorch. PyTorch is TensorFlow's friendly rival; the two are always trying to outdo each other like competing chefs in a cooking show. Installing PyTorch is almost as simple as TensorFlow, but you need to select the configuration that suits your environment (especially if you are using CUDA for GPU support). Head over to the PyTorch website (**https://pytorch.org**), and you will see an easy widget to help you construct the installation command. However, for a general Python installation, this command should work:

```
pip install torch torchvision
```

You are now equipped with both TensorFlow and PyTorch.

The intricate web of artificial neural networks

Alright, let us wade into the realm of artificial neural networks. Think of ANNs as an intricate web of neurons, not unlike the human brain, where each neuron gets to play its part in processing information. This powerful architecture is the foundation of deep learning, helping machines make sense of the complex, messy world around them. From recognizing a cat in an image to translating languages, ANNs play a pivotal role in teaching machines to carry out tasks that require human-like intelligence.

Mimicking the human brain with artificial neurons

The artificial neuron is often referred to as a node or unit. In the human brain, a neuron typically receives input signals, processes them, and produces an output signal. Artificial neurons do something similar. They take in a bunch of numbers (let us keep it simple and call these numbers inputs), perform complex mathematical operations on them, and then spurt out another number (or set of numbers) called **output**.

Each input is assigned a weight that signifies its importance. These inputs are then combined into a weighted sum, to which a bias is usually added (think of it as an extra nudge). Finally, an activation function is used to transform this sum meaningfully, like squeezing it into a range between 0 and 1. The resulting value is what is sent out as the output.

Intriguingly, artificial neurons are inspired by our own biology. Biological neurons have dendrites to receive signals, a cell body to process them, and an axon to send signals out to other neurons. Similarly, artificial neurons receive input through its many channels, combine them to make sense of it and, using an activation function, decide the output.

What is truly impressive is when you start connecting these artificial neurons together, forming an entire network. These artificial neural networks are capable of learning from data, which is, in essence, adjusting the weights and biases to make better predictions or decisions. The potential here is enormous, from recognizing human speech to detecting diseases in medical imaging.

Layers of an artificial neural network

The structure of an ANN can be thought of as a web, intricately woven to form connections between layers of neurons. At the forefront of an ANN is the input layer, which takes in the raw data, much like our senses pick up stimuli from the environment. Hidden within the network are the hidden layers, the workhorses that perform the complex calculations. They are like the wizards behind the curtain, working their magic to bring sense to the information. Finally, we reach the grand finale: the output layer. Here, the final piece of information or prediction is presented.

Think of the input layer as the receiving area in an office building. The raw data is like the parcels that arrive. The hidden layers are the different departments that process the parcels. They make sense of what is in them, repackage them, or send them to another department for further processing. The output layer is the mailing room, where the final package, now ready to be sent out, emerges. This department ensures that the parcel reaches its intended destination, whether that is a probability, a class label, or any other form of output.

This network of layers is deeply interconnected. Neurons from one layer are connected to neurons in the next layer through weighted links. Each neuron performs calculations and passes on the output to the next neuron through an activation function. This process continues until the information reaches the output layer. This whole architecture and flow of data are crucial to how ANNs process information and learn from it.

Now, the number of hidden layers and the number of neurons in each layer can vary widely. A network with many hidden layers is called a **deep neural network** (**DNN**). The choice of architecture can affect the network's ability to learn complex patterns. Designing the architecture of an ANN is more of an art than a science, and it often involves experimentation to find the most effective structure for a given problem.

The art of learning in neural networks: Weights, biases, and beyond

How does an ANN learn? Think of a budding artist learning to paint. At first, the paintings might look like abstract chaos, but with practice, the strokes become refined, and masterpieces emerge. The ANN follows a similar process.

In an ANN, the artists are the neurons, and the brushes and techniques they use are the weights and biases. Weights are like the different brush strokes, and biases are like the color palettes; together, they shape the raw input data into something meaningful.

When an ANN starts learning, it is like the artist beginning with random brush strokes. The weights are initially set to random values, and as the network is exposed to training data, it slowly adjusts these weights and biases. But how does it know which direction to adjust them in? That is where the learning process comes into play.

One of the central characters in this learning tale is the loss function. Think of it as a critical art teacher who is always pointing out flaws. The loss function measures how far off the network's predictions are from the actual targets. The network's mission is to minimize this loss, much like how our artist wants to satisfy the critical art teacher.

Now, to improve the painting (or in this case, predictions), the ANN needs to change its brush strokes and colors gently. That is where the concept of backpropagation and gradient descent comes into play. Backpropagation helps in calculating the gradient, or how much the weights and biases need to be adjusted. Gradient descent, on the other hand, is like the artist stepping back, looking at the painting, and knowing where to add a touch of blue or reduce the intensity of red.

During training, this process is repeated, with the network consistently adjusting weights and biases. As it iterates over the training data, the magic unfolds: the ANN begins to learn from the patterns, making its predictions more accurate. The artist evolves through practice, and the paintings blossom into works of art.

As you can see, ANNs learn by experiencing data and constantly refining their weights and biases, just like an artist honing their skills. And when the network is well trained, it can create some impressive masterpieces in the form of highly accurate predictions!

Steering ANNs with loss functions, optimizers, and epochs

So, you have designed an ANN, and now it is time to make it learn from the data. Let us dive into the nitty-gritty of how training happens. When an ANN starts learning, it is like a newborn, knowing nothing about the data it is about to receive. The heart of this learning process is an interplay between loss functions, optimization algorithms, and epochs.

Let us talk about the loss function first. The purpose of the loss function is to measure how well the ANN is performing. Think of it as a teacher grading a student. It gives a numerical value that tells us how far the predictions made by the ANN are from the actual outcomes. The lower this value, the better. Common loss functions are **mean squared error** (**MSE**) for regression problems and cross-entropy loss for classification problems.

Next up are optimization algorithms. These are the strategies used to improve the network's performance. They are like the guidelines that the student follows to improve their grades. The most widely used optimization algorithm is gradient descent. It works by adjusting the weights and biases of the network in a direction that minimizes the loss. There are also many variants and improvements of gradient descent, such as **Stochastic Gradient Descent** (**SGD**), Adam, RMSprop, and Adagrad. Each has its own set of pros and cons, and the choice of an optimizer may depend on the problem at hand.

Now, let us discuss **epochs**. An epoch is when the entire dataset is passed through the network, both forward and backward, exactly once. It is like studying the whole syllabus once. Too few epochs could mean underfitting, and too many could lead to overfitting. The number of epochs is generally set through trial and error. You should keep an eye on the performance of your network on a separate validation set to know when to stop training.

We must also talk about learning rate, batch size, and momentum. The learning rate controls how big the steps are during optimization. It is like deciding whether the student should take baby steps or giant leaps in learning. Batch size defines the number of samples that will be propagated through the network at a time. Momentum helps accelerate optimizers and dampens oscillations; think of it as a wind behind the student's back.

You are well on your way to becoming an ANN training maestro. It might seem overwhelming at first, but once you get the hang of it, it is incredibly rewarding to see your network learn and improve.

Exploring activation functions and backpropagation in ANNs

We have already discussed the fascinating structure of ANNs and how they learn by adjusting weights and biases. We have not talked about the role of activation functions yet. Activation functions, along with backpropagation, are like the hidden magic spells that breathe life into a neural network, enabling it to learn from complex patterns and make astounding predictions. They are the nuts and bolts that make a neural network capable of solving nonlinear problems. In this section, we will unmask these mysterious entities, that is, activation functions and backpropagation, and explore how they work in harmony to make ANNs the powerful learning machines they are. So, buckle up as we venture into the electrifying world of activation functions and unravel the enigma of backpropagation.

Activation functions: The spark that ignites neural networks

Have you ever wondered how our brains can make sense of the complex world around us? How can they decipher intricate patterns or make snap decisions? Neural networks are inspired by our brains, and activation functions are the little wizards that help them do something similar. In essence, activation functions decide how much signal should be passed through the network.

Consider activation functions as filters in a system. They determine which signals should proceed and which ones should be blocked, according to specific criteria. In neural networks, these rules dictate whether a neuron should be activated. Activation functions add the nonlinearity to the network that is essential for learning complex patterns. Without them, neural networks would be just a linear regression model, unable to learn much.

There are several activation functions, each with its unique flavor. The **rectified linear unit (ReLU)** function, for instance, has become quite popular. It is simple and computationally efficient. ReLU replaces all negative values with zero and leaves positive values unchanged. Then there is the sigmoid function, which squashes values between 0 and 1. It is like that cautious friend who never goes to extremes. The tanh function is sigmoid's hyperbolic twin, and it ranges from -1 to 1.

Choosing the right activation function can be an art. It is like choosing the right ingredients for a recipe. Sometimes you might want the spice of a ReLU, other times the smoothness of a sigmoid. Knowing which one to choose comes with experience and a bit of experimentation. Activation functions are truly the magical spells that give power to neural networks.

Exploring top activation functions in neural networks

Now that we have peeked into the world of activation functions, let us learn about sigmoid, tanh, ReLU, and softmax. These activation functions are like the different gears in a car, each bringing its own set of attributes to the ride. Let us delve into what makes each of them tick.

First up, let us meet sigmoid. Mathematically, it squashes values between 0 and 1. Imagine an s-shaped curve; that is sigmoid for you. It is great for binary classification but has its quirks. For example, it suffers from the vanishing gradient problem, which basically means it can have a hard time learning when inputs are too high or too low.

Next on the stage is tanh, the hyperbolic tangent function. It is similar to sigmoid but stretches from -1 to 1. It is generally considered an improvement over the sigmoid function as it deals with the vanishing gradient problem more gracefully.

The ReLU function is straightforward and effective. It transforms all negative values to zero and maintains all positive values as they are. ReLU's non-saturating nature makes it less likely to run into the vanishing gradient problem, which is why it is all the rage these days. However, be cautious, as ReLU can sometimes fall into a coma and stop learning; this is known as the dying ReLU problem.

Finally, softmax is especially popular in the final layer of a network for multi-class classification. It converts raw scores to probabilities, ensuring that they sum up to 1. It ensures that the output is a nice probability distribution over the classes.

In summary, choosing an activation function is like choosing the right tool for the job. Sigmoid is great for binary classification, but watch out for those gradients. Tanh is like a buffed-up sigmoid. ReLU is the simple and powerful workhorse, and softmax is your go-to for multi-class party time.

Backpropagation and gradient descent in neural networks

In the captivating world of neural networks, learning is an art. Like a composer creating a symphony or a dancer mastering their steps, the neural network learns to perfect its predictions through a mesmerizing dance of algorithms. Among the most graceful dancers in this ballet are backpropagation and its choreographer, gradient descent.

Let us first take a closer look at backpropagation, the star of this performance. Imagine a classroom where a teacher explains concepts to students. The students, trying to grasp the information, make mistakes initially. The teacher, upon seeing this, adjusts the explanation until most students get it right. Backpropagation is like this teacher. It plays a critical role in adjusting the weights of the network to reduce the error in predictions.

However, backpropagation is mathematical. It uses the chain rule from calculus to compute the gradient of the loss function with respect to each weight. Essentially, it is calculating how a change in weights affects the overall error. This information, known as the gradient, tells us the direction in which the weights need to be changed to minimize the error.

Now, enter the elegant maestro, gradient descent. As backpropagation calculates how the error changes with respect to the weights ($\partial L/\partial W$), gradient descent uses this information to make the actual adjustments.

Think of the error as a landscape with hills and valleys. We aim to reach the lowest point in this landscape, where the error is minimal. Gradient descent uses the gradient information from backpropagation to know which direction to move in. It is like having a compass that tells us the direction to the lowest point.

The weight update formula in gradient descent is like the guide to this landscape. It is as follows:

$W\_new = W\_old - \alpha * \partial L/\partial W,$

W_new is the updated weight, *W_old* is the current weight, α is the learning rate, and $\partial L/\partial W$ is the gradient or the slope.

Here, the learning rate, α, is the show director, determining the size of the steps taken. Setting the right learning rate is crucial as it controls the pace. Too high, and we might overshoot the lowest point. Too low, and we will be inching our way, taking forever to reach the destination.

Together, backpropagation and gradient descent create a stunning ballet. Backpropagation sets the stage by calculating how error changes with respect to weights. Then, gradient descent takes the lead, using this information to elegantly adjust the weights, minimize the error, and craft a neural network that makes stunning predictions.

So, as you dive into the enchanting waters of deep learning, take a moment to appreciate the intricate choreography behind the scenes. Through the harmonious dance of backpropagation and gradient descent, neural networks evolve, learn, and thrive in the mesmerizing world of artificial intelligence. It is a performance that is as breathtaking as it is mathematically beautiful. You are not just a spectator but an artist in the making, ready to choreograph your ballet in the world of neural networks.

Importance of data and feature engineering in deep learning

As we have embarked on our deep learning journey, exploring the intricacies of neural networks, backpropagation, and gradient descent, it is time to address the very lifeblood of these networks: data. But data in its raw form is much like a rough diamond; it needs to be cut and polished to reveal its true brilliance. This is where the art and science of data and feature engineering come into play. With carefully crafted features and meticulously prepared data, we can amplify the potential of our neural networks, ensuring that they learn from the most informative and representative examples available.

Unlocking deep learning's potential with pristine data

Picture yourself as a chef. To create a delectable dish, you need the freshest and finest ingredients. Well, in deep learning, data is the key ingredient. The quality of data fed into your neural networks is of paramount importance, much like the ingredients in a gourmet meal.

When you have high-quality data, you give your neural network the best possible information to learn from. Imagine teaching a child to read using a book filled with errors. They might learn something, but it would not be efficient or accurate. On the other hand, if you provide a well written, informative book, the child is much more likely to excel at reading.

In deep learning, the neural network thrives on patterns and correlations. With clean, well structured data, the network can focus on relevant features and create more accurate models. It is not just about the quantity; a smaller dataset that is rich and meaningful can outperform a much larger but noisy and irrelevant dataset.

On the flip side, poor data quality can lead to many problems. The model might overfit, underfit, or, even worse, develop biases that can have real-world consequences. Not only will this affect the model's performance but it can also make the results unreliable or misleading.

In a nutshell, good data is like fuel to the deep learning engine. It is the foundation upon which the intricate layers of neural networks are built. So, investing time and resources into acquiring and preprocessing quality data will lay the groundwork for a high-performance deep learning model. Remember, the success of your model starts with the quality of the data you put into it. Like a wise chef selecting the perfect ingredients, be discerning and vigilant in your data choices.

Prepping data for the deep learning forge

Let us start with data cleaning. You might recall the good old garbage in, garbage out adage. The same principle holds true for deep learning. In the deep learning workshop, we often deal with mammoth datasets. These can have missing values or noisy data, which are like dents in our raw material. Techniques such as interpolation or using pretrained embeddings, especially for NLP tasks, are akin to smoothing out these dents so that our neural network can learn efficiently.

Next up, let us add a dash of normalization to the mix. When working with deep learning, we are often handling immense datasets with features that may have different scales. Imagine trying to forge a sword with materials that do not heat evenly. Normalization, as you already know, is the process of rescaling features to a standard scale. This ensures that all features contribute evenly to the learning process. This is especially important for image data, where pixel values can range widely, and ensuring that all the pixels have a similar scale can be vital for the neural network's performance.

Lastly, let us talk about a fascinating technique that is particularly dear to deep learning: data augmentation. Think of this as a blacksmith adding intricate designs to make a weapon not just effective but stunning. In deep learning, data augmentation is the craft of generating new training samples by applying transformations like rotation, scaling, or cropping. For instance, with image data, by flipping or rotating the images, we create new examples that help the model generalize better. This magic trick is particularly useful for preventing overfitting when our treasure chest of data is not as bountiful as we would like it to be.

So, there you have it, the triad of crafts: cleaning, normalization, and augmentation. These are the skills you will need to refine the raw materials before they are ready for the deep learning forge. As we shape our data into fine steel, our neural networks will be eternally grateful for the care we have put into preparing their training grounds.

Feature crafting versus self-learning

In traditional machine learning, we had to play the role of an alchemist, carefully combining and transforming ingredients (or features) to concoct the perfect potion (or model). That is what manual feature engineering is all about, selecting and transforming features, essentially crafting potions by hand. You would sit down with your data, do some domain research, and extract the relevant features to feed to your algorithm. Think of it as handcrafting a bow and arrows.

Deep learning, on the other hand, is more like wielding magic. Enter automatic feature learning, where the neural network plays the role of the sorcerer. Rather than painstakingly crafting the features, the network learns the most useful features from the data on its own. It is like having a magic wand that conjures up the bow and arrows for you.

In deep learning, as data passes through layers of the network, each layer learns to recognize increasingly complex features. For example, in image recognition, the first layer might learn to recognize edges, the next layer might learn to recognize textures, and so on, until the higher layers can recognize complex objects like faces or trees. The network is conjuring up features from the raw data, like a sorcerer summoning magical entities.

Now, does this mean manual feature engineering is a relic of the past? Not quite. Sometimes, the sorcerer needs a guiding hand. In certain scenarios, combining deep learning with some manual feature engineering can lead to even more powerful models. It is like combining alchemy with sorcery, the best of both worlds.

Managing overfitting and complexity in deep learning

In exploring deep learning, we have delved into the concepts of artificial neurons, activation functions, and the importance of quality data. Now, let us shift our focus to two interlinked components that hold significant importance in the effectiveness of a deep learning model: hyperparameters and the notion of overfitting. Hyperparameters, as we know, are the levers we adjust to optimize our model's learning process. However, overzealous tuning can lead to overfitting, a scenario where our model becomes an overachiever, mastering the training data but faltering when presented with new, unseen data. In this section, we will journey into the intricacies of hyperparameters, unravel the concept of overfitting, and learn how to strike the right balance for optimal model performance.

The role of hyperparameters in deep learning

In the realm of deep learning, the subject of hyperparameters acquires a new depth of complexity and significance. Here, hyperparameters take on roles akin to a cast of characters in a well crafted novel, their interactions and adjustments determining the narrative's progression.

In our previous encounter with hyperparameters during our journey through machine learning, we understood them as key settings in our algorithm that we tweak to optimize performance. The essence remains the same in the context of deep learning, but the intricacies are more profound.

For instance, the learning rate, in the deep learning context, is the narrative's pace setter. It dictates how much we adjust the weights of our neural network with respect to the loss gradient. Too slow a pace, and we risk a slow and inefficient learning process; too quick, and we may skip over our optimal solution altogether.

The batch size, akin to the number of pages we read at a time, determines the number of training examples our model reviews before making a weight update. A smaller batch size means our model updates frequently, making it responsive but also susceptible to noise in the data. Conversely, a larger batch size offers more stable updates but demands more computational resources.

Then, we have the number of layers and neurons in a neural network, which together form the ensemble's size. More layers and neurons enable the model to learn more complex patterns, akin to introducing more plot twists in our novel. But, as with any good story, overcomplication can lead to confusion, or in the case of our model, overfitting.

Adjusting these hyperparameters and striking the right balance forms an integral part of working with deep learning models. It is like fine-tuning the elements of a novel to create a compelling narrative, capturing the reader's attention from beginning to end.

Overfitting: A deep learning perspective

Deep learning, a subset of machine learning, is not immune to overfitting, a common pitfall that haunts many ML models. Overfitting refers to the situation where our model becomes an over-enthusiast, impressively acing the training data but stumbling regarding new, unseen data.

You may remember the overzealous student analogy from our discussions on ML. Consider a student who memorizes every single word in the textbook. They will perform brilliantly if the questions in the exam are directly from the book, right? But what happens when they encounter questions that need them to apply the principles they have learned rather than repeating text word-for-word? Often, they stumble. The same applies to our deep learning models. A model that is overfitting has spent too much time memorizing the training data and has, consequently, failed to generalize the underlying patterns for use on new, unseen data.

In the context of deep learning, overfitting takes on even more significance. The larger and more complex nature of deep learning models, think layers upon layers of interconnected neurons, amplifies the problem. These models have a larger capacity to memorize the training data, especially if the data is sparse or if the model is over-engineered.

The ramifications? A model that excels in training but disappoints in the real world. A model that does not overfit, one that generalizes well, is valuable in deep learning. And to find it, we need to better understand overfitting and learn strategies to avoid it.

Dodging the overfitting bullet in deep learning

The haunting shadow of overfitting may loom over our deep learning models, but we are not without defenses. Just like in the world of strategy games, having a robust line of defense can make all the difference. And so, let us equip ourselves with some of the most effective strategies to combat overfitting in deep learning.

Our first line of defense? More data. A model trained on a larger dataset is like a well-traveled person: they have seen more, they understand better, and they can generalize better. By exposing our model to a broader range of data, we improve its ability to identify the underlying patterns instead of memorizing the specifics of the training data. In practical terms, this can mean collecting more data, if feasible, or using techniques to expand our existing dataset synthetically.

One such technique is something we have already talked about: data augmentation. Think of it as a form of virtual traveling for our model. We create variations of our existing data, such as slightly rotated or zoomed versions of images in a dataset, thereby expanding the range of data our model gets to learn from.

Sometimes, the key to avoiding overfitting is simplifying the model itself. Reducing the complexity of our model, such as decreasing the number of layers or neurons in an ANN, can help prevent the model from becoming an over-enthusiast. Remember, an overly complex model is like a student who insists on memorizing even the page numbers; they are focusing on the wrong details.

And then, we have dropout, one of the most popular techniques for preventing overfitting in neural networks. Let us delve a bit deeper into dropout, which has proven to be an extremely effective technique for preventing overfitting.

Dropout is a form of regularization in deep learning models inspired by biological neural networks. It was introduced by *Geoffrey Hinton*, a renowned computer scientist often called the godfather of deep learning, and his team. The idea is deceptively simple but is potent in its effect.

Consider a team where one superstar carries out the most important tasks while the other members become complacent, relying on this key player. If that star player were to unexpectedly leave, the team would struggle. Similarly, in our artificial neural network, if specific neurons become too influential, the network's performance can falter when it encounters new data that does not match its learned patterns.

This is where dropout comes into the picture. During the training phase, dropout randomly switches off a fraction of neurons in a layer at each step, which effectively means that they do not contribute to the forward pass, nor do they get updated during the backward pass. This fraction is often set to 50%, but it is a hyperparameter that you can tune.

Randomly disabling neurons in this way forces the network to learn more robust features that are useful in conjunction with different random subsets of the other neurons. The network becomes less sensitive to the specific weights of neurons, leading to a model that generalizes better.

Think of it as a form of ensemble learning happening within a single model. Each time a subset of neurons is dropped out, a mini-model is trained. The final trained model is, therefore, an ensemble of all these mini-models.

This way, dropout introduces some noise into the network, mitigating the overfitting problem and helping our model become a more versatile player in the field of unseen data.

Implementing dropout in TensorFlow or PyTorch is straightforward, with built-in functions that allow you to specify the dropout rate. But as with all things in deep learning, careful implementation and testing are vital to ensuring its success.

So, there you have it, four strategies that can fortify your deep learning models against overfitting. Implementing these strategies can make the difference between a model that is a mere training superstar and one that shines in the real world as well.

Convolutional neural networks

Shifting gears, we now move from densely connected neural networks into the world of convolutional neural networks, often abbreviated as CNNs. These special kinds of neural networks have an architecture incredibly well-suited for processing grid-like data, with images being the most notable example.

CNN revolutionized the field of computer vision, turning tasks such as image classification, object detection, and facial recognition from near impossible challenges into routine tasks. They have the extraordinary ability to extract features from images, learn spatial hierarchies, and reduce the amount of preprocessing required. So, let us roll up our sleeves and dive into the colorful universe of CNNs.

The art and architecture of convolutional neural networks

The fascinating structure of convolutional neural networks is designed to mimic the process of human visual perception, and to understand it, we will need to delve into the mechanisms of its different layers: the convolutional layer, the pooling layer, and the fully connected layer.

The convolutional layer is the first stop in the information processing journey. In this layer, small, learnable filters are passed across the input image. The filters act like small windows, observing portions of the image and generating feature maps. Each filter is designed to detect a specific feature in the image, such as edges, shapes, or textures. When a filter is passed over the image, it performs a convolution operation, a mathematical process of combining two functions to produce a third function. This operation is performed by sliding the filter across the image, and calculating the dot product of the filter values and the original pixel values of the image. The resulting matrix forms a feature map or convolved feature. This process is repeated with multiple filters, creating a stack of feature maps that capture different aspects of the original image. The beauty of this process lies in its ability to retain the spatial relationships between pixels by learning image features using small squares of input data.

After the convolution operation, the feature maps pass through a ReLU activation function. The role of the ReLU layer is to introduce non-linearity into the network, enabling it to learn and predict more complex functions. The ReLU function simply converts all negative pixel values in the feature map to zero; the output is a rectified feature map.

The next layer is the pooling or subsampling layer, which is critical in a convolutional neural network. It follows the convolutional layer and reduces the dimensionality of the feature maps, thereby controlling overfitting and reducing computational cost. This layer operates independently on each depth slice of the input, applying an aggregation function over a small window of values.

There are two common types of pooling: max pooling and average pooling. Max pooling returns the maximum value from a particular window, effectively capturing the most prominent characteristic in that region. On the other hand, average pooling calculates the average of all the values within the window, distributing the representation equally among all features. Both these methods help maintain the spatial invariance of the image, meaning the network will recognize a feature regardless of where it is located in the image.

Lastly, we have the **fully connected (FC)** layer, which acts as a classifier on top of these extracted high-level features. The role of this layer is to take the output of the previous layers and make a final decision about the input image's class. It connects every neuron in one layer to every neuron in another layer (hence the term fully connected).

Think of the fully connected layer as a mastermind that has been fed data from various sources and whose job is to make the final, most informed decision. It uses the features from the pooling layer, each representing a high-level attribute of the image, and combines them in various ways to recognize more complex patterns. For instance, it might recognize that a combination of a round shape, the color red, and a stalk signifies an apple.

The FC layer uses functions such as the **softmax activation function** for classification. The softmax function outputs a vector that represents the probability distribution of a list of potential outcomes. It is a way of highlighting the most probable class while maintaining a relative ranking of the other classes.

With all these layers working together, the CNN can effectively learn hierarchical representations, allowing it to process complex visual information in a more efficient and effective manner.

Image data processing with convolutional neural networks

CNNs have truly transformed the field of image processing and recognition, setting new standards for accuracy and computational efficiency. The secret to their success lies in how they handle image data and extract meaningful features from it, and to understand this, we need to delve into the architecture and functioning of CNNs.

At the core of CNNs' success with image data is their ability to maintain the spatial structure of the image. Unlike traditional machine learning models that treat input data as a flat vector of features, CNNs maintain image in their original grid structure. This means that CNNs work with three-dimensional data: the height, width, and depth (color channels) of an image. By preserving the spatial relationships between pixels, CNNs can extract localized features such as edges, textures, and shapes, which are crucial in image recognition tasks.

A major highlight of CNNs is their convolutional layers, which apply a set of learnable filters or kernels to the input image. Each filter is small spatially but extends through the full depth of the input volume. As the filter slides, or convolves, across the width and height of the input image, it is dot-multiplied with the part of the image it is currently covering, producing a two-dimensional activation map. This operation enables the network to learn filters that activate when they see some specific type of feature at some spatial position in the input. This is how CNNs can automatically and adaptively learn spatial hierarchies of features: lower layers may learn simple features such as edges, while deeper layers combine these to learn more complex patterns.

Additionally, using pooling layers contributes to the efficiency and effectiveness of CNNs in handling image data. By progressively reducing the spatial size of the input, pooling layers help control overfitting, reduce the computational cost, and create a form of translation invariance, meaning the network will recognize a feature regardless of where it appears in the image.

Lastly, the fully connected layers take the high-level representations produced by the convolutional and pooling layers and translate them into final outputs, such as classification scores. The softmax function is often applied in the final fully connected layer, converting raw score outputs into probabilities for each class in a multi-class problem.

In summary, the reason why CNNs excel in image recognition tasks is their unique architectural decisions, specifically the use of convolutional and pooling layers that effectively capture spatial hierarchies, positional invariance, and complex patterns in the data, while preserving the original structure of the image. This combination of features enables CNNs to deliver high accuracy, efficiency, and generalizability when dealing with image data.

CNNs in action: Revolutionizing industries with visual intelligence

From the digital assistants in our pockets to autonomous vehicles on the road, CNNs are being applied in a plethora of fields, creating a significant impact. Their exceptional ability to analyze and interpret visual data has opened up possibilities that were once thought to be firmly in the realm of science fiction.

Firstly, image and video recognition is a massive application area for CNNs. From social media filters that recognize faces to medical diagnostic tools that can detect abnormalities in **Magnetic Resonance Imaging (MRI)** scans, CNNs are significantly transforming the landscape of visual data interpretation. They are used in security systems for surveillance, in agriculture for identifying diseased plants, and even in astrophysics to classify galaxies.

Furthermore, CNNs are integral to the booming field of autonomous vehicles. Self-driving cars use CNNs for object detection, understanding the road layout and identifying important visual cues such as traffic lights and pedestrian crossings.

In the world of entertainment, CNNs have found a significant role in the gaming industry, where they are used to create AI opponents that understand visual inputs. Similarly, in virtual reality systems, CNNs are applied to track users' motions and generate corresponding visual feedback.

In the retail sector, CNNs have led to innovative advancements like virtual try-on, where customers can visualize how clothes, glasses, or makeup will look on them without physically trying them on. In the real estate industry, CNNs aid in creating virtual tours of properties.

Finally, CNNs are crucial in modern robotics, where robots use these networks to understand their environment, recognize objects, and interact appropriately.

In summary, the practical applications of CNNs are far-reaching and revolutionizing, serving as a testament to their transformative power.

Implementing CNNs on MNIST with Keras

Let us go through a simple example of a CNN using Keras. We will use the famous **Modified National Institute of Standards and Technology (MNIST)** dataset, which consists of handwritten digits, for this demonstration.

The MNIST dataset is foundational in the field of machine learning. It is a collection of handwritten digits, ranging from 0 to 9, and is frequently used to demonstrate and evaluate various machine learning techniques, especially in image recognition tasks. Each image in the dataset is a 28x28 grayscale image, representing a handwritten digit, and is labeled with the digit it represents.

Our primary objective with this CNN is to train a model to identify and classify these handwritten digits accurately. In other words, when presented with an image of a handwritten number, our model should be able to recognize and output the correct numerical value.

Let us go through the implementation step by step:

1. **Import the necessary libraries**

   Before diving in, we need to ensure that we have the right tools. This step focuses on importing the necessary Python libraries that empower us to load the dataset and build and evaluate the neural network model. Execute the following code:

   ```
   import numpy as np
   import matplotlib.pyplot as plt
   from tensorflow.keras.datasets import mnist
   from tensorflow.keras.models import Sequential
   from tensorflow.keras.layers import Dense, Flatten, Conv2D,
   MaxPooling2D
   from tensorflow.keras.utils import to_categorical
   ```

2. **Load the MNIST dataset**

   Now, we are going to fetch the dataset. Keras provides easy-to-use utilities that allow us to quickly load datasets like MNIST. This step will give us our training and test sets, which are essential for building and evaluating our model.

   ```
   (x_train, y_train), (x_test, y_test) = mnist.load_data()
   ```

3. **Preprocess the data**

   Data preprocessing is a crucial step in machine learning. We will reshape our images to fit the model's expectations and convert our target labels to one-hot encoded vectors. One-hot encoding transforms our numeric labels into vectors of 0s and 1s, making it suitable for a classification task. Use the following code:

   ```
   # Reshape data to fit the model

   x_train = x_train.reshape(60000, 28, 28, 1)

   x_test = x_test.reshape(10000, 28, 28, 1)


   # One-hot encoding for target column

   y_train = to_categorical(y_train)

   y_test = to_categorical(y_test)
   ```

4. **Build the CNN model**

   With our data in hand and preprocessed, we will now construct our CNN. CNNs are especially potent for image-related tasks. We will start by adding convolutional layers that detect patterns in our images, then use a pooling layer to reduce dimensionality, and finally, flatten our data for the dense output layer that predicts the digit represented by each image using the following code:

   ```
   # Initialize the model

   model = Sequential()  # This initializes a linear stack of layers


   # Add a convolutional layer with 64 filters, a 3x3 window, and ReLU
   activation function.

   model.add(Conv2D(64, kernel_size=3, activation='relu', input_
   shape=(28, 28, 1)))


   # Add another convolutional layer

   model.add(Conv2D(32, kernel_size=3, activation='relu'))


   # Add a max pooling layer

   model.add(MaxPooling2D(pool_size=(2, 2)))


   # Flatten the 2D arrays for fully connected layers

   model.add(Flatten())


   # Add a dense layer with 10 neurons (for the 10 digits we have in
   the dataset) and softmax activation.

   model.add(Dense(10, activation='softmax'))
   ```

5. **Compile the model**

   Compiling the model prepares it for training. We will specify an optimizer that adjusts our model parameters, a loss function that measures how well our model is performing, and metrics like accuracy to give us an intuitive understanding of our model's performance during training. Use the following code:

   ```
   model.compile(optimizer='adam', loss='categorical_crossentropy',
   metrics=['accuracy'])
   ```

6. **Train the model**

   Now, we will train our compiled model on the preprocessed training data. Training is where the magic happens. Our model will learn the best parameters to predict the digit from an image. Use the following code:

   ```
   model.fit(x_train, y_train, validation_data=(x_test, y_test), ep-
   ochs=5)
   ```

7. **Evaluate the model**

   After training, we must evaluate our model on unseen data (test data) to determine how well it might perform in real-world scenarios. This step provides an accuracy score that tells us the percentage of images our model correctly classified. Use the following code:

   ```
   loss, accuracy = model.evaluate(x_test, y_test)

   print(f"Test Loss: {loss:.4f}")

   print(f"Test Accuracy: {accuracy*100:.2f}%")
   ```

You will end up with a superb test accuracy of 98%.

With this, you have taken a significant step into the world of CNNs using Keras. Remember, understanding the fundamental steps and the reasoning behind each is key to harnessing the full power of deep learning.

Recurrent neural networks

While previously discussed networks like ANNs and CNNs process inputs independently, RNNs stand apart with their ability to process sequences of data, making them particularly suited for dealing with time-series data or any data where order matters. From language translation to stock market prediction, RNNs shine in scenarios where understanding the context or temporal dynamics is crucial. In this section, we will unlock the inner workings of RNNs, understand why they are essential for tasks involving sequential data, and explore their practical applications in various industries.

The power of recurrence: Unfolding the RNN architecture

Within the vast family of neural networks, RNNs claim a distinctive spot, thanks to their unique structure. Unlike their feedforward siblings, RNNs possess loops that allow information to flow from one step in the network to the next. Think of it as having a conversation, where what you say next largely depends on the previous sentences. RNNs mirror this conversational memory in a manner that is immensely helpful when dealing with sequential data.

These loops give the RNN a form of memory. Each neuron or unit in an RNN receives input not just from the preceding layer, as in a typical feedforward network, but also from itself at the previous time step. This forms the central architecture of RNNs: loops that pass information along the network across time steps. The primary benefit? This setup allows the RNN to incorporate its understanding of the previous context into its interpretation of the current input.

However, do not let the simplicity of this description deceive you. These loops result in complex internal states that adapt based on input, allowing RNNs to process sequences of varying lengths, a feat out of reach for traditional feedforward networks.

In summary, the looping, recurrent architecture of RNNs is what imbues them with their sequential data prowess. Whether it is predicting the next word in a sentence, the future price of a stock, or the next note in a melody, RNNs leverage their unique structure to excel in tasks that require an understanding of context and sequence.

The utility of recurrent neural networks in sequential data

RNNs are the go-to neural network model for handling sequential data, and for good reason. Sequential data, whether text in a novel, a sequence of stock prices, or time-stamped sensor data, has an inherent order that carries significant meaning. Understanding this order, the context, and how the parts of the sequence interact is paramount to making accurate predictions or deriving meaningful interpretations.

Take language, for instance. The meaning of a sentence often hinges on the order of the words. Change the order, and you risk changing the meaning entirely. RNNs excel in tasks like this because they are designed to recognize patterns over time. They accomplish this by retaining a sort of memory of previous inputs in the sequence while considering the current input. This ability allows them to create a context-sensitive analysis of the input sequence, which is instrumental in tasks such as language translation, sentiment analysis, and even predictive text input.

Similarly, consider time-series data such as stock prices. Predicting future prices is not merely about understanding the current price or volume of trading; it is also about understanding trends, fluctuations, and patterns over time. The memory of an RNN allows it to incorporate this historical context into its predictions, making it a suitable choice for this type of tasks.

In essence, RNNs shine in sequential data due to their unique design. They not only consider the current input but also the historical context, thereby unveiling the complex, time-dependent patterns that exist within such data. This ability sets them apart from other neural networks and cements their role in dealing with sequential data.

RNNs: Tackling the hurdles of vanishing and exploding gradients

Despite their impressive capabilities, RNNs are not without their share of challenges, and one of the most prominent among these is the issue of vanishing and exploding gradients. To truly appreciate this issue, let us delve deeper into the learning process of an RNN.

We know that RNNs, like all neural networks, learn by tweaking their parameters in response to the errors they make in their predictions, a process carried out through backpropagation. The gradient we often mention is a measure of the error's sensitivity to changes in the network's parameters: the steeper the gradient, the more the parameters need to be adjusted.

Now, when dealing with long sequences, we are essentially multiplying these gradients over many time steps during backpropagation. This is where things can go awry. If the gradient is small (less than 1), these multiplications across time steps can cause it to shrink exponentially toward zero, leading to a scenario known as the vanishing gradient problem. When this happens, the parameters of the early layers in the network are barely updated, causing them to learn extremely slowly, if at all.

If the gradient is large (greater than 1), it can grow exponentially during these multiplications and become extremely large: the exploding gradient problem. This can result in wildly fluctuating parameter values and unstable network performance, as the network weights may take on extreme values.

Both these issues pose substantial challenges when training RNNs. They prevent the network from learning effectively, impacting the model's performance. In the following sections, we will explore how these problems can be mitigated and how new RNN architectures like LSTM and **Gated Recurrent Unit (GRU)** networks have been designed to overcome these problems. So, while these gradient issues may seem like formidable obstacles, do not worry; the AI community has devised some clever workarounds.

Putting RNNs to work: Real-world applications

Recurrent neural networks, with their proficiency for handling sequential data, have found applications in a multitude of sectors. Let us unpack some of them to give you a better idea of how these networks are making a difference in the real world.

One of the most commonly discussed applications of RNNs is in the realm of NLP. NLP encompasses many tasks, such as language translation, sentiment analysis, and text generation, all of which involve sequences, sequences of words to be precise. Given their ability to maintain context over long sequences, RNNs have become a cornerstone in this field. For example, in language translation, an RNN can ingest an entire sentence in one language and produce its equivalent in another, maintaining grammatical and contextual accuracy.

Next up is time-series prediction, which is particularly important in finance and weather forecasting. The sequential nature of this data (stock prices, weather conditions, and so on.) lends itself well to the strengths of RNNs. They can predict future stock prices based on historical data or forecast tomorrow's weather considering past conditions.

RNNs also shine in speech recognition systems. Your voice assistant? It is using an RNN (or a variant) to interpret your commands. By recognizing patterns over time in audio signals, these models can accurately convert spoken language into written text.

In the healthcare industry, RNNs have been employed to predict the progression of diseases over time. By analyzing patient data like symptoms, treatment responses, and test results recorded over periods, RNNs can predict future health status or disease progression, aiding doctors in creating personalized treatment plans.

The common thread across all these applications? Sequential data. It is this ability to process and learn from sequences that makes RNNs an incredibly powerful tool for these and many other applications. As we continue to generate more and more sequential data, the significance and utility of RNNs will only grow.

Deciphering sentiments: Implementing a basic RNN with Keras

The IMDb dataset is a standard dataset in the machine learning community, especially for sentiment analysis tasks. It contains 50,000 movie reviews: 25,000 labeled for training and 25,000 labeled for testing. Each review is marked as positive or negative based on the sentiment.

We aim to train an RNN to understand the underlying sentiment of a movie review. Given a text review, the model should classify it as positive or negative, thereby demonstrating the power of RNNs in understanding the sequence and context of textual data.

Let us go through the implementation step by step:

1. **Dataset loading and preprocessing**

   First, we will load the IMDb dataset from Keras and preprocess it by padding each sequence to the same length. Use the following code:

   ```
   from tensorflow.keras.datasets import imdb
   ```

```
from tensorflow.keras.preprocessing import sequence

# Load dataset
(train_data, train_labels), (test_data, test_labels) = imdb.load_
data(num_words=10000) # Limiting to top 10,000 frequent words

# Pad each sequence to the same length (let's use a max length of
500)
maxlen = 500
train_data = sequence.pad_sequences(train_data, maxlen=maxlen)
test_data = sequence.pad_sequences(test_data, maxlen=maxlen)
```

2. **Building the recurrent neural network model**

   Now, let us define our RNN model. We will use an embedding layer to convert our word indices into dense vectors, followed by a simple RNN layer. Use the following code:

```
from tensorflow.keras.models import Sequential
from tensorflow.keras.layers import Embedding, SimpleRNN, Dense

# Initialize the model
model = Sequential()

# Add an embedding layer
model.add(Embedding(10000, 32, input_length=maxlen))

# Add an RNN layer
model.add(SimpleRNN(32))

# Add a dense layer for classification
model.add(Dense(1, activation='sigmoid'))
```

3. **Compiling and training the model**

   With the model constructed, we will now compile it and start the training process. Use the following code:

```
# Compile the model
model.compile(optimizer='rmsprop', loss='binary_crossentropy', met-
rics=['accuracy'])

# Train the model
model.fit(train_data, train_labels, epochs=10, batch_size=128, vali-
dation_split=0.2)
```

- **Evaluating the model**

  After our RNN model is trained, we will evaluate its performance on the test dataset. Use the following code:

  ```
  # Evaluate the model on test data
  test_loss, test_acc = model.evaluate(test_data, test_labels)
  print("Test Accuracy:", test_acc)
  ```

  The test accuracy in this case will be around 80%.

Long short-term memory networks

Having explored the incredible potential of RNNs, we have also acknowledged their Achilles' heel: the notorious vanishing and exploding gradient problems that can hamper their learning from long sequences. This is where LSTMs, a special kind of RNNs, come to the rescue. LSTMs have an edge over traditional RNNs as they are explicitly designed to combat the gradient problem, enabling the network to learn from sequences of substantial length. In the upcoming sections, we will dive deep into the architecture of LSTMs, understand how they handle the gradient problem, and explore their applications in real-world scenarios.

Diving deep into LSTM networks

Long short-term memory networks, or LSTMs, are a unique type of RNNs that bring a new perspective to handling sequential data. The standard RNN should be able to connect information through long sequences using its looping mechanism. However, the vanishing gradient problem throws a wrench into this idea, making it hard for the RNN's to learn from long sequences.

LSTMs share the RNNs' recurrent structure but with a twist. The traditional simple neuron is replaced by an intricate cell structure called an LSTM cell. Think of these cells as miniature RNNs within the main RNN, giving the LSTM its ability to selectively read, write, and delete information from its memory.

Now, let us dive deeper. Each LSTM cell is a combination of multiple components: a cell state, which carries information across the sequence, and three gates, which are input, forget, and output gates, that control the flow of information into, out of, and within the cell. The brilliance of LSTMs lies in these gates. They use sigmoid functions, which output values between 0 and 1, enabling them to decide the proportion of information to let through. It is like having a mini quality control mechanism for data.

This way, LSTMs make a significant departure from standard RNNs. They retain the core concept of processing sequential data while adding an additional layer of complexity to better manage the storage and flow of information. This allows them to keep track of long dependencies in sequences, hence the name long short-term memory.

Cracking the long-term dependency problem with LSTM

The problem of long-term dependencies in sequential data is a challenge that traditional RNNs have grappled with for a long time. This problem arises when the network needs to learn from information that is a significant distance away from the point of interest in a sequence. In other words, if a piece of critical information and the point where it is needed are too far apart, a regular RNN tends to forget it.

LSTMs brilliantly overcome this challenge; let us understand how.

Suppose you are reading a long novel, and a key event occurs in the first few pages that influences the climax. As an LSTM network, you have the ability to store that early event in your memory, thanks to your input gate and cell state. The cell state is like a conveyor belt that runs through all cells, carrying along important information. The input gate determines what new information in the current input needs to be stored in the cell state.

Now, let us say irrelevant events occur throughout the book. Forget gate comes into play, deciding what details to erase from the cell state. It is like highlighting important facts and erasing trivial information in a study guide.

Finally, when you reach the climax of the novel, the output gate helps you recall the stored event from the beginning, allowing you to understand the significance of the climax. This allows an LSTM to keep critical information handy, even across long gaps in sequences.

Therefore, LSTMs, with their unique cell structure and gating mechanism, can handle the problem of long-term dependencies, giving them a significant edge over traditional RNNs when dealing with complex sequential data.

LSTM gates: The secret sauce of long memory

The LSTM cell structure differs from a standard RNN in that it has these three gates, each a type of neural network, that control the flow of information into, within, and out of the cell. These gates are decision-making mechanisms that determine how much of each type of information should be allowed to pass through. The real power of LSTMs lies in the balance and interplay among these three gates.

Let us briefly understand each gate:

- **The forget gate**: This gate is like the cell's guardian, deciding which information to throw away or keep. For instance, if the LSTM cell is processing a book and it comes across information that is not important (like a random sub-plot), the forget gate learns to discard this.

- **The input gate**: Following the forget gate, the input gate's job is to update the cell state with new information it deems important. It is like a filter, deciding which values from the input should be used to update the cell's state.

- **The output gate**: This is the final gate that dictates what the next hidden state should be. Remember, the hidden state contains information about past inputs. The output gate determines what information the cell outputs to the next LSTM cell.

In short, the beauty of an LSTM cell is that it has the ability to forget irrelevant parts, learn to store important information, and then output the parts of this information that will be useful in the future. The complex orchestration of these three gates gives LSTMs their unique ability to process and remember information over long periods of time and across sequences of inputs.

Where LSTMs shine: A glimpse of practical applications

LSTM networks have proven to be incredibly valuable in various applications, showcasing their strength in dealing with sequence prediction problems. So, let us delve into some of the fascinating use cases where LSTMs have marked their territory.

The most commonly touted application of LSTMs is in NLP tasks. They have been instrumental in language translation, often called **machine translation**. Here, LSTMs can capture the context and semantics of an entire sentence in one language and effectively translate it into another.

Another domain is text generation, where LSTMs, due to their memory-retention ability, can generate coherent and contextually relevant sentences or even entire stories. They can be taught to write like *Shakespeare* or generate new movie scripts in the style of a certain director.

In speech recognition, LSTMs are a popular choice. They can understand the temporal dependencies in our speech, allowing for the effective transcription of spoken words into written text. This is the technology behind virtual assistants like **Siri** and **Alexa**.

LSTMs also play a vital role in the field of time-series prediction. Be it stock price forecasting, weather prediction, or predicting sales in the retail sector, LSTMs' ability to remember long-term dependencies helps them predict future values based on past data.

Lastly, the world of music has also seen the impact of LSTMs. They are used for music composition by understanding and memorizing the pattern or sequence in a piece of music and then generating similar music.

These are just some of the many ways LSTMs are used to solve complex problems. Their ability to handle long-term dependencies in sequence data really comes to the forefront in these applications, making them an excellent tool in the deep learning toolkit.

Sentiment analysis on IMDB movie reviews with LSTM

We have already done sentiment analysis on the IMDB movie review dataset using an RNN. Let us try the exact same thing using an LSTM. As you will now see, most of the code is very similar; consider the following code:

```
import numpy as np

from tensorflow.keras.datasets import imdb

from tensorflow.keras.models import Sequential

from tensorflow.keras.layers import LSTM, Dense, Embedding

from tensorflow.keras.preprocessing import sequence

# Load the dataset
max_features = 10000

(X_train, y_train), (X_test, y_test) = imdb.load_data(num_words=max_features)

# Pad the sequences to have a uniform length
maxlen = 80   # Only consider the first 80 words of each movie review

X_train = sequence.pad_sequences(X_train, maxlen=maxlen)

X_test = sequence.pad_sequences(X_test, maxlen=maxlen)

model = Sequential()

# Starting off with an efficient embedding layer which maps our vocab indices into embedding_dims dimensions
embedding_dims = 128

model.add(Embedding(max_features, embedding_dims, input_length=maxlen))

# Adding LSTM layer with 128 memory units
model.add(LSTM(128, dropout=0.2, recurrent_dropout=0.2))

model.add(Dense(1, activation='sigmoid'))  # Because this is a binary classification problem

model.compile(loss='binary_crossentropy', optimizer='adam', metrics=['accuracy'])

print(model.summary())

model.fit(X_train, y_train, batch_size=32, epochs=3, validation_data=(X_test, y_test))

print("Training complete!")
```

Conclusion

In wrapping up our exploration of deep learning, we journeyed through the foundations of neural networks, dipped our toes into the intricacies of their architecture, and climbed the higher slopes of more complex network types, such as CNNs, RNNs, and LSTMs.

We saw how these powerful models capture intricate patterns in diverse types of data, with CNNs excelling at image-processing tasks, and RNNs and LSTMs ruling the roost when it comes to sequence data. We dissected their structures and operations and understood why they are the way they are. We also discussed how we can tune and tweak these models with hyperparameters and discussed ways to combat overfitting, ensuring that our models not only learn well but can generalize their learning to unseen data.

Furthermore, we looked at the significance of quality data and the role of feature engineering in deep learning, emphasizing that good data is just as important as a good model. We touched on the issues and hurdles, such as the vanishing gradient problem in RNNs, and looked at how we have managed to build solutions such as LSTMs to overcome these.

Deep learning is a vast and exciting field, and what we covered in this chapter is just the tip of the iceberg. There is so much more to explore, from **Generative Adversarial Networks (GANs)** to autoencoders, from transfer learning to reinforcement learning. But with the knowledge you now have, you are well equipped to dive deeper into this fascinating ocean of possibilities.

In the next chapter, we will learn how to process and analyze textual data, perform sentiment analysis, classify text, and uncover hidden patterns through topic modeling and named entity recognition, unlocking the potential to extract valuable insights from unstructured text.

Points to remember

- Deep learning utilizes neural networks with many layers (hence, deep) to model and understand complex patterns in datasets.

- Neural networks consist of interconnected neurons (nodes) arranged in layers: an input layer, one or more hidden layers, and an output layer. Each connection has a weight that gets adjusted during learning.

- Convolutional neural networks are designed to automatically and adaptively learn spatial hierarchies of features from data, making them excellent for image processing tasks.

- Recurrent neural networks are used for sequential data and have loops that allow information to be carried across sequences. They, however, can suffer from vanishing and exploding gradient problems.

- Long short-term memory networks, a type of RNN, are designed to avoid the long-term dependency problem (the issue of maintaining information over long sequences) that traditional RNNs face.

- Hyperparameters like learning rate, batch size, number of layers, and number of neurons need to be set before training, and their optimal values can be found through a process known as hyperparameter tuning.

Multiple choice questions

1. **What are convolutional neural networks particularly good at handling?**

    a. Sequential data

    b. Tabular data

    c. Image data

    d. Audio data

2. **What problem are long short-term memory networks specifically designed to solve?**

    a. Vanishing and exploding gradient problems

    b. Overfitting

    c. Long-term dependency problem

    d. None of the above

3. In a neural network, what is the function of an activation function?

    a. To normalize the output

    b. To introduce non-linearity into the model

    c. To speed up training

    d. To reduce the number of layers

4. **What is a common strategy to avoid overfitting in a deep learning model?**

    a. Increase model complexity

    b. Increase the learning rate

    c. Apply dropout

    d. Increase batch size

5. **What are recurrent neural networks best suited for?**

   a. Image classification

   b. Tabular data

   c. Sequential data

   d. Clustering

6. **In the context of deep learning, what is the purpose of data normalization?**

   a. To handle missing data

   b. To ensure that different features contribute proportionally to the final prediction

   c. To convert categorical variables into numerical ones

   d. None of the above

Answers

   1. c

   2. c

   3. b

   4. c

   5. c

   6. b

Questions

   1. How does the architecture of a CNN differ from that of a standard ANN?

   2. What are the advantages of using a RNN for sequential data? What problems might arise when training an RNN, and how do LSTMs address these issues?

   3. Can you explain the concept of overfitting in the context of deep learning and describe some strategies for mitigating it?

   4. What is the role of activation functions in an artificial neural network, and can you provide examples of some commonly used activation functions?

   5. What are hyperparameters in the context of deep learning? Describe a few examples and their roles in the training process.

CHAPTER 15

Word Play: Text Analytics and Natural Language Processing

Introduction

As we step into the world of text analytics and **natural language processing (NLP)**, we open their potential when combined with the power of **Machine Learning** (ML) and **Artificial Intelligence (AI)**.

We will dive deep into the process of transforming raw text into a format that our models can understand, discovering along the way how to extract meaningful features from the text. We will delve into the heart of sentiment analysis, learning how to harness the power of language to draw out the sentiment behind the words. Our journey will lead us to the door of topic modeling and named entity recognition, where we will learn to automatically detect topics and named entities in a body of text.

Structure

In this chapter, we will discuss the following topics:

- Text processing and tokenization
- The transformative journey: From text to features
- Decoding emotions: Sentiment analysis and text classification
- Topic modeling and named entity recognition

Objectives

By the end of this chapter, we aim to provide you with a comprehensive understanding of textual data and its complexities, elucidating why it requires unique processing techniques. We would like to familiarize you with the key stages of text preprocessing and tokenization. Further, the chapter will explain how these processes make text understandable to machine learning models. Moreover, we will help you gain a thorough understanding of various text representation methods and feature extraction techniques, which transform the complexities of human language into a format that can be processed by machines. As the chapter progresses, we will dive into sentiment analysis and text classification, aiming to equip you with a comprehensive understanding of their role in deriving insights from text data. Lastly, we will explore the fascinating fields of topic modeling and named entity recognition, illuminating their capabilities in unraveling structure and meaning from textual data. Through all these topics, we will be connecting theories to practical applications, underscoring the power and utility of NLP in the real world.

Text processing and tokenization

Stepping into text analytics and NLP, we must first understand the initial stage of handling textual data: text processing and tokenization. It is easy to underestimate the complexity of our everyday language, but remember that machines do not share our innate grasp of context, grammar, or slang. Thus, raw text data must be cleaned and structured so that models can be understood. This first section will guide you through these crucial preprocessing steps, which lay the foundation for all further text analysis tasks, making it easier for our machine learning models to discern patterns and extract meaningful insights from raw, unstructured text.

The intricacies of textual data in natural language processing

Textual data, also known as **unstructured data**, is arguably one of the most complex forms of data we deal with in data science. Unlike structured data, which is usually numeric and fits neatly into database tables or spreadsheets, textual data is less rigid and more complex, much like the human language it originates from.

At the heart of textual data's complexity are several key characteristics, which are listed as follows:

- **High dimensionality:** Textual data has an extremely high dimensionality. Consider, for example, a corpus of text documents: The vocabulary of these documents, including different forms of the same word, can easily run into thousands or even tens of thousands of unique words. Each of these unique words forms a different dimension in our data.

- **Sparsity:** Textual data is often sparse due to its high dimensionality. This means that while there could be thousands of unique words in our documents, only a handful of them appear in each document. This results in a data representation where there are more zeros than actual values.

- **Temporal and contextual dependence:** Textual data, particularly when dealing with sentences or documents, have a temporal dimension. This means that the order in which words appear matters and can dramatically change the meaning of the text. The meaning of a word often depends on its context: the words that appear before and after it.

- **Varied length:** Unlike numerical data, where each instance usually contains the same number of features, textual data can be of varied lengths. One document might contain a few words, while another could contain thousands.

- **Language nuances:** Textual data comes loaded with a host of language-specific nuances. This includes the use of idioms, slang, and cultural references. Additionally, language has syntax (grammatical structure) and semantics (meaning), which need to be understood for effective analysis. Synonyms and homonyms further add to the complexity.

- **Noisy:** Textual data is often noisy, containing errors, abbreviations, special characters, and non-standard language use.

Refining the raw: Text preprocessing essentials

Our exploration of text analytics begins with the crucial task of managing and processing raw textual data, often unruly and unstructured in its original form.

First, let us start with casing. Textual data can be a mix of uppercase and lower case words. Since TEXT, Text, and text all represent the same word, we usually convert all text to lower case to maintain consistency and reduce the dimensionality of our data. This process is known as **case normalization**.

Next comes the removal of punctuation. Punctuation marks might be important in English grammar, but when it comes to text analytics, they are usually just noise that can interfere with our algorithms. Therefore, we remove these punctuation marks to keep only the actual words in the text.

Moving on, we encounter stop words. These are common words like is, the, and, etc . that occur frequently in all documents but do not contribute much information for text analytics tasks. These words can take up a lot of space and computational resources while providing little to no benefit, so they are typically removed.

Some other preprocessing steps you might consider are as follows:

- **Stemming and lemmatization:** These techniques reduce words to their root form. For example, running, runs, and ran can all be reduced to run. This helps in reducing the dimensionality of the data and grouping similar words.

- **Handling numbers and special characters:** Depending on the task, numbers and special characters might be removed, replaced, or treated in a special way.

- **Spell correction:** Textual data, especially if it is user-generated (like tweets or reviews), might contain spelling errors. We may correct these errors as part of our preprocessing.

In essence, text preprocessing is all about cleaning and standardizing your textual data, reducing noise and complexity, and transforming your text into a form that is easier for machine learning models to digest.

Chopping blocks of text: The art of tokenization

Once the text data is well refined through the preprocessing steps, we can start slicing and dicing it into digestible pieces. This process of chopping text into smaller units is known as **tokenization**. The most common forms of tokenization in text analytics are sentence tokenization and word tokenization.

Sentence tokenization is the process of breaking down a text into sentences. On the surface, it might sound like a trivial task: we can split the text every time we encounter a full stop, right? But what about periods used in abbreviations or decimal numbers, or exclamations and interrogations? What about languages where punctuation rules for sentence termination are different? The process can quickly get complex, requiring efficient algorithms and sometimes even an understanding of the language syntax to perform accurately.

Word tokenization, on the other hand, is the task of splitting sentences into individual words or tokens. This is a crucial step because the word is typically the primary unit of analysis in text analytics. While it might seem as simple as splitting by spaces, it can get complicated when considering punctuation, contractions like do not, and language-specific rules. In some languages, such as German or Finnish, words can be combined to form compound words, which might need to be split further.

These tokenization processes form the backbone of most natural language processing tasks, transforming a raw text string into a more structured and analyzable format. It is like breaking a wall into individual bricks that can be studied, understood, and then rearranged to create new structures.

Pruning words to their roots: Unraveling stemming and lemmatization

Post tokenization, we are left with a bag of words. But even then, our work in processing is not done. Language is riddled with inconsistencies and redundancies. For instance, run, runs, and running all stem from the same idea but are different words. If we treat them as separate entities, we end up with a vast and sparse vocabulary that might impede our machine learning model. To address this issue, we use techniques like stemming and lemmatization.

Stemming is like a gardener pruning the branches of a word, cutting it down to its root form. For instance, running, ran, and runner might all be cut down to run. However, this process can sometimes be a bit reckless, and the stems might not always be recognizable words; it is more of a crude chopping technique.

Lemmatization, in contrast, is a more scholarly approach. It is like having a linguist carefully reconstruct the base form of each word. The lemma of is, was, or been is the word be. Lemmatization considers the grammatical structure and uses a detailed dictionary or vocabulary to return the base or dictionary form of a word.

Choosing between stemming and lemmatization depends on the application. If you are working on a task where the meaning of words is crucial, such as sentiment analysis, you may opt for lemmatization. If you are more concerned about grouping similar words, like in a search algorithm, stemming could be your choice.

By reducing words to their base forms, both stemming and lemmatization help consolidate different forms of a word to a common base. This can be particularly helpful in feature representation, improving both the efficiency and effectiveness of text analytics models.

Assigning roles to words: Unveiling parts-of-speech tagging

After stemming or lemmatization, we use a more standardized set of words. This brings us to another essential step in text preprocessing: **parts-of-speech** (**POS**) tagging. POS tagging involves categorizing each word in our text based on its role in the sentence, such as whether it is a noun or verb or adjective and so on.

Knowing the role of a word can offer critical insights. For instance, consider the word run. In *I run every morning*, run is a verb, but in *This is a run*, it is a noun. By identifying the part of speech, we can understand the context better and differentiate between these usage types.

POS tagging is not just a one-size-fits-all labeling task. Various algorithms, from rule-based to stochastic and transformation-based, can be used to achieve accurate POS tagging. These algorithms consider the contextual information and syntax of the sentences to categorize the words accurately.

By enriching our understanding of the text, POS tagging paves the way for more complex NLP tasks like named entity recognition and dependency parsing. It is like assigning roles in a play; once you know who the protagonist, antagonist, and supporting characters are, you are better equipped to understand the plot.

Text cleaning and tokenization using natural language toolkit and spaCy in Python

The beautiful dance of language holds secrets that algorithms aspire to unlock. But before we start, let us introduce **natural language toolkit (NLTK)** and spaCy, the two key libraries we will use.

NLTK is a leading platform for building Python programs to work with human language data. It provides easy-to-use interfaces to over 50 corpora and lexical resources and a suite of text-processing libraries for classification, tokenization, stemming, tagging, parsing, and semantic reasoning.

Spacy, on the other hand, is an open-source library for NLP in Python. It is designed specifically for production use, and it offers pre-trained neural networks for various languages.

To install these libraries, you can use pip, the Python package installer. Open your terminal or command prompt and execute the following code:

```
pip install nltk spacy
```

In this code example, we assume that we are working with a dataset of reviews, possibly from a product or service, where each review is a piece of text written by a user. This is a common scenario in NLP and text analytics tasks.

The goal of this task is to preprocess and tokenize this raw textual data into a form that can be easily understood and analyzed by machine learning algorithms. Text preprocessing and tokenization are crucial first steps in any NLP pipeline, as they transform unstructured data into a structured form.

After installing NLTK, you need to download the *punkt* and *wordnet* packages, which are used for tokenization and lemmatization, respectively. Run the following in your Python environment:

```
import nltk
nltk.download('punkt')
nltk.download('wordnet')
nltk.download('stopwords')
```

For spaCy, after installation, you need to download a language model. We will use the English model for this example. To download the model, type the following in your command prompt or terminal:

```
python -m spacy download en_core_web_sm
```

Once you have the above packages installed, let us proceed with our text preprocessing and tokenization example. Follow the given steps:

1. Import the necessary modules and packages using the following code:

```
from nltk.corpus import stopwords
from nltk.stem import WordNetLemmatizer
from nltk.tokenize import word_tokenize, sent_tokenize
import spacy
```

Here, we import the necessary functions from NLTK for tokenization, lemmatization, and stop word removal. We also import spaCy , which we will use later in the process.

2. Load spaCy 's English language model:

```
nlp = spacy.load("en_core_web_sm")
```

We are loading spaCy 's English model, which includes part-of-speech tags, dependency parse, and named entities.

3. Initialize the NLTK's **lemmatizer** and define a list to hold processed reviews. Use the following code:

```
lemmatizer = WordNetLemmatizer()
processed_reviews = []
```

Here, we initialize the **WordNetLemmatizer** from NLTK. We also create an empty list, **processed_reviews**, to hold our processed review text after pre-processing.

Now we are all set for the main preprocessing steps, which will occur in a loop for each review.

4. Loop through each review and the review into sentences. Execute the following code:

```
for review in reviews:
sentences = sent_tokenize(review)
```

We start a loop that will go through each review in our dataset, and then we use NLTK's **sent_tokenize** function to split the review into individual sentences.

5. Loop through each sentence in the review and then tokenize the sentence into words:

```
for sentence in sentences:
sentences = sent_tokenize(review)
```

We use NLTK's **word_tokenize** function to split the sentence into individual words.

6. Remove punctuation and convert words to lower case:

```
words = [word.lower() for word in words if word.isalpha()]
```

We use a list comprehension to iterate through each word in the sentence. We remove any punctuation and convert all words to lower case using the **isalpha** and lower functions.

7. Remove stop words using the following code:

```
words = [word for word in words if not word in stopwords.words('english')]
```

Stop words are common words like is, the, a, and so on that do not carry much meaning. We use another list comprehension to remove these words from our list.

8. Lemmatize words using the following code:

```
words = [lemmatizer.lemmatize(word) for word in words]
```

Lemmatization is the process of converting a word to its base form. For example, the lemma of running is run. We use another list comprehension and NLTK's **WordNetLemmatizer** to do this.

9. Join the words back into a sentence and add it to our list of processed reviews using the following code:

```
processed_review = ' '.join(words)
```

```
processed_reviews.append(processed_review)
```

We use the join function to join the words back into a sentence and then add this processed review to our list of processed reviews.

By following these steps, you can transform raw text data into a form that is ready to be used in NLP tasks. You can adjust these steps to fit the needs of your specific task.

The transformation journey: From text to features

As we move beyond the basic processing and organization of textual data, our next focus is on representing and extracting features from the text. At the core of text analytics and NLP is the challenge of transforming unstructured text into a format that machine learning algorithms can understand. This involves converting the text into numerical representations or features that capture the necessary information from the text. In this section, we will explore several widely used techniques to accomplish this, such as **bag-of-words (BoW)**, **Term Frequency-Inverse Document Frequency (TF-IDF)**, word embeddings, and more, each with its unique advantages and applications.

Bag-of-words: Turning words into numbers

BoW model is one of the simplest yet most effective techniques in NLP. As the name suggests, this technique converts text into a bag of individual words. This is a simple but powerful approach to converting textual data into a format that can be easily analyzed or fed into machine learning algorithms.

Let us look at how it works.

First, we perform tokenization and split the given text into individual elements with semantic meaning. For instance, consider the sentence *I love reading books*. Tokenization would break this down into the following list of words: (I, love, reading, books). Each of these words, known as **tokens**, serves as an independent unit that the algorithm can understand and analyze.

The next step is building a vocabulary from the corpus, which is the entire dataset of text you are working with. The vocabulary is a set containing all unique words from the corpus.

For example, let us say, our corpus contains two sentences: *I love reading books*, and *I love playing games*. The vocabulary built from these sentences would be (I, love, reading, books, playing, games).

After building the vocabulary, the text data is converted into numerical vectors. Each document or sentence is represented as a vector in a space where each dimension corresponds to a word from the vocabulary. The value at each dimension in the vector represents the count of occurrences of the corresponding word in that document.

Continuing with our example, the sentence *I love reading books* would be converted into a vector based on the vocabulary we created. The corresponding vector would be (1, 1, 1, 1, 0, 0), where each value corresponds to the count of the word at the respective index in the vocabulary. For instance, I appears once, love appears once, reading appears once, and so on. The two zeros at the end of the vector correspond to the words playing and games from our vocabulary, which do not appear in the sentence *I love reading books*.

These steps effectively convert textual data into a format that can be readily used for machine learning or statistical analysis.

The advantage of this model lies in its simplicity and efficiency. It can handle large volumes of text and turn them into a numerical vector that machine learning algorithms can work with. However, its limitations are equally important. The lack of context sensitivity and the inability to capture semantic and syntactic relationships between words can lead to inaccurate models, especially for complex NLP tasks.

Weighing words with TF-IDF: Balancing frequency and importance

While bag of words allows us to represent text data for machines, it misses out on one key aspect: the relevance of words. Not all words are created equal, and some carry more information than others. This is where TF-IDF shines, adding a layer of sophistication to our text representation.

TF-IDF is a statistical measure used to evaluate the importance of a word in a document relative to a collection of documents, known as a corpus. It does this by multiplying two metrics: **Term Frequency (TF)** and **Inverse Document Frequency (IDF)**.

Term frequency is just how often a word appears in a document. It operates on the same principle as bag of words. However, words like is, the, and an may appear frequently but offer little informational value. To mitigate this, TF-IDF uses the inverse document frequency. This measure decreases the weight for commonly used words and increases it for words that are not used very often in a collection of documents. Thus, words unique to a document become more significant.

For example, consider the sentence, *The cat sat on the mat*. In a corpus where documents talk about various animals, the word *cat* would be more significant than the, despite the appearing more often in the document.

It is worth mentioning that TF-IDF brings us a step closer to understanding the context and relevance, although it still does not capture the order of words.

Embedding semantics with Word2Vec and GloVe

Building on the idea of word relevance, we cannot ignore the importance of context in human language. While BoW and TF-IDF provide a good start, they fail to capture the semantic relationships between words. Now, word embedding methods, such as Word2Vec and GloVe, not only map words to numerical vectors but also do so in a way that captures their semantic meanings and relations to other words.

Word2Vec, developed by researchers at Google, uses a shallow neural network to learn these word vectors. It operates under the assumption that words appearing in the same contexts share semantic meaning. Word2Vec can be implemented in two ways: **continuous bag of words (CBOW)**, where we predict a word given its context, and skip-gram, where we predict the context given a word.

Global Vectors for Word Representation (GloVe) is a project from Stanford that also constructs word embeddings but with a different approach. GloVe aims to directly optimize the vector representations so that their dot product equals the logarithm of the words' probability of co-occurrence.

A key point is that Word2Vec and GloVe generate word vectors that capture semantic meaning. For example, the vector operations *King - Man + Woman* could result in a vector very close to Queen, capturing the gender relationship in this instance.

The adoption of word embeddings has been a major milestone in NLP, paving the way for more complex models that can understand and generate human language more effectively.

ELMo and BERT: The rise of context in word embeddings

As we have explored, Word2Vec and GloVe provide powerful tools for capturing word semantics. Yet, they have a limitation: they assign a single vector to each word, ignoring the fact that the meaning of a word can change depending on its context. Consider the word bank. In *I bank on you* and *I sat by the river bank*, bank has entirely different meanings. Static word embeddings like Word2Vec and GloVe cannot capture this nuance. This is where contextualized word embeddings like ELMo and BERT come into play.

Embeddings from language models (**ELMo**) addresses this problem by generating word representations that consider both the syntax and semantics of words, taking into account their context. This means that the same word can have different ELMo vectors depending on its usage in a sentence. ELMo accomplishes this using a bi-directional **Long Short-Term Memory** (**LSTM**) network trained on a large text corpus. The word embeddings are the output from the LSTM, which has learned to understand context due to its sequential input processing.

Bidirectional Encoder Representations from Transformers (**BERT**), another method for creating contextualized word embeddings, further improves upon ELMo by using a transformer model instead of LSTMs. The transformer architecture allows BERT to consider the context from both left and right directions simultaneously (hence, bidirectional); due to this, BERT has achieved state-of-the-art results on various NLP tasks.

These advancements in contextualized word embeddings significantly enhance our ability to capture the nuances of language, enabling more sophisticated language understanding models.

Navigating text data: Bag of words, TF-IDF, and Word2Vec

To illustrate the concept of text representation tangibly, let us imagine we are working on a text classification problem. We will use a sample of sentences to represent typical text data. Then, we will transform this data using several text representation techniques: Bag of words, TF-IDF, and Word2Vec.

Our data might be as follows:

```
corpus = [
    'The cat sat on the mat.',
    'The dog sat on the log.',
    'Cats and dogs are great pets.',
    'I have a cat; I have a dog.'
]
```

Bag-of-words

In bag-of-words, each unique word in the text is considered a feature. The number of times each word occurs in the document will be its value. Execute the following code:

```
from sklearn.feature_extraction.text import CountVectorizer

vectorizer = CountVectorizer()
X = vectorizer.fit_transform(corpus)

print(vectorizer.get_feature_names_out())
print(X.toarray())
```

In this code, we use the **CountVectorizer** class from **sklearn.feature_extraction. text** to implement the **BoW** model. The **fit_transform** function learns the vocabulary of the corpus and returns a document-term matrix. Each row of the matrix corresponds to one document, and each column corresponds to a unique word in the corpus. The value in each cell is the count of the word (column) in the document (row).

Term Frequency-Inverse Document Frequency

TF-IDF is a numerical statistic that reflects how important a word is to a document in a corpus. It increases proportionally to the number of times a word appears in the document but is offset by the number of documents in the corpus that contain the word. Execute the following code:

```
from sklearn.feature_extraction.text import TfidfVectorizer

vectorizer = TfidfVectorizer()
X = vectorizer.fit_transform(corpus)

print(vectorizer.get_feature_names_out())
print(X.toarray())
```

Here, we are using the **TfidfVectorizer** class from **sklearn.feature_extraction. text** to implement the TF-IDF model. The usage is similar to **CountVectorizer**, but the resulting matrix contains TF-IDF scores instead of word counts.

Word2Vec

Word2Vec is a recent model that embeds words in a lower-dimensional vector space using a shallow neural network. The result is a set of word vectors where vectors close together in vector space have similar meanings based on context, and word vectors distant from each other have differing meanings.

We will use the Gensim library to illustrate Word2Vec.

Gensim is an open-source library for unsupervised topic modeling and NLP using modern statistical machine learning. Gensim is designed to handle large text collections using data streaming and incremental online algorithms. This makes it different from most machine learning software packages that only target batch and in-memory processing.

Installing Gensim is a straightforward process. Open your terminal or command prompt and enter the following command:

```
pip install gensim
```

Since Word2Vec requires sentences as its input, we first have to tokenize our corpus using the following code:

```
from gensim.models import Word2Vec
from nltk.tokenize import sent_tokenize, word_tokenize

# Tokenizing our corpus
sentences = [word_tokenize(sent) for sent in corpus]

# Training Word2Vec model
model = Word2Vec(sentences, min_count=1)

# Summary of the model
print(model)
```

In the preceding code, we are tokenizing our corpus into sentences and then into words using the **nltk.tokenize** module. We then train the Word2Vec model on these sentences using the **gensim.models.Word2Vec** class.

For the Word2Vec model, the result is not a vector space that can be easily printed, but you can access the vector representation of individual words using the **model.wv** attribute.

Decoding emotions: Sentiment analysis and text classification

In the universe of NLP, sentiment analysis and text classification serve as powerful tools, enabling machines to understand, interpret, and generate human language in a valuable way. Sentiment analysis, often referred to as opinion mining, delves into the emotional tone behind words to understand the attitudes, opinions, and emotions of a speaker or writer. Meanwhile, text classification is the process of assigning tags or categories to text according to its content; it is one of the fundamental tasks in NLP. Sentiment analysis and text classification, with their respective functionalities, offer a broad spectrum of applications in today's data-driven world, from filtering spam emails to analyzing customer feedback or social media conversations.

Navigating the sea of opinions with sentiment analysis

The widespread use of social media and other online communication channels has led to an unprecedented explosion in the volume of digital text. In such a scenario, a critical need arises to understand and analyze these massive amounts of text data effectively. Sentiment analysis, an integral part of NLP and machine learning, fills this gap.

Sentiment analysis, often associated with opinion mining, is a systematic process that leverages NLP, text analysis, and computational linguistics to extract and identify subjective information from source materials. The primary objective is to determine the attitudes, opinions, and emotions of a speaker or writer on a specific topic or toward a contextual polarity within a document. The analysis provides a sentiment score, typically ranging from extremely negative to extremely positive.

The essence of sentiment analysis lies in its ability to extract subjective elements, such as opinions, beliefs, evaluations, appraisals, and emotions, from text data. While humans can instinctively form an understanding of sentiment upon reading or hearing text, teaching a machine to understand sentiment requires training it on a large dataset with predefined sentiments, enabling it to detect patterns and make associations.

The rise in social media usage has made sentiment analysis a valuable tool in various fields like marketing, customer service, and product analytics. For instance, businesses use sentiment analysis to gauge customer responses to their products or campaigns, providing valuable insights to improve their strategies. Additionally, in a customer service setting, it helps identify unhappy customers and their grievances, enabling timely and effective resolution.

As a comprehensive field, sentiment analysis consists of various techniques and approaches, which can be broadly classified into three categories: knowledge-based techniques, statistical methods, and hybrid methods. Knowledge-based techniques leverage publicly available resources to conduct the analysis, while statistical methods rely on machine learning algorithms. Hybrid methods, as the name suggests, combine both knowledge-based and statistical techniques to achieve more accurate results.

Mastering text classification

Text classification is a cornerstone of NLP and is essential in many real-world applications. It is a supervised learning method and, at its heart, involves assigning predefined categories (or labels) to text. This procedure makes way for an organized and structured way of handling vast amounts of unstructured data, making it more understandable and easier to analyze.

Text classification begins with creating a training dataset, where each document is associated with one or more labels. This labeled data is used to train a machine learning model. After the model has been trained, it can predict the labels for new, unseen documents based on the patterns and associations it learned during training.

The power of text classification extends to numerous applications. For example, in the world of news, it can automatically categorize articles based on their content, such as sports, politics, or entertainment. In customer service, it can direct customer queries to the appropriate department based on the issue mentioned in the text. It is also a vital tool in social media management for identifying and tracking topics of interest or sentiment, and it helps in email filtering systems, distinguishing between spam and non-spam emails.

Several machine learning models can be employed for text classification, ranging from traditional methods like Naïve Bayes, **Support Vector Machines (SVM)**, and decision trees to more advanced models like **convolutional neural networks (CNN)** and **recurrent neural networks (RNN)**. Each of these methods has its strengths and weaknesses, and their effectiveness can vary depending on the nature of the text data and the specific task at hand.

The key to a successful text classification model lies in the feature extraction stage, where meaningful attributes are derived from raw text to represent the documents. Methods such as BoW, TF-IDF, and word embeddings are commonly used for feature extraction in text classification tasks.

Bringing sentiment analysis and text classification to life with Python

Alright, now that we have covered the theory of sentiment analysis and text classification, let us put that knowledge into practice with some Python code. We will be using NLTK and scikit-learn.

Before we begin, you need to make sure you have those installed.

In this example, we will be using a simple dataset of movie reviews.

The movie reviews dataset in this code example is a built-in dataset available in the NLTK corpus. NLTK provides several such sample datasets, which are useful for learning and exploring natural language processing tasks without worrying about collecting and cleaning data. The movie reviews dataset, in particular, is a collection of 2,000 movie reviews labeled as positive or negative, making it an excellent resource for practicing sentiment analysis and text classification.

Our goal is to create a model that can accurately predict the sentiment of a review. Follow the given steps:

1. Import the necessary libraries and load the data using the following code:

```
import nltk

from nltk.corpus import movie_reviews

from sklearn.model_selection import train_test_split

from sklearn.feature_extraction.text import CountVectorizer

from sklearn.naive_bayes import MultinomialNB

from sklearn.metrics import accuracy_score

# Download movie reviews from nltk corpus

nltk.download("movie_reviews")

# Now you can load the reviews and labels

reviews = [movie_reviews.raw(fileid) for fileid in movie_reviews.file-
ids()]

labels = [movie_reviews.categories(fileid)[0] for fileid in movie_
reviews.fileids()]
```

In this step, we import the necessary libraries, download and load the movie review data from NLTK. We also separate the reviews (the features) from their corresponding labels (the target).

2. Preprocess the data and create a BoW representation using the following code:

```
# split data into training and test set

X_train, X_test, y_train, y_test = train_test_split(reviews, labels,
test_size=0.2, random_state=42)

# create a bag of words representation

vectorizer = CountVectorizer(stop_words='english')

X_train_vectorized = vectorizer.fit_transform(X_train)

X_test_vectorized = vectorizer.transform(X_test)
```

In this step, we split the data into a training set and a test set. We then create a BoW representation of our data using scikit-learn's **CountVectorizer**, which also conveniently removes English stop words.

3. Train a Naïve Bayes classifier using the following code:

```
# train a Naive Bayes classifier
clf = MultinomialNB()
clf.fit(X_train_vectorized, y_train)
```

Here, we create and train a Naïve Bayes classifier. This type of classifier works particularly well with text data.

4. Evaluate the model using the following code:

```
# predict the labels for the test set
y_pred = clf.predict(X_test_vectorized)

# print the accuracy of the model
print("Accuracy: ", accuracy_score(y_test, y_pred))
```

In the final step, we use our trained model to predict the labels for the test set and print the model's accuracy.

Topic modeling and entity recognition

As we wade deeper into text analytics, we encounter more sophisticated techniques for understanding and extracting insights from text data. Among these are topic modeling and **named entity recognition** (**NER**). Topic modeling is a technique that automatically identifies topics present in a text object and derives hidden patterns exhibited by a text corpus. On the other hand, named entity recognition is a process wherein an algorithm takes a string of text (sentence or paragraph) as input and identifies relevant nouns (people, places, and organizations) that are mentioned in that string.

Introduction to topic modeling

Understanding what a document is about is a common task in many applications. Still, the process becomes daunting when the data size scales up to thousands or even millions of documents. Enter topic modeling, a suite of algorithms that interpret a corpus to discover the main themes or topics that run throughout.

In essence, topic modeling is an unsupervised machine learning technique that is employed to identify the topics that are present in a document body, giving us the ability to pinpoint the major themes in a large collection of texts. It is a statistical model with the fundamental assumption that any document consists of a mixture of topics, each consisting of a set of words with certain probabilities. A key aspect to remember is that the definition of a topic here is a bit abstract. A topic can be regarded as a cluster or group of words found together more often.

For example, in a corpus related to the news industry, we may find topics related to politics, sports, technology, and entertainment. Each of these topics would contain words most representative of the theme. For instance, the politics topic might include words like government, policy and election, while the sports topic might contain words like team, score and tournament. The model assigns each document a mixture of these topics, with each topic contributing a certain proportion to the document.

The beauty of topic modeling is that it does not require any prior annotations or labeling of the documents. It works well on large text corpora and is excellent for exploring data, finding a structure, and understanding the main themes in the data. One of the most popular techniques for topic modeling is **Latent Dirichlet Allocation (LDA)**, which assumes that the documents are produced from a combination of topics and those topics then generate words based on their probability distribution.

Unearthing context with named entity recognition

The world comprises countless entities: people, places, organizations, and even time-specific phrases. Identifying and classifying these entities in text is what we call **NER**. It is a key component of many natural language processing tasks, offering valuable context to understand the semantic richness of text.

NER is a form of information extraction that seeks to locate and classify named entities within a text into predefined categories such as person names, organizations, locations, medical codes, time expressions, quantities, monetary values, and percentages. For instance, in the sentence *Microsoft has its headquarters in Seattle,* NER identifies Microsoft as an organization and Seattle as a location.

NER plays an important role in several applications, including question-answering systems, text summarization, and machine translation. By identifying the entities in the text, these applications gain a deeper understanding of the context, improving their accuracy and effectiveness.

The complexity of NER lies in its ability to distinguish between general and specific terms within a text. For instance, while spring could refer to a season, in another context, it might refer to a mechanical device. Understanding the context is key to successful entity recognition.

NER can be performed using several rule-based and machine learning methods. Rule-based approaches create rules and use them to identify named entities in text. Machine learning methods, on the other hand, train models on a labeled dataset to perform the task. Deep learning techniques have also been successfully applied to NER, using architectures such as RNNs and their variants like LSTM networks.

Cracking topics and entities: A Python code walkthrough

To demonstrate topic modeling and NER, let us use the popular Python libraries Gensim and spaCy. We will perform topic modeling using the LDA method from the Gensim library. For NER, we will use the spaCy library.

LDA is a popular technique for topic modeling. This algorithm seeks to find clusters of words (that is, the topics) that frequently occur together in documents. LDA treats each document as a mix of various topics and each topic as a mix of various words. This way, topics can be understood by looking at the most prominent words in them. A key aspect of LDA is that it allows each document to be a mix of topics, where the weightage of each topic determines its relevance to that document. LDA makes two key assumptions:

- Documents that have similar words often have similar topics.

- Documents with groups of words frequently occurring together often have the same topic.

Before we dive in, ensure that both libraries are installed in your Python environment.

Once installed, you can download the necessary language model for spaCy with the following command:

```
!python -m spacy download en_core_web_sm
```

Now, we have a corpus of documents, and we want to determine the topics within these documents and identify any named entities. Execute the following code:

```
# import the necessary libraries
import gensim
from gensim import corpora
from gensim.models.ldamodel import LdaModel
import spacy

# load the spacy model
nlp = spacy.load('en_core_web_sm')

# suppose 'documents' is a list of text documents
documents = ["The quick brown fox jumps over the lazy dog",
             "John bought a new car",
             "The new car is beautiful",
             "Python is a great programming language"]
```

```python
# perform basic preprocessing (lowercase, tokenization, stopword removal)
texts = [[token for token in doc.lower().split() if token not in gensim.
parsing.preprocessing.STOPWORDS] for doc in documents]

# create a dictionary representation of the documents
dictionary = corpora.Dictionary(texts)

# convert the list of texts to a list of vectors
corpus = [dictionary.doc2bow(text) for text in texts]

# perform topic modelling using LDA
lda_model = LdaModel(corpus=corpus, id2word=dictionary, num_topics=2)

# print the topics
topics = lda_model.print_topics(num_words=4)
for topic in topics:
    print(topic)

# perform named entity recognition using spacy
for doc in documents:
    spacy_doc = nlp(doc)
    for ent in spacy_doc.ents:
        print(ent.text, ent.start_char, ent.end_char, ent.label_)
```

In the preceding code, we first perform basic preprocessing on the documents, which includes lowercasing, tokenization, and stop word removal. We then create a dictionary representation of the documents and convert the list of texts to a list of vectors. And, of course, we use LDA to perform topic modeling.

By setting **num_topics=2**, we instruct the LDA model to find two topics in our corpus. The model then associates each word in our corpus to one of the two topics based on the frequency of the word in each topic. The result of the LDA model is a set of topics, each represented as a distribution of words.

The **lda_model.print_topics(num_words=4)** line prints the four most frequently used words in each of the two topics. These are the words that the LDA model has found to be most indicative of each topic.

Conclusion

Our journey in this chapter took us through the fascinating realm of text analytics and natural language processing. We began by delving into the intricacies of text data, uncovering the process of transforming raw text into meaningful, digestible pieces of information through tokenization and text preprocessing techniques. This knowledge was then applied to represent text in various formats suitable for machine understanding, from the straightforward bag of words and TF-IDF to the more nuanced word embeddings and their contextualized counterparts. Further, we explored how this understanding can power applications like sentiment analysis and text classification. Finally, the chapter unveiled the methods for discerning topics within a sea of text using topic modeling and identifying specific entities using NER.

Now, as we transition to the next chapter, we will shift our focus to recommendation engines, where we will explore content-based filtering, matrix factorization techniques like **Singular Value Decomposition (SVD)**, and the art of creating hybrid recommender systems. This will provide personalized suggestions and enhance user experiences across various domains.

Points to remember

- **Text processing and tokenization:** This is a critical step in text analytics and NLP, where raw text data is cleaned and segmented into manageable units known as tokens.

- **Text representation:** Text representation techniques such as bag-of-words, TF-IDF, and word embeddings transform the text into numerical vectors that machine learning algorithms can understand.

- **Sentiment analysis and text classification:** Leveraging machine learning, these techniques identify and categorize opinions expressed in a piece of text, particularly to determine the writer's attitude toward a particular topic, product, and so on.

- **Topic modeling and named entity recognition:** Topic modeling identifies the abstract topics that occur in a collection of documents, while named entity recognition seeks to locate and classify named entities in text into predefined categories such as person names, organizations, and locations.

Multiple choice questions

1. **Which of the following is not a technique used for text representation?**

    a. Bag-of-words

    b. Term Frequency-Inverse Document Frequency

    c. Word embeddings

    d. Named entity recognition

2. **Sentiment analysis is mainly used to do which of the following?**

   a. Identify topics in a document

   b. Tokenize text data

   c. Determine the sentiment or attitude of the writer toward a particular topic

   d. Classify named entities in the text

3. **What is the role of tokenization in text analytics and NLP?**

   a. It helps in topic modeling.

   b. It transforms raw text data into manageable units.

   c. It classifies text into different sentiments.

   d. It recognizes named entities in the text.

4. **In the context of this chapter, what does LDA stand for, and what is it used for?**

   a. Linear Discriminant Analysis; used for dimensionality reduction

   b. Latent Dirichlet Allocation; used for dimensionality reduction

   c. Latent Dirichlet Allocation; used for topic modeling

   d. Linear Discriminant Analysis; used for topic modeling

Answers

1. d

2. c

3. b

4. c

Questions

1. What are the key differences between the bag-of-words and TF-IDF techniques for text representation?

2. What is named entity recognition, and why is it important in text analytics?

3. Can you explain the importance of preprocessing in NLP and some common preprocessing steps?

## CHAPTER 16

Crafting Recommender Systems

Introduction

In an era characterized by large amounts of data and digitization, the demand for personalization is higher than ever. Whether it is online shopping, music streaming, or even content consumption on social media platforms, the concept of personalized suggestions or recommendations is a defining feature of our digital experiences. It is no wonder that recommender systems have emerged as a crucial element in many applications and industries. In the modern digital economy, recommender systems have become the pioneers of personalization.

In this chapter, we will look into the fascinating world of recommender systems, understanding the underlying algorithms and techniques that power these systems. We will explore collaborative filtering, content-based filtering, matrix factorization, and hybrid recommender systems in depth, equipping you with the knowledge and tools you need to create your recommender systems.

Structure

In this chapter, we will discuss the following topics:

- Collaborative filtering
- Content-based filtering

- Matrix factorization and Singular Value Decomposition
- Hybrid recommender systems

Objectives

By the end of this chapter, you should understand the significance of recommender systems and differentiate between various techniques used in these systems. You can implement these techniques using Python and assess their performance using suitable metrics, equipping you with the skills to create personalized user experiences that enhance engagement and satisfaction.

Introduction to collaborative filtering

In the vast universe of recommender systems, collaborative filtering is one of the most effective and commonly used methods. Its success lies in its inherent ability to provide personalized recommendations by leveraging the power of collective behavior. This innovative technique operates on the assumption that if users X and Y have agreed in the past, they are likely to agree again in the future. In other words, users with similar tastes and preferences in the past will likely have similar preferences moving forward.

Collaborative filtering focuses on finding patterns and similarities between user interactions, rather than the content of items, to make these recommendations. This sets it apart from content-based methods, which primarily focus on the attributes of items. As a result, collaborative filtering enables us to predict a user's interests by collecting preferences from many users.

It is important to note that collaborative filtering is broadly categorized into two types: user-based and item-based. User-based collaborative filtering, as the name suggests, finds similarity between users, whereas item-based collaborative filtering calculates similarity between items. Both techniques have their advantages and use cases, and the choice of which one to use depends on the specific problem at hand.

User-based collaborative filtering

Imagine walking into a book club meeting, and a member with whom you have shared similar book preferences in the past raves about a newly published novel they just finished reading. Given your shared interests, you would likely consider checking out this novel. In essence, this is the simple yet powerful idea behind user-based collaborative filtering: leveraging the power of shared preferences to provide personalized recommendations.

User-based collaborative filtering, one of the key methods in recommender systems, works by finding users who are similar to the target user (often based on past behavior like ratings, purchases, or views) and then recommends items that these similar users have liked or interacted with in the past. The fundamental assumption here is that if two users agreed in the past, they are likely to agree again in the future.

The process of user-based collaborative filtering typically involves the following steps:

1. Calculate the similarity between all pairs of users. This is often done using measures such as cosine similarity or pearson correlation coefficient.

2. For a given user, find the most similar users, often called **neighbors**. The number of neighbors chosen can vary based on the specific application.

3. Predict the target user's rating for an item (that they have not yet interacted with) based on the ratings given to that item by the neighbors.

4. Recommend the items with the highest predicted ratings.

There are some significant advantages to using user-based collaborative filtering. Firstly, because it is based on the behavior of real users, the recommendations it provides are often easy to explain (User A liked this, so you might too!). Secondly, it can help users discover new items they may not have found, broadening their horizons.

However, user-based collaborative filtering is not without its challenges. For one, it can struggle with scalability: in a large system with many users, finding the most similar users can be computationally expensive. Additionally, it can suffer from a problem known as **user churn**, where the system's performance decreases as users continually change their behavior. Lastly, it is not effective for dealing with cold-start problems, where it is difficult to make accurate recommendations for new users who have little to no history in the system.

Despite these challenges, user-based collaborative filtering has proven to be a highly effective method in many recommender systems, driving personalization and enhancing the user experience. As we move forward in this exciting field, new techniques and optimizations continue to be developed to address its limitations and improve its performance.

Decoding item-based collaborative filtering

This method, instead of focusing on the similarity between users, concentrates on the likeness between items. The reasoning here is that if users liked a certain item, they will likely enjoy similar items.

Item-based collaborative filtering operates in the following way:

- First, it computes the similarity between each pair of items. This calculation can be based on various metrics, such as cosine similarity or pearson correlation coefficient.

- Once the similarity matrix is established for a given user, the algorithm predicts their potential interest in an item they have not interacted with yet. This prediction is based on the weighted average of the user's previous ratings on the most similar items.

- The items with the highest predicted interest are then recommended to the user.

Now, why should we care about item-based collaborative filtering? Well, there are some noteworthy advantages. It is more stable and less prone to the user churn issue that plagues user-based collaborative filtering. This is because user preferences change more rapidly and drastically than item attributes. Also, item-based collaborative filtering is typically more scalable since the number of items is often smaller than the number of users, especially in large-scale systems.

That said, item-based collaborative filtering also has its share of challenges. One main issue with this method is that it also suffers from the cold-start issue when dealing with new items. Since new items lack interaction history, the algorithm struggles to compute similarities and make accurate recommendations. Furthermore, this method may oversimplify user interests by assuming that their preference for one item can be directly transferred to similar items.

Despite these challenges, item-based collaborative filtering has shown prowess in various settings, from movie recommendations to product suggestions, enhancing user experiences and personalization. It is a testament that collaborative filtering's power goes beyond user similarities and can be harnessed effectively by focusing on items. As we continue to journey through the world of recommender systems, the charm of item-based collaborative filtering only grows stronger, and its utility becomes more apparent.

Measuring similarities in recommender systems

The journey into the heart of collaborative filtering brings us to a critical stop: similarity scores. We are diving deep into the mathematical terrain, unearthing the formulas that power the concept of similarity in data science. It is through these similarity scores that collaborative filtering systems determine who shares tastes with whom or which items are like each other.

First up, we have the cosine similarity. Picture two vectors in multi-dimensional space. The cosine similarity measures the cosine of the angle between these vectors. The closer the cosine value is to 1, the smaller the angle and the greater the match between the two vectors. Mathematically, it is calculated as the dot product of the vectors divided by the product of their magnitudes. If A and B are our vectors, our formula would look something like this:

```
cosine_similarity = dot_product(A, B) / (norm(A) * norm(B))
```

In pearson correlation, we are looking at the covariance of the two vectors divided by the product of their standard deviations. This gives us a value between -1 and 1, indicating the strength and direction of the association. Consider the following code:

```
pearson_correlation = covariance(A, B) / (std_dev(A) * std_dev(B))
```

Lastly, the Jaccard index comes into play when dealing with sets of items rather than numerical ratings. It calculates the ratio of the intersection of the sets to their union, essentially giving us the proportion of shared items. In the language of mathematics, for sets **A** and **B**, we have the following:

```
jaccard_index = intersection(A, B) / union(A, B)
```

With these formulas, we can calculate similarity scores in collaborative filtering. Remember, the road to successful recommendations is paved with accurate similarity measures. Let us continue our journey with Python code examples applying these concepts.

Sparsity and scalability in collaborative filtering

Let us consider the flip side of the recommendation systems coin: the challenges, specifically the twofold trouble of sparsity and scalability.

Sparsity in the context of collaborative filtering comes from the fact that not all users rate all items. When you think about it, even the most fervent movie buff could not watch all the movies on Netflix, right? So, we have a lot of unknowns in our user-item matrix. This results in sparsity, a major challenge because our algorithms rely on existing ratings to predict the unknowns. Techniques like matrix factorization, where we decompose our user-item matrix into the product of lower-dimensional matrices, can help us predict these unknown ratings and handle sparsity effectively.

But that is just one half of the problem. Next, we have to deal with scalability. As the number of users and items grows, so does the size of our user-item matrix and, hence, the computational resources we need. The situation can get out of hand quickly with large-scale systems like Amazon or Netflix. We have a couple of strategies up our sleeve to combat this. We could use dimensionality reduction techniques, such as SVD, to reduce the size of our data. We can opt for a more localized approach, such as using nearest neighbors, limiting our focus to a subset of similar users or items instead of the entire database.

Keep in mind that these are just some of the ways to handle sparsity and scalability in collaborative filtering. In the vast landscape of recommendation systems, numerous other techniques are waiting to be explored. Next, we will look at code examples to implement these concepts.

Building your first collaborative filtering systems in Python

Surprise stands for simple Python recommendation system engine. It is a powerful, easy-to-use Python library designed specifically for building and analyzing recommender systems. You can install it via **pip** with this simple command:

```
pip install scikit-surprise
```

Having installed surprise, we will also need a dataset to work with. For our purposes, we will use the MovieLens dataset, which is a classic in the realm of recommender systems. It consists of movie ratings provided by users and is renowned for its quality and variety: it is an excellent resource for our exploration. Surprise has it prepackaged for our convenience.

Let us delve into building our first user-based collaborative filtering system.

User-based collaborative filtering

Take a look at the following code:

```
from surprise import KNNBasic, Dataset, Reader, accuracy
from surprise.model_selection import cross_validate, train_test_split

# Load the movielens-100k dataset
data = Dataset.load_builtin('ml-100k')

# Sample random trainset and testset
# Test set is made of 25% of the ratings.
trainset, testset = train_test_split(data, test_size=.25)

# Use user_based true/false to switch between user-based or item-
based collaborative filtering
algo = KNNBasic(sim_options={'user_based': True})

# Train and test reporting the RMSE and MAE scores
algo.fit(trainset)
predictions = algo.test(testset)

# Then compute RMSE
accuracy.rmse(predictions)
```

With just a few lines of code, we have built a user-based collaborative filtering system. It is that simple with surprise.

Item-based collaborative filtering

Now, let us move on to building an item-based collaborative filtering system. It will be very similar to the user-based system we built, with one crucial difference. Use the following code:

```
# Use user_based true/false to switch between user-based or item-
based collaborative filtering
algo = KNNBasic(sim_options={'user_based': False})

# Train and test reporting the RMSE and MAE scores
algo.fit(trainset)
predictions = algo.test(testset)

# Then compute RMSE
accuracy.rmse(predictions)
```

With just a few tweaks to a single parameter, you can switch between user-based and item-based collaborative filtering, broadening the capabilities of your recommender systems.

Congratulations, you have made significant strides in building personalized recommender systems. As we continue, we will delve deeper into the possibilities and functionalities of Python's surprise library.

Personalized proposals: Understanding content-based filtering

Content-based filtering represents another core strategy for building recommender systems. Unlike collaborative filtering, which leverages collective patterns among users, content-based filtering focuses on the properties or features of the items. It is like having a personal shopper who knows your tastes and preferences in intricate detail. They know you enjoy reading mystery novels, so they are more likely to suggest the latest bestseller in that genre. Likewise, if you have given high ratings to a string of action-packed films, a content-based recommender would suggest more of the same. This approach does an excellent job when you have rich item metadata or when dealing with new users. It is time to unveil how this process works, how to implement it, and when to use it to your advantage.

The harmony of user and item profiles

Content-based filtering is like a well-choreographed dance between user and item profiles. Let us step into this dance and observe the intricate movements.

User profiles are where we document the preferences of each individual. These preferences might be explicitly stated, like ratings given to movies or books. Alternatively, they can be inferred from past actions: Did our user read many articles about space exploration? If so, it is a hint that they might be interested in astronomy.

Item profiles, on the other hand, describe the characteristics of the items in our catalog. If we are talking about books, an item profile might include the genre, the author, and key themes. For a movie, consider the director, the actors, and the film's genre.

Now, imagine these profiles as points in a multi-dimensional space. The magic of content-based filtering happens when we calculate how close or similar these points are to each other. This process, known as **similarity matching**, allows us to predict which items a user will like based on their past preferences.

As we journey through content-based filtering, remember this dance. It is key to understanding how to make personalized recommendations at scale.

Understanding feature extraction and selection

Regarding content-based filtering, the power lies in the features we choose to represent our items. It is like creating a culinary masterpiece; each ingredient or feature adds unique flavor and depth to the dish, and the right combination can make it a hit.

Feature extraction is the process of identifying these key ingredients. For a book, for example, the genre, author, and publisher might be relevant features. If we are dealing with movies, we might extract features such as director, genre, actors, and the year of release. The quality of these features significantly influences the quality of our recommendations.

The next stage is **feature selection**, and this becomes discerning chefs. Not every ingredient is essential to our recipe; some may even spoil the flavor if added. Similarly, not every feature extracted is useful for our recommendation system. We may have hundreds of potential features, but not all will contribute meaningfully to predicting a user's preference. Feature selection helps us to reduce dimensionality and choose only those features that improve the performance of our recommendation system.

Feature extraction and selection, therefore, are pivotal steps in content-based filtering, like fine-tuning a recipe until we have the perfect dish. With these tools, we can develop a sophisticated recommendation system that precisely understands and caters to our users' preferences.

The pros and cons of content-based filtering

Content-based filtering brings a unique flavor to the recommender system banquet, providing some tantalizing benefits but also certain limitations to consider.

The key advantage of content-based filtering is its ability to recommend niche items that few users have interacted with. It is like an eagle-eyed restaurant critic that can pick out a hidden gem of a dish on a menu that most patrons overlook. By focusing on item properties, it can identify potential matches even for rare, unique, or new items, thereby providing users with a wider array of options.

Moreover, content-based filtering is a master of independence. Unlike its cousin, collaborative filtering, it does not need data about other users to make recommendations. It is like a diner who is confident in their taste buds and does not need to know what everyone else in the restaurant is eating. This makes it a particularly good fit for new users, for whom we have limited interaction data.

However, content-based filtering is not without its challenges. One of its major disadvantages is its tendency to recommend items that are too similar to those the user has already interacted with. It is like a cautious chef who only cooks with familiar ingredients, limiting the range of flavors they can produce. This can lead to a lack of diversity in the recommendations, potentially stifling the discovery of new or different items that the user might also enjoy.

Finally, content-based filtering relies heavily on the quality of the item descriptions, which can be difficult to obtain or extract for certain types of items. It is akin to trying to cook a meal without knowing the quality of your ingredients. Without detailed, relevant item profiles, the performance of content-based filtering can suffer.

So, while content-based filtering brings some exciting advantages to the table, it is also important to be aware of its limitations to ensure that it is the right fit for your specific use case.

Breaking the filter bubble and enriching content analysis

Overcoming the challenges of content-based filtering often feels like a quest for the recommender systems. It is all about finding that balance between familiarity and novelty, between simplicity and complexity. Let us delve into two primary hurdles, over-specialization and limited content analysis, and learn how to navigate through these potential pitfalls.

Overspecialization, or the filter bubble, is a common problem where the system overfocuses on matching content similar to that of a user's past behavior. It is like eating your favorite pasta every day; eventually, you will crave for a change. To break this bubble, introduce diversity in your recommendations. One way to do that is to incorporate a certain level of randomness or include some less similar items in your recommendations. You could also combine content-based filtering with collaborative methods (opt for a hybrid approach) so that your system can leverage the power of the crowd to bring in some variety.

Limited content analysis is another hurdle where the system can only recommend items based on available content or features. Imagine being at a restaurant with a limited menu; you will be left longing for more options. To enhance content analysis, work on enriching your item profiles. For instance, you could use web scraping or APIs to gather more data or employ techniques like **natural language processing (NLP)** or computer vision to extract more sophisticated features from unstructured data like text or images.

Overcoming these challenges is a journey that demands continuous tweaking and experimentation. Remember, a great recommender system is like a five-star dining experience. It is not just about serving what the diner ordered but surprising them with flavors they never knew they would love!

Building content based recommendations in Python

Let us delve into the exciting world of Python, where we will create our own content-based recommender system. We will harness the power of TF-IDF for feature extraction and cosine similarity for item recommendation.

We will use the scikit-learn library for its feature extraction and similarity computation utilities, and we will use pandas for data handling.

Suppose we have a dataset of movies, where each movie has a description. Our goal is to recommend movies based on the similarity of their descriptions. Follow the given steps:

1. **Feature extraction**

   Here, we employ TF-IDF, a technique that quantifies the importance of a word in a document relative to its frequency in a corpus (group of documents). We can easily implement this in Python with scikit-learn's **TfidfVectorizer**, using the following code:

   ```
   from sklearn.feature_extraction.text import TfidfVectorizer

   tfidf = TfidfVectorizer(stop_words='english')  # Remove English stop words

   movie_descriptions = df['description']  # assuming our dataframe is df and it has a 'description' column

   tfidf_matrix = tfidf.fit_transform(movie_descriptions)
   ```

2. **Compute similarity scores**

   Once we have our TF-IDF matrix, we can compute similarity scores. We will use cosine similarity, a measure that calculates the cosine of the angle between two vectors. Execute the following code:

```
from sklearn.metrics.pairwise import linear_kernel
cosine_sim = linear_kernel(tfidf_matrix, tfidf_matrix)
```

3. **Create a recommendation function**

Finally, we will create a function that takes a movie title as input and outputs a list of the most similar movies. Take a look at the following code:

```
indices = pd.Series(df.index, index=df['title']).drop_
duplicates()  # mapping movie titles with their indices

def recommend_movies(title, cosine_sim=cosine_sim):
    idx = indices[title]  # getting the index of the movie
    sim_scores = list(enumerate(cosine_
sim[idx]))  # getting the similarity scores
    sim_scores = sorted(sim_
scores, key=lambda x: x[1], reverse=True)  # sorting the scores
    sim_scores = sim_
scores[1:11]  # getting the top 10 most similar movies
    movie_indices = [i[0] for i in sim_
scores]  # get the movie indices
    return df['title'].iloc[movie_
indices]  # return the top 10 most similar movies
```

We have created a simple content-based recommender using Python. Once a movie title is inputted, the system can recommend similar movies based on their descriptions.

Matrix factorization and SVD in recommender system

Matrix factorization and SVD are powerful techniques often employed in building advanced recommender systems. At their core, they transform our high-dimensional user-item interaction matrix into lower-dimensional but denser matrices. This helps unearth hidden correlations between users and items and can help in getting more precise recommendations. Leveraging these techniques, recommender systems can handle larger and sparser datasets, combat the cold start problem, and provide more nuanced recommendations.

Introduction to matrix factorization

Matrix factorization serves as a magic decoder ring in the world of recommendation systems.

When applied to a user-item interaction matrix, matrix factorization unveils two lower-dimensional matrices. Think of these as hidden features representing the preferences of users and attributes of items. By multiplying these lower-dimensional matrices, we get an approximation of the original matrix but with the bonus of having populated previously unknown or missing interactions. It is like having a snapshot of user-item interactions that never happened, making it a prime tool in recommendation systems.

Singular value decomposition

SVD is a powerful factorization method in linear algebra that has found great utility in recommender systems.

SVD decomposes a given matrix into three other matrices. So, if you start with matrix A, applying SVD would yield matrices U, Σ, and V-transpose. The core idea is that every matrix has a singular value decomposition.

In simpler terms, suppose we have a matrix A of size m x n. When we apply SVD, it gives us three resultant matrices: U, an m x m orthogonal matrix; Σ, an m x n diagonal matrix; and V, an n x n orthogonal matrix. The elements on the diagonal in Σ are known as the singular values of the original matrix A.

In the context of recommendation systems, SVD provides a method to approximate a matrix, filling in the unknowns, as we discussed in the section on matrix factorization.

The singular values in Σ represent the strength of different latent features. By only keeping the top k largest singular values, we choose to keep the k most important latent features, a process called **dimensionality reduction**. This is incredibly useful because it reduces the noise and gives us a cleaner, simpler approximation of the original matrix.

Through SVD, we can predict unknown user-item interactions, and these predictions can then be used to make personalized recommendations. So, while the math behind SVD might be complex, the outcome is incredibly valuable: a robust, effective recommendation system that does an excellent job of personalizing user suggestions.

Breaking down the user-item matrix into latent factors

Diving deeper into our journey through matrix factorization, we now need to look at the actual decomposition process of the user-item matrix into latent factors. The user-item matrix is the matrix where rows represent users, columns represent items, and each cell contains the rating a particular user has given to a particular item.

The goal here is to uncover the latent (hidden) factors that explain the ratings the users give. These latent factors can represent anything, such as genre in the case of movies or authors' writing style in the case of books.

So, how does this process work?

We begin with our user-item matrix, R, filled with many unknown values (ratings not yet provided by users). Then, we factorize this matrix into two lower dimensional matrices; let us call them P and Q. The P matrix has the dimensions of the number of users by some number of k latent factors, and the Q matrix has the dimensions of the same number of latent factors by the number of items.

This k is a parameter we choose, representing the number of latent factors. For example, for movie ratings, the latent factors could include dimensions such as the amount of action, romance, comedy or drama.

The aim is to find P and Q so their product approximates R. This can be done by minimizing the difference between the actual ratings in R and the estimated ratings obtained by multiplying P and Q.

Mathematically, we can represent this as minimizing the following cost function:

$$|| R - PQ ||^2 + \lambda (|| P ||^2 + || Q ||^2)$$

In this equation, the first part, $|| R - PQ ||^2$, represents the sum of squared differences between the actual ratings and the predicted ratings for all user-item pairs for which R has a known rating. The second part, $\lambda (|| P ||^2 + || Q ||^2)$, is a regularization term that helps prevent overfitting by penalizing the magnitudes of the components of P and Q.

To find the optimal P and Q, we can use techniques like **Stochastic Gradient Descent (SGD)** or **Alternating Least Squares (ALS)**.

This decomposition process helps us in estimating the unknown ratings, which ultimately aids us in recommending items to the users.

Pros and cons of matrix factorization and SVD

The pros are as follows:

- **Handling sparse data:** Matrix factorization and SVD excel in dealing with sparse data, which is often a challenge in collaborative filtering. They can predict missing values in the user-item interaction matrix, helping discover the hidden interests of users.

- **Uncovering latent factors:** Matrix factorization and SVD can identify latent features underlying the interaction processes. These are the features that drive the user-item interaction but are not explicit in the data. For instance, in movie recommendations, these factors could be a certain genre, director's style, or a specific actor's presence.

- **Scalability:** These methods are highly scalable and can be used to handle very large datasets, making them popular in the industry.

The cons are as follows:

- **Cold start problem:** Like most recommendation techniques, matrix factorization and SVD also suffer from the cold start problem. They struggle to recommend items to new users or to recommend new items that lack interaction data.

- **Difficulty interpreting latent factors:** While the ability to uncover latent factors is a strength, it is also a challenge. The latent factors are mathematical constructs that do not always have a clear, interpretable meaning.

- **Sensitivity to outliers:** Matrix factorization techniques can be sensitive to outliers. A single very high or very low rating can significantly impact the factors.

- **Overfitting:** Without proper regularization, these models can be overfitted to the training data, leading to poor generalization to unseen data.

Tackling sparsity with matrix factorization

A significant challenge faced with collaborative filtering, particularly with large datasets, is the issue of sparsity. In real-world scenarios, users interact with a minuscule fraction of the available items. This means the user-item interaction matrix, the central piece of data used in collaborative filtering, tends to be filled with more empty spaces or zeros than actual data. In simple terms, this matrix is sparse, and sparsity increases as the number of users and items grows.

Sparsity is problematic for a couple of reasons. Firstly, it means we have a lot of missing data. Recommender systems need data to make good predictions, and a sparse matrix provides less data. Secondly, it is computationally expensive. Even though most of the matrix is empty, the computational resources are required to scale with the size of the matrix, not with the amount of actual data.

So, how does matrix factorization help here? Matrix factorization algorithms take this sparse matrix and break it down into the product of two lower-dimensional matrices. This process, akin to compressing data, results in dense matrices that are easier to work with and represent the same data in a more compact form.

The magic of matrix factorization lies in its ability to fill in the missing values in these lower-dimensional matrices. It can infer the likely ratings a user would give to an item they have not interacted with based on the latent factors derived from the decomposition process. This way, matrix factorization tackles the issue of sparsity, making it possible to make recommendations even with scarce user-item interactions.

Cracking latent factors: TruncatedSVD in action with Python

Alright, let us roll up our sleeves and dig into some coding. We will use the **TruncatedSVD** class from scikit-learn, a popular **Machine Learning** (**ML**) library in Python, to apply matrix factorization on a user-item interaction matrix. Do not worry if this sounds a bit overwhelming; we will walk through the steps individually.

First, let us assume that we have a user-item interaction matrix named **user_item_matrix**. We will perform matrix factorization on it using **TruncatedSVD**. Here is how you do it:

```
from sklearn.decomposition import TruncatedSVD

# Number of latent factors
n_factors = 20

# Create a TruncatedSVD instance
svd = TruncatedSVD(n_components=n_factors)

# Fit and transform the user-item matrix
user_factors = svd.fit_transform(user_item_matrix)
```

This **fit_transform** method does two things: it first learns the latent factors by fitting the SVD model on our **user_item_matrix**, and then it transforms our matrix into a new matrix with reduced dimensionality. The **user_factors** matrix now represents our users in terms of the learned latent factors.

But what are these latent factors? They are hidden characteristics inferred from the user-item interactions. For instance, in a movie recommendation scenario, a latent factor could represent a genre like action or a feature like the movie's era. We do not exactly know what these factors represent; they are latent, after all! But the power lies in how they help capture user preferences.

With the **user_factors** matrix, we can make predictions for a user. Here is an example of how to predict the ratings a user (let us say user 0) would give to all items:

```
import numpy as np

# Item factors (transposed)
item_factors = svd.components_

# Predicted ratings for user 0
predicted_ratings = np.dot(user_factors[0], item_factors)
```

We use the dot product between the user factors and item factors to calculate the predicted ratings. We now have a prediction for every item for our user.

Synergy in recommendation: Hybrid systems

Hybrid recommender systems are a step up from the basic approaches we have discussed thus far. These systems cleverly combine the strengths of collaborative filtering and content-based filtering to provide more accurate and personalized recommendations. The crux of the hybrid approach lies in its ability to fill the gaps left by the singular models, capitalizing on the advantages of each while diminishing their inherent weaknesses. In this chapter, we will delve into the world of hybrid recommender systems, understanding their mechanics, advantages, and various implementation techniques.

Understanding hybrid recommender approaches

Alright, we are now about to dip our toes into the distinct flavors of hybrid recommender systems. Each system possesses a unique methodology and approach to harnessing the power of both collaborative and content-based filtering. Let us take a look at each system:

- **Weighted hybrid systems** balance the recommendations from both collaborative and content-based methods by assigning them varying degrees of importance. Picture a seesaw, where the balance shifts depending on the weight assigned to each side.

- **Mixed hybrid systems** go a step further. They amalgamate recommendations from both systems into a single list, giving the user a wholesome view of what they might like. It is like a buffet that combines the best dishes from two different cuisines.

- **Switching hybrid systems** are a bit picky. Depending on the situation or the user's context, they switch between collaborative and content-based filtering. It is as if they have an internal compass that directs them to the best route at any given time.

- **Feature combination hybrid systems** merge features from both methodologies into one system, treating both sets of features equally. It is a great example of teamwork, where every feature gets a chance to shine.

- **Cascade hybrid systems** have a hierarchical approach. First, they use one method to make a preliminary set of recommendations and then use the other to refine them. It is a two-step dance, ensuring precision at every turn.

- **Meta-level hybrid systems** employ an innovative technique where one method creates a model, which is then fed into the second method for refinement. Think of it as crafting a sculpture where one method forms the basic structure, and the other method adds the finishing touches.

It is crucial to note that these are just starting points: the magic lies in how they can be tweaked and combined to fit different scenarios.

Overcoming limitations for superior recommendations

Standalone systems, as proficient as they might be, often come with their own challenges. Let us take collaborative filtering, for instance. It tends to fall prey to the cold start problem where new users or items without interaction history struggle to receive accurate recommendations. Then, there is the issue of sparsity and scalability that we discussed earlier. On the other hand, content-based filtering has its Achilles' heel: the limitation of analyzing content beyond its scope and the danger of over-specialization, suggesting only a certain type of content.

Introducing hybrid recommender systems, which integrate the strengths of both content-based and collaborative filtering approaches, effectively addressing the limitations inherent in each. For instance, the cold start problem, often encountered in collaborative filtering, can be mitigated in hybrid systems through content-based techniques, enabling recommendations for new users or items. Additionally, challenges like sparsity and scalability are addressed using matrix factorization methods. Hybrid systems also overcome issues related to over-specialization and limited content analysis by incorporating the broader recommendation diversity found in collaborative filtering.

And it does not end there. By offering a seamless fusion of both systems, hybrid recommender systems bring to the table richer and more personalized recommendations. This means a more comprehensive user experience, leading to increased user engagement and satisfaction. These systems are like the superhero team-ups of the recommender system universe, bringing together the best of both worlds for an epic result.

Hybrid recommender systems in action

Let us delve into the exciting realm of real-world applications of hybrid recommender systems. It is time to see these powerful recommendation titans in action:

- **Netflix: The entertainment maestro**

  If you have ever binged a series on Netflix, then you have experienced hybrid recommender systems firsthand. Netflix employs a combination of content-based filtering, collaborative filtering, and deep learning to serve those on-point recommendations. For instance, if you watch a lot of sci-fi movies, Netflix will suggest similar genres while also considering what other users with similar tastes have watched. Their famed competition, Netflix Prize, sought to improve their algorithm, and matrix factorization techniques played a huge role in the winning entry.

- **YouTube: The video sensation**

  YouTube's recommendation engine is as hybrid as it gets. It uses content-based filtering to gauge the topics of the videos you watch and collaborative filtering to see what else is hot among viewers with tastes akin to yours. Deep learning models help further refine the recommendations. The result is the infamous YouTube rabbit hole, where you start by watching a music video and end up learning about the mysteries of the universe.

- **Amazon: The retail giant**

  Amazon, the behemoth of e-commerce, employs hybrid recommender systems to make sure you find the products you never knew you needed. By blending content-based filtering with collaborative filtering, Amazon makes recommendations based on your browsing and purchasing history as well as those of customers with similar behavior. Have you ever noticed the *customers who bought this item also bought* section? That is the hybrid recommender system hard at work.

- **Spotify: The music aficionado**

  Spotify uses hybrid recommender systems to curate playlists and suggest songs. It combines content-based filtering, using features like tempo and genre, with collaborative filtering, reflecting listener behavior. Additionally, Spotify uses NLP to analyze text data, like blogs and articles, to capture the buzz around different tracks.

- **Google News: The information hub**

  Google News uses a hybrid approach to ensure that the news articles you see are relevant and diverse. Using content-based filtering to match your interests and collaborative filtering to factor in trending topics, Google News ensures a personalized and well-rounded briefing.

  These real-world examples give us a glimpse of how hybrid recommender systems have effectively changed the landscapes of entertainment, retail, music, and information dissemination. It is like having a personal concierge in each domain, meticulously catering to your tastes and preferences.

Crafting a hybrid recommender with Python: Step-by-step guide

Now, let us create a simple hybrid recommender system that combines the techniques we have learned so far. As you know, we will be using the MovieLens dataset.

First, we will import the required libraries using the following code:

```
import pandas as pd
import numpy as np
```

```
from surprise import Dataset, Reader, KNNBasic, SVD
from surprise.model_selection import cross_validate, train_test_split
from sklearn.feature_extraction.text import TfidfVectorizer
from sklearn.metrics.pairwise import linear_kernel
```

Next, we will load our dataset using the following code:

```
data = Dataset.load_builtin('ml-100k')
trainset, testset = train_test_split(data, test_size=0.25)
```

We will create our collaborative filtering model first; consider the following code:

```
user_based_cf = KNNBasic(sim_options={'user_based': True})
user_based_cf.fit(trainset)
```

Then, we will create our content-based model. For this example, we will keep it simple and assume that we have a dataframe (**df_movies**) of movies and their descriptions. Execute the following code:

```
tfidf_vectorizer = TfidfVectorizer(stop_words='english')
tfidf_matrix = tfidf_vectorizer.fit_transform(df_movies['description'])

cosine_sim = linear_kernel(tfidf_matrix, tfidf_matrix)
```

And finally, we will create an SVD model using the following code:

```
svd = SVD()
svd.fit(trainset)
```

Now, to create a hybrid model, we can make predictions from these three models and combine them. For example, we can simply average the predictions; consider the following code:

```
def hybrid_model(user_id, item_id):
    u_pred = user_based_cf.predict(user_id, item_id)
    i_pred = cosine_sim[user_id][item_id]
    svd_pred = svd.predict(user_id, item_id)

    return (u_pred.est + i_pred + svd_pred.est) / 3
```

In the preceding code, **user_based_cf.predict** and **svd.predict** return a prediction object with an **est** attribute containing the estimated rating. For the item-based prediction, we are directly using the similarity score.

This is a simple example of a hybrid system that averages the predictions from three different types of recommender systems. In practice, you might want to assign different weights to different systems based on their performance.

Again, remember that a real-world implementation of a hybrid recommender system can get complex depending on the amount and type of data, and the specific needs of your application. This simple example should provide a good starting point for understanding how these systems work.

Conclusion

In this enlightening chapter, we navigated through the intricacies of recommender systems, unraveling various methodologies and techniques employed to craft personalized experiences. From understanding the basics of collaborative filtering and content-based, through to the matrix factorization and hybrid recommender systems, we dissected the inner workings of these systems. We also delved into the strengths and weaknesses of each technique, shedding light on the necessity of hybrid systems in overcoming standalone limitations. Through hands-on examples using Python, you gained a practical understanding and appreciation of the recommender systems, setting a solid foundation for future exploration. As we wrap up, remember, the journey to mastering recommender systems is iterative and continuous: keep learning, experimenting, and above all, enjoy the process!

In the next chapter, we will explore data storage, SQL, Python libraries for database interaction, data storage formats, serialization and deserialization, and the concepts of data warehousing and data lakes, equipping you with the skills needed to efficiently manage and access your data for various analytical tasks.

Points to remember

- **Collaborative filtering** relies on the premise that users who agreed in the past will agree in the future. It is of two types: **user-based** and **item-based**.

- **Content-based filtering** recommends items by comparing the content of the items to a user profile, with the content being represented as a set of descriptors or terms.

- **Matrix factorization**, particularly SVD, helps in reducing a matrix into constituent parts, which makes it easier to calculate more complex matrix operations.

- **Hybrid recommender systems** combine different recommendation techniques, helping improve recommendation performance by overcoming the limitations of a single approach.

- **Practical implementation** of recommender systems in Python often employs libraries like surprise and scikit-learn, and datasets like MovieLens provide a convenient playground for testing out various methods.

Multiple choice questions

1. **What is collaborative filtering?**

   a. A recommendation method that relies solely on item content

   b. A recommendation method that leverages historical user behavior

   c. A matrix reduction technique for improved calculations

   d. A way to combine different recommendation methods

2. **What is the main drawback of content-based filtering?**

   a. It requires user behavior history.

   b. It can lead to over-specialization, recommending only similar items.

   c. It struggles with large datasets.

   d. It cannot handle sparse data.

3. **In the context of recommendation systems, what is matrix factorization used for?**

   a. Balancing the weight between different recommendation methods

   b. Switching between different recommendation methods

   c. Dividing a matrix into its constituent parts to uncover latent factors

   d. Combining the features of different recommendation methods

4. **Which technique helps overcome the limitations of standalone recommender systems?**

   a. Collaborative filtering

   b. Content-based filtering

   c. Matrix factorization

   d. Hybrid recommendation approach

5. **What is the surprise library used for?**

   a. Feature extraction in content-based filtering

   b. Building recommendation systems in Python

   c. Reducing sparsity in collaborative filtering

   d. Dealing with scalability in collaborative filtering

Answers

1. b

2. b

3. d

4. d

5. b

Questions

1. Explain how the process of content-based filtering works and discuss one advantage and one disadvantage of this technique.

2. What are the steps involved in applying matrix factorization on a user-item interaction matrix, and how can this technique address the problem of sparsity in collaborative filtering?

3. Can you provide a brief overview of the different methods used to develop hybrid recommender systems, and discuss why these systems are crucial in overcoming the limitations of standalone recommender systems like collaborative and content-based filtering?

Join our book's Discord space

Join the book's Discord Workspace for Latest updates, Offers, Tech happenings around the world, New Release and Sessions with the Authors:

https://discord.bpbonline.com

## CHAPTER 17

Data Storage Mastery: Databases and Efficient Data Management

Introduction

In this chapter, we will cover everything related to data storage and management, a core skill for anyone working with data. Our journey will start with a deep dive into databases, both relational and NoSQL, as we explore their benefits and optimal use cases. We will take you on a tour of SQL and the Python libraries that make interacting with databases a breeze. We will then move on to various data storage formats, including CSV, JSON, XML, and Parquet, discussing their unique characteristics and applications. Moving on, we will delve into the essentials of data serialization and deserialization, exploring how they enable efficient storage and exchange of data. Finally, we will summarize the chapter with an overview of data warehousing and data lakes, the differences between them, and their roles in modern data architecture.

Structure

In this chapter, we will discuss the following topics:

- Introduction to databases
- SQL and Python libraries for database introduction
- Data storage formats

- Data serialization and deserialization
- Data warehousing and data lakes

Objectives

The objective of this chapter is to provide you with a comprehensive understanding of data storage and management, arming you with the knowledge to handle a wide variety of data efficiently. By delving into relational and NoSQL databases, you will gain valuable insights into how they function and when to use each. We aim to equip you with practical SQL skills and familiarize you with Python libraries for interacting with databases. Understanding different data storage formats and their uses will enable you to choose the most efficient one based on your needs. Additionally, we will uncover the process of data serialization and deserialization, helping you manage complex data structures effectively. We will introduce you to data warehousing and data lakes, which are essential components of big data architecture, broadening your understanding of data handling at scale. By the end of this chapter, you should be able to confidently navigate the landscape of data storage and management in any data science project.

Exploring database types: Relational and NoSQL databases

Databases, the backbone of data-driven industries, come in many shapes and sizes. In this section, we will delve into the heart of data storage, exploring the two main types of databases: relational databases, epitomized by SQL, and NoSQL databases. We will analyze their structure and working mechanisms, and we will see where they fit in the grand scheme of data storage. Our goal is to understand how they help in managing data efficiently, providing a foundation for our further exploration of data management.

Data housekeepers: The role of databases in data science

Databases are truly the unsung heroes of the data science world. They silently house, organize, and manage the precious data that data scientists turn into insights. Each piece of information, whether it is a simple integer or a complex unstructured text, finds a home within a database. This systematic storing and retrieving of data makes it easier for businesses to make informed decisions, drive sales, and even predict future trends.

But why are databases so important, especially in data science? Suppose you are a detective. The data you need to solve your case is all there, but it is strewn around in different places, unorganized. Databases step in here, acting like a well-maintained filing system that keeps your clues structured, accessible, and ready for analysis.

Data scientists depend on these organized datasets to build their models, validate hypotheses, and debug issues. Databases provide not just a storage mechanism but a systematic and efficient way to manipulate and retrieve data. As such, a deep understanding of databases forms a cornerstone of learning data science.

SQL and NoSQL: Two sides of the database coin

There are different types of databases, each with its unique strengths and designed to cater to specific needs.

First up, we have relational databases, which are also referred to as SQL databases. These databases are like well-organized filing cabinets with clearly defined compartments. They store data in tables, with each table consisting of rows (records) and columns (attributes). Relational databases enforce a schema, which is a blueprint defining how data is organized. They are excellent for handling structured data and complex queries, and they excel in maintaining data integrity.

On the flip side, we have NoSQL databases. If SQL databases are like filing cabinets, NoSQL databases are more like a group of post-it notes: flexible and easily adaptable. NoSQL does not insist on a fixed schema, and these databases are comfortable dealing with semi-structured or unstructured data. They are particularly known for their ability to scale horizontally and handle large volumes of data, making them a darling for big data and real-time applications.

Choosing between SQL and NoSQL is not about deciding which one is better but about which one fits your needs better. It is like choosing between a sedan and an SUV. Each has its strengths, and the choice depends on your unique needs.

Breaking down relational databases: Tables, rows, columns and keys

Dive into the world of relational databases, and you will find it structured, organized, and efficient, like a well-oiled machine. It is as if every piece of data has its designated spot. Understanding this precise structure is key to leveraging the power of relational databases, and it all starts with tables, rows, columns, and keys.

A table in a relational database is like a spreadsheet. It is a structured set of data made up of rows and columns. Rows, or records, represent individual entries in the table. Each row holds related data. For example, in a table of books, each row might represent a single book.

Columns, or attributes, are the different categories of data that exist in the table. In our books table, the columns might be title, author, publication date, and genre. Each column describes a characteristic of the data entries.

Now, let us talk about keys, the super navigators of relational databases. Primary keys are unique identifiers for each row. They are like a students' roll number in a class: each one is unique and identifies one student and one student only. Foreign keys, on the other hand, are columns that create a link between the data in two tables. They are like the mutual friends who introduce people in different social groups.

Finally, we have indices. An index in a database is similar to an index at the end of a book. It allows the database to find and retrieve data faster than it otherwise could. Just like you would use a book index to locate specific information quickly, a database index allows the database system to quickly find data without having to search every row in the database table every time a database table is accessed.

All these components come together like puzzle pieces, creating a highly organized and efficient system for storing and retrieving data.

Diversifying your data storage: NoSQL databases

NoSQL is a broad term that encompasses a wide variety of database technologies. They were developed in response to the limitations of traditional relational databases, particularly when it comes to handling big data and real-time applications. You will find that NoSQL databases are quite different from relational ones, but each has its unique charm.

The first island we visit is the land of document-based databases. Rather than tables, rows, and columns, these databases store data as documents in formats like JSON. Each document can have a different structure, which provides immense flexibility. If relational databases are like neatly arranged lockers, document-based databases are more like personalized backpacks, with each one potentially containing different types of items.

Our next stop is the realm of key-value databases. This is the simplest type of NoSQL database, where each value is associated with a unique key. Just like you have a unique key to your locker, in key-value databases, you can only access the data if you have the associated key.

Column-based databases, our third stop, take a unique approach. They organize data by columns instead of rows. Think of a warehouse where items are arranged by type, not individual shipments. This structure is particularly beneficial when dealing with analytics, as it allows more efficient data retrieval for certain queries.

Finally, we arrive at graph databases, which are often regarded as the network hubs of NoSQL databases. In these, data is stored in nodes and relationships. If data were people at a party, a graph database would not just remember who was there; it would also remember who talked to whom, who arrived together, who spent most of the time near the snacks, and so on.

Each NoSQL database type, from document-based to graph, offers unique features and capabilities. In the world of data science, it is important to pick the right tool for the right job, and understanding these different types of databases is a key part of that process.

Choosing between SQL and NoSQL

We have explored the landscape of SQL and NoSQL databases, but how do we decide where to settle? In the world of databases, it is not about which type is inherently better but about which one is more suitable for your specific needs. Like you would pick the right gear based on your destination, you will pick your database based on your data and application requirements.

Imagine that you are planning a road trip. If you are following a well-known route and have a clear roadmap (or, in our case, a schema), a relational database or SQL could be your trusty sedan. With its predefined schema, SQL databases are a good fit for applications where data integrity and consistency are crucial. They excel in complex querying, making them great for applications that require multi-row transactions like banking systems or any other financial operations. SQL databases are like your go-to recipe, reliable and predictable.

On the other hand, if you are off-roading, exploring new terrains with unpredictable paths, a NoSQL database might be your rugged 4x4. Its schema-less structure makes it flexible and adaptable to change. When dealing with large volumes of rapidly changing, diverse data, a NoSQL database is a solid choice. You will see these databases being used in real-time analytics, content management systems, IoT applications, and more. Think of NoSQL databases like your experimental recipe, ready to adapt and change with the ingredients at hand.

Of course, these are not hard and fast rules but general guidelines to inform your choice. Remember, the best database for your project is the one that fits your needs and plays well with your data.

Database showdown: An overview of popular choices

Let us take a short and scenic route through the land of popular databases:

- **MySQL:** MySQL is an open-source relational database that is versatile and has a robust performance. It is widely used for web applications and is backed by a vast community.

- **PostgreSQL:** Consider it to be the multi-faceted gem of the database world, offering more sophistication with advanced features and strict compliance with SQL standards. Its extensibility and ability to handle complex, large-scale applications make it a favorite among developers.

- **Oracle:** This is the heavy-duty machinery in the world of databases. Oracle is renowned for its robustness, enterprise-grade capabilities, and knack for handling massive data amounts. It is often the choice for big corporations with complex database requirements.

- **MongoDB:** Stepping into the NoSQL territory, MongoDB is the trailblazer. As a document-based database, it is perfect for handling diverse data that does not fit neatly into tables. It is an ideal choice for content management, real-time analytics, and mobile applications.

- **Cassandra:** This is the skyscraper of databases, built for height and scale. As a column-based database, Cassandra shines in managing colossal data across many commodity servers. Its promise of scalability and high availability without compromising performance makes it a preferred choice for big data solutions.

- **Redis:** Wrapping up with the swift athlete of databases, Redis is an in-memory key-value store known for its superior performance and versatility. It is a superb fit for caching, real-time analytics, queuing, and chat/messaging functionalities.

While there are many more databases out there, these are some renowned ones you would likely consider in your data science journey.

Python meets SQL: Mastering database interaction

Navigating the vast world of databases is a critical skill in the toolkit of any data scientist, but equally important is the ability to interact with these databases. SQL, or **Structured Query Language**, serves as the standard language for communicating with relational databases. However, Python, with its ease of learning and extensive library support, has emerged as a preferred tool for database interaction. Libraries like **SQLAlchemy** and **SQLite3** provide convenient and powerful interfaces for executing SQL commands directly from Python scripts. This section aims to introduce these indispensable tools, unraveling the nuances of SQL syntax and exploring the functionalities offered by Python libraries for smooth database interaction.

Exploring SQL: Definition, maipulation, and control

As we know, databases are the lifeblood of data management. To access, manipulate, or control the data stored within them, we rely on SQL. SQL is incredibly powerful and diverse in its applications, including three main categories: **data definition language (DDL)**, **data manipulation language (DML)**, and **data control language (DCL)**.

DDL is the foundation of your database structure. Using DDL, you define or modify your database structure. The key commands under DDL include **CREATE**, **ALTER**, and

DROP. **CREATE** is used to define a new table or database. **ALTER** modifies existing database structures like tables, whereas **DROP** deletes entire tables or databases.

DML, as the name suggests, is all about manipulating data. It is used to insert, update, or delete data in your tables. The most common DML commands include **SELECT**, **INSERT**, **UPDATE**, and **DELETE**. For instance, **SELECT** retrieves data, **INSERT** adds new data, **UPDATE** modifies existing data, and **DELETE** removes data.

Finally, we have DCL, which controls access to your data. If you are working in a team or your database is accessed by multiple users, DCL becomes quite important. The fundamental DCL commands include **GRANT** and **REVOKE**. **GRANT** is used to provide privileges to users, while **REVOKE** is used to take back any granted privileges.

Together, DDL, DML, and DCL provide the comprehensive toolset you need to define, manipulate, and control your data using SQL. Once you have got these basics, you will have a strong foundation for managing your data effectively.

Unleashing SQL's potential: Joins, subqueries, indexes, and stored procedures

Mastering SQL is not merely about understanding DDL, DML, and DCL. To fully wield SQL's potential, it is important to venture further into more advanced topics like joins, subqueries, indexes, and stored procedures.

Let us start with joins. Joins in SQL are used to combine rows from two or more tables based on a related column between them. There are various types of joins: **INNER JOIN**, **LEFT JOIN**, **RIGHT JOIN**, and **FULL JOIN**. **INNER JOIN** gives us rows that have matching values in both tables, **LEFT JOIN** returns all records from the left table, and the matched records from the right table, **RIGHT JOIN** does the opposite, and **FULL JOIN** effectively combines **LEFT** and **RIGHT JOINS**.

Next, we have subqueries. A subquery, also known as an inner query or nested query, is a query within another SQL query. Subqueries can be used to return data that will be used in the main query as a condition to further restrict the data to be retrieved. They can be very powerful tools for manipulation and transformation of data.

Now, let us tackle indexes. Indexes in SQL are used to retrieve data from the database more quickly than otherwise. They are similar to indexes in the back of a book. They are incredibly useful for improving the speed of data retrieval operations on a database table, but remember, creating an index also takes up storage space, and updating a table with indexes takes more time than updating a table without them. It is all about finding the right balance.

Finally, stored procedures are prepared SQL codes that you can save so that the code can be reused multiple times. Stored procedures can encapsulate logic, such as manipulation of data or maintaining data integrity, and are like a guide to your database, steering you away from the cliffs of syntax errors.

By understanding these advanced concepts, you will be ready to fully harness the power of SQL in your data science journey.

Navigating databses in Python: SQLAlchemy, SQLite3, PyMango

Building on our understanding of SQL and NoSQL databases, let us now explore how we can leverage the power of Python to interact with these databases. Python, with its rich ecosystem of libraries, provides us with several tools that make it easier to execute database operations. Among these tools, SQLAlchemy, SQLite3, and PyMongo are some of the most commonly used ones.

Let us start with SQLAlchemy. It is a SQL toolkit and **Object-Relational Mapping (ORM)** system for Python that provides a full suite of well-known enterprise-level persistence patterns. It is designed for efficient and high-performing database access, adapted into a simple and Pythonic domain language. So, you can execute SQL statements in Python as if writing them directly in an SQL environment.

Next is SQLite3, a built-in Python module that you can use to create, populate, and query databases entirely in memory. It is excellent when you need a lightweight disk-based database that does not require a separate server process. SQLite3 can be integrated with Python applications without any additional setup.

Finally, we have PyMongo, which is a Python driver for MongoDB, a document database that provides high performance, high availability, and easy scalability. PyMongo enables us to work with MongoDB in Python, allowing us to create, retrieve, update, and delete records (documents).

By learning to use these libraries, you can harness Python's simplicity and readability to manage your database operations effectively.

Talking to databases with Python: A hands-on guide

As a data scientist, you will often be tasked with extracting insights from vast data. Much of this data will not be in neat CSV files but in complex databases that require a bit more finesse to navigate. Python, known for its extensive ecosystem, offers several libraries to help you connect to these databases, execute queries, and retrieve results. It is high time we roll up our sleeves and put these tools to the test.

Before we start, we must ensure that the relevant libraries are installed. For SQLite, no installation is necessary as the SQLite3 module comes with Python. However, if you want to work with other databases, such as PostgreSQL, MySQL, or MongoDB, you must install the corresponding Python libraries. Here is how you can do it using **pip**:

```
# For PostgreSQL
pip install psycopg2-binary
```

```
# For MySQL
pip install mysql-connector-python
```

```
# For MongoDB
pip install pymongo
```

Now that we have the right tools, let us discuss connecting to a database. For this example, we will use SQLite via the SQLite3 module. SQLite is a light, file-based database engine, ideal for small projects or learning purposes. Here is how to establish a connection:

```
import sqlite3
conn = sqlite3.connect('example.db')
```

Once connected, we need a cursor object to execute SQL commands:

```
c = conn.cursor()
c.execute('''CREATE TABLE stocks
            (date text, trans text, symbol text, qty real, price real)''')
```

You have created a table in your SQLite database using Python. To add data or execute queries, you can use the same cursor object:

```
c.execute("INSERT INTO stocks VALUES ('2023-06-28','BUY','RH
AT',100,35.14)")
conn.commit()  # Remember to commit your changes!
c.execute("SELECT * FROM stocks")
print(c.fetchall())  # Fetches and prints all rows
```

The SQLite3 module allows us to use Python-like syntax to interact with an SQLite database, hiding many underlying complexities. This trend continues with other libraries, such as SQLAlchemy for SQL databases or PyMongo for MongoDB, which we will explore later.

The language of data: CSV, JSON, XML, Parquet, and Excel

Data storage formats, such as CSV, JSON, XML, Parquet, and Excel, each come with unique characteristics that can greatly affect the efficiency and simplicity of your data science tasks. CSV, which stands for comma-separated values, is a human-readable and broadly compatible format for tabular data. JSON, short for JavaScript object notation, presents a flexible structure that can accommodate complex, nested data. At the same time, XML, or **eXtensible Markup Language**, provides another approach to storing hierarchical information with an emphasis on self-description and broad system interoperability.

Parquet is a binary format that is optimized for efficient, columnar storage, making it highly suitable for big data scenarios due to its compression and performance benefits. Similarly, Excel files are indispensable in many business contexts, allowing for data storage in a format that is both familiar to non-technical users and capable of supporting complex data types and multi-sheet documents.

Understanding the strengths and limitations of these data storage formats, namely CSV, JSON, XML, Parquet, and Excel, is essential in choosing the most effective tool for your data science endeavors.

Weighing the options: Advantages and drawbacks of different data formats

When it comes to storing data, the format we choose to store it in can significantly impact our data analysis and processing tasks. Each data format has its unique set of characteristics, which are designed to serve different needs and scenarios. Let us understand these briefly:

- **Comma-Separated Values (CSV)** is the simplest type of format. It is lightweight and easy to use – which is why we have used it extensively in the book. Its data is tabular and plain text, making it universally readable across different programs. CSV files are easy to import and analyze in data analysis software such as Excel, Google Sheets, or any SQL-based database system. However, CSV struggles with complex, hierarchical data, as it does not support nesting. Plus, it does not maintain types - everything is just a string, which can lead to problems if the data is not consistently formatted.

- **JavaScript object notation (JSON)**, on the other hand, excels with complex, nested data structures. It is a format widely used for APIs and web applications because of its compatibility with JavaScript and other programming languages. JSON maintains types and supports complex, nested data, which gives it an edge over CSV when dealing with such data structures. However, JSON is not ideal for tabular data and can be more challenging to analyze using traditional data analysis tools.

- **XML** is another data format that supports complex, nested data. XML is self-descriptive, meaning it includes metadata in its syntax. This feature makes it suitable for document markup and data interchange in applications where the data structure is complex and may change over time. However, this flexibility comes at a cost: XML files are verbose, leading to large file sizes and slower parsing times than CSV or JSON.

- **Parquet** is a columnar storage file format optimized with Apache Hadoop, a popular big data processing framework. Unlike row-based files like CSV or JSON, Parquet stores data by column, which allows it to achieve high compression ratios and improved query performance. Parquet is excellent when working with big data because it supports advanced nested data structures, and its columnar nature allows for more efficient storage and querying. However, Parquet's binary format makes it less human-readable and harder to manipulate using simple text processing tools.

- **Microsoft Excel (XLSX)**: As one of the most widely used tools for data storage and analysis, Excel files (**.xlsx**) are indispensable for their versatility and user-friendly interface. They support complex data types, formulas, and multiple sheets, making them a go-to for diverse data manipulation tasks. However, Excel's proprietary format is not ideal for large datasets and can be less efficient for processing compared to formats like Parquet.

When choosing a data format, it is important to consider the nature of the data you are working with, the kind of analyses you will be performing, the tools you will be using, and the scalability requirements of your data infrastructure.

Python data format handling: CSV, JSON, XML, Parquet, Excel

Let us look at some hands-on examples of how to read and write data in different formats using Python. We will use some popular libraries: pandas for CSV and Parquet, and JSON and **xml.etree.ElementTree** for JSON and XML, respectively.

First, let us tackle CSV files using pandas. To read a CSV file, use the following code:

```
import pandas as pd

# Reading a CSV file
df = pd.read_csv('filename.csv')

# This will display the first 5 rows of the DataFrame
print(df.head())
```

To write to a CSV file, use the following code:

```
# Writing to a CSV file
df.to_csv('new_filename.csv', index=False)
```

Next up are JSON files. Here is how we can read and write JSON data in Python:

```
import json

# Reading a JSON file
with open('filename.json', 'r') as f:
    data = json.load(f)

# Printing the data
print(data)

# Writing to a JSON file
with open('new_filename.json', 'w') as f:
    json.dump(data, f)
```

XML files are a bit trickier due to their hierarchical nature. Let us see how we can deal with them. Execute the following code:

```
import xml.etree.ElementTree as ET

# Reading an XML file
tree = ET.parse('filename.xml')
root = tree.getroot()

# Printing the data
for elem in root:
    for subelem in elem:
        print(subelem.text)

# Writing to an XML file is a bit more in-
volved as you need to build the tree
root = ET.Element("root")
doc = ET.SubElement(root, "doc")
```

```python
field1 = ET.SubElement(doc, "field1")
field1.text = "some value1"

field2 = ET.SubElement(doc, "field2")
field2.text = "some vlaue2"

tree = ET.ElementTree(root)
tree.write("new_filename.xml")
```

Now, let us look at Parquet files. Execute the following code:

```python
import pandas as pd

# Reading a Parquet file
df = pd.read_parquet('filename.parquet')

# Writing to a Parquet file
df.to_parquet('new_filename.parquet')
```

Finally, let us look at a quick example of how to read an Excel file using Pandas:

```python
import pandas as pd

# Reading an Excel file into a pandas DataFrame
excel_file = 'data.xlsx'  # Replace with your file path
df = pd.read_excel(excel_file)
```

Now, you know how to work with different data formats in Python. Remember, selecting the correct data format can significantly influence your data analysis efficiency and insights.

Unpacking serialization: Moving and storing data efficiently

Let us dive into the world of data serialization. Data serialization converts complex data structures into a format that can be easily stored or transmitted and reconstructed later. In a data-driven world where systems continually exchange information, serialization allows data to move seamlessly from one system or application to another. For example, you could serialize a Python object into a JSON format to send it over a network or store it in a file or a database. Conversely, the data can be deserialized back into its original structure.

Most programming languages, including Python, have built-in capabilities or libraries for serialization and deserialization. Python uses **pickle** for serializing (pickling) and deserializing (unpickling) Python objects. Use the following code:

```
import pickle

# Here's a simple Python object - a dictionary
data = {"name": "John", "age": 30, "city": "New York"}

# Now, let's serialize (pickle) it
serialized_data = pickle.dumps(data)

# Now, let's deserialize (unpickle) it
deserialized_data = pickle.loads(serialized_data)

# And we're back to the original data
print(deserialized_data)
```

We have successfully serialized and then deserialized a Python object. However, keep in mind that pickle is specific to Python and is not suitable for long-term storage as it does not guarantee backward compatibility. For these situations, use standard data exchange formats like JSON or XML.

So, in a nutshell, serialization is a powerful tool to have in your data science toolbox. It helps you to exchange data efficiently between different parts of your software architecture, store it, or transmit it over networks.

Journey through serialization formats: Pickle, JSON, MessagePack

Let us extend our journey in serialization by examining a few popular formats. You will find that each has its distinct features, uses, and potential drawbacks. The key players we will cover are pickle, JSON, and MessagePack. Let us briefly understand each:

- **Pickle:** As a native Python module, pickle provides a simple way to serialize (and deserialize) Python objects, which can be incredibly useful when you want to save the state of your Python objects or share data between Python processes. Pickle is Python-specific, which is unsuitable for communicating with applications written in other languages. Moreover, it is not secure against erroneous or maliciously constructed data, and its output is not human-readable. If these are factors in your use case, pickle may not be the best option.

- **JSON:** Moving on to a more universal option, JSON is a lightweight data-interchange format that is easy for humans to read and write and for machines to parse and generate. It is language-independent and is widely used for storing and exchanging data on the web. Python's JSON module can help you convert Python objects into JSON strings (serialization) and vice versa (deserialization). However, JSON has limitations in the data types it can handle (for example, no support for binary or date/time data), and large JSON files can be slow to parse.

- **MessagePack:** This is where MessagePack comes in. It is like JSON, but fast and small. MessagePack is an efficient binary serialization format that is like JSON but faster and smaller. It lets you exchange data among multiple languages like JSON but quicker and in a more compact manner. It supports a broader set of data types than JSON, including binary data. The tradeoff is that, unlike JSON, MessagePack-encoded data is not human-readable. Python's **msgpack** module provides an API similar to **json** for easy (de)serialization.

Execute the following code:

```
import msgpack

# Here's a simple Python object - a dictionary
data = {"name": "John", "age": 30, "city": "New York"}

# Now, let's serialize it
serialized_data = msgpack.packb(data)

# Now, let's deserialize it
deserialized_data = msgpack.unpackb(serialized_data)

# And we're back to the original data
print(deserialized_data)
```

As we have seen, the best serialization format for your use case will depend on your need: interoperability, security, human-readability, performance, or support for specific data types.

Data warehouses and data lakes: A comprehensive guide

As we traverse the vast terrain of data management, it is time we cast our sights on the monumental constructs of data warehousing and data lakes. By the end of this journey, you should have a basic understanding of both and, more importantly, a clear idea of when and why to use one over the other.

Data warehouses and data lakes are two different yet complementary approaches for storing large volumes of data. The primary distinction boils down to the state of the data they hold and the purpose they serve. A data warehouse is a structured data repository optimized for analysis and reporting. It is where data goes to be understood, bearing the result of transformations to become clean, reliable, and readily interpretable.

Contrast this with a data lake, which is a vast pool that stores data in its raw, unprocessed form, including structured, semi-structured, and unstructured data. It is designed to be a cost-effective, one-size-fits-all solution for storing an organization's data. But with great power comes great responsibility: without proper data management practices, a data lake can quickly descend into poor quality, inaccessible data.

In the subsequent sections, we will delve deeper into the specific features, advantages, disadvantages, and appropriate use cases for both data warehouses and data lakes. By the end, you will be well equipped to decide which one suits your data needs.

Exploring Google BigQuery and Amazon Redshift

Stepping into the arena of data warehousing solutions, we will come across various options offered by various tech powerhouses, each flaunting a unique blend of capabilities, advantages, and use cases. Among the crowd, Google BigQuery and Amazon Redshift have emerged as two leading data warehousing solutions, beloved by many data professionals and businesses.

Google BigQuery is an enterprise-grade **Infrastructure as a Service (IaaS)** data warehouse. What sets BigQuery apart is its inbuilt capacity to leverage the comprehensive power of Google's robust infrastructure to run analyses on large datasets in real time. BigQuery has a strong appeal for data scientists and businesses due to its ability to execute SQL queries over large amounts of data swiftly and its seamless integration with an assortment of other Google services that many are familiar with.

Pivoting to Amazon Redshift, another formidable player in the market, we encounter a data warehouse product that is part of the larger cloud-computing platform, **Amazon Web Services (AWS)**. As a columnar storage database, Redshift handles data at the petabyte scale, making it an ideal choice for high-performance analysis and reporting of large data sets. Its broad compatibility with SQL-based clients and business intelligence tools, plus its easy integration with other services within the AWS ecosystem, has earned it an extensive and loyal user base.

Both Google BigQuery and Amazon Redshift offer scalable, robust, and flexible options for handling, managing, and analyzing data, even at petabyte scales. Their capability to support a wide variety of SQL queries, their scalable infrastructure, and the cost-effective, pay-as-you-go model have positioned these services as highly effective solutions for businesses of all sizes.

Hadoop: The cornerstone of data lakes and big data management

Hadoop, an open-source project by Apache, shook the data world with its innovative approach to handling big data. It presents a unique framework that allows us to process and store large amounts of data across multiple machines, bringing a robust and cost-effective solution to the data management problem.

This is made possible by its key components: the **Hadoop Distributed File System (HDFS)** and MapReduce. HDFS is the heart of Hadoop, a distributed file system designed to run on commodity hardware. It is highly fault-tolerant and is designed to be deployed on low-cost hardware. HDFS provides high throughput access to application data and is suitable for applications that have large data sets.

MapReduce, on the other hand, is the brain of Hadoop. It is a programming model for large-scale data processing. The term MapReduce refers to two separate tasks. The **Map** job takes a set of data and converts it into another set of data, where individual elements are broken down into tuples (key/value pairs). Secondly, the **Reduce** job takes the output from a map as input and combines those data tuples into a smaller set of tuples.

Beyond the core of Hadoop, there is an entire ecosystem of auxiliary tools that extends and enriches its capabilities. **Hive**, for example, allows data analysts familiar with SQL to work with Hadoop data, abstracting the underlying complexity. Then there is **Pig**, a platform for creating complex data transformations with a scripting language called **Pig Latin**. **HBase** is another component that provides real-time access to your data in Hadoop, whereas tools like Mahout offer **Machine Learning (ML)** capabilities to derive advanced analytics.

Each component of the Hadoop ecosystem has specific strengths and weaknesses. Choosing the right tool depends on your specific requirements and the nature of your problem. However, the comprehensive nature of the Hadoop ecosystem makes it an excellent foundation for building and understanding data lakes.

Conclusion

As we conclude this chapter on data storage mastery, it is clear that understanding databases, data storage formats, serialization, and the concepts of data warehouses and lakes is critical to being a proficient data scientist. The way we store and manage data can significantly impact the efficiency, performance, and scalability of our data-driven solutions. From traditional SQL databases to NoSQL alternatives, each has its unique strengths and potential use cases. Similarly, various data storage formats and serialization protocols serve different purposes, ranging from inter-system communication to efficient data storage and retrieval. Lastly, with the rising tide of big data, tools and concepts like Hadoop, data warehousing, and data lakes become essential for handling such voluminous and complex data landscapes.

In the next chapter, we will put all the knowledge and skills we have gathered throughout this journey into practice. We will embark on a comprehensive end-to-end data science project, where you will learn how to define a data science problem, collect and prepare data, select, train, and evaluate models, communicate results effectively, and finally deploy, monitor, and maintain a model, giving you a holistic understanding of the data science workflow from start to finish.

Points to remember

- Databases are foundational in data management. Understanding the differences between SQL and NoSQL databases and their appropriate use cases is crucial.

- SQL remains a powerful language for interacting with databases, with Python libraries providing useful interfaces to execute SQL queries and manage databases.

- Different data storage formats like CSV, JSON, XML, and Parquet have distinct characteristics and are chosen based on the specific requirements of data size, complexity, and required operations.

- Data serialization, the process of converting data into a format that can be stored or transmitted and then reconstructed is an important aspect of efficient data storage and communication.

- Data warehousing and data lakes provide different approaches to storing and analyzing big data. While data warehouses provide structured, cleaned data for business analytics, data lakes retain all data in raw format for diverse big data operations. Tools like Hadoop form the basis of many data lakes, providing a distributed processing system that handles vast amounts of data.

Multiple choice questions

1. **Which of the following is a key-value store NoSQL database?**

    a. MySQL

    b. Oracle

    c. Redis

    d. PostgreSQL

2. **What SQL command would you use to retrieve data from a database?**

    a. **INSERT**

    b. **UPDATE**

    c. **SELECT**

    d. **CREATE**

3. **What is the main advantage of a Parquet file over a CSV file?**

   a. Parquet is human-readable.

   b. Parquet supports schema evolution.

   c. Parquet does not support complex data structures.

   d. Parquet has a larger file size.

4. **In the context of data storage, what does the serialization process do?**

   a. Converts data into a machine-readable format

   b. Converts data into a human-readable format

   c. Both a and b

   d. Neither a nor b

5. **What is the key difference between a data lake and a data warehouse?**

   a. Data warehouse stores raw data, while data lake stores processed data.

   b. Data lake stores raw data, while data warehouse stores processed data.

   c. Both store raw data.

   d. Neither store raw data.

Answers

1. c

2. c

3. b

4. a

5. b

Questions

1. What are the main differences between SQL and NoSQL databases, and in what scenarios might you choose to use each one?

2. Describe how Python libraries like SQLAlchemy and PyMongo can be used to interact with databases.

3. What are the advantages of using a data warehousing solution like Google BigQuery or Amazon Redshift?

Join our book's Discord space

Join the book's Discord Workspace for Latest updates, Offers, Tech happenings around the world, New Release and Sessions with the Authors:

https://discord.bpbonline.com

CHAPTER 18

Data Science in Action: A Comprehensive End-to-end Project

Introduction

In the preceding chapters, we delved deep into the intricacies of data science, from understanding its foundational concepts to exploring advanced techniques. As we stand on the brink of the final chapter, it is time to combine everything into one comprehensive project. Our goal is not only to apply what we have learned but also to mimic the real-world challenges and decision-making processes that data scientists face daily.

In the world of hospitality, the ability to predict hotel booking cancellations can be a transformative asset. With this foresight, hotels can optimize room allocation, improve revenue, and enhance guest experiences. In this chapter, we will explore a hotel bookings dataset from Kaggle, rich with details about each reservation. Our primary aim is to predict the likelihood of a hotel booking being canceled, allowing us to witness the entire lifecycle of a data science project.

Structure

In this chapter, we will discuss the following topics:

- Defining a data science problem
- Data collection and preparation

- Model selection, training and evaluation
- Communication of results
- Deployment, monitoring, and maintenance of a model

Objectives

Through this chapter, we aim to provide a comprehensive view of a real-world data science project, from problem definition to deployment. By tackling the challenge of predicting hotel booking cancellations, readers will experience firsthand the decisions, challenges, and steps involved in bringing a data-driven solution to fruition.

Defining a data science problem

As we embark on our data science journey, the first step is to define the problem we aim to solve. This is crucial as it shapes our entire approach to the project, from data collection to the final deployment of the model. Using our hotel booking demand dataset, we will tackle a challenge faced by many in the hospitality industry: predicting future booking demand. Let us explore how to refine this general problem statement into a defined data science problem that can guide our subsequent steps.

Understanding the business context

Let us begin by understanding the business context. In any data science endeavor, understanding the broader business context or domain is paramount. It shapes the foundation upon which the entire project stands. For industries like hospitality, this involves grasping the delicate balance between optimizing guest experiences and ensuring profitability. Within our dataset, the challenge emerges prominently: overbooking is a prevalent strategy to offset anticipated cancellations, but it comes with its risks. Predicting cancellations with higher accuracy can significantly reduce the chances and costs associated with overbooking, such as compensating guests when no rooms are available.

Formulating the problem statement

A clear, well-defined problem statement is the compass that guides the course of the project. It ensures that the team remains focused on a specific objective. Drawing from our hotel bookings dataset, the problem we seek to address is this: How can we leverage the available data to predict the likelihood of a hotel booking being canceled?

Identifying key stakeholders and understanding their expectations

Every project has stakeholders: individuals or groups deeply invested in the outcome. Recognizing these stakeholders and aligning with their expectations can be pivotal for a project's success. When it comes to hotel booking cancellations, stakeholders range from hotel management and front desk staff to the marketing team. Hotel management might prioritize accuracy and profitability, the front desk staff would value real-time predictions for efficient guest management, and the marketing team could seek insights to shape promotions.

Establishing success metrics

Once the problem is laid out and the stakeholders identified, it is essential to determine how success will be measured. These metrics should resonate with the project's objectives and offer tangible value to stakeholders. For our hotel booking prediction challenge, accuracy stands out as the primary KPI. However, considering the business implications, other metrics like precision, recall, or the F1-score may also hold importance. Specifically, understanding the impact of false positives and negatives can guide which metric to prioritize.

Understanding the business context, formulating the problem statement, identifying key stakeholders, understanding their expectations, and establishing KPIs are not just preliminary steps; they form the very core of a data science project. They provide the direction, set the benchmarks, and ensure that the project's outcomes align effectively with the business objectives. Without these, a project can easily become a case of garbage in, garbage out, where irrelevant input produces irrelevant output.

Data collection and preparation

A successful data science project is invariably built on the foundation of good-quality data. Thus, data collection and preparation become two of the most crucial steps in any data science pipeline. They involve gathering data from varied sources, identifying its relevancy, addressing missing values, and transforming it into a format that is ready for analysis.

Dataset attribution

The data used in this project is taken from the **Hotel booking demand** dataset[1], hosted on Kaggle and prepared by *Jesse Mostipak*.

After clicking on the link, we need to go to the top right and click **Download** to download it on our local machine. Before exploring the following topics, spend some time reading about dataset[2] and looking at the preview provided below. The interface looks like the following figure:

---

[1] *https://www.kaggle.com/datasets/jessemostipak/hotel-booking-demand. The dataset is shared under the Attribution 4.0 International (CC BY 4.0) license.*
Original data and the idea are from the article Hotel Booking Demand Datasets, written by Nuno Antonio, Ana Almeida, and Luis Nunes for Data in Brief, Volume 22, February 2019.
[2] *Special acknowledgments to Thomas Mock and Antoine Bichat for downloading and cleaning the dataset for the #TidyTuesday project during the week of February 11th, 2020.*

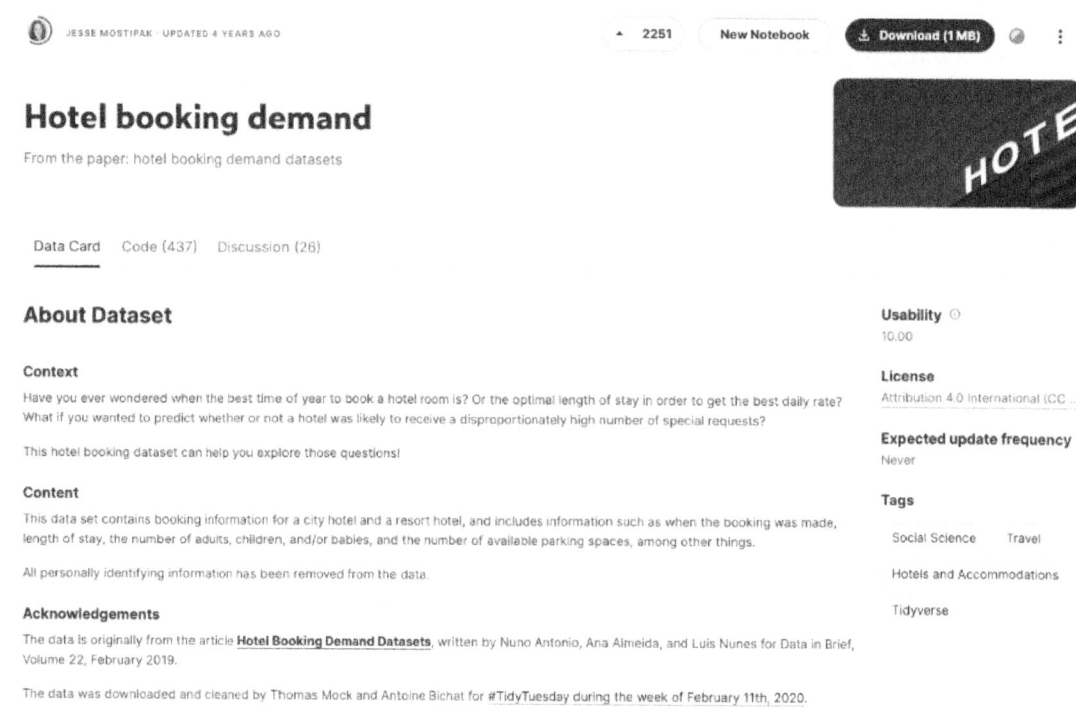

Figure 18.1: Our dataset on Kaggle

From source to solution: The journey of data collection

In the vast universe of data science, it is often said that data is the new oil. But just like crude oil needs refining before it is usable, raw data needs meticulous preparation before revealing its treasures.

Imagine being an explorer, setting foot on uncharted territory. Consider the problem statement as your compass and the right data being the treasure. Now, data can be hiding anywhere: in spreadsheets forgotten on old servers, online repositories, or even in paper records stacked in a dusty archive. The challenge is to know where to look and how to extract what you need.

Typically, data sources can be broadly classified into the following categories:

- **Primary sources:** Data collected firsthand for a specific purpose. This could be through surveys, interviews, or direct observations.

- **Secondary sources:** Data initially collected for another purpose but relevant to the current problem. This encompasses databases, online repositories, and previously conducted studies.

Once the source is identified, the method of collection comes into play. While automated tools and web scrapers can pull data from online sources, manual efforts might be needed for offline or non-digitized data.

For our hotel bookings dataset, we are working with secondary data sourced from Kaggle. Kaggle is a goldmine for data enthusiasts, hosting datasets across various domains. The original collectors of this dataset might have extracted the data from hotel management systems or **customer relationship management** (**CRM**) tools. Since it is already in a digitized form of **comma-separated values** (**CSV**), the collection is straightforward. However, it is essential to recognize the effort behind such datasets. Someone, somewhere, took the time to compile, clean, and anonymize the data to ensure that it is ready for our exploration.

But as we dig deeper, remember that every dataset has a story, a history. Understanding this can offer valuable context. It can be the difference between a good model and a great one. After all, in data science, context is the key that unlocks truly insightful solutions.

Polishing the mirror: The art of data cleaning

Imagine finding an old, tarnished mirror at an antique shop. At first glance, it might seem dull and unremarkable. But with some polishing and care, its true beauty shines through. Similarly, our raw dataset, while valuable, might have imperfections that obscure its true potential. It is time to roll up our sleeves and get polishing.

Let us start by peeking into our dataset and spotting any blemishes.

Handling missing values

Missing data is like those patches of tarnish on our antique mirror. Let us first identify how many and where these missing values are by using the following code:

```
# load the dataset
hotel_bookings = pd.read_csv("hotel_bookings.csv")


# Check for missing values again
missing_values = hotel_bookings.isnull().sum()
# Filter out columns that have missing values for further examination
missing_values = missing_values[missing_values > 0]

print(missing_values)
```

Upon closer examination, we have identified several potential culprits:

- **Children:** 4 missing values
- **Country:** 488 missing values
- **Agent:** 16,340 missing values
- **Company**: 112,593 missing values

These gaps in data can trip us up, so let us address them:

- **Children:** Given the context, it is reasonable to assume that if the number of children is not specified, it is likely that no children are part of the booking. We can fill these missing values with 0.

- **Country:** Missing country values could be filled using various methods like mode imputation, but for now, let us label them as *Unknown* to keep it simple.

- **Agent and company:** These columns represent IDs for travel agencies and companies.

  Since a large percentage of values are missing here, the tendency is to drop these columns altogether. But, as mentioned under the **Data Attribution** section, this dataset is based on an article entitled hotel booking demand datasets. In the article, there is a sentence that addresses the missing values in these two columns.

  In some categorical variables like Agent or Company, "NULL" is presented as one of the categories. This should not be considered a missing value but as "not applicable". For example, if a booking "Agent" is defined as "NULL", it means that the booking did not come from a travel agent. So, we are going to replace these missing values with 0.

Let us make these imputations using the following code:

```
# Imputing missing values
hotel_bookings["children"].fillna(0, inplace=True)
hotel_bookings["country"].fillna("Unknown", inplace=True)
hotel_bookings["agent"].fillna(0, inplace=True)
hotel_bookings["company"].fillna(0, inplace=True)

# Verify that there are no more missing values
missing_after_imputation = hotel_bookings.isnull().sum().sum()
```

And just like that, our dataset is free from missing values. It is like filling in the gaps of a puzzle, bringing the whole picture into clearer focus.

Data type mismatch

After sorting out the missing values, we must ensure that each column has the appropriate data type. This will help ensure that numerical operations can be performed on numerical columns and string operations on categorical columns. Let us inspect the data types of each column using the following code:

```
# Check data types of each column
data_types = hotel_bookings.dtypes

print(data_types)
```

The output is displayed in the following figure:

```
hotel                           object
is_canceled                      int64
lead_time                        int64
arrival_date_year                int64
arrival_date_month              object
arrival_date_week_number         int64
arrival_date_day_of_month        int64
stays_in_weekend_nights          int64
stays_in_week_nights             int64
adults                           int64
children                       float64
babies                           int64
meal                            object
country                         object
market_segment                  object
distribution_channel            object
is_repeated_guest                int64
previous_cancellations           int64
previous_bookings_not_canceled   int64
reserved_room_type              object
assigned_room_type              object
booking_changes                  int64
deposit_type                    object
agent                          float64
company                        float64
days_in_waiting_list             int64
customer_type                   object
adr                            float64
required_car_parking_spaces      int64
total_of_special_requests        int64
reservation_status              object
reservation_status_date         object
dtype: object
```

Figure 18.2: Data types for the hotel bookings dataset

Here, the datatype of one feature or column jumps out: **reservation_status_date**. This appears to be a date but is currently an object (string). Converting it to a datetime data type would be more appropriate. Let us execute the following code to do this:

```
# Convert 'reservation_status_date' to a datetime data type
hotel_bookings['reservation_status_date']        =        pd.to_datetime(hotel_
```

```
bookings['reservation_status_date'])
```

Logical consistency

It is essential to ensure that the data is logically consistent. As an example, ensure the following for a hotel booking system:

- The number of adults, children, and babies should not all be zero for a booking.

- The total stay (weekend nights + weeknights) should be greater than zero unless it is a canceled booking.

Let us check for these inconsistencies using the following code:

```
# Check for bookings with no guests
no_guests = hotel_bookings[(hotel_bookings['adults'] == 0) &
                           (hotel_bookings['children'] == 0) &
                           (hotel_bookings['babies'] == 0)]


# Check for bookings with zero total stay but not cancelled
zero_stay = hotel_bookings[(hotel_bookings['stays_in_weekend_nights'] == 0)
&
                           (hotel_bookings['stays_in_week_nights'] == 0) &
                           (hotel_bookings['is_canceled'] == 0)]


print(len(no_guests), len(zero_stay))
```

This bit of code will print out 180 and 680. With that, these are the inconsistencies we can find:

- There are 180 bookings with no guests (that is, the number of adults, children, and babies is zero). This might be a data entry error.

- There are 680 bookings where the total stay (both weekend and weeknights) is zero but the booking is not marked as canceled. This might also be a data entry error or an indication of bookings made just for amenities or events at the hotel, without an overnight stay.

Now, let us address these inconsistencies.

Bookings with no guests

- **Option 1:** We can exclude these records from the dataset.

- **Option 2:** If we assume that it is a data entry error, we can replace the number of adults with 1 (assuming that at least one adult made the booking).

Bookings with zero total stay but not canceled

- **Option 1:** We can exclude these records from the dataset.

- **Option 2:** If these bookings are for amenities or events without an overnight stay, they might be valid. In this case, we can leave them as is or create a new category (for example, *day use*) to label them.

In our case, since we do not have any further information, we will choose option 1 for both inconsistencies and exclude these records. Execute the following code:

```
# Removing inconsistent records

# Remove bookings with no guests
hotel_bookings = hotel_bookings[~((hotel_bookings['adults'] == 0) &
                    (hotel_bookings['children'] == 0) &
                    (hotel_bookings['babies'] == 0))]

# Remove bookings with zero total stay but not cancelled
hotel_bookings = hotel_bookings[~((hotel_bookings['stays_in_weekend_
nights'] == 0) &
                    (hotel_bookings['stays_in_week_nights'] == 0) &
                    (hotel_bookings['is_canceled'] == 0))]
```

We also need to be on the lookout for values that look like they are out of place in the dataset. To do that, let us check the unique values of all the categorical columns using the following code:

```
# Categorical columns

cat_columns = ['hotel', 'is_canceled', 'meal', 'country', 'market_segment',
'distribution_channel', 'is_repeated_guest', 'reserved_room_type', 'assigned_
room_type', 'deposit_type', 'customer_type', 'reservation_status']

# Unique values in each categorical column

print(f"Unique values by categorical columns\n".upper())

for cat_column in cat_columns:
    unique_values = hotel_bookings[cat_column].unique()
    print(f"\n{cat_column}: \n{unique_values}\n")
    print('-' * 70)
```

When you run this particular bit of code, you might notice that there are values in the **meal** feature. They are ['BB' 'FB' 'HB' 'SC' 'Undefined'].

However, the category **Undefined** actually corresponds to **SC** (self catering, that is, no meals are included), as defined in the original article. Therefore, we will replace its value with **SC**. Execute the following code:

```
#Replacing 'undefined' meal with 'SC'

hotel_bookings['meal'].replace(to_replace = 'Undefined', value = 'SC', in-
place = True)
```

Duplicates

The next step is to check for any duplicate rows in the dataset. Duplicate rows can skew our analysis and may indicate data entry errors or issues with data collection methods. To identify these duplicates, execute the following code:

```
# Check for duplicate rows
duplicate_rows = hotel_bookings[hotel_bookings.duplicated()]

# Number of duplicate rows
num_duplicate_rows = len(duplicate_rows)

print(num_duplicate_rows)
```

There are 31,926 duplicate rows in the dataset. These duplicates can affect the accuracy of our analysis. To address this, we can remove the duplicate rows to ensure that each booking is represented only once.

If the duplicates have significance (for example, multiple similar bookings by different customers), we can keep them. However, given the large number of duplicates, it is more likely that these are data entry errors or issues with data collection.

Let us proceed by removing these using the following code:

```
# Removing duplicate rows
hotel_bookings = hotel_bookings.drop_duplicates()
```

After removing the duplicate rows, we have 86,662 records remaining in the dataset. We are done cleaning our dataset. Next on our agenda is data exploration.

Unearthing data treasures: The power of exploration

Data exploration is akin to a treasure hunt. Imagine stepping onto an untouched island, armed with a map, a compass, and a relentless curiosity. With every step, you discover clues, unearthing secrets buried deep within the sands of data. This process is the essence of data exploration.

Statistical summaries

We will begin by providing descriptive statistics for the numerical columns in the dataset. This will give us an overview of the central tendency, dispersion, and shape of the dataset's distribution. Use the following code:

```
# Statistical summaries for numerical columns
statistical_summaries = hotel_bookings.describe()

print(statistical_summaries)
```

Here are the statistical summaries for the numerical columns in the dataset:

- **lead_time:** The average time between the booking and the stay is 80 days. Some bookings are made more than 700 days in advance.

- **adults, children, babies:** Most bookings are for 1 or 2 adults. The average number of children and babies is close to zero, but there are bookings with up to 10 children or babies.

- **stays_in_weekend_nights**, **stays_in_week_nights:** On average, guests stay for about one weekend night and almost three weeknights.

- **Average Daily Rate (ADR):** The average rate is about 107 units (likely in currency, for example, dollars or euros). There is an unusual minimum value of -6.38, which might be an error or represent some form of discount or compensation.

- **previous_cancellations**, **previous_bookings_not_canceled:** Most guests have not canceled before, but some have canceled up to 26 times.

- **booking_changes:** Most bookings do not have changes, but some have been changed up to 18 times.

- **days_in_waiting_list:** Most bookings are not on a waiting list, but some have waited up to 391 days.

- **required_car_parking_spaces:** Most bookings do not require a parking space, but some need up to 8 spaces.

- **total_of_special_requests:** On average, bookings have less than one special request, but some have up to five requests.

Data visualizations

Next, let us visualize some of this data to understand the distributions and relationships better. We will create the following visualizations:

- Histograms of numerical variables to understand the distribution

- Heatmap of the correlation matrix to visually represent correlations

- A few scatter plots for selected pairs of variables with high correlations to visualize their relationships

Let us start with the histograms for a few select numerical variables using the following code:

```
# Set up the figure and axes
fig, axes = plt.subplots(nrows=2, ncols=3, figsize=(18, 10))
fig.suptitle('Histograms of Numerical Variables', fontsize=16)

# List of variables to plot
variables = ['lead_time', 'adr', 'stays_in_weekend_nights', 'stays_in_week_
nights', 'adults', 'total_of_special_requests']

# Plot histograms
for ax, variable in zip(axes.ravel(), variables):
    sns.histplot(hotel_bookings[variable], bins=30, ax=ax, kde=True)
    ax.set_title(variable.replace("_", " ").title())
    ax.set_ylabel('Frequency')

plt.tight_layout()
plt.subplots_adjust(top=0.90)
plt.show()
```

The result is shown in the following figure:

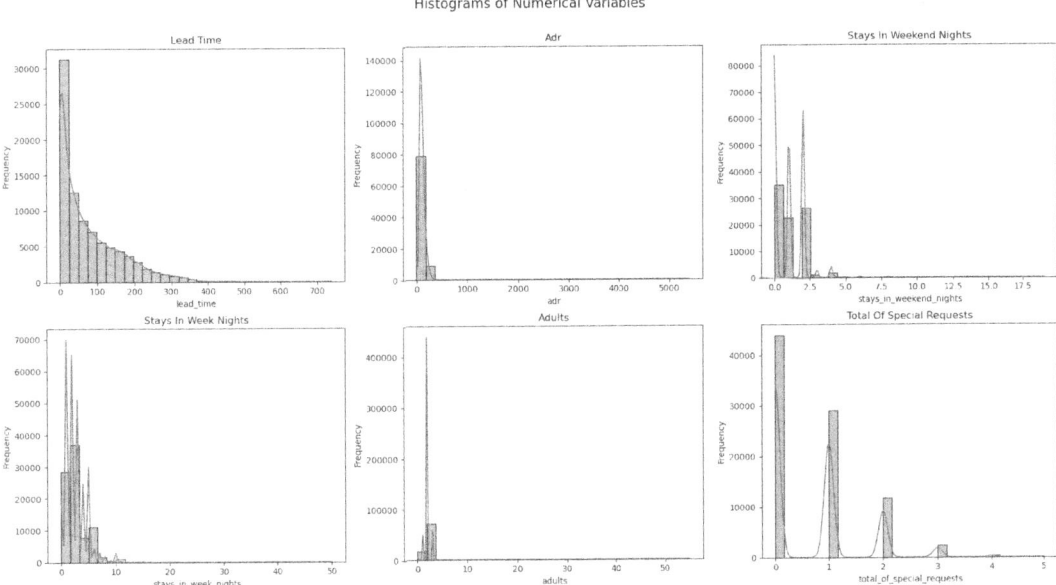

Figure 18.3: Histogram of numerical variables in the dataset

These are some of the observations from the histograms:

- **Lead time**: Most bookings are made with a short lead time (close to the stay date), but there are several bookings made hundreds of days in advance.

- **ADR:** Most bookings have an ADR between 50 and 150. There are some outliers, particularly on the higher end.

- **Stays in weekend nights:** Most guests stay for 1 or 2 weekend nights, with a significant number not staying over the weekend at all.

- **Stays in** weeknights: A large number of guests stay for just 1 or 2 weeknights. However, there are bookings spanning multiple weeknights.

- **Adults:** The majority of bookings are for 1 or 2 adults. There are a few bookings with a larger number of adults, but they are less common.

- **Total of special requests:** Most bookings have no special requests or just one. Few bookings have multiple special requests.

Next, let us visualize the correlation matrix as a heatmap to get a visual representation of the relationships between variables using the following code:

```
# Filter out non-numeric columns
numeric_columns = hotel_bookings.select_dtypes(include=['float64', 'int64'])
```

```
# Compute correlations for numeric columns
correlation_matrix_new = numeric_columns.corr()
correlation_matrix = numeric_columns.corr()
plt.figure(figsize=(18, 14))
sns.heatmap(correlation_matrix,    annot=True,    cmap='coolwarm',    vmin=-1,
vmax=1)
plt.title('Heatmap of Correlation Matrix', fontsize=16)
plt.show()
```

The **heatmap** is shown in the following figure:

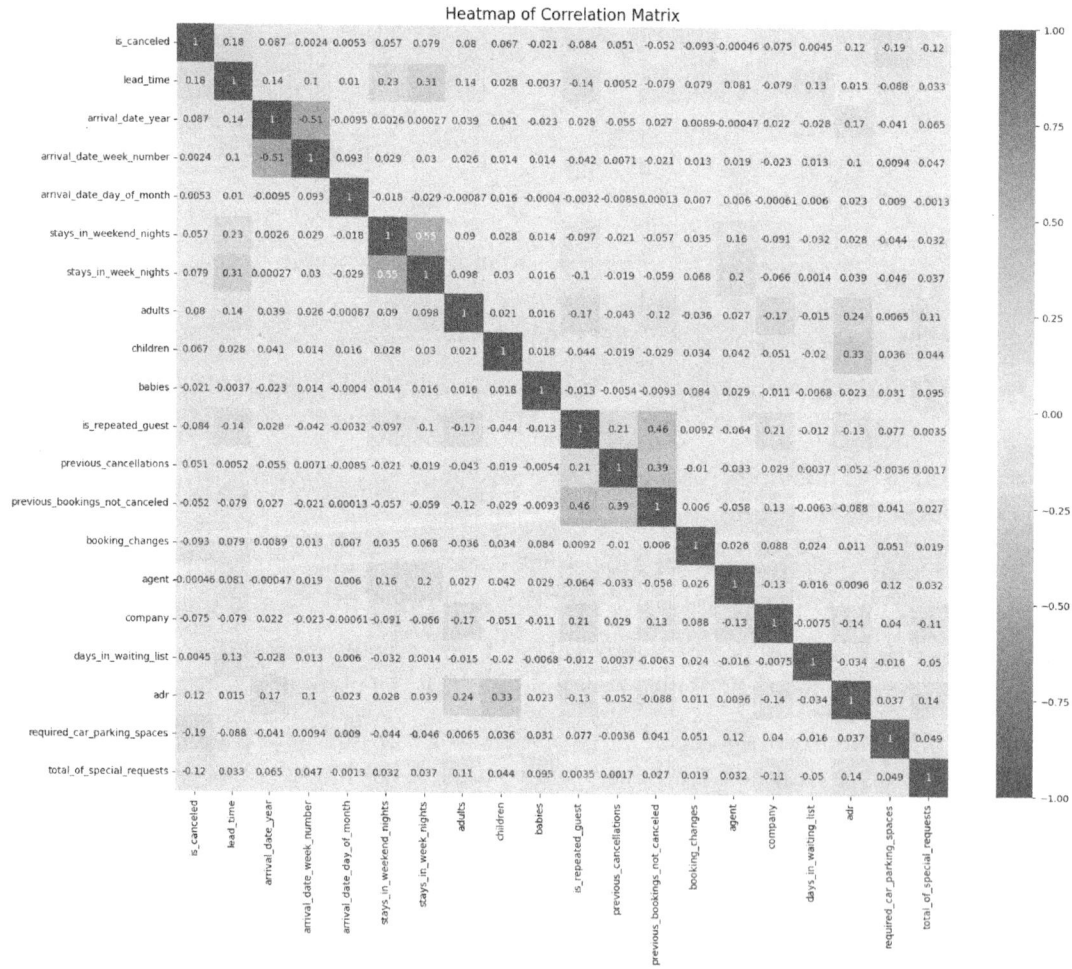

Figure 18.4: Correlation heatmap[3]

---

[1] *Note: Please refer to Figure 18.4 in the provided Image bundle for a colored version of this image.*

The heatmap provides a visual representation of the correlation matrix. Here is what we can infer from it:

- Darker shades of blue indicate strong positive correlations.

- Darker shades of red indicate strong negative correlations.

- Lighter shades (near white) indicate weak or no correlations.

Some observations are as follows:

- **arrival_date_year** and **arrival_date_week_number** show a strong negative correlation (-0.51), which is expected since the week number resets each year.

- **stays_in_weekend_nights** and **stays_in_week_nights** have a positive correlation (0.55), indicating that longer stays often span both weekends and weekdays.

- **adr** shows a positive correlation with adults (0.24) and a negative correlation with **is_repeated_guest (-0.14)**.

Lastly, let us create scatter plots for a few pairs of variables with notable correlations to visualize their relationships further. We will look at the following:

- **stays_in_weekend_nights** versus **stays_in_week_nights**

- **adr** versus **adults**

Execute the following code:

```
# Scatter plots for selected pairs of variables

# Set up the figure and axes
fig, axes = plt.subplots(nrows=1, ncols=2, figsize=(18, 6))
fig.suptitle('Scatter Plots of Selected Variable Pairs', fontsize=16)

# Plot for stays_in_weekend_nights vs. stays_in_week_nights
sns.scatterplot(data=hotel_bookings, x='stays_in_weekend_nights', y='stays_
in_week_nights', ax=axes[0], alpha=0.5)
axes[0].set_title('Stays in Weekend Nights vs. Stays in Week Nights')
axes[0].set_xlabel('Stays in Weekend Nights')
axes[0].set_ylabel('Stays in Week Nights')

# Plot for adr vs. adults
sns.scatterplot(data=hotel_bookings, x='adr', y='adults', ax=axes[1],
alpha=0.5)
axes[1].set_title('Average Daily Rate (ADR) vs. Adults')
```

```
axes[1].set_xlabel('Average Daily Rate (ADR)')
axes[1].set_ylabel('Adults')

plt.tight_layout()
plt.subplots_adjust(top=0.85)
plt.show()
```

The output is shown in the following figure:

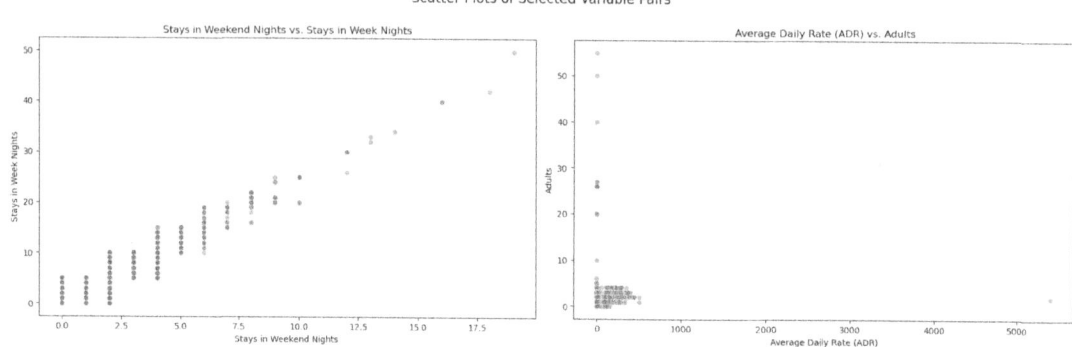

Figure 18.5: Scatter plot of selected variables

From the above plots, we can identify the following things:

- **Stays in weekend nights versus stays in week nights:** The scatter plot shows that bookings can range from only weekend stays to only weeknight stays. There is a concentration of points near the origin, indicating a significant number of short stays. Many guests stay for a combination of both weekend and weeknights.

- **ADR versus adults:** The scatter plot displays a general upward trend, which confirms the positive correlation between the number of adults in a booking and the average daily rate. Most bookings, as expected, fall within the 1-3 adults range. There are some outliers in the ADR, as noted previously.

Sculpting data: The craft of feature engineering

In the domain of data science, feature engineering is analogous to the meticulous work of a sculptor presented with an unrefined block of marble. To the uninitiated, this marble is merely a stone. Yet, to the discerning eye, it represents a latent form, brimming with potential, awaiting the sculptor's touch. Similarly, feature engineering is the process of shaping, refining, and optimizing raw data to reveal its inherent value and insights.

For our dataset, there are three things we will be doing in this section, as follows:

- Creating new features

- Encoding categorical variables

- Feature scaling

Creating new features

- **Total guests:** One of the simplest yet effective new features we can create is the total number of guests for a booking. By summing the number of adults, children, and babies, we can get a comprehensive view of the total number of guests per booking.

  Let us create this new feature:

  ```
  # Create a new feature 'total_guests'
  hotel_bookings['total_guests'] = hotel_bookings['adults'] + hotel_
  bookings['children'] + hotel_bookings['babies']
  ```

- **Booking duration:** This feature can be created by summing the **stays_in_ weekend_nights** and **stays_in_week_nights** columns. It will provide the total duration of each booking. Execute the following code:

  ```
  # Booking duration
  hotel_bookings['booking_duration'] = hotel_bookings['stays_in_
  weekend_nights'] + hotel_bookings['stays_in_week_nights']
  ```

- **Booking change rate:** By dividing the **booking_changes** column by **total_ guests**, we can understand how many changes were made per guest. Use the following code:

  ```
  # 2. Booking Change Rate
  hotel_bookings['booking_change_rate']   =   hotel_bookings['booking_
  changes'] / hotel_bookings['total_guests']
  ```

Encoding categorical variables

Encoding categorical variables correctly is essential to ensure that **Machine Learning (ML)** algorithms can make sense of the data. Let us delve deeper into the encoding techniques available and decide on the best strategy for each categorical variable:

- **hotel**

  o **Type:** Nominal

  o **Encoding strategy:** One-hot encoding

- **arrival_date_month**
  - o **Type:** Ordinal (Months have an inherent order)
  - o **Encoding strategy:** Label encoding (January=1, February=2, ...)
- **meal**
  - o **Type:** Nominal
  - o **Encoding strategy:** One-hot encoding
- **country**
  - o **Type:** Nominal
  - o **Encoding strategy:** One-hot encoding

Note: This can lead to a large number of columns. A strategy we could use involves grouping countries into broader categories based on certain criteria. For instance, we could group less frequent countries into an 'Other' category, keeping only the top N most frequent countries as separate categories.

- **market_segment**
  - o **Type:** Nominal
  - o **Encoding strategy:** One-hot encoding
- **distribution_channel**
  - o **Type:** Nominal
  - o **Encoding strategy:** One-hot encoding
- **reserved_room_type**
  - o **Type:** Nominal
  - o **Encoding strategy:** One-hot encoding
- **assigned_room_type**
  - o **Type:** Nominal
  - o **Encoding strategy:** One-hot encoding
- **deposit_type**
  - o **Type:** Ordinal (There is an inherent order: *No Deposit < Refundable < Non Refund*)
  - o **Encoding strategy:** Label encoding

- **customer_type**

  o **Type:** Nominal

  o **Encoding strategy:** One-hot encoding

- **reservation_status**

  o **Type:** Nominal (Although it might seem ordinal, the categories do not have a clear order in terms of cancellations)

  o **Encoding strategy:** One-hot encoding

- **reservation_status_date**

  o **Type:** Date

  o **Encoding strategy:** This feature can be split into separate year, month, and day columns for a more granular representation.

Let us implement these encoding strategies using the following code:

```
# Encode the 'hotel' column using label encoding
hotel_bookings['hotel_encoded'] = hotel_bookings['hotel'].map({'City
Hotel': 0, 'Resort Hotel': 1})

# One-Hot Encoding for nominal features
nominal_features = ['hotel', 'meal', 'market_segment', 'distribution_
channel',
                    'reserved_room_type', 'assigned_room_type', 'customer_
type', 'reservation_status']

hotel_bookings= pd.get_dummies(data=hotel_bookings, columns=nominal_
features, drop_first=True, dtype=int)

# Label Encoding for 'arrival_date_month'
month_ordering = ['January', 'February', 'March', 'April', 'May', 'June',
                  'July', 'August', 'September', 'October', 'November',
'December']
month_mapping = {month: i+1 for i, month in enumerate(month_ordering)}
hotel_bookings['arrival_date_month_encoded'] = hotel_bookings['arrival_
date_month'].map(month_mapping)

# Label Encoding for 'deposit_type'
deposit_mapping = {'No Deposit': 0, 'Refundable': 1, 'Non Refund': 2}
```

```python
hotel_bookings['deposit_type_encoded'] = hotel_bookings['deposit_type'].
map(deposit_mapping)


# Splitting 'reservation_status_date' into year, month, and day columns
hotel_bookings['reservation_status_year'] = pd.to_datetime(hotel_book-
ings['reservation_status_date']).dt.year

hotel_bookings['reservation_status_month'] = pd.to_datetime(hotel_book-
ings['reservation_status_date']).dt.month

hotel_bookings['reservation_status_day'] = pd.to_datetime(hotel_book-
ings['reservation_status_date']).dt.day


# Frequency distribution of the 'country' feature to get top 10 countries
country_counts = hotel_bookings['country'].value_counts()

top_10_countries = country_counts.head(10).index.tolist()


# Group countries outside the top 10 into 'Other'
hotel_bookings['country_grouped'] = hotel_bookings['country'].apply(lambda
x: x if x in top_10_countries else 'Other')


# One-Hot Encoding for the 'country_grouped' column
hotel_bookings = pd.get_dummies(data=hotel_bookings, columns=["country_
grouped"], drop_first=True, dtype=int)


# Drop the encoded columns
hotel_bookings.drop(["country", "arrival_date_month", "deposit_type", "res-
ervation_status_date"], axis=1, inplace=True)


# Display the first few rows to verify the one-hot encoding
hotel_bookings.head()
```

Partitioning data: Carving out training, validation, and test sets

In data science, consider the analogy of a chef preparing an intricate three-course meal. For the final dish to meet culinary standards, the chef must sample each course during its preparation. Similarly, in the development of a machine learning model, it is imperative to assess its performance at multiple stages to ensure that its predictions are both accurate and reliable.

We will proceed with the data splitting process as described:

1. Separate the dataset into features (X) and the target variable (y).

2. Split the data into training (70%) and a temporary set (30%) using stratified sampling based on the **is_canceled** column.

3. Further split the temporary set into validation (50%) and test sets (50%), ensuring a similar distribution of the **is_canceled** column.

Now, execute the following code:

```
from sklearn.model_selection import train_test_split

# Features and target variable using the correct column name
X = hotel_bookings.drop('is_canceled', axis=1)
y = hotel_bookings['is_canceled']

# Splitting the data into training (70%) and temporary set (30%)
X_train, X_temp, y_train, y_temp = train_test_split(X, y, test_size=0.3,
stratify=y, random_state=42)

# Splitting the temporary set into validation (50%) and test sets (50%)
X_val, X_test, y_val, y_test = train_test_split(X_temp, y_temp, test_
size=0.5, stratify=y_temp, random_state=42)
```

From selection to evaluation: Charting the model's journey

In the vast ecosystem of data science, choosing the right model is akin to selecting the ideal tool for a craftsman's masterpiece. Not every tool, or in our case, model, fits all tasks. Once the model is chosen, it embarks on a rigorous training regimen, learning from the data and honing its predictive abilities. This training culminates in evaluation, where we critically assess the model's performance, ensuring it is ready to tackle real-world challenges.

Hotel booking analysis: Choosing the right classifier

In our journey with the hotel bookings dataset, our mission is clear: predict whether a booking will be canceled. This task of determining one of two possible outcomes places us squarely in the realm of binary classification.

Given the nature of our dataset, which encompasses a variety of features from booking details to customer preferences, the choice of algorithm becomes paramount. Some might argue for the simplicity and interpretability of logistic regression: a classic choice for binary outcomes. It resembles a hotel concierge relying on years of experience to predict whether a guest might cancel.

Yet, the complexity of human behavior, especially regarding decisions like canceling bookings, might demand more intricate models. Decision trees or random forests could come into play, diving deeper into the intricacies of the data, much like a detective piecing together various clues. These models, with their hierarchical decision-making structure, can consider a myriad of factors, from lead time to deposit type, to predict cancellations.

Of course, the power of **support vector machines** (**SVM**) should not be overlooked. SVMs, with their ability to handle nonlinear boundaries, might prove adept at handling the nuances and intricacies of our dataset.

As we stand at the crossroads of algorithmic choice, it is essential to remember that while the allure of complex models is tempting, simplicity often holds its charm. The ultimate choice should hinge on not just accuracy but also interpretability, especially if we aim to provide insights to hotel management.

Assessing predictions: The hotelier's guide to model metrics

Imagine being the hotel manager, eagerly awaiting the weekly performance report. You would not be satisfied with just a single number. Instead, you would want a comprehensive breakdown of occupancy rates, guest feedback, revenue, and so on. Similarly, when evaluating our machine learning model, especially with our hotel bookings dataset, a single metric rarely tells the full story. It is the ensemble of metrics that truly paints the picture.

In the context of our hotel bookings dataset, where we are trying to predict cancellations (a binary classification problem), the choice of metric largely depends on the business objective and the potential costs associated with false predictions.

Here are a few considerations:

- **The business impact of false positives versus false negatives**

    o A **false positive** means predicting a booking will be canceled when it will not be. This could lead to overbooking rooms and potentially turning away guests if the hotel is full.

    o A **false negative** means predicting a booking will not be canceled when it actually will be. This could result in vacant rooms, lost revenue, and wasted resources.

Depending on which scenario is more costly or detrimental to the hotel's operations, we might prioritize precision (to minimize false positives) or recall (to minimize false negatives).

- **Dataset imbalance**

  o If there is a significant imbalance in the number of canceled versus non-canceled bookings, accuracy might not be a reliable metric. In such cases, the F1-Score, which balances precision and recall, becomes more valuable.

  o The area under the **receiver operating characteristic curve (AUC-ROC)** is also a good metric for imbalanced datasets as it evaluates the model's ability to distinguish between the classes at various thresholds.

- **Stakeholder preference**

  o Sometimes, the choice of metric is influenced by stakeholder preference or industry standards. For instance, if the hotel management is particularly concerned about falsely predicting cancellations (due to overbooking risks), they might prioritize precision.

- **Interpretability**

  o Metrics like accuracy are straightforward and easy to explain. However, in situations where the nuances of false positives and false negatives are crucial, the confusion matrix and derived metrics (precision, recall) offer a more detailed perspective.

- **Recommendation**

  o Given the potential business implications of both false positives and false negatives in our context, using a combination of metrics is recommended. The F1-Score provides a balance between precision and recall, making it a good starting point. Additionally, the ROC-AUC score can give insights into the model's overall discriminatory power. Finally, a detailed look at the confusion matrix will provide a granular view of where the model is making mistakes.

Exploring the hotel bookings landscape with four models

In exploring hotel booking predictions, we have access to various machine learning models. Each model has its own strengths and unique characteristics. Our task is to train and evaluate them to determine which one performs the best.

- **Logistic regression: The trusty concierge**

  Let us begin with logistic regression, the reliable concierge of the modeling world. It is straightforward, easy to implement, and often serves as a solid baseline. Given its linear nature, it can identify clear-cut patterns in our data. Training it on our dataset, we are essentially asking it to weigh the importance of each feature, like lead time, deposit type, or room type, in predicting cancellations.

- **Decision trees: The meticulous housekeeper**

  Next up is the decision tree, akin to a meticulous housekeeper who follows a strict checklist. It asks a series of questions, branching out based on the answers until it reaches a decision. For our dataset, it might start by inquiring about the deposit type and then delve into lead times, systematically narrowing down the possibilities. Its visual nature makes it interpretable, but there is a catch: It can be a bit too strict, sometimes overfitting to our data.

- **Random forests: The coordinated service team**

  Building on decision trees, we have random forests. Think of it as a coordinated team of service staff, each member slightly different but working harmoniously. Random forests ensemble multiple decision trees, each trained on random subsets of our data. The idea? To build a robust model that captures diverse patterns, reducing the overfitting risk that individual trees might face.

- **Support vector machines: The discerning chef**

  Lastly, there is SVM, the discerning chef of our model lineup. With a knack for drawing boundaries, it carefully separates canceled from non-canceled bookings, even when the patterns are intricate. Especially with the kernel trick, it can carve out nonlinear decision boundaries, capturing the subtle nuances in our dataset.

- **Training and testing: The crucial taste test**

  Much like taste-testing dishes before they reach the guests, training and testing our models is crucial. We have already split our data, so it is about feeding them to our models, adjusting their parameters, and evaluating their performance. Which model predicts cancellations most accurately? Which one offers insights that resonate with our hotel's operations? These evaluations will guide our choice, ensuring that we pick the model that best serves our hotel's needs.

Let us train and test each of these models on our dataset. Here is the plan:

- **Data preparation:** We have already preprocessed and split the data into training, validation, and test sets. We will use the training set for training and the validation set for model evaluation.

- **Model training**

  o Train a logistic regression model.

  o Train a decision tree classifier.

  o Train a random forest classifier.

  o Train a support vector machine classifier.

- **Model evaluation:** We will evaluate the models on the validation set using accuracy, confusion matrix, f1-score and ROC-AUC scores.

We will first train the models using their default hyperparameters. To do that, let us import all the models from scikit-learn, along with the metrics, using the following code:

```
# Importing all the models
from sklearn.linear_model import LogisticRegression
from sklearn.tree import DecisionTreeClassifier
from sklearn.ensemble import RandomForestClassifier
from sklearn.svm import SVC


# Importing metrics

from sklearn.metrics import accuracy_score, confusion_matrix, roc_auc_score
```

Then, we will train each model on our dataset, beginning with logistic regression. Execute the following code:

```
# Train Logistic Regression
log_reg = LogisticRegression(random_state=42)
log_reg.fit(X_train, y_train)
```

Once that is done, we will print out three metrics: the accuracy score, the confusion matrix, and the ROC-AUC score of the model on our validation dataset. Use the following code:

```
# Accuracy on validation data

log_reg_val_acc = accuracy_score(y_val, log_reg.predict(X_val))
print("Logistic Regression Accuracy on Validation Data - ", log_reg_val_
acc)

# Confusion Matrix on validation data
cm_log_reg = confusion_matrix(y_val,log_reg.predict(X_val))
print("Logistic Regression Confusion Matrix - \n", cm_log_reg)

# F1 Score
log_reg_f1 = f1_score(y_val, log_reg.predict(X_val))
print("Logistic Regression F1- Score on Validation Data - ", log_reg_f1)

# ROC-AUC score
print("Logistic Regression ROC-AUC Score on Validation Data - ", roc_auc_
score(y_val, log_reg.predict(X_val)))
```

The output is shown in the following figure:

```
Logistic Regression Accuracy on Validation Data -  0.7969074544195708
Logistic Regression Confusion Matrix -
 [[8900  498]
 [2142 1459]]
Logistic Regression F1- Score on Validation Data -  0.5250089960417417
Logistic Regression ROC-AUC Score on Validation Data -  0.6760876170040728
```

Figure 18.6: Logistic regression scores on validation data

This is a good beginning, even though the false positives or the cases in which the actual booking was *not canceled* but the model incorrectly predicted them as canceled, are pretty high.

Next up is a decision tree. Execute the following code:

```
# Accuracy on validation data


dt_val_acc = accuracy_score(y_val, decision_tree.predict(X_val))
print("Decision Tree Accuracy on Validation Data - ", dt_val_acc)


# Confusion Matrix on validation data
cm_dt = confusion_matrix(y_val, decision_tree.predict(X_val))
print("Decision Tree Confusion Matrix - \n", cm_dt)


# F1 Score
decision_tree_f1 = f1_score(y_val, decision_tree.predict(X_val))
print("Decision Tree F1- Score on Validation Data - ", decision_tree_f1)


# ROC-AUC score
print("Decision Tree ROC-AUC Score on Validation Data - ", roc_auc_score(y_val, decision_tree.predict(X_val)))
```

The results of this are really surprising. Take a look at the following figure:

```
Decision Tree Accuracy on Validation Data -  1.0
Decision Tree Confusion Matrix -
 [[9398    0]
 [   0 3601]]
Decision Tree F1- Score on Validation Data -  1.0
Decision Tree ROC-AUC Score on Validation Data -  1.0
```

Figure 18.7: Decision tree scores on validation data

The model apparently seems to be able to give perfect predictions. This is an extremely rare scenario, unless something is not right.

To explore this further, let us look at the features this particular model believes to be the most important when predicting booking cancellations. Execute the following code:

```
# Feature importance

pd.DataFrame(data = decision_tree.feature_importances_*100,
                    columns = ["Importances"],
                    index = X_train.columns).sort_values("Importances", as-
cending = False)[:15].plot(kind = "barh", color = "r")

plt.xlabel("Feature Importances (%)")
plt.show()
```

The resulting graph clearly tells you the problem. Refer to the following figure:

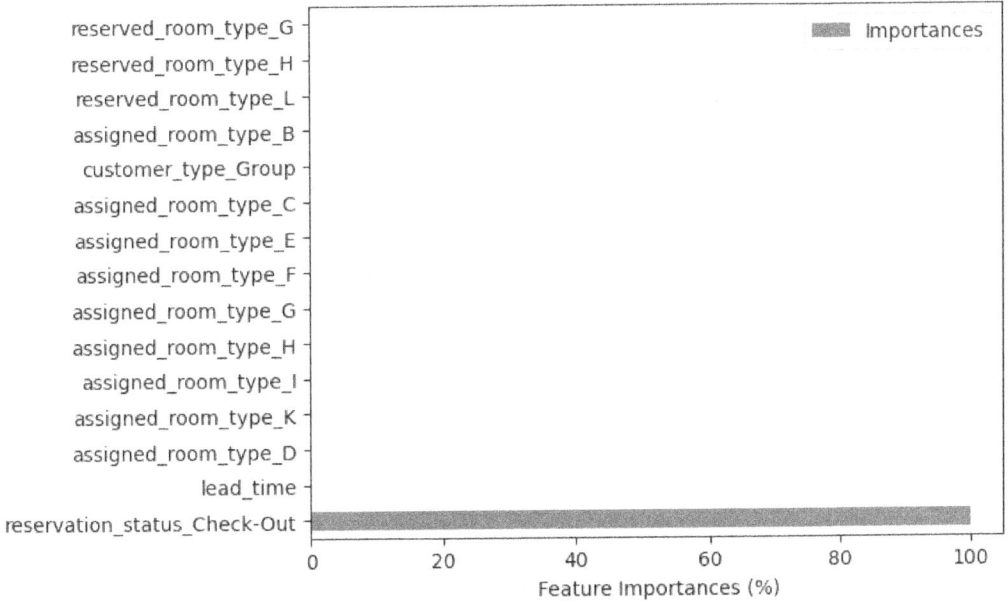

Figure 18.8: Decision tree feature importances

You can see that the entire predictive power comes from one particular feature: **reservation_status_Check-Out**.

When you look at it further, you will notice that this particular feature mimics the **is_canceled** feature and hence, is able to predict everything perfectly.

This is an unexpected bump in the road and means that the model is not taking any other feature into account. To ensure that we have a robust model, we will need to drop this particular feature from the dataset and try again. Execute the following code:

```
from sklearn.model_selection import train_test_split

# Features and target variable using the correct column name
X = hotel_bookings.drop(['is_canceled', 'reservation_status_Check-Out'],
axis=1)

y = hotel_bookings['is_canceled']

# Splitting the data into training (70%) and temporary set (30%)
X_train, X_temp, y_train, y_temp = train_test_split(X, y, test_size=0.3,
stratify=y, random_state=42)

# Splitting the temporary set into validation (50%) and test sets (50%)
X_val, X_test, y_val, y_test = train_test_split(X_temp, y_temp, test_
size=0.5, stratify=y_temp, random_state=42)
```

Now that we have dropped the feature in question, let us try all the models again, starting with logistic regression. Execute the following code:

```
# Train Logistic Regression
log_reg = LogisticRegression(random_state=42)
log_reg.fit(X_train, y_train)

# Accuracy on validation data

log_reg_val_acc = accuracy_score(y_val, log_reg.predict(X_val))
print("Logistic Regression Accuracy on Validation Data - ", log_reg_val_
acc)

# Confusion Matrix on validation data
cm_log_reg = confusion_matrix(y_val,log_reg.predict(X_val))
print("Logistic Regression Confusion Matrix - \n", cm_log_reg)

# F1 Score
log_reg_f1 = f1_score(y_val, log_reg.predict(X_val))
print("Logistic Regression F1- Score on Validation Data - ", log_reg_f1)

# ROC-AUC score
print("Logistic Regression ROC-AUC Score on Validation Data - ", roc_auc_
score(y_val, log_reg.predict(X_val)))
```

This bit of code gives the following output:

```
Logistic Regression Accuracy on Validation Data -  0.78082929456112
Logistic Regression Confusion Matrix -
 [[9202  196]
 [2653  948]]
Logistic Regression F1- Score on Validation Data -  0.3995785036880927
Logistic Regression ROC-AUC Score on Validation Data -  0.6212023521640055
```

Figure 18.9: Logistic regression (updated) scores on validation data

The results are slightly worse accuracy and ROC-AUC scores and a much worse F1-Score, but it is very similar to the previous attempt. Now, let us try the decision tree again; consider the following code:

```
# Train Decision Tree

decision_tree = DecisionTreeClassifier(random_state=42)

decision_tree.fit(X_train, y_train)


# Accuracy on validation data


dt_val_acc = accuracy_score(y_val, decision_tree.predict(X_val))

print("Decision Tree Accuracy on Validation Data - ", dt_val_acc)


# Confusion Matrix on validation data

cm_dt = confusion_matrix(y_val, decision_tree.predict(X_val))

print("Decision Tree Confusion Matrix - \n", cm_dt)


# F1 Score

decision_tree_f1 = f1_score(y_val, decision_tree.predict(X_val))

print("Decision Tree F1- Score on Validation Data - ", decision_tree_f1)


# ROC-AUC score

print("Decision Tree ROC-AUC Score on Validation Data - ", roc_auc_score(y_val, decision_tree.predict(X_val)))
```

Take a look at the following output; refer to the following image:

```
Decision Tree Accuracy on Validation Data -  0.9308408339103008
Decision Tree Confusion Matrix -
 [[8942  456]
 [ 443 3158]]
Decision Tree F1- Score on Validation Data -  0.8753984753984755
Decision Tree ROC-AUC Score on Validation Data -  0.9142288275720153
```

Figure 18.10: Decision tree (updated) scores on validation data

Even though the scores are still very high, the results are much more believable.

Up next, we have random forest; use the following code:

```
# Train Random Forest
random_forest = RandomForestClassifier(random_state=42)
random_forest.fit(X_train, y_train)


# Accuracy on validation data


rf_acc = accuracy_score(y_val, random_forest.predict(X_val))
print("Random Forest Accuracy on Validation Data - ", rf_acc)


# Confusion Matrix on validation data
cm_rf = confusion_matrix(y_val, random_forest.predict(X_val))
print("Random Forest Confusion Matrix - \n", cm_rf)


# F1 Score
rf_f1 = f1_score(y_val, random_forest.predict(X_val))
print("Random Forest F1- Score on Validation Data - ", rf_f1)


# ROC-AUC score
print("Random Forest ROC-AUC Score on Validation Data - ", roc_auc_score(y_
val, random_forest.predict(X_val)))
```

These are the results:

```
Random Forest Accuracy on Validation Data -  0.9336872067082084
Random Forest Confusion Matrix -
 [[9242  156]
 [ 706 2895]]
Random Forest F1- Score on Validation Data -  0.870414912808178
Random Forest ROC-AUC Score on Validation Data -  0.8936720363139533
```

Figure 18.11: Random forest (updated) scores on validation data

The results here are very similar to the decision tree.

Finally, we have the support vector machine. Execute the following code:

```
# Train Support Vector Machine
svm = SVC(random_state=42)
svm.fit(X_train, y_train)


# Accuracy on validation data

svm_acc = accuracy_score(y_val, svm.predict(X_val))
print("SVM Accuracy on Validation Data - ", svm_acc)


# Confusion Matrix on validation data
cm_svm = confusion_matrix(y_val, svm.predict(X_val))
print("SVM Confusion Matrix - \n", cm_svm)


# F1 Score
svm_f1 = f1_score(y_val, svm.predict(X_val))
print("SVM F1- Score on Validation Data - ", svm_f1)


# ROC-AUC score
print("SVM ROC-AUC Score on Validation Data - ", roc_auc_score(y_val, svm.
predict(X_val)))
```

The lazy learning model takes a bit more time to churn through this task than the others, and eventually, this output is generated:

```
SVM Accuracy on Validation Data -  0.722978690668513
SVM Confusion Matrix -
 [[9398    0]
 [3601    0]]
SVM F1- Score on Validation Data -  0.0
SVM ROC-AUC Score on Validation Data -  0.5
```

Figure 18.12: SVM (updated) scores on validation data

SVM seems to be easily the worst of the lot.

Based on these results, the decision could be between a decision tree and random forests. Given the options, the preference might lean toward random forests, primarily because it is a more complex model. There is a possibility that further performance improvements could be achieved through hyperparameter tuning.

Given the complexity of hotel booking data, with its mix of categorical and numerical features, it makes sense that random forest came out on top. It can capture intricate patterns that might be missed by a simpler model, and it is especially adept at handling datasets with high dimensionality, which can be the case after encoding categorical variables.

Hyperparameter tuning

A random forest has several hyperparameters that can be adjusted to optimize its performance for a specific dataset. For our hotel bookings dataset, we might consider tuning the following:

- **n_estimators**: This refers to the number of trees in the forest. More trees typically allow the model to capture more nuances in the data but can also increase computation time.

- **max_depth**: This is the maximum depth of each tree. A deeper tree can capture more details but is also more prone to overfitting.

- **max_features**: This is the number of features to consider when looking for the best split. This can help in randomizing the trees further, adding to the model's robustness.

Given the importance of accurately predicting cancellations, we want a model that is both accurate and interpretable. Random forests offer a good balance. By tuning their hyperparameters, we can ensure that they is well suited to our specific dataset without overfitting. A slight tuning rather than an exhaustive search can provide us with a robust model without excessive computation time.

Now, we will utilize **GridSearchCV** from scikit-learn to perform the hyperparameter tuning; consider the following code:

```
from sklearn.model_selection import GridSearchCV

param_grid = {
    'n_estimators': [150, 250, 500],
    'max_features': ['sqrt', 'log2', None],
    'max_depth': [3, 6, 9, 12, 15],
}

grid_search = GridSearchCV(RandomForestClassifier(random_state=42, ver-
bose=2),
                          param_grid=param_grid,
                          n_jobs=-1)
```

```
grid_search.fit(X_train, y_train)
print(grid_search.best_estimator_)
```

Here, the grid includes three potential tree counts (150, 250, 500), three methods to determine the number of features for splits (**max_features**: *sqrt, log2,* and considering all features), and five varying tree depths from 3 to 15. The **GridSearchCV** function, configured with parallel processing (**n_jobs=-1**), exhaustively trains the model on all 45 possible combinations of these parameters. Once complete, the best-performing model configuration can be extracted, providing a fine-tuned random forest classifier ideally suited for predicting hotel booking cancellations.

Now, let us test the tuned model on the validation dataset using the following code:

```
# Accuracy on validation data

rf_gs_acc = accuracy_score(y_val, grid_search.predict(X_val))
print("Random Forest (Tuned) GS Accuracy on Validation Data - ", rf_gs_acc)


# Confusion Matrix on validation data
cm_gs_rf = confusion_matrix(y_val, grid_search.predict(X_val))
print("Random Forest (Tuned) Confusion Matrix - \n", cm_gs_rf)


# F1 Score
rf_gs_f1 = f1_score(y_val, grid_search.predict(X_val))
print("Random Forest (Tuned) F1- Score on Validation Data - ", rf_gs_f1)


# ROC-AUC score
print("Random Forest (Tuned) ROC-AUC Score on Validation Data - ", roc_auc_
score(y_val, grid_search.predict(X_val)))
```

The output of this code block is shown in the following image:

```
Random Forest (Tuned) GS Accuracy on Validation Data -  0.947919070697746
Random Forest (Tuned) Confusion Matrix -
 [[9319   79]
 [ 598 3003]]
Random Forest (Tuned) F1- Score on Validation Data -  0.8986981894358821
Random Forest (Tuned) ROC-AUC Score on Validation Data -  0.9127644871057135
```

Figure 18.13: Random forest (tuned) scores on validation data

As you can see, there is a definite improvement over the untuned model.

Finally, we must see if we get similar results on the unseen test dataset. If we do, that is an excellent indicator of a robust model. Execute the following code:

```
# Accuracy on testing data
```

```
rf_gs_acc = accuracy_score(y_test, grid_search.predict(X_test))
print("Random Forest GS Accuracy on Test Data - ", rf_gs_acc)

# Confusion Matrix on validation data
cm_gs_rf = confusion_matrix(y_test, grid_search.predict(X_test))
print("Random Forest Confusion Matrix on Test Data - \n", cm_gs_rf)

# F1 Score
rf_gs_f1 = f1_score(y_test, grid_search.predict(X_test))
print("Random Forest (Tuned) F1- Score on Test Data - ", rf_gs_f1)

# ROC-AUC score
print("Random Forest ROC-AUC Score on Test Data - ", roc_auc_score(y_test,
grid_search.predict(X_test)))
```

Take a look at the following figure:

```
Random Forest (Tuned) GS Accuracy on Test Data -  0.9456153846153846
Random Forest (Tuned) Confusion Matrix on Test Data -
 [[9312   86]
 [ 621 2981]]
Random Forest (Tuned) F1- Score on Test Data -  0.8939871045134203
Random Forest (Tuned) ROC-AUC Score on Test Data -  0.9092224484777617
```

Figure 18.14: Random forest (tuned) scores on test data

The results are completely in line with what we were expecting. With this, we have a robust model that we can use to predict cancellations in our hotel dataset. It is encouraged to tune the model further, as there are many more hyperparameters that you can play around with.

Communication of results

In data science, developing a powerful model is just one part of the puzzle. Equally vital is the ability to effectively communicate the results, insights, and implications of that model to various stakeholders, from technical experts to business leaders. Clear communication ensures that the value and impact of the analysis are understood, fostering informed decision-making and strategic planning. As we delve into the outcomes of our random forest model on the hotel bookings dataset, we will explore the art and science of presenting the results in a compelling, transparent, and actionable manner.

Crafting understandable narratives for all stakeholders

Whether you are presenting to a team of data scientists or business leaders, the goal remains the same: conveying the essence, significance, and implications of your analysis. Yet, the approach can differ significantly based on the audience's familiarity with technical jargon and data science concepts. Let us navigate this delicate balance using our hotel bookings dataset as a backdrop.

- **Speaking to the technical audience:** For those well-versed in the world of data, diving deep into the specifics can be necessary and appreciated. Discuss the intricacies of the random forest model, the hyperparameters fine-tuned, and the rationale behind the chosen metrics. Visualizations like feature importance plots or confusion matrices can provide a comprehensive view. In our context, you might delve into why certain features, like lead time or deposit type, played a pivotal role in predicting cancellations. The discussion could further venture into challenges, such as handling missing data or encoding categorical variables, and the solutions employed.

- **Engaging the non-technical audience:** For stakeholders less acquainted with the technical nuances, it is crucial to shift the focus from *how* to *why* and *what*. Start with the bigger picture: *We aimed to predict hotel booking cancellations to optimize room allocation and enhance guest experience*. Use simple, relatable analogies. For instance, compare the model to a detective gathering clues (features) to predict an outcome (cancellation). Visual aids can be invaluable; consider using simplified charts, infographics, or even storyboards. Highlight key findings, such as bookings made months in advance are more likely to be canceled, and discuss their business implications. End with actionable insights or recommendations, such as considering flexible booking policies for long lead time bookings.

Regardless of the audience, authenticity and clarity are paramount. Be prepared to answer questions and address concerns. For uncertainties or areas of future exploration, be transparent. Remember, the goal is not just to inform but to inspire confidence, action, and collaboration.

Translating findings into actionable steps

In the vast landscape of data science, the final frontier is not just about understanding data but transforming that understanding into actionable strategies. Think of it as reading a map; once you have discerned the terrain, the next step is to chart the best course forward. Using our hotel bookings dataset as a guide, let us explore how to convert model results into tangible insights and recommendations.

This is the feature importance chart of our final model; take a look at the following figure:

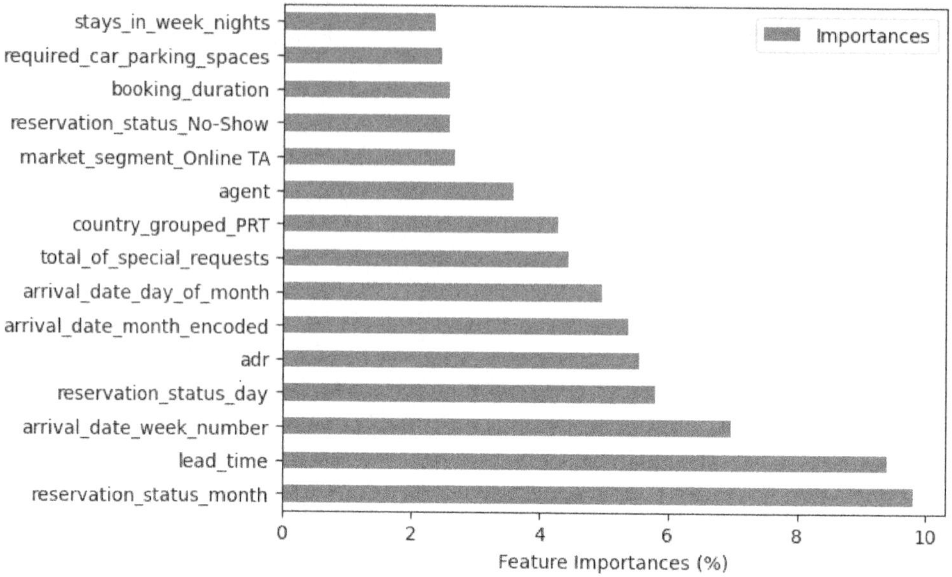

Figure 18.15: Feature importances of the final model

Let us delve into the insights and potential implications of these top features:

1. **reservation_status_month**

   o **Insight:** The month in which the reservation status was last updated appears to be a significant predictor of cancellations.

   o **Implication:** Certain months might have higher cancellation rates due to various reasons, such as seasonal trends, holidays, or events. It is crucial to understand these monthly fluctuations to anticipate and mitigate potential cancellations.

   o **Recommendation:** Consider running targeted promotional campaigns in months with historically high cancellation rates to secure bookings. Alternatively, offer flexible rebooking options for guests who may need to change their plans.

2. **lead_time**

   o **Insight:** The time between the booking date and the arrival date is a strong predictor of cancellations.

   o **Implication:** Longer lead times might be associated with a higher likelihood of cancellations. This could be because guests who book well in advance are more uncertain about their plans.

o **Recommendation:** Implement dynamic pricing or loyalty incentives for early bookings to encourage guests to commit. Alternatively, consider flexible cancellation policies for bookings made with a long lead time.

3. **arrival_date_week_number**

o **Insight:** The week number of the year when the guest arrives has a significant influence on cancellations.

o **Implication:** Certain weeks, possibly during peak holiday seasons or major events, might see a surge in cancellations.

o **Recommendation:** Analyze which specific weeks have high cancellation rates and adjust marketing strategies or offer special packages during those periods to retain bookings.

4. **reservation_status_day**

o **Insight:** The day on which the reservation status was last updated plays a role in predicting cancellations.

o **Implication:** Some days of the week might witness more cancellations, potentially due to guests reviewing and altering their plans.

o **Recommendation:** Send reminder emails or offers a few days before these high-cancellation days to reduce the likelihood of guests canceling their bookings.

5. **ADR**

o **Insight:** The average daily rate of bookings is a key factor in predicting cancellations.

o **Implication:** Higher or lower rates might influence guests' decisions to cancel. It is possible that guests might find better deals elsewhere or feel that the rate does not offer value for money.

o **Recommendation:** Regularly benchmark your hotel's rates against competitors. Consider offering value-added services or perks for certain rate tiers to enhance perceived value and reduce cancellations.

Remember, while these features are influential in predicting cancellations in the model, it is essential to corroborate these findings with business insights and consider external factors that might also influence guest behaviour.

Deployment, monitoring and maintenance of a model

In the grand symphony of data science, deploying a model is akin to presenting the final performance after countless rehearsals. However, the show does not end with the deployment; it marks the beginning of a continuous journey of monitoring and maintenance. As our model begins to interact with real-world data in a live environment, it is paramount to ensure that it remains robust, accurate, and relevant. In the following sections, we will investigate the intricacies of deploying our hotel booking prediction model and the subsequent steps to monitor its performance and ensure its longevity.

Exploring model deployment platforms

Embarking on the model deployment journey can feel like selecting the perfect stage for a grand theatrical performance. The model, after all, is our star performer, and the choice of deployment platform sets the stage for its public debut. Let us explore the fascinating world of deployment options using our hotel booking prediction model as a guiding star:

- **Cloud platforms:** The cloud is the modern-day equivalent of a grand amphitheater, offering scalability, flexibility, and many tools. Platforms like **AWS SageMaker**, **Google Cloud ML**, and **Azure ML Studio** allow for seamless model deployment with just a few clicks. In the context of our hotel bookings model, a cloud deployment would be ideal if we target a broad audience, perhaps a chain of hotels spread globally. The cloud ensures that our model is accessible from anywhere, scales with demand, and offers robust security protocols.

- **On-premise servers:** Sometimes, the performance is more intimate, tailored for a specific audience. On-premise deployment is akin to a private theater, where the model resides within the organization's infrastructure. For a single hotel or a local chain, an on-premise deployment might be more appropriate. It offers full control over the data, ensuring privacy and compliance, especially if sensitive guest data is involved.

- **Edge devices:** Imagine a roving troupe performing in various nooks and corners of a city. Deploying on edge devices is similar, where the model runs on local hardware (like IoT devices) close to the data source. While our hotel booking model might not be the typical candidate for edge deployment, think of scenarios where real-time predictions are crucial, like instant room recommendations based on sensor data from a smart hotel room.

- **Hybrid approaches**: Occasionally, a blend of grand stages and intimate settings creates the perfect ambiance. Hybrid deployments combine the best of cloud and on-premise, offering flexibility and control. For instance, preliminary data processing might occur on-premise, while the heavy-duty predictions are offloaded to the cloud.

The choice of deployment platform hinges on various factors: the scale of operations, data sensitivity, required computational power, and, of course, budgetary considerations. Whether it is the vast expanse of the cloud, the controlled environment of on-premise servers, or the immediacy of edge devices, each platform offers a unique flavor to our model's performance. As we prepare our hotel booking model for its grand debut, the key is to select a stage that complements its strengths and ensures a lasting impression on the audience.

Crafting application programming interfaces for seamless access

Imagine the grandeur of a theater's main entrance, ornate doors ushering guests into a world of wonder and awe. In machine learning, **application programming interfaces (APIs)** play a similar role, serving as the grand gateway that allows applications to access the magic of our model. Let us embark on a journey to understand how APIs become the bridge between our hotel booking model and the outside world.

At its core, an API is a set of rules and protocols that allows one software application to interact with another. In the context of our hotel booking model, an API would enable various hotel management systems, booking platforms, or even mobile apps to tap into our model's predictions. Instead of interacting directly with the model's intricate code, they would make a simple API call and receive predictions in return.

Consider Flask as the stage crew, setting the scene for our model's performance. Flask is a lightweight web framework often used to wrap machine learning models into APIs. By integrating our hotel booking model with Flask, we can create endpoints that receive booking data and return predictions. It is like having a dedicated ticket booth where guests provide their details and instantly receive their showtime.

The beauty of an API lies in its simplicity. A hotel's booking system, for instance, could send a JSON payload with booking details to our API. Behind the scenes, our model processes the data, predicts whether the booking might be canceled, and then the API gracefully returns the result, all in real-time.

Scaling with containers: To ensure that our model's performance remains smooth even under heavy demand, we can employ containers like **Docker**. Think of Docker as the grand auditorium's seating arrangement, ensuring that every guest (or API call) has its designated space and resources. By containerizing our Flask API, we ensure scalability, reproducibility, and efficient resource utilization.

An API, like a theater, must ensure the safety and comfort of its guests. Implementing authentication mechanisms, such as **API keys** or **OAuth**, ensures that only authorized systems can access our model. Additionally, rate limiting can be set up to prevent overwhelming the system with too many requests, akin to managing the inflow of guests during peak showtimes.

Crafting an API for our hotel booking model is akin to rolling out the red carpet, offering a seamless, secure, and efficient pathway for various systems to experience the model's prowess. As we unveil our model's capabilities to the world, the API ensures that the magic remains accessible, scalable, and, above all, awe-inspiring.

Embracing model versioning and rollback

Our hotel booking model, like any machine learning model, is not static. As we gather more data, uncover new patterns, or fine-tune our algorithms, we naturally want to update the model to improve its accuracy. However, each update carries a risk: What if the new version performs worse in certain scenarios? Model versioning allows us to keep track of these iterations, ensuring that we can always return to a previous state if needed.

Several tools, such as **MLflow** or **DVC**, offer robust model versioning capabilities. Think of these tools as the meticulous script supervisors of our theatre production, diligently noting each change. In the context of our dataset, every time we retrain our model with new booking data or tweak its parameters, these tools store the model's version, along with relevant metadata like training data, hyperparameters, and performance metrics.

The ability to revert to a previous model version is akin to having a safety net. If a newly deployed version of our hotel booking model starts generating a higher rate of false predictions, we do not have to panic. With a well-implemented rollback mechanism, we can swiftly switch back to a previous, more reliable version, ensuring minimal disruption to hotel operations.

Versioning and rollback are not just about storing old models. It is vital to maintain consistency in data preprocessing steps, feature engineering, and even the software environment. If our hotel booking data transforms into a new model version, rolling back to an older model would require reverting to the previous data processing pipeline as well.

Best practices are as follows:

- **Frequent checkpoints:** Regularly save model versions during development, especially before major updates or changes.

- **Detailed documentation:** We need to maintain detailed logs of changes, reasons for updates, and performance metrics for each version.

- **Automate rollbacks:** Implement automated mechanisms to quickly switch to a previous model version if anomalies are detected in real-time predictions.

Detecting drifts and setting retraining rhythms

Just as audience preferences evolve, the data our model encounters in the real world might deviate from the data it was initially trained on. This phenomenon, known as **data drift**, can gradually erode our model's accuracy. For instance, if there is a sudden trend of last-minute hotel bookings due to a new travel app, our model, which was trained on older booking patterns, might struggle to make accurate predictions.

Monitoring tools like TensorFlow Model Analysis or Amazon SageMaker Model Monitor act as our vigilant stage managers, constantly observing the model's predictions against real outcomes. If there is a significant deviation, say, a surge in false positives for booking cancellations, it is a cue that our model might be facing data drift. In the context of our hotel bookings, regularly comparing the distribution of features like `lead_time` or `adr` between the training data and incoming real-world data can offer clues about potential drifts.

Retraining a model is not just about reacting to drifts; it is about anticipating them. Setting clear policies or thresholds for retraining is crucial. For our hotel booking model, we might decide to retrain in the following cases:

- If the false prediction rate surpasses a set threshold

- If there's a significant shift in the distribution of key features

- If the hotel introduces new booking policies or services not present in the initial training data

In the fast-paced world of hotel bookings, waiting for manual interventions might not be ideal. Implementing automated drift detection and retraining pipelines ensures that our model remains agile. Think of it as having an understudy ready to step in immediately, ensuring that the show goes on seamlessly.

Establishing feedback loops with the end users (in this case, the hotel management or booking platforms) provides invaluable insights. They can flag unexpected booking prediction behaviors or provide context to sudden shifts in booking trends, offering a richer perspective than data alone.

Ensuring the model's longevity and relevance

Let us think of our hotel booking prediction model as a seasoned actor, celebrated for its stellar performances on the grand stage of data science. However, like any artist, it requires consistent care, periodic refreshers, and adaptation to evolving scripts to maintain its star status. Over time, as the dynamics of hotel bookings change due to evolving traveler preferences or global events, our model's predictions might start to wane. This phenomenon, known as **model decay**, is an inevitable challenge, but it can be managed with regular maintenance.

One of the most effective ways to combat this decay is by periodically retraining the model with fresh data, much like an actor rehearsing with a revised script. By introducing it to the latest booking trends and traveler behaviors, we ensure that it remains attuned to the current hospitality landscape. For our dataset, this might mean monthly or even quarterly retraining sessions, incorporating the latest booking records to keep the model's predictions sharp.

Yet, the upkeep does not end there. Just as an actor relies on a supportive crew, our model is intertwined with various software libraries and dependencies. As these libraries evolve, there is the ever-present risk of compatibility issues. Regular updates, while ensuring no disruptions to our model's performance, become crucial to ensure that the entire ecosystem functions harmoniously.

Feedback, the lifeblood of any performance, plays a pivotal role. Robust feedback mechanisms, capturing insights directly from hotel staff or booking platforms, can be invaluable. They might highlight patterns that the model misses or suggest new features, guiding targeted updates to align the model with user needs.

In the bustling world of hotel bookings, manual interventions might not always be feasible. This is where automated monitoring tools come into play, acting as vigilant overseers that alert us to potential model decay or performance drops. With these tools in place, we can ensure that our model remains agile, responsive, and ever-ready to adapt to the ever-shifting sands of the hotel booking landscape.

Conclusion

In this book, we explored the diverse landscapes of data science, from its fundamental concepts to advanced techniques and real-world applications. We have honed our skills, navigated complex datasets, and honed our abilities to extract meaningful insights from the sea of information.

Data science is a field that thrives on curiosity, innovation, and exploration. It is a discipline where learning never ceases, where challenges are opportunities, and where data-driven solutions can transform industries and improve lives. As you close this book, remember that the world of data science is boundless, with new horizons waiting to be discovered.

Continue to explore, experiment, and innovate. Share your knowledge and insights with others, for collective learning propels our field forward. Above all, relish the joys of unraveling the mysteries hidden within data and the satisfaction of crafting solutions that make a difference.

The world of data science is vast, and your quest for knowledge and impact is bound to leave an indelible mark. Keep pushing the boundaries, for the possibilities are limitless. Farewell, and may your data-driven adventures be both fulfilling and enlightening.

Points to remember

- Data science is not just about building models; it is about understanding the problem, ensuring data quality, and continuously refining the model based on real-world feedback.

- Establishing feedback loops with stakeholders and end users is essential. It not only helps in refining the model but also in capturing the evolving nuances of the domain.

- A model, once deployed, is not set in stone. Regular monitoring, addressing model decay, and periodic retraining ensure its longevity and relevance.

Index

Printed in Great Britain
by Amazon

53250252R00231